PERENNIAL VEGETABLES

PERENNIAL VEGETABLES

From Artichoke to 'Zuiki' Taro,
a Gardener's Guide to Over 100
Delicious, Easy-to-Grow Edibles

Eric Toensmeier

Chelsea Green Publishing
White River Junction, Vermont

Editor: Ben Watson
Project Manager and Copy Editor: Collette Leonard
Proofreader: Laura Jorstad
Design: Robert Yerks, Sterling Hill Productions
Design Assistant: Abrah Griggs, Sterling Hill Productions
Printed in the United States
First printing, May 2007
10 9 8 7 6 5 4 3 2 1

Our Commitment to Green Publishing
Chelsea Green sees publishing as a tool for cultural change and ecological sterwardship.
We strive to align our book manufacturing practices with our editorial mission, and to
reduce the impact of our business enterprise on the environment. We print our books
and catalogs on chlorine-free recycled paper, using soy-based inks, whenever possible.
Chelsea Green is a member of the Green Press Initiative (www.greenpressinitiative.org),
a nonprofit coalition of publishers, manufacturers, and authors working to protect the
world's endangered forests and conserve natural resources.
   Perennial Vegetables was printed on New Life Opaque, a 30 percent post-consumer-
waste recycled paper supplied by RR Donnelley–Willard, OH.

Library of Congress Cataloging-in-Publication Data

Toensmeier, Eric.
Perennial vegetables : from artichoke to zuiki taro, a gardener's guide to over 100 delicious,
easy-to-grow edibles / by Eric Toensmeir [sic].
      p. cm.
Includes bibliographical references and index.
ISBN-13: 978-1-931498-40-1
ISBN-10: 1-931498-40-7
1. Vegetables. 2. Vegetable gardening. 3. Perennials. I. Title.

SB320.9.T64 2007
635—dc22   2006102256

Chelsea Green Publishing Company
Post Office Box 428
White River Junction, Vermont 05001
(802) 295-6300
www.chelseagreen.com

Contents

Part III:
Resources

Preface

In the summer of 2002, in a rented RV dubbed Maxine, four friends and I drove the length of Florida. My good friend and plant geek extraordinaire Craig Hepworth was our guide, and took us to wonders like ECHO, the Fruit and Spice Park, and the legendary Grimmel Grove in the Keys. In a mere six days we sampled a remarkable 62 species of fruit. While driving through the Everglades, I mentioned that Ben Watson of Chelsea Green had asked me to write a book on perennial vegetables. By the end of an hour my friends had me convinced that I should go for it. Without their support I would not be typing these words right now. To Craig, Jonathan, Darini, and Scott, thank you.

When in 1989 I first discovered permaculture and the "agriculturally productive ecosystems" it promoted, I was sure that comprehensive lists of perennial vegetables had been developed. But as I investigated further in college, it became clear that, unlike fruits and nuts, there was no one place to turn for information on perennial vegetables. I began to piece together information from various sources, with help from Steve Breyer of Tripple Brook Farm and my trusty copies of *Cornucopia* and *Hortus Third*. To fill the gap, I founded and ran the Perennial Vegetable Seed Company for several years. While a nice idea, it turned out that it was a bit before its time—and that I was clearly not cut out for the seed business.

It was during the years of the seed company that Jonathan Bates came to live with me. He quickly became my gardening partner and fellow plant geek. He carried much of the weight of the seed company in its last and most successful year, and together we grew out many perennial vegetables—several were from seeds imported from Europe. We learned how they grew, how they looked, and how they tasted (some terrible!). We stayed for three years, and then moved our whole garden to our current home, where we have quite a nice little garden (most of the photos in this book come from our garden, including many of the tropicals). So thanks, Jonathan, for sharing the excitement, for being such a swell, reliable guy, and putting up with the craziness of my writing for these past years.

Water lotus is not only an outstanding ornamental, but also an important root crop in much of Asia.

Thanks to my parents, who both helped out with the challenging financial aspects of writing at key times, which made this book possible in a very real way. My mother came and spent many weekends, keeping me company while I wrote. Visits to my father in Arizona, and his fantastic cactus garden, built my understanding of arid-climate gardening.

Thanks as well to the crew at Chelsea Green Publishing. As I write the process is not quite complete, but I can say a big thanks to senior editor Ben Watson for proposing the book several times over the years, and sticking with me through a good bit longer than the year of writing we initially anticipated. The whole production and editing team has been great to work with—thus far John Barstow and Collette Leonard have been especially helpful. I am grateful to President Margo Baldwin for raising the flag of permaculture at Chelsea Green—they have become the premier North American permaculture publisher. Thanks also to Elayne Sears for her fantastic illustrations. Having worked with her on *Edible Forest Gardens*, I knew what she was capable of and was able to build the book around the visual element.

Thanks to my pals Dave Jacke, Craig Hepworth, Jonathan Bates, Michelle Wiggins, and my mom, who reviewed several drafts. Thanks also to everyone who supplied photographs, including Ethan Rowland, Dave Jacke, Craig Hepworth, Judy Dolmach, Jay Ram, Brock Dolman, and Jonathan Bates. My coworker Jaime Iglesias, and friend and farmer Fermín Galarza, along with so many others from Nuestras Raíces, have shared with me many stories of life in rural Puerto Rico, and the role of many perennial vegetables in home gardens and homesteads there. Author, farmer, and teacher Miranda Smith has been a great guide through the whole writing and publishing process for this book (and for my previous one).

There are a few organizations out there that have pioneered work on perennial vegetables. They still stand out as demonstration centers, researchers, writers, and nursery sources for rare but important plants. Educational Concerns for Hunger Organization (ECHO) in Fort Myers, Florida, hosted me, allowed me to use their fantastic library, and was the location for most of my best photos as well as home of an inspirational edible landscape. Special thanks to the very busy Dr. Martin Price, who granted me a valuable interview in person, and site manager Danny Blank, who has provided special tours for me over many years. Plants for a Future in Cornwall, England, an organization that I visited in 1997, has done so much to promote temperate-climate perennial crops, including a great demonstration site, nursery, book, and online database. The Occidental Arts and Ecology Center in Occidental, California, likewise has amazing gardens, a nursery offering great perennial vegetables, and courses and workshops to promote permaculture. They have been great with me on the phone, and I hope to visit someday. Finally, though now defunct, Triades in Hawaii did incredible work, particularly publishing the *Tropical Perennial Vegetable* series, promoting species suited to Pacific island farms and gardens. Their work is being carried on by Agrinom in Hakalau, Hawaii.

Also thanks to the Internet radio station Delicious Lo-fi Lounge on Live365. com, which I listened to while writing essentially all of the species profiles. Give it a try while you are reading!

A special thanks to the memory and family of Robert Wagner. Bob was a dedicated plant enthusiast who had an incredible collection of plants and books he collected in travels around the world. When he died a few years ago, the cold climates of the world lost an amazing resource. My thanks to his brother, who donated Bob's seed collection to Seed Savers Exchange and his books to the New England Small Farm Institute Library, as well as some tropical titles and duplicate copies to my own collection. These resources greatly improved this book—including rarities like *Vegetables of the Dutch East Indies* and a battered copy of Vilmorin-Andrieux's *The Vegetable Garden*. I hope that this book can pass Bob's legacy to the wider audience he deserved.

Much appreciation to my sweetheart Marikler Girón Ramirez, who has been so good to me, and has generously shared me with this book even when we would have rather been together.

I hope that this small work can be a humble contribution to permaculture and all forms of ecological gardening. Now that we have a guide to the species, we can experiment and find the best ways to incorporate them into our gardens. And let's get breeding!

ERIC TOENSMEIER
Holyoke, Massachusetts
December 7, 2006

Part I

Gardening with Perennial Vegetables

CHAPTER ONE

A New Class of Food Plants

I just had a delicious meal of cooked greens from my garden. This abundant harvest of leaves came in an appetizing array of colors, from light green to rich emerald to gray-blue, and diverse flavors: lemony 'Profusion' sorrel; nutty, cabbage-like sea kale; the sweet yet pungent garlic flavor of wild leeks; tender, tasty shoots of water celery; and the mustardy, arugula-like bite of Turkish rocket greens in spring. What was remarkable was that I planted all of these vegetables four years ago, and today they are producing better than ever. I am a lazy gardener with a bad back, but with a bit of mulching and weeding these vegetables have yielded abundantly and have required very little care over the years.

With the exception of asparagus and rhubarb, perennial vegetables are largely unknown to American and Canadian gardeners. These plants produce vegetable crops for many years without replanting, taste delicious, yield abundantly, and can be harvested when annual garden crops aren't available. This book will introduce you to over 100 of the best perennial vegetables that deserve more attention and a place at the gardener's table.

Many of the species profiled here can grow in niches of your garden where you have never been able to grow food crops before. Some thrive in full shade, others grow in poor or waterlogged soils, and some will even grow in your water garden. Once established, these crops will bear for years, some for decades! Plant some perennial vegetables, including beautiful edible trees, shrubs, and vines, and in a few years' time you can become a forager in your own backyard Garden of Eden. When combined with berry bushes and fruit and nut trees, perennial vegetables allow you to create an attractive and productive edible landscape.

To grow most of these plants, you probably won't need many skills you don't already possess. Part I of this book will teach you the few additional tricks you might want to learn, and give you some ideas about incorporating perennial vegetables into your garden. After all, what gardener can resist learning about new and interesting plants?

The edible shoots, or "fiddleheads," of ostrich fern.

The Species Profiled in This Book

I'm not the world's most sophisticated gardener, but I do know my plants. I have spent many years researching, growing, and cooking with perennial vegetables, and I have traveled quite a bit to sample species that won't grow in my region. In this book I have compiled the vegetables I believe to be the very finest that can be grown in Canada and the United States, including Hawaii.

Several criteria were used in selecting the species in this book. Most importantly, all of the species listed here are both *perennial* and used *as a vegetable.* In this book the word *perennial* means any plant that lives for three or more years. It can include the herbaceous species we usually call perennials, as well as trees, bulbs, shrubs, cacti, bamboos, grasses, and vines. Some of these plants will stay in one place while others will form large colonies. While a few are fairly short-lived, others (in the words of Liberty Hyde Bailey) ". . . may remain long after the house they were planted around falls down." All plants listed here also give perennial harvests—in other words, I have not included species that are killed by harvesting (like perennial root crops that form a single tuber).

I have focused on plants that a gardener would actually want to eat as a vegetable. Culinary herbs and minor edible "novelty" plants are not included. The vegetables profiled here include those grown for green parts like leaves, leafstalks, stems, and shoots; roots, tubers, bulbs, and other underground parts; flowers and flowerbuds; and pods and beans. I have also included some fruits that are eaten as vegetables. While this is a bit of a gray area, I have selected those fruits that are used in salads or cooked dishes like tomatoes or cucumbers, rather than dessert fruits like strawberries.

In addition, I have tried to include plants suitable for a wide range of climates. Some of the tropical species listed can be grown in colder climates as annuals or dieback perennials, allowing northern gardeners to give them a try as well. I have chosen species that are adapted to as much of the United States and Canada as possible. Since most of those areas have some frost, I have de-emphasized the many excellent tropical perennial vegetables. Thus a hardy crop like stinging nettle, which is probably only minor in the great scheme of things, gets a major write-up, while the tropical-only sissoo spinach, which in a tropical book would get a major write-up, is treated as a minor crop here.

Benefits of Perennial Vegetables

Perennial vegetables are low-maintenance

Think about how much work your perennial flowerbed takes compared with your annual vegetable garden. In a busy year your perennial garden largely sails through despite neglect. Once your perennials are established, and if they are suited to your climate and site conditions, they can be virtually indestructible. An annual vegetable garden, as we all know, requires much more watering, weeding, and work to get a good crop. Once established perennial vegetables are often more resistant to the attacks of pests due to their reserves of energy stored in their roots.

Many readers undoubtedly grow, or have grown, asparagus. In fact, asparagus is the only perennial vegetable most people can think of. Let's take a moment to reflect on your experiences with asparagus. Every year it comes back, providing a long and delicious season of harvest. Sure, it needs some weeding and fertilizing. But I know a lot of people who neglect their asparagus terribly and still have good harvests. Many other perennial vegetables are a lot tougher than asparagus. In fact, some perennial vegetables fend for themselves so well that they require frequent harvesting to keep them from becoming weeds. This phenomenon of little care for multiple years of harvests is,

Types of Perennial Vegetables

Edible Leaves

There are many perennial vegetables with edible leaves, stems, and leafstalks. These include some fascinating trees, shrubs, and woody vines.

Water Celery. This celery-flavored green thrives in water gardens or makes a great groundcover in sun or shade.

Edible Fruits Used as Vegetables

Just as there are many annual fruits used as vegetables (like tomatoes and eggplants), some perennials have fruits that are cooked or used in meals.

Chayote. This vine produces tasty pear-sized squash. They have a mild, nutty flavor and are used like zucchini and summer squash.

JUDY DOLMACH

Edible Shoots

This includes many crops with edible, tender new growth.

Asparagus. The most popular perennial vegetable in cold climates, fresh-picked asparagus is surely one of the world's finest meals.

Edible Pods and Beans

Many perennial legumes have edible beans and pods.

Scarlet Runner Bean. In England scarlet runners are the most popular green bean. Runner beans can bear for 20 years and can be grown as perennials in Zone 8 or even 7 with protection.

CHELSEA GREEN PUBLISHING STOCK PHOTO

BROCK DORMAN

Edible Flowers and Flowerbuds

Some vegetables are flowers and flowerbuds, like broccoli and cauliflower.

Globe Artichoke. This gourmet vegetable is a perennial in California, and new varieties mean gardeners can grow their own artichokes as annuals in a much larger area.

Colony-Forming Root Crops

Many perennial root crops form large colonies, which can be harvested for decades.

Sunchoke. This relative of native sunflowers, also commonly known as Jerusalem artichoke, has enormous yields of sweet, crisp roots.

Aerial Root Crops

Air potato and some other yam species actually produce tubers on vines above ground.

Air Potato. This unique vegetable grows apple-sized roots on climbing vines, which can be picked just like a fruit! They are among the few root crops that require no digging.

Plant/Replant Root Crops

These vegetables are the least perennial of the plants profiled in this book. They form clumps with multiple tubers. When you harvest them you just replant a few to ensure next year's harvest.

Oca. This "lost crop of the Incas" produces sweet, tart tubers in beautiful colors.

in my mind, the number one reason to grow perennial vegetables.

Their deep roots and soil-building abilities make perennials more self-sufficient in terms of watering, and their canopies, which leaf out so much earlier than annuals, better suppress the growth of weeds. What else can these remarkable plants do?

Perennial vegetables are great soil-builders

Perhaps the greatest ecological benefit from perennials is their beneficial effect on soil. Bare soil quickly dries out and can be eroded by wind and rain, especially in sloping gardens. Tillage also kills many beneficial elements of the soil food web, particularly some of the best kinds of mycorrhizae (beneficial fungi that share nutrients with crop plants). Well-mulched perennials don't need any tilling once they are established.

But the soil benefits of perennials come not just from the absence of tillage. Perennials improve the soil's organic matter, structure and porosity, and water-holding capacity through the slow and steady decomposition of their roots and leaves. Perennial vegetable gardens build soil the way nature intended—allowing the plants to add more and more organic matter without tillage, and letting the worms do the work of mixing it all together.

Perennials provide ecosystem benefits

Perennials, especially trees, moderate microclimates, making the areas around them cooler and moister. Large numbers of trees can moderate the climates of whole regions in a similar fashion. The root systems of perennials catch and store water and nutrients that would otherwise be washed away. Perennials provide critical habitat to a number of animal, fungal, and other life-forms, many of which are highly beneficial in gardens.

Perennial vegetables combat global warming

Perhaps most critically, no-till perennials help moderate climate change by capturing atmospheric carbon from carbon dioxide and sequestering it in long-term storage as soil humus and perennial plant parts. With climate change poised to create dramatic changes in all of our lives, converting as much of our food production as possible to no-till perennials is an important step.

Perennial vegetables extend the harvest season

Perennials often have different seasons of availability from annuals, which helps spread the season of harvest throughout more of the year. While you are starting seeds indoors, or transplanting tiny, vulnerable seedlings out to the garden, which must be watered and weeded frequently, many perennials are already in robust growth or even ready for harvesting. In my own garden I begin eating the first tender perennial shoots not long after the snow melts. Later, in the heat of mid-summer, I visit the sweltering hot beds along my driveway to harvest some delicious tropical heat-loving greens. Perennial vegetables can provide food during those times of year when your annual garden doesn't have much to offer.

Perennial vegetables often can perform multiple functions in the garden

In addition to years or decades of low-maintenance yields and soil-building benefits, perennial vegetables can do other important jobs in the garden. Many are beautiful ornamental plants that can contribute to attractive edible landscapes. Some species can function as hedges, groundcovers, or erosion control for steep slopes. Others provide free fertilizer for themselves and their neighbors by fixing atmospheric nitrogen or accumulating subsoil nutrients. And some help out with pest control, by providing habitat or food for predatory and other beneficial insects. Vines like chayote and perennial cucumber can be grown over trellis frames to create "edible shade houses," creating a cool place to snack out of the sun. See page 15 for tables of multifunctional perennial vegetables.

Drawbacks of Perennial Vegetables

No crop is perfect, and perennial vegetables are no exception. Here are some of the disadvantages of growing perennial vegetables.

- Some perennial vegetables are slow to establish and may require several years of growth to begin yielding well. Asparagus is a classic example.
- Like annual crops, some perennial greens become bitter once they flower. Thus their greens are available only early in the season. Perennial vegetables are not meant to replace annuals, but to complement them. In this case, perennial greens are available early in the season, providing greens until the annuals are up and running.
- Many of the minor perennial vegetables have rather strong flavors, especially those adapted to cold climates.
- Many perennial vegetables are so low-maintenance that they can become weeds in your garden, or escape and naturalize in your neighborhood.
- Perennial vegetables will not fit into your ordinary annual garden management plan and will need an area just for them (like you probably do now for asparagus, globe artichokes, or rhubarb).
- Perennials have special disease challenges. First, you can't use crop rotation to minimize diseases. Second, once they have a disease they often have it for good—for example, plant viruses are problematic with some perennial crops that are vegetatively propagated (cut or divided for multiplication).

You will find suggested solutions for each of these challenges in chapter 4, "Techniques."

"Perennials Grown as Annuals"

One occasionally sees a crop described as a "perennial grown as an annual" (some of these crops are referred to here as "plant/replant perennials"; see page 53). Sometimes there are good reasons to grow perennials as annuals. For example, if left in the same place year after year, potatoes would build up terrible disease pressure. On the other hand, many crops usually grown as annuals make fine perennials (such as skirret, which actually has better flavor when grown as a perennial). In some cases, we just don't know what would happen to these crops if they were allowed to persist for multiple years. Perhaps new techniques would need to be developed to manage them in this fashion. It is my hope that readers of this book will get excited about experimenting with species like oca or multiplier onions as perennials just to see what happens.

Why You've Probably Never Heard of These Crops Before

Why are asparagus, rhubarb, and globe artichokes the only perennial vegetables most gardeners have heard of? I have a few practical answers, and some speculative ones.

Lack of information

When I first became interested in perennial vegetables, I found that I had to fish for little bits of information here and there. There was no single book or Web site devoted to perennial vegetables. One could read many gardening books, review issues of garden magazines, and never get an inkling of this other class of vegetable crops that exists. My sincere hope is that

The Origins of Annual Agriculture in North America

In the United States and Canada most of our gardening traditions come from Europe, where there are few perennial crops (except fruits and nuts). However, much of our landmass is well suited to crops from warm and tropical regions where, it turns out, there are numerous perennial vegetables. So why haven't people been growing perennial vegetables in the United States and Canada for centuries? In the tropics there are many more perennial vegetables. Why were so few perennials domesticated in colder and temperate climates? The answer may have its roots in the multiple independent origins of agriculture itself and the historical peculiarities of the areas where crops were domesticated.

In tropical areas of Africa, Asia, and Latin America, agriculture developed strongly around root and starchy fruit crops as staples. This enabled crops to be grown in mixtures of trees, vines, perennials, and annuals. Cold and temperate Eurasian agriculture was built around annual grains and legumes. Why did this happen? Partly it is a question of the plants available as raw material for domestication—perhaps, with a far greater diversity to choose from, more perennial candidates were available in the tropics.

But, remarkably, Europeans actually took some perennial wild edible plants and bred them into annual crops, such as beets and brassicas. In contrast, ancient Andean people domesticated the perennial, rather than annual, forms of arracacha. In fact, a strikingly high number of perennial vegetables originated in the tropical Americas, like chayote, chaya, and perennial beans.

One possible explanation is that the Americas were without domesticated draft animals to pull plows. All farmwork had to be done with hand tools, allowing different parts of the farm to get custom treatment with no real extra energy cost. In most of the Old World draft animals were used to plow up large areas. Growing perennials would have required areas set aside for different management systems. Perhaps this explains the "annualizing" of perennial wild crops like beets and brassicas.

Jared Diamond's *Guns, Germs, and Steel* gives an intriguing history of agriculture. It turns out that agriculture in Eurasia began in the Mediterranean, in a winter rain–summer drought climate that favored annuals. These crops were adopted in Europe, and may have superseded any development of perennials that might otherwise have occurred.

Another factor could be that the early crop domesticator's most important goal was getting enough food to eat. Perhaps raw material from annuals gave quicker rewards than perennials, particularly in cold climates where a short growing season often means that perennials require several years before they begin bearing.

Whatever the origin of our neglect, there is certainly no longer a valid reason to ignore these useful and productive crops. Perennial vegetables can (and should) be made much more widely available, and I believe that a network of gardeners will prove them to be an important new component of food production in the United States and Canada in the coming years.

the publication of this book will help to rectify that situation.

The chicken-and-egg problem

Only a small number of nurseries and seed companies offer even the best perennial vegetables! In fact, some are still commercially unavailable in the United States and Canada even as I write this book. These plants will never have the chance to become popular if no one can acquire them. On the other hand, nurseries and seed companies will never offer them if there is no demand.

Readers of this book can break us out of this cycle by requesting (nay, demanding!) perennial vegetables from your favorite seed companies and nurseries. With your help, these useful and delicious plants will soon become more widely known and grown.

CHAPTER TWO

Design Ideas

There are lots of ways to use perennial vegetables in your garden, from traditional garden styles to edible water gardens to the integrated edible ecosystems of the future. Take a look at the design ideas presented here. How might they fit into the climate and garden traditions of your region? Which are suited to the backyard, community garden parcel, abandoned urban lot, or rural homestead where you will be gardening? Consider trying something completely different in your garden this year. To learn about the process of garden design spend some time with *Edible Forest Gardens Vol. II: Design and Practice for Temperate-Climate Permaculture.*

Perennial Vegetables in the Annual Vegetable Garden

Many gardeners already set aside a space in their vegetable garden for perennials like globe artichoke, rhubarb, and asparagus. You can use the same technique for most of the species profiled in this book. Perennial vegetable beds are often ideal to plant as a border at the edge of your annual vegetable garden so that they are out of the way of when you need to rototill. You may also want to incorporate coppice beds (see page 49), grow perennial vegetable vines on fences or arbors, or plant some edible trees (to the north of your garden so they don't cast shade).

Left: Rhubarb is one of the most widely grown perennial vegetables.

Right: Perennial vegetable border in San Francisco featuring rhubarb, globe artichoke, goldenberry, asparagus, pepino melon, and tree collards.

Edible Landscaping

Edible landscaping is just what it sounds like—incorporating food plants into ornamental landscapes. There are some great books on the subject, notably Rosalind Creasy's *Complete Book of Edible Landscaping* and Robert Kourik's *Designing and Maintaining Your Edible Landscape Naturally* (see Recommended Reading in Part III). Until now, edible landscaping has largely relied on growing fruit and nut trees along with annual vegetables. However, perennial vegetables have tremendous potential to enrich the palette for edible landscapers throughout North America.

Perennial edible landscapes are appropriate for suburban yards, public parks, the edges of urban community gardens—almost anywhere that plants can be grown. There are species suited to virtually any climate and site: See table 1 for suggested species.

A plaza in Phoenix with edible landscape featuring nopale cactus and '7 Year' lima bean with hedges of moringa and chaya, plus an edible-podded mesquite tree and wild chiltepine peppers.

Table 1: **Ornamental Perennial Vegetables for the Edible Landscape**

Bulbs	Groundcovers	Ornamental Grasses & Bamboos	Ornamental Shrubs
camass	Chinese artichoke	clumping bamboos	cassava
daylily	daylily	pitpit	chaya
garlic chive	fuki	running bamboos	cranberry hibiscus
Welsh onion	New Zealand spinach		edible hibiscus
wild hyacinth	Okinawa spinach		katuk
	ostrich fern		nopale cactus
	sheep sorrel		saltbush
	sissoo spinach		
	sweet potato		
	water celery		

Ornamental Vines	Showy Herbaceous Perennials	Specimen Trees
air potato	achira	banana & plantain
basket vine	aroids	basul
bitter gourd	arracacha	breadfruit
cache bean	asparagus	clumping bamboos
chayote	belembe	fragrant spring tree 'Flamingo'
Chinese yam	giant Solomon's seal	linden
groundnut	globe artichoke	papaya
lablab bean	Okinawa spinach	
lima bean	pokeweed	
Malabar spinach	purple tree collards	
mashua	rhubarb	
perennial cucumber	sea kale	
runner bean	skirret	
winged bean	tannier	
yams	taro	
	Turkish rocket	
	udo	
	yacon	
	yellow asphodel	
	water celery	

ECHO: A Subtropical Edible Landscape

As I write, I am sitting on the porch of the library at Educational Concerns for Hunger Organization (ECHO) in Fort Myers, Florida. I have been doing interviews and library research at this world-class collection of useful tropical plants. A midday rainstorm is pouring down on the leaves and into the pond. A cool breeze is blowing where a few minutes ago it was hot and humid. Sitting here in a comfortable chair on the veranda, protected from the rain, an edible landscape seems the most natural thing in the world. Around the buildings and in the courtyard between, virtually every plant in the landscape is a food plant. Vegetable shrubs include edible hibiscus, nopale cactus, variegated cassava, katuk, and cranberry hibiscus. Taro and lemongrass form attractive clumps, and Okinawa spinach is used as a low groundcover. Tree fruits include jakfruit, citrus, jaboticaba, guava, and banana. Lovely monstera fruit vines climb the railing. The idea just seems to make such perfect sense that I can't believe everyone isn't doing it.

ECHO is a Christian nongovernmental organization that sends free seeds of useful plants to tropical development projects all over the world. Their headquarters in Fort Myers is a world-class education center demonstrating techniques for urban rooftops, hill and mountainside farming, and tropical monsoon, rain forest, dry-land, and humid lowland biomes. Their nursery is currently one of the only U.S. mainland sources for many tropical perennial vegetables. They don't ship their plants, but it is worth a trip to Florida just to tour their farm and nursery! ECHO's mail-order seed company also offers many perennial vegetables. See Sources of Plants and Seeds in Part III for their contact information.

Edible landscape at ECHO featuring taro, cranberry hibiscus, variegated cassava, numerous tropical fruits, and an aquaculture fishpond.

More edible landscaping at ECHO with Okinawa spinach and tannier in the foreground as well as fruits including *Monstera deliciosa* and grumichama in the background.

Perennial vegetables in the edible landscape at ECHO's parking lot, featuring Okinawa spinach and cranberry hibiscus.

The Edible Water Garden

Water gardening is becoming incredibly popular. Spend some time sitting beside one on a summer day and you'll find it's not hard to see why. The quiet stillness brings a tranquil feeling. I can watch the fish, snails, and dragonflies in mine for hours. It turns out that many of the most common water garden plants are actually edible. Many other perennial vegetables are suited to water gardens as well. Edible water gardens can be extremely productive and will become a focal point in any landscape design. See the section beginning on page 60, and take a look at the books on general water gardening in Part III. I have found a few books that briefly talk about edible water gardens, including Ken Fern's *Plants for a Future* and Joy Larkcom's *Oriental Vegetables*.

Perennial Polycultures

A polyculture is a mixture of different species grown together, planted in such a way that each species benefits. When done right polycultures allow you to produce more food on the same amount of land by growing complementary plants together. Plants in a polyculture share resources—for example, shade-loving perennials like wood nettles could be grown beneath the shade of a fragrant spring tree. These plants are sharing the limited resource of sunlight, and each one gets what it needs without harm-

An edible water garden in Washington, DC, that features water lotus, watercress, water chestnut, and arrowhead, plus cattails.

Table 2: **Multifunctional Perennial Vegetables for Polycultures**

Nitrogen-Fixing Species	Nutrient Accumulators	Insect Nectaries	Groundcovers
basul	chicory	arracacha	Chinese artichoke
cache bean	dandelion	fuki	daylily
groundnut	sorrels	lovage	fuki
lablab bean	stinging nettle	Okinawa spinach	New Zealand spinach
lima bean	watercress	scorzonera	Okinawa spinach
runner bean		skirret	ostrich fern
water mimosa		sunchoke	sheep sorrel
winged bean		udo	sissoo spinach
		water celery	sweet potato
		yacon	water celery

ing the other. You can use table 3, Perennial Vegetables with Special Tolerances (page 23) to find plants with compatible sun and shade tolerances. Plants in polycultures also support one another through various kinds of ecological interactions, including:

- **Nitrogen fixation.** Some plants work with soil bacteria to turn nitrogen from the air into a usable fertilizer. These plants not only don't compete with their neighbors for nitrogen, but actually make it available to others over time through root and leaf decomposition.
- **Nutrient accumulation.** The roots of certain species reach deep into the subsoil to bring up nutrients like calcium, phosphorus, and potassium. Like nitrogen-fixers nutrient-accumulating plants compete less, and over time they increase soil fertility for their neighbors.
- **Insect nectary plants.** Many kinds of beneficial insects eat pests in the garden. A number of them like to have nectar from flowers to fuel their hunting. Certain families of plants are best at providing

that nectar—notably the Apiaceae and Asteraceae. Stocking your garden with nectary plants will help keep pest populations under control.
- **Groundcovers.** These plants form dense carpets and inhibit the germination and growth of undesired weeds.

There are perennial vegetables that fill each of these roles. *Note:* Not all species in a polyculture need to be multifunctional—some are just plain edible!

You can design polycultures that consist only of perennial vegetables. A simple example is grown at the ECHO demonstration site in Fort Myers, Florida. Perennial winged beans are grown on trellises just like ordinary pole beans. Below them, sweet potato vines cover the ground and suppress weeds. In their intense subtropical heat, sweet potatoes can grow just fine with a bit of shade. The sweet potatoes help winged beans help the sweet potatoes by fixing nitrogen.

Perennial vegetables can also play a role in polycultures that include other types of plants, such as fruit and nut trees. Shade-loving

Permaculture and Perennial Polycultures

"Permaculture (permanent agriculture) is the conscious design and maintenance of agriculturally productive ecosystems which have the diversity and resilience of natural ecosystems. It is the harmonious integration of landscape and people providing their food, energy, shelter, and other material and non-material needs in a sustainable way."

—Bill Mollison, from *Permaculture: A Practical Guide for a Sustainable Future*, 1990

Permaculture is a design tool to help you take all the garden elements you want (e.g., greenhouse, vegetables, shed, small fruits, pond) and integrate them in such a way that they become more than the sum of their parts. Permaculture is not about any particular type of food production, although it helped to develop and popularize the notion of perennial polycultures. The simple elegance of this idea has captivated me for the last 17 years. Whenever I am driving, walking, or riding my bike, I imagine the landscape around me converted to perennial polycultures.

Try to imagine polycultures of useful plants growing in public spaces everywhere. Vibrant ecosystems would surround our homes and neighborhoods, producing

- a diverse array of foods, from staple protein and carbohydrates to fruits, leaves, and roots;
- timber, bamboo, and other construction materials;
- grazing, browsing, and fodder for livestock;
- medicinal and culinary herbs;
- outdoor habitat for humans and wildlife;
- fuelwood for heat and cooking;
- fertilizers, compost feedstocks, and botanical pesticides;
- biofuels like vegetables oils to run diesel engines; and
- plant-based petroleum and plastic substitutes.

We're not there yet. In fact, while some tropical areas have farmed this way for centuries, it is not yet certain that this vision is even possible for the frostier climates most readers of this book live in. But there is only one way to find out—to start experimenting on whatever land we have access to.

It isn't enough to grow food sustainably—it has to be distributed equitably as well, and that's going to take a lot more than perennial polycultures. We need political and economic systems that prioritize human beings and the environment over short-term greed and oppression. In such a scenario permaculture systems could provide the abundant basis of life in a "post-scarcity" agriculture. Perennial food systems could mean less work, less petroleum use, and more free time to enjoy life—that is, after the first few decades of working the bugs out and getting those trees to grow to maturity!

Ultimately, permaculture offers a vision of how humanity can participate in—rather than damage—our planet's ecosystems and the process of evolution itself. When seen in this context, perennial vegetables are not just a novelty for the garden: They may just have a humble role to play in the future of our species and its relationship to the planet it calls home.

For further reading, see Bill Mollison and Reny Mia Slay's *Introduction to Permaculture* and David Holmgren's *Permaculture: Principles and Pathways Beyond Sustainability*.

This perennial vegetable polyculture at ECHO features winged bean on tipi trellises above a groundcover of sweet potato.

vegetables like sissoo spinach and ramps can be grown in the shade of fruit and nut trees. Clumping bamboos and trees with edible leaves can take their place in the canopy of such food forests. Globe artichokes, bush cherries, and tree collards can tower above a low carpet of 'Flamingo' water celery. Wherever you live, you can intermingle your perennial vegetables with locally adapted fruit and nut trees, nitrogen-fixing plants, and other ornamental and functional plants.

To learn more about designing polycultures, spend some time with *Edible Forest Gardens Vol. II: Ecological Design and Practice for Temperate-Climate Permaculture.*

Naturalizing Perennial Vegetables

When grown in amenable conditions, some perennial vegetables will make themselves at home in your garden, thriving and spreading on their own. Some are resilient enough that they can be released to fend for themselves, forming naturalized colonies that you can harvest from as a forager rather than a gardener. For example, you may want to permit water lotus to fill up a constructed pond, or allow bamboo to stabilize an eroded hillside.

Of course there are issues involved in releasing plants into the wild (see the discussion in the article Rethinking Nonnative Plants on

Perennial polyculture: An edible forest garden in Seattle with fragrant spring tree 'Flamingo', skirret, sea kale, water celery, and Welsh onion, plus Saskatoon berry and sea buckthorn.

Naturalized native perennial vegetables in Montreal, including ostrich fern, arrowhead, sunchoke, groundnut, wood nettle, and linden.

page 31). Certainly one should feel good about reintroducing native perennial vegetables into neighboring wild areas. For example, in my area ramps (*Allium tricoccum*) were once widespread. Hundreds of years of clearing and grazing left only fragmented populations of this woodland species. Everywhere I drive I see moist deciduous woods (a perfect habitat for this plant) without ramps. Transplanting ramp bulbs to these areas can help to reestablish viable populations.

"Guerrilla gardening" is the planting of food and other plants in areas that do not belong to you. The goal is not necessarily to form viable colonies, but simply to grow some figs or tree collards (for example) in an empty urban lot. Guerrilla gardening is an effort to make our neighborhoods more human-friendly. In the highly disturbed areas where most guerrilla gardening takes place, there is little native vegetation left to displace. As long as you are not planting species that disperse aggressively by seed, I don't see any ecological problem with this technique. For much more discussion of this topic, read *Food Not Lawns: How to Turn Your Yard into a Garden and Your Neighborhood into a Community* by H. C. Flores (see the bibliography). What I would discourage is planting nonnative perennial vegetables in "wild" areas. Let's leave our healthy ecosystems (such as they are) alone. This is especially critical with aquatic plants, as it is far too easy for aquatic plants to spread rapidly.

CHAPTER THREE

Selecting Species

Well over 100 species are profiled in this book. How can you determine which ones are best suited to your garden's unique conditions and to your specific needs? First, consider where you are going to be gardening. Are the soils wet, dry, or just right? Rich and fertile or poor and unproductive? Is it sunny or shady, or does it have patches of both? And, most importantly, what is the overall climate in your region?

This information about your garden site places important constraints over what perennial vegetables you can grow. There are probably species profiled in this book that are well suited to whatever conditions you currently have. But you are not entirely at the mercy of your garden—many conditions can be made more favorable for your desired crops. For example, you can improve poor soils, provide irrigation, and find or create protected microclimates for tender crops. Also, many tropical perennial vegetables can be grown virtually anywhere as annuals.

Unfortunately, you can only modify your garden so far. Bananas and breadfruit are just not going to produce well in your Omaha garden. If you are determined to raise a particular species not suited to your particular climate, your only option is a serious greenhouse or other climate-controlled structure, at which point I wish you good luck, but this book won't help you much in that venture: I am focusing on growing crops outdoors with only minimal protection.

Once you have determined the potential pool of crops that you can grow, find the ones that you would most like to raise and eat. You may also be selecting for garden or ecological functions, such as a good groundcover for your edible landscape, a nitrogen-fixer for an experimental polyculture, or a vine to cover an arbor in your garden.

Part III includes the list Perennial Vegetables for Each Climate Type, which can help you with this process. It has information on the climate suitability of all the species profiled in this book. You may also want to review the tables in Part I,

Once cooked, the spring shoots of nettles are
rich, nutritious, and lose their sting.

notably the tables on ornamental and multi-functional species in the "Design Ideas" chapter, the special tolerances and tropical plants as annuals tables, and the table of aquatic perennials in the "Techniques" chapter.

Of course, if you are like me you will do this whole process backward. You will want to read all of the profiles to find which get you most excited. That's just fine. Each profile features a little map demonstrating the range where the crop can be grown as a perennial, and in some cases where its range can be extended as an annual. The profiles also include detailed information on climate, soils, and other requirements.

Sun, Soils, and Water

Many perennial vegetables can grow in adverse growing conditions that tomatoes or broccoli can't go near. Some even perform better in shade or poor soils. Regardless, it is important to review the requirements of any species before including it in your garden. Match species to the conditions in different areas of your garden, or modify your conditions to accommodate desirable species. To learn how see Site Preparation in the "Techniques" chapter. Consult table 3, Perennial Vegetables with Special Tolerances, to find species for troublesome spots.

Climate

Most gardeners already know their hardiness zone using the USDA or Canadian system. The hardiness zone system is somewhat limited, as it only measures minimum winter temperatures. Clearly, many other factors are at play in the survival of plants. For example, mashua, an Andean root crop, is hardy to USDA Zone 7 or 8 as far as minimum temperatures are concerned, but it cannot tolerate hot summers and prefers cool, misty weather. Although

Seattle and Atlanta both have acceptable winter minimum temperatures, mashua is only suited to the Pacific Northwest.

In recent years a more sophisticated climate map for the United States has been developed. The *Sunset National Garden Book* system incorporates factors including summer heat, timing and quantity of rainfall, and length of growing season. It has been reprinted as a set of regional guides. For more of these details of your regional climate, check out the *Southern Living Garden Book*, *Sunset Western Garden Book*, *Sunset Northeastern Garden Book*, or *Sunset Midwestern Landscaping Book* (see the bibliography).

You Might Be Surprised by What You Can Grow

Wherever you live, you can probably grow lots of great plants that you thought were too tender for your climate. Hardiness is more complex than you might think, and you can do a lot to protect plants from less-than-ideal conditions.

- First, many species, or certain varieties of them, are hardier than they are given credit for. For example, while most true yams (*Dioscorea* spp.) are tropical or subtropical, several edible species including Chinese yam (*D. batatas*) are hardy to Zone 4!
- Second, different parts of plants are hardy in different ways. The leaves, stems, and roots of a plant, for example, will be killed at vastly different temperatures. The leaves and stems of moringa trees will be killed to the ground in a hard frost—but as long as it was not cold enough to freeze the ground, the tree will put up multiple shoots 15 feet high again when it warms up, providing a long season of nutritious greens!
- Third, while you have a hardiness zone on paper, microclimate varies enormously. Proper siting in a location protected

Table 3: Perennial Vegetables with Special Tolerances

Dry Soils	Wet Soils (See page 64 for aquatic perennial vegetables)	Poor Soils
'7 Year' lima bean	achira	achira
bull nettle	arrowhead	basul
cassava	belembe	cassava
chaya	canebrake bamboo	chaya
daylily	chufa	chicory
lablab bean	daylily	dandelion
moringa	fuki	daylily
New Zealand spinach	groundnut	goldenberry
nopale cactus	ostrich fern	groundnut
saltbush	ramps	Haitian basket vine
sheep sorrel	skirret	mashua
spurge nettle	tannier	moringa
sylvetta arugula	taro	New Zealand spinach
Turkish rocket	violet-stem taro	pitpit
	water celery	pokeweed
	water mimosa	saltbush
	water spinach	sweet potato
	watercress	sylvetta arugula
		ulluco

Partial Shade			Full Shade
achira	lovage	sissoo spinach	fuki
arracacha	mountain sorrel	skirret	giant Solomon's seal
basket vine	musk mallow	sorrels	katuk
belembe	nettles	tannier	linden
bitter gourd	New Zealand spinach	taro	ostrich fern
camass	Okinawa spinach	Turkish rocket	ramps
Chinese artichoke	papaya	udo	ramson
clumping bamboos	perennial cucumber	violet-stem taro	wood nettle
cranberry hibiscus	perennial sweet leek	walking onion	
daylily	pokeweed	water celery	
edible hibiscus	running bamboos	wild hyacinth	
good king Henry	scorzonera	wolfberry	
groundnut	sea beet	yellow asphodel	

Guidelines and Inspiration for Each Climate Type

For the purposes of this book I have divided the United States and Canada into eight basic climate types. Find your home on the map and read the overview for your garden's potential. For a complete list of species that can grow in each climate type, see Perennial Vegetables for Each Climate Type in Part III.

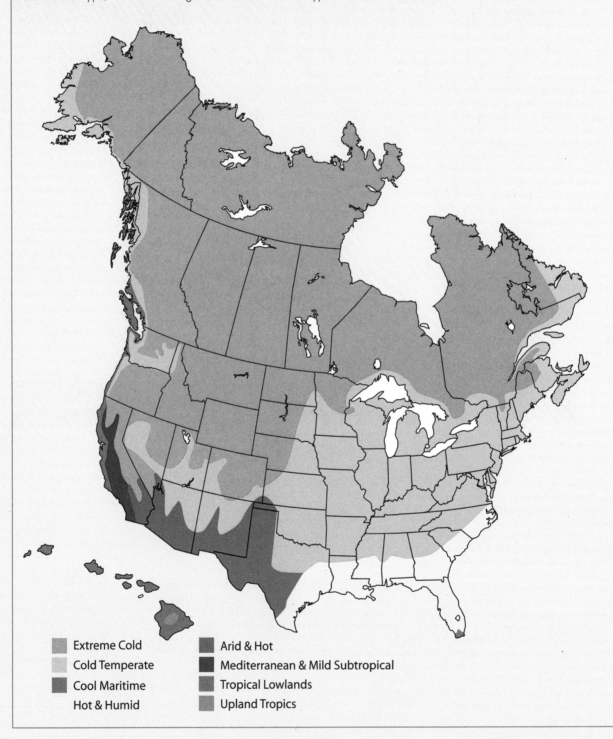

Extreme Cold

Cold Temperate

Cool Maritime

Hot & Humid

Arid & Hot

Mediterranean & Mild Subtropical

Tropical Lowlands

Upland Tropics

Extreme Cold: High Mountains and Frozen Northlands

Gardeners of the frozen mountains and northlands of central and eastern Canada and the northern U.S. plains and the Rockies, take heart! A surprising number of perennial vegetables thrive in your climate; in fact, many of the best are from extreme cold regions. Some highlights: rhubarb, hardy to an unbelievable −50°F; sunchoke, ostrich fern, and watercress, to USDA Zone 2; and many others to Zone 3, including asparagus, as well as many greens like sorrel, pokeweed, and good king Henry; plus roots like groundnut and arrowhead. Snow cover is likely to be so deep that herbaceous plants will actually experience a relatively mild winter—at least compared with trees and shrubs! The issue really becomes what crops can mature in your short season. Consider pushing the limits with more tender edible greens and shoots in protected locations, especially where they will be deeply buried under snow. This region corresponds with USDA Zones 1–3 and Sunset Zones 1, 44, and 45.

Cold Temperate: East, Midwest, and Mountain West

While cold-climate gardeners cannot grow the flashy crops of the tropics, there are many perennial vegetables we can grow that are productive and delicious. Many more are excellent raw material just waiting for the attention of backyard breeders to fully come into their own. Sea kale, asparagus, arrowhead, sorrel, and chicory are reliable and tasty components of the hardy perennial vegetable garden. Wood nettle, ramps, and good king Henry are shade-lovers well suited to growing in edible forest gardens beneath fruit and nut trees. We can also grow many of the finest tender species as annuals, such as cranberry hibiscus, runner beans, and Malabar spinach. This region corresponds with USDA Zones 4–7 and Sunset Zones 2–4, 6, 11, and 32–43.

Cool Maritime: The Pacific Northwest

From San Francisco north to Vancouver and the Alaska panhandles lies a narrow, highly populated coastal region. The Northwest is characterized by mild rainy winters and dry, warm summers. Many native wild edibles of this area are perennial, including camass and arrowhead. Many crops from coastal Europe can be grown here, including the magnificent shrub-like perennial kales. The Northwest is also a good area for growing high-altitude tropical plants as annuals, such as mashua and oca. Mix perennial vegetables with berries, hazels, and the apples that grow so well in your region. This region corresponds with USDA Zones 8–9 and Sunset Zones 5 and 17.

Hot and Humid: The Southeast

This region can grow almost everything colder regions can, plus many tropical and subtropical perennial vegetables. The Gulf Coast and parts of Florida can grow 'Rajapuri' bananas and chayote. These warmer parts of the region can experiment with tropical crops such as yams, katuk, and perennial beans as dieback perennials. These same crops are worth experimenting with in the colder parts of Zone 8 with protection. Taro is actually fully hardy through this zone and even a bit colder. Whether you are in the peach belt or the citrus belt, you will be able to grow many of the world's best perennial vegetables. This region corresponds with USDA Zones 8–9 and Sunset Zones 26–28 and 31.

Arid and Hot: The Southwest

Some of the finest perennial vegetables are ideally adapted to the Southwest. Moringa trees and chaya shrubs can be grown as dieback perennial leaf crops. Of course the spineless nopale cactus is already grown by many gardeners in the region. Several perennial beans are drought-lovers, including the highly productive '7 Year' lima bean. These perennials could be components of an edible xeriscape, combined with fruiting cacti, pomegranates, and mesquite. This region can also grow a great many warm-climate and tropical perennials as long as sufficient irrigation is provided. This region includes much of inland California, an area we don't usually think of as arid due to extensive irrigation. This region corresponds with USDA Zones 8–10 and Sunset Zones 10, 12, 13, 29, and 30.

Mediterranean and Mild Subtropical: Southern and Coastal California

From San Francisco and southward the climate of the coast and adjacent inland areas is among the world's best areas for growing globe artichokes. Other crops that thrive here include pepino melon, the delicious edible shrub saltbush, and goldenberry. The edible canna achira should thrive here. Many tropical perennial vegetables can be grown here with minimal protection as dieback perennials, including some edible groundcovers like Okinawa and sissoo spinach. More inland areas, while colder in winter, have a long growing season enabling the protected production of yams and many other tropical vegetables. This region corresponds with USDA Zones 8–10 and Sunset Zones 7–9, 14–16, and 18–25.

Tropical Lowlands: Hawaii and South Florida

It is in the tropics that the full promise of perennial vegetables is already fulfilled. Trees and shrubs with edible leaves abound, from moringa to edible hibiscus. The magnificent breadfruit will only grow in Hawaii and the Florida Keys—apparently it finds Miami winters a bit too chilly. Winged beans and chayote provide beans and squash to complement the many perennial leaf and root crops. Here giant clumping bamboos can produce high yields of crisp shoots. Tropical perennial vegetables are ideal for growing in polycultures between and beneath coconut, mango, and other tree crops. This region corresponds with USDA Zones 10–12 and Sunset Zone 25.

The Hawaiian Upland Tropics

Although only this tiny portion of the entire United States and Canada is in upland tropics, globally this is an important biome. Mild, frost-free temperatures permit the cultivation of many interesting crops. Some, such as the remarkable tree bean basul will only grow here. Many of the Andean crops are at their best here, like achira, yacon, oca, ulluco, arracacha, and mashua. This region corresponds with USDA Zones 10–12 and is not included in the Sunset zone system. For the purposes of this book, upland tropics begins above 6,600 feet.

---

from wind or next to the wall of a heated building can effectively gain you a full zone (10°F) in warmth. This effect can also make your growing season remarkably longer.

- Fourth, protecting your plants, with a thorough mulching or other low-tech technique, can gain you another full zone!

Some plant enthusiasts have been able to overwinter taro (*Colocasia esculenta*), usually considered quite the tropical, in Zone 6. It turns out that many taro varieties (perhaps all) are hardy to Zone 7. With a protected location and plenty of mulch it can be done. A northern growing season is still not long enough to mature taro as a root crop in a single year, but one could eat roots at the end of the second year, or just harvest the edible leaves. To learn more about this fascinating subject, read the excellent *Palms Won't Grow Here and Other Myths: Warm-Climate Plants for Cooler Areas* (see the bibliography).

Manipulating microclimate

Any gardener knows that certain areas in their garden are hotter, colder, or more protected from wind than others. These small areas are called microclimates, and utilizing them efficiently is important if you want to grow crops that are not ideally suited to your climate. The first step is to identify areas where the microclimate is different. South-facing walls will be the warmest and will have the longest growing season. This might be a good or a bad thing depending on what you are trying to accomplish. The reverse is true for north-facing exposures. Large objects like buildings and walls will absorb heat during the day and release it at night. Large bodies of water will moderate extremes of temperature.

Table 4: Tropical Species That Can Be Grown as Annuals in Cold Climates

Species That Can Be Grown from Seed as Annuals		Species That Can Be Overwintered Indoors as Tubers or Corms (*Note:* Some of these have day-length issues and are better suited to the Northwest than the central and eastern cold regions)	
bitter gourd	New Zealand spinach	achira	runner bean
cache bean	pepper	aroids (for use as leaf crops)	sweet potato
cranberry hibiscus	runner bean		ulluco
goldenberry	tomato	Chinese arrowhead	water chestnut
lablab bean	winged bean 'Day Length Neutral'	mashua 'Ken Aslet'	winged bean 'Day Length Neutral'
lima bean		oca	
Malabar spinach		potato	yacon
moringa			

Species That Can Be Overwintered as Houseplants (from cuttings or small divisions)	Surprisingly Hardy "Tropical" Species
katuk	air potato
Okinawa spinach	banana 'Rajapuri'
perennial cucumber	taro
tree collards	water lotus
sissoo spinach	water celery

Plants, buildings, and other landscape features can affect crop exposure to sun, rain, and wind. Besides taking advantage of preexisting microclimates, you can also deliberately create them: for example, by planting a windbreak for protection on windy sites.

For assistance in determining the best microclimates in your garden, I highly recommend the aforementioned *Palms Won't Grow Here*, as well as *The Weather-Resilient Garden* (see the bibliography in Part III).

What if my garden is still too cold to grow my favorite tender perennial vegetables?

It is an unavoidable fact that, at this point in history, most of the best perennial vegetables are tropical or subtropical. There are plenty of good hardy species, but tropical farmers have

been selecting their perennial crops for thousands of years, and it is going to take the rest of us awhile to catch up.

There are several strategies you can try at this point. (Besides moving somewhere warmer!) Many tropical perennials, like Malabar spinach, can be grown successfully as annuals in colder climates. You can store roots or tubers indoors in a cool, dark place, just like you store dahlias or potatoes (this also works well with water chestnuts). You can also take cuttings from some species and overwinter them as houseplants, planting them out again in spring. Some of the tender species listed here, like chaya, grow well as container plants that are put outside for the summer and brought back indoors for winter. See Overwintering Tender Perennials on page 49. Of course perennial vegetables can also be

Tropical Trees as Dieback Perennials in Zones 8 and 9

Many of the best woody leaf crops are tropical and killed by frost. For those of you living in Hawaii or southern Florida, congratulations. You have some incredible plants available to you, like chaya, katuk, moringa, and cranberry and edible hibiscus. Get planting! As for the rest of us, these edible-leaved trees and shrubs have potential in a great swath of the United States as dieback perennials. While their growth is killed to the ground in a frost, most can recover just fine and send up vigorous new growth, as long as the ground does not freeze. While many fruit trees will do the same, they usually do not have enough time to set fruit before being killed back again. Thus, tropical trees and shrubs with edible leaves are uniquely suited to production as dieback perennials in Zone 9, because their food product is immediately available once their shoots emerge. These crops are even worth trying in Zone 8 with some protection from microclimate, copious mulch, or both. These nutritious, low-maintenance vegetables could become important vegetables in places like Atlanta, Florida and the Gulf Coast, much of Texas, the desert Southwest, and most of the populated parts of California.

grown in cold frames or greenhouses to allow them to be grown even farther outside their range. I encourage gardeners to do so, but this subject is outside of the scope of this book.

Growing Native and Nonnative Species

Many gardeners and environmentalists are concerned over the introduction and escape of species that are not native to their regions. Currently a very rigid "anti-exotic" stance has come into vogue. I wish I could tell you that there were hundreds of great native perennial vegetables to choose from. However, most of the best perennial vegetables are not from here, and in fact have escaped from cultivation somewhere in the United States or Canada. But is that such a bad thing? In my own region of western Massachusetts asparagus is a major crop. Wild asparagus is sometimes found along roadsides, in meadows, and in disturbed areas. It is not growing in huge monocultures, wiping out entire communities. It has simply made itself at home in the neighborhood. True "super-competitive" invasive weeds are rare. I, for one, am always delighted to pick some wild asparagus spears when out for a spring walk. Perhaps the pendulum needs to swing back a bit to an appreciation for the benefits that nonnative plants can offer us. I understand that this issue is important to many readers. I encourage you to read the accompanying article for more background. Meanwhile, the following section gives you information that can help you select or rule out species based on their native and naturalization status.

The plants discussed in this book fall into the following categories as far as this issue is concerned:

- **Species native somewhere in the United States or Canada.** Our continent is rich in fruit and nut species, but has a somewhat weak selection of perennial vegetables worth cultivating. This book profiles what I believe to be the best we have to offer, including some unique and productive crops. *Please note:* These species may also naturalize outside of their native range.
- **Nonnative plants that are not known to have escaped from cultivation and naturalized.** Although two-thirds of all nonnative plants ever introduced to North America fall into this category, only a fairly small group of the crops profiled here do.
- **Sterile or otherwise harmless varieties of normally "invasive" plants.** Many of the best perennial vegetables are quite weedy.

Sunchokes, also called Jerusalem artichokes, are a native perennial vegetable with sweet, crisp tubers.

Fortunately, varieties that do not set seed or are otherwise not able to naturalize are available for some of these crops, including the worldwide garden and farm weed chufa and perennial cucumber, the scourge of Hawaii.

- **Plants that have naturalized somewhere in the United States or Canada to a mild or moderate degree.** Most of the species in this book fit in this category. The majority of perennial vegetables are herbaceous species of mid-succession stages, including many vines. Ecologists call plants using this strategy competitors since they have evolved to disperse their seeds widely and then grow aggressively to secure a niche for themselves. It's no small wonder that the majority of perennial vegetables have escaped from cultivation and made themselves at home here. If they are already established in your neighborhood, you certainly might as well take advantage of them since planting a few more is hardly going to change the situation. Certain techniques can also minimize the potential of these species to escape your garden—like planting aquatic vegetables in containers and plastic ponds rather than establishing them in natural ponds and waterways. Otherwise I leave this ethical call up to you. Please consult the article Rethinking Nonnative and Recommended Reading in Part III if you are interested in this issue.

This book does *not* include:

- **Plants that are known to be very aggressive naturalizers and/or noxious weeds.** I have excluded some very useful plants for

this reason, including the delicious singhara ling water chestnut (*Trapa* spp.) and oyster nut squash (*Telfaria pedata*). To my mind, I simply cannot recommend planting these species at this time, with the following exceptions:

- **Water spinach,** an incredibly productive and tasty aquatic vegetable. Water spinach, a tender tropical, can be cultivated in cold areas or artificial ponds in such a way that it can't escape. This species is illegal to grow in the United States without a permit, but is legal in Canada.
- **Air potato** is unique—a root crop that produces tubers on vines above ground, as if they were fruits. The wild form has toxic tubers, and has naturalized extensively in Florida. The cultivated variety is less aggressive, although still quite vigorous. Because of the incredible potential of this plant to produce starchy tubers without digging and disturbing the soil, I believe it to be a crop of great importance.

Each profile indicates where the species is native, and whether it may naturalize.

Please note: There is a big difference between plants that are "invasive" on the ecological level (plants that escape gardens to form viable populations in the wild) and plants that spread aggressively in your garden. For instance, running *Phyllostachys* bamboos with edible shoots are not native. However, they almost never set seed, and thus won't start growing hundreds of miles away from seed carried by birds or in the cracks of car tires. But you can be sure they will form a huge colony and take over your garden if given the chance!

Rethinking Nonnative Plants

It seems that you can't discuss any interesting plant species these days without someone wanting to know within the first three minutes whether it is native or exotic and, if it is exotic, is it invasive.

Many gardeners and environmentalists are concerned that exotic invaders are outcompeting native plant species and communities. I have personally witnessed salt cedar, melaleuca, and Japanese knotweed growing in dense, virtually monocultural stands where native plant communities once grew. I have seen kudzu, bittersweet, and wild air potato smothering the very life out of mature native trees. Certainly I would hate to be responsible for the introduction of such a "super-competitive" species.

Numerous books and articles in recent years indicate the groundswell of public concern about this issue. To me this expresses a very legitimate concern about the health of our environment. It is heartening to see that so many people are taking action against the destruction of the native flora and fauna of our countries. Alan Burdick's *Out of Eden* gives an eloquent and open-minded review of the issue.

For many years my own position was to advocate the planting of native plants wherever possible, and the use of nonnative species known or likely not to escape from cultivation only if there were no native species that could perform the functions you were looking for.

Then came David Theodoropoulos's *Invasion Biology: Critique of a Pseudoscience*. An environmentalist, ecologist, and plant lover, Theodoropoulos offers a very different perspective on the issues. Though they may be unpopular in some circles, I think Theodoropoulos's ideas are a critical and largely unheard voice in this dialogue, and need to be widely heard and discussed.

Theodoropoulos is concerned that the native plant movement is becoming rigid and reactionary. Imagine our North American gardens and cuisine without peaches, apples, or carrots. Yet if you attempted to introduce these species today, you would face resistance, and perhaps even legal barriers. And indeed, all three species have naturalized here to varying degrees. Nonnative perennial vegetables could similarly become a part of our agriculture and cuisine, but could potentially escape

from cultivation. What is one to think? Let's review some aspects of the issue that have been neglected in the dialogue, and return to the question.

What exactly is a native plant?

The native plant movement in the United States and Canada generally defines *native* as a plant that was growing here in 1492. But plant populations move and always have. Plants have always traveled around the globe, often dispersed by far-flying birds. It seems likely that the bottle gourd floated across the Atlantic Ocean from West Africa to South America thousands of years ago and established itself there. Climate changes cause tremendous movements of plants. Fifteen thousand years ago my garden was buried under a mile-high glacier, and north Florida was home to spruce forests similar to those that you would now find north of Montreal. As continents move and come into and out of contact with each other, massive waves of species travel among them. Animals that we consider native, such as grizzly bears and moose, have in reality only arrived from Eurasia within the last 13,000 years—just the blink of an eye in ecological time. Tim Flannery's *The Eternal Frontier* is a fascinating account of the last 65 million years of North American history. It describes waves of species arriving and emigrating over and over, offering a very different perspective on what is native. In this context, the arrival of new species is not a new phenomenon. The difference is the dispersal vector (humans), and the rate of new species arriving (although this is also not without historical precedent). This perspective of evolutionary biology has largely been missing from discourse on invasives.

Invasive plants defined

Invasive species must meet two criteria. First, they must not be native according the criteria discussed above. Second, they must be growing in the wild without human assistance. Most definitions would also say that invasive plants are those that have not only naturalized, but also done so successfully enough to outcompete natives and cause ecological harm (Theodoropoulos critiques the way invasion biologists define *harm* as well). Remember that most nonnative plants do not escape from cultivation, and those that do rarely become "super-weeds."

Invasive plants are indicators of disturbance

Most invasive plants are adapted to colonizing disturbed areas. They have a much more difficult time becoming established in healthy, intact ecosystems. Unfortunately, there are not many healthy, intact ecosystems left. But invasive species are a symptom of ecological disturbance, not its cause. It is easy to look at western riverbanks and get upset about salt cedar displacing native willows and cottonwoods. What is a bit trickier to see is that the widespread use of dams has disrupted the flooding cycle that willows and cottonwoods are adapted to. This intense disturbance changes conditions and sets up natives to be outcompeted by salt cedar.

Scapegoating invasive plants

It's not invasive plants that dammed western rivers. They didn't cause global warming or acid rain either. Short-term thinking motivated by greed has caused tremendous damage to our world's ecological systems. When we turn our eyes solely on invasive plants we miss the real cause of ecological destruction—governments and corporations acting for short-term profit to "benefit" a tiny segment of the population. These plants may be a mechanism for the loss of diversity due to disturbance, but they are not its cause.

Follow the money

Not many people know that the anti-invasive-plant movement has been extensively bankrolled by herbicide companies. A Monsanto executive in charge of developing new markets sits on the U.S. National Invasive Species Council. Herbicide companies have funded many books and conferences on this issue. In a somewhat ironic twist, companies that helped to cause the environmental crisis are now profiting from the spraying of herbicide in national parks in the name of environmentalism.

Regulation and control of the world's plant resources

Federal, state, and provincial governments prohibit the importation of certain species known to be invasive. In many cases useful species are being banned—in others the species being banned are native by some definitions. In my own state of Massachusetts the black locust would be banned under proposed legislation. Black locust fixes nitrogen, is a rot-resistant wood that is a perfect replacement for toxic, pressure-treated lumber, and grows as a native less than 200 miles away. While perhaps laudable, these regulations clearly need a bit of revision.

This policy of blacklisting specific plants may give way to proposed white-list legislation (in the United States at least), which would ban importation of new species unless proven innocent. Any proposed process of demonstrating that a plant will not become invasive is not only on shaky ground scientifically, but would be extremely expensive.

Meanwhile, a small number of so-called life science multinationals (with pharmaceutical, genetic engineering, agrichemical, and seed divisions) are rapidly gaining control of the world's food plant diversity. Monopolies may be good for business, but in the long term it is not in anybody's best interest for a few corporations to own and control the very seeds the world depends on for food. White-list legislation would make introduction of new species so expensive that only these giants could do it—putting more power into their hands. To learn more about consolidation in the seed industry and corporate control of plant genetic resources contact the Action Group on Erosion, Technology and Concentration (listed in Part III).

The real enemies of native ecosystems

It is ironic that the same governments and corporations that are pushing the regulation and extermination of invasive plants are not concerned with the potential ecological damage caused by genetically engineered plants and other organisms (GMOs). Plants have spread around the world for millions of years, but GMOs are completely unprecedented. While GMOs may have the potential to develop interesting new crops in the hands of "life science" corporations, this technology is being used to seize greater control of the plant genetic resources necessary to human survival.

Spraying herbicide on naturalized plants won't solve the root cause of the environmental crisis—this is an irrational economic system that puts profits above air, water, people, and ecosystems. It will only make the real culprits richer and add more poison to our environment. There is currently a lot of human energy being put into the invasive issue at the grassroots level. I think more of this energy needs to be directly aimed at the causes, not the symptoms, of ecological destruction.

I sympathize deeply with people's legitimate concerns about the destruction of the environment. However, we need to pay attention to these larger issues, and not allow our emotions to be manipulated by the forces that are the real enemies of native ecosystems.

The environmental argument for introducing new species

In the global economy, food, timber, and other plant products are shipped around the world. Apples are grown in China and freighted to New York for less than it costs to produce them in orchards just a few hours outside of the city. The result is a heavy toll on small farmers around the world. The enormous amount of fossil fuels required to fuel this "free" trade system has the side effects of global warming and global war. And that is to say nothing of the petroleum needed for the tractors and fertilizers that are the basis of our annual agriculture, and the environmental and human health impacts of pesticides and other agrichemicals.

An alternative is for each region to produce the majority of what they need in a sustainable fashion. I believe that to do this effectively we will need to utilize plants from around the world (particularly perennials!). In this case clearly the environmentalist platform is to welcome nonnative species. See the profile for air potato (page 136) for an example.

Ecosynthesis

David Holmgren, one of the founders of permaculture, argues that naturalized plants are integrating with native species to form new hybrid ecosystems that are better able to respond to the changed conditions human disturbance has caused. He calls this ecosynthesis and will explore this idea in his forthcoming book *Weeds or Wild Nature?* You can read a short article on ecosynthesis at Holmgren's Web site, listed in Part III.

So how do I know what to plant?

All of this certainly does not mean we should be indiscriminate in introducing new species to our regions. There is very clearly a real phenomenon occurring, which is causing changes in plant communities. But the situation is more complicated than we believed, and invisible causes need to be investigated.

When a species successfully naturalizes in its new environment there is often a population explosion. In time, a balance is restored as local herbivores and pathogens learn to take advantage of this new food resource. This process can take decades or even centuries. Meanwhile, our already fragmented ecosystems are already hurting, and more aggressively successful naturalizers are probably the last thing they need.

I urge anyone who cares about plant invasion to read Theodoropoulos's *Invasion Biology* and get acquainted with his ideas. Even if he is reacting too strongly to what he sees as unscientific and dangerous ideas, his perspective is of critical importance at this point in history and needs to be debated widely in gardening and environmental circles. We need to arrive at a more balanced perspective through a frank, ethical, and science-based discussion of this issue.

So should you plant species that may naturalize? I would discourage readers from planting anything where there is a real danger of explosive naturalization. You will have to make your own judgment call as to whether you are willing to plant species that have naturalized somewhere to some degree—although if they are already present in your region you may decide to take advantage of it and plant them. Certainly you should feel free to plant native species and noninvasive nonnatives. There are a fair number of such species to choose from profiled here.

CHAPTER FOUR

Techniques

Growing perennial vegetables uses techniques that many readers will be familiar with, but it does put a unique spin on even common practices. Here we review a range of techniques and the unique ways they apply to perennial vegetables. For more practical details, I recommend ECHO's excellent *Amaranth to Zai Holes: Ideas for Growing Food Under Difficult Conditions*; Robert Kourik's *Designing and Maintaining Your Edible Landscape Naturally*; and *Edible Forest Gardens*, a two-volume work on forest gardening theory and practice that I coauthored with Dave Jacke. Throughout this section you will find references to these and other gardening books. Information on all of them can be found in Part III.

Site Preparation

Perennials crops can live for a long time, and you want to give them the best start you can.

It is important to take the time to choose the right location, thoroughly eliminate perennial weeds, and build long-term fertility. This is an area where perennial vegetables are quite different from annuals. While it may seem like a lot of work, remember that this is a one time investment that will pay off with years or decades of harvests.

Improve your soil fertility, drainage, and compaction

You want to provide your plants with the best soil you can, so they will produce well and resist pests and diseases. Soil preparation is even more important with perennials, since it is harder to improve soils once your plants are in the ground. Follow these steps to ensure bountiful harvests for years to come.

French sorrel is a traditional European perennial vegetable.

Test your soil

Start by getting a soil test—contact your local extension service or a commercial testing company. You want to find out the percentage of organic matter, nutrient levels, and any possible contaminants such as lead. To learn more about your soils and how to improve them, I highly recommend *Start with the Soil* by Grace Gershuny.

Improve your pH if necessary

pH is a measure of the acidity or alkalinity of your soil. It is represented on a scale with 7 being neutral, lower meaning acidic, and higher indicating alkaline. Too far on either end of the scale and nutrients are no longer available to your plants. Between pH 6.2 and 7.5 your nutrients will be most available, with 6.5 as the ideal. If your pH is out of line, your soil test will recommend the proper amount of lime or sulfur to bring it toward 6.5. Test again the year after adjusting pH to make sure all is well.

Provide the necessary soil nutrients

In addition to sunlight and water, your perennial vegetables require certain nutrients to survive and thrive. The three major nutrients are required in large quantities. Nitrogen (N) is essential for vegetative growth. Often the lack of nitrogen prevents other nutrients from being used. Phosphorus (P) is necessary for flowering and fruiting. The form of phosphorus used by plants is called phosphate. Potassium (K) is essential to root growth. Potash is the form of potassium used by plants. Calcium, sulfur, and magnesium are the secondary or minor nutrients, essential in small quantities. Finally, there are several micronutrients necessary, but only in trace quantities. All these nutrients must be present in roughly the right quantities, but also in the right balance, and too much of any of them can be as bad as too little.

Your soil test results will tell you how your nutrient levels are, and make recommendation for adding nutrients. Use table 5 to find the right fertilizers for you. Rock powders and organic fertilizers are most appropriate for perennial vegetable gardens: They release nutrients more slowly than conventional fertilizers, and resist leaching away in the rain; also, they won't damage your soil food web (see below).

Add organic matter

Outside of nutrient deficiencies, organic matter is the cure for almost every problem your soil can have: It helps fight soil diseases and nematodes; it improves drainage and water-holding capacity; it brings both acidic and alkaline soils toward a neutral pH; it improves soil with too much clay or too much sand; and it helps your soil hold on to its fertility over the long term. The best way to increase organic matter is to add lots of compost or well-rotted manure. You can incorporate organic matter into your soil with a shovel or tiller, or add it in layers (see Sheet Mulching on page 39). Your soil test will tell you the percentage of organic matter in your soil. The desired amount of organic matter is different in different soils and regions, but you almost always want to bring it up.

Nourish your soil food web

Unnoticed beneath our feet, billions of tiny organisms swarm in the soil—fungi, earthworms, tiny insects, and bacteria. Among the work they do for us are the following: improving drainage, breaking down organic matter, making nutrients available to your plants, suppressing soil diseases, and more. They are especially important for their role in improving soil structure, making the "crumbs" and spaces between that allow water and air to reach plant roots. We want to keep these critters happy. To do so, we need to minimize tillage (not a problem with perennials!), mulch, use slow-release organic fertilizers, and avoid herbicides, fungicides, and pesticides.

Table 5: **Soil Amendments: Which, When, and How Much**

| Material | Benefits | N–P–K | Average Application Rate per 1000 sq ft when soils test: | | | Notes |
			Low	Moderate	Adequate	
alfalfa meal	organic matter, nitrogen	5–1–2	50 lbs.	35 lbs.	25 lbs.	contains a natural growth stimulant plus trace elements
blood meal	nitrogen	15–1.3–0.7	30 lbs.	15 lbs.	7 lbs.	lasts 3–4 months
bonemeal	phosphate	3–20–0	60 lbs.	25 lbs.	10 lbs.	also has good calcium
colloidal phosphate	phosphate	0–2–2	60 lbs.	25 lbs.	10 lbs.	adds to soil reserves as well as available quantity
compost	organic matter, soil life	Variable (0.5 to 3 for each N-P-K)	200 lbs.	100 lbs.	50 lbs.	adds balanced nutrients and the soil life to make them available
Epsom salts	magnesium, sulfur		5 lbs.	3 lbs.	1 lb.	use when magnesium is so low that other sources won't work
fish emulsion	nitrogen	4–1–1	2 oz.	1 oz.	1 oz.	can be used as a foliar feed too; mix 50:50 with liquid seaweed and dilute to half the recommended strength
granite meal (rock dust)	potash, trace nutrients		100 lbs.	50 lbs.	25 lbs.	rock powders add to long-term soil fertility and health; contain 19 trace elements
greensand	potash, trace elements		100 lbs.	50 lbs.	25 lbs.	excellent potash source; contains 32 trace elements
kelp meal	potash, trace elements	1.5–0.5–2.5	20 lbs.	10 lbs.	5 lbs.	best for spot applications where extra potash is needed
lime—calcitic	improves acidic soils, calcium	variable	variable	variable	variable	use in soils with adequate magnesium and low calcium
			——— consult soil test results ———			
lime—dolomitic	improves acidic soils, calcium, magnesium	variable	variable	variable	variable	use in soils with low magnesium and low calcium
			——— consult soil test results ———			
rock phosphate	phosphate	0–3–3	60 lbs.	25 lbs.	10 lbs.	apply when you start the garden and every 4 years once soil phosphate levels are adequate; contains 11 trace elements
soybean meal	nitrogen	7–0.5–2.3	50 lbs.	25 lbs.	10 lbs.	excellent soil amendment during the second half of the season
Sul-Po-Mag	sulfur, potash, magnesium	0–0–22	10 lbs.	7 lbs.	5 lbs.	use only if magnesium levels are low but never with dolomitic lime
sulfur	improves alkaline soils, acidifies	variable	variable	variable	variable	excessive quantities harmful to soil life
			——— consult soil test results ———			

Adapted from Miranda Smith, *Complete Home Gardening* (Creative Homeowner, 2006).

If you have lead contamination

Many urban and suburban soils have lead contamination. If your soil test indicates low levels, you can safely bind up your lead by adding organic matter and bringing your pH close to neutral. At that point the main danger is from dust, not from eating vegetables, so make sure to mulch to keep the dust down. If you have higher lead levels, you could build some serious raised beds with imported soil, grow in containers, or put in an artificial water garden. The alternative is to grow only vegetables with edible fruits—lead is present in leaves and roots but in the not fruits of plants growing in contaminated soils. For more information contact the American Community Garden Association (see Part III).

Improve drainage

Most plants are more susceptible to root rots and other soilborne diseases in poorly drained soils. If your drainage issues are mild, adding organic matter may be enough. But in poorly drained areas, it is probably best to build raised beds in order to keep your plants from getting "wet feet." Don't forget, there are lots of perennial vegetables that actually prefer wet soils (see page 23).

Combat compaction

Compaction is a common problem, especially in urban and suburban soils. Compacted soils can't "breathe," creating conditions for disease and poor plant health. Once again, adding organic matter helps—especially if you till it in. You may also want to spend a year planting cover crops with deep-rooted plants to break up the soil before introducing your perennials. Double-digging, though quite labor-intensive, is very effective at improving compacted soils and building spectacular fertility. John Jeavons's *How to Grow More Vegetables* can show you this technique.

Going with the flow

So far we have discussed modifying and improving your site to make it suited to your crops. However, it is likely there are already perennial vegetables that are suited to even your worst site conditions. For example:

- goldenberry actually produces more fruit in poor soils;
- water celery thrives in wet, waterlogged areas (even shady ones); and
- ramps will form extensive colonies in full shade.

Table 3, Perennial Vegetables with Special Tolerances (page 23), offers some choices of species that are well adapted to conditions most vegetables cannot tolerate. You may choose to save some work and leave at least some of your garden unimproved.

Nuke the weeds

The other key issue in site preparation is removing weeds, especially perennial weeds. In your annual beds you can let the weeds get a bit out of control, because it all gets tilled in at the end of the year anyway. Not so with perennials. Some perennial weeds are extremely pernicious (like quack grass and bindweed), and will thrive in the same conditions as your crops. Thus it is critical to thoroughly remove perennial weeds before planting. Techniques include hand removal, cover cropping, solarization (see Plant-Parasitic Nematodes on page 58), herbicides, and mulching for a year with carpeting or black plastic. See Sheet Mulching: Instant Eden (page 39) to learn about my personal favorite technique.

Other site preparation issues

Gardeners in warmer climates may want to pay special attention to techniques to kill nematodes (again, see the Plant-Parasitic Nematodes

Sheet Mulching: Instant Eden

Sheet mulching combines soil improvement, weed removal, and long-term mulching in one fell swoop. This technique, also known as lasagna gardening, can build remarkable soils in just a few years. There are several key components. First, a weed barrier like cardboard is laid down to smother weeds. In theory (and quite often in practice) the cardboard decomposes after the weeds have all died and turned into compost. The second ingredient is to add compost, or build a layered compost pile that will enrich your new garden bed. The third step is to add a thick layer of mulch on top, to keep new weeds from getting established. I have had great results with sheet mulching, although sometimes the first year is a bit rough on delicate species, until the raw materials break down. You can use sheet mulching to turn lawns or weedy waste areas into gardens in just a few hours, or even to build soil from scratch inside built frames for raised beds. Sheet mulch can range from just a few inches thick to 2 feet or more, depending on how bad your soil is and how much raw material you have available (it will cook down and settle quite a bit). For more information see Patricia Lanza's *Lasagna Gardening*, or *Edible Forest Gardens*.

The author's Massachusetts front yard before sheet mulching. The soils are very poor fill from new construction.

Addition of rotted leaves below thick paper bags as a weed barrier with a layer of compost and mulch on top—just a few hours of work.

By mid-summer the garden is thriving with sweet potato, taro, edible hibiscus, and hardy bananas (yes, they overwinter in Massachusetts, but they don't fruit here).

Jonathan Bates enjoys the results of our first year of sheet mulching. This garden has just gotten better each year. Note the fantastic growth of hyacinth beans!

Simple Steps to Sheet Mulching

1. Mow or cut your lawn, weeds, or other vegetation right down to the ground.
2. Plant any crops that will require a large planting hole (including woody plants, perennials in large pots, and large transplants).
3. Add soil amendments (as determined by your soil test).
4. Water the whole area thoroughly. You are going to be putting a layer of cardboard or newspaper over it, and rain and irrigation won't soak through very well until that weed barrier breaks down. Water also helps the decomposition process get going.
5. If you have compost materials that may contain weed seeds (like fresh manure, leaves, or hay), spread them in layers on the ground. Put a dry, carbonaceous layer of hay or shredded leaves below any manure layer. Avoid thick layers, and make sure to get a good carbon-to-nitrogen ratio just as if you were building a compost pile (see *Start with the Soil* or other gardening books for details). Water this layer well.
6. Lay down a weed barrier. I prefer to use large sheets of cardboard from appliance stores, because these last longer and are quicker to lie down. You can use layers of wet newspaper too. Make sure to have a 4- to 6-inch overlap where sheets meet so buried weeds can't find a route to the surface. If you have already planted crops, or have other preexisting plants, don't mulch over them. Cut holes in the cardboard to make some breathing space for each plant (or leave some room around each plant when laying newspaper).
7. Now you can add your weed-free organic materials. I like to keep it simple, and just add a nice layer of compost. You can also do some sheet composting here, alternating layers of nitrogen-rich materials like fresh grass clippings with carbonaceous materials like weed-free straw.
8. Now you add your final top mulch layer, at least 3 inches thick. Water the whole bed thoroughly once again. Your sheet mulch bed is complete.
9. You can plant right into your bed if you like. To plant tubers or potted plants, just pull back the top layers until you get to the weed barrier. Cut an X in the cardboard or newspaper. If you are transplanting a large plant, peel back the corners of the X. Throw a double handful of compost in the planting hole and then put in the plant. Pull the layers and top mulch back around the plant, water well, and you're all set. Planting seeds is easy too. Just pull back the top mulch to the compost layer and plant your seeds. You may want to cut through the weed barrier below first, depending on weed pressure below the barrier. If you are planting seeds, be sure to water regularly, as compost on top of cardboard can dry out quickly.

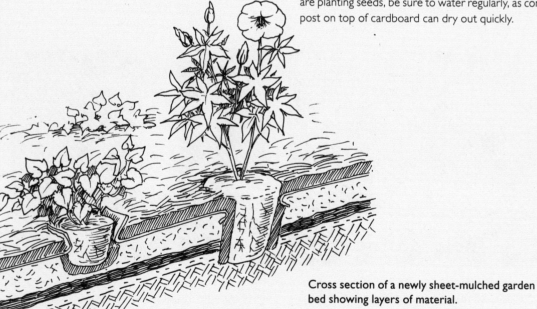

Cross section of a newly sheet-mulched garden bed showing layers of material.

Table 6: **Materials for Sheet Mulching**

Sheet mulch can be as simple as three layers: cardboard, compost, and straw. But compost isn't cheap, and it can be fun and thrifty to add layers of organic materials that will break down to make compost on their own. When doing so, you want to alternate layers of high-nitrogen material (greens) with high-carbon material (browns), just like the recipe you use to build an ordinary compost pile. You want to have more carbon materials than nitrogen: The ideal ratio by weight is 30:1 carbon to nitrogen, which translates roughly to two to three times as much carbon bulk as nitrogen. Keep these layers thin (3 inches at most) and they will break down more quickly. Some items should be shredded first—leaves because they mat, and large items like cornstalks so they break down more quickly. Remember also that some materials must be kept below the root barrier because they may contain viable seeds.

Below the Weed Barrier: Seed-Containing Materials		Above the Weed Barrier: Seed-Free Materials	
High-Nitrogen	**High-Carbon**	**High-Nitrogen**	**High-Carbon**
aged but seedy manure	dried leaves	aquatic weeds & algae	pine needles
fresh manure	dried plant stalks	coffee grounds	sawdust
legume hay (e.g. alfalfa)	grass hay	aged, seed-free manure	shredded newspaper
vegetable kitchen waste	*Note:* You can use	grass clippings	straw
weeds	seed-free carbon	seaweed	wood chips
	sources if these are		(top mulch only)
	not available		

article). You may also have other microclimate modifications in mind, like cutting trees to allow in more sun, or planting a windbreak. All of these steps are much more easily achieved before planting.

Planting and Establishment

Plant your perennial vegetables with love. Give each one the time and tenderness that you would give a cherished fruit tree that will live for 100 years. Planting perennial vegetables is usually not an act of mass production. Instead of seeding out 100 annuals, you may be planting only a few plants. Follow these tips and you will be repaid with years of kindness.

Give your plants room to grow

I am always planting my perennial vegetables too close together. I am usually working with tiny seedlings or small mail-order plants, and it is just hard to imagine that in a few years my Turkish rocket is going to be as big as a mid-sized shrub. This means that I am always digging plants up and moving them later—a disturbance that some of them resent heavily, and often delays growth in even the most resilient. I have also lost some plants that were too close to neighboring giants. The silly thing is that I know better: The rules for plant spacing are quite simple.

Space clumping plants at "crowns-touching" distance at a minimum

Clumping plants are plants that stay put, perhaps growing a wider clump each year but not spreading aggressively. Space your clumpers so when mature they will not be touching any other vegetation. This helps to increase airflow, preventing diseases and competition for light. *Note:* Lower groundcovers may touch the base of the plant, and plants in higher layers (for example, trees above) may cast shade on shade-tolerant plants.

Plant runners cautiously

Running plants make their way around the garden. Give them room to spread. Plant at such a distance that they will fill in over 12 to 18 months. You can mix runners and clumpers as long as the maximum height of the runners is lower than the clumpers. Particularly aggressive or tall runners may need to be constrained with rhizome barriers (see below).

Planting

A few general tips on planting are in order. Dig a hole at least twice as wide as the rootball, but shallow enough that the ground line of the plant will be level with the soil when all is said and done. In compacted soils, use a garden fork to loosen up the soil at the bottom and sides of the hole, so that roots have room to grow. Save your soil amendments and compost and add them on top of the soil once you finish: If you make too rich a soil in the hole, your plant's

roots will never leave and the hole will function like a pot placed in the ground.

Aftercare

Water your plants in thoroughly. Mulch right away to avoid letting weed seeds get any ideas. If you will be using drip, soaker, or pitcher irrigation, now is the time to connect up your system. Some perennials are slower to establish than the annual vegetables you are used to and need to be protected a bit more until established. Make sure that you keep the soil around your plants consistently moist for the first few weeks, and water thoroughly on a weekly basis thereafter. Give the plants some extra weeding attention in this early phase as well. Some perennials will need a few years until they can be harvested; others you will have to race to keep up with!

Rhizome barriers

Some plants are likely to be a bit *too* successful in your garden. Rhizomatous species like sunchokes and running bamboos can spread rapidly and become a real nuisance.

Rhizome barriers from left: arrowhead limited by dry soils; giant Solomon's seal limited by mowing strip; Chinese artichoke with 12-inch plastic rhizome barriers; running bamboo with 24-inch plastic barriers.

Use underground rhizome barriers or inhospitable habitat to prevent their spread. The larger and more aggressive the plant, the more serious barrier you need. For some plants a short mowed strip will suffice, whereas running bamboos require a serious underground barrier. Underground barriers should be 12–18 inches deep or more, and constructed of 60-mil HDPE plastic or ferro-cement (thin cement slabs reinforced with steel mesh). Barriers should stick at least 2 inches above ground, tilt away from the plants, and have no sharp corners where aggressive roots can break through.

Maintenance

Watering

Like annual vegetables, perennial crops will produce better with adequate water. The general rule of thumb is an inch of water per week, though in warmer climate zones you probably need more. Drip irrigation is ideal for perennial vegetables for several reasons. First, once established it requires little work (a lot less than standing out there with a hose!), and this fits into the low-maintenance philosophy of perennial vegetable gardening. Second, as perennials these crops are more vulnerable to diseases. Wet leaves and overhead irrigation can help diseases spread to and between your plants, whereas drip systems provide water right to the roots. Finally, drip irrigation only waters where you want it wet—so competing weeds don't get watered, and you'll conserve water too. *Note:* Whatever system you use, watering in the morning will also help keep diseases to a minimum.

Several other techniques also meet the challenges of perennial vegetables. Soaker hose is made of a spongy material, and seeps water along the length of the hose. It is less complicated to set up than drip, and sometimes less expensive, although it does not deliver water with the same pinpoint accuracy.

Pitcher irrigation has been used in arid climates for thousands of years. Unglazed ceramic pots are buried in the garden and filled with water. Crops are planted next to the pots, and water seeping from the pots meets their needs. You simply refill the pots every few days.

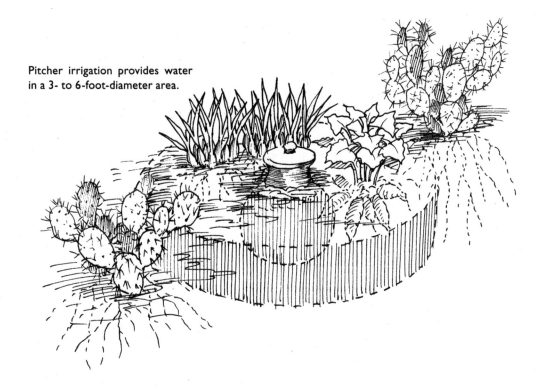

Pitcher irrigation provides water in a 3- to 6-foot-diameter area.

Pots between 1.5 and 2.5 gallons are ideal. A unique feature of this technique is that the more water the plants need, the more seeps out of the pot.

For more information consult Robert Kourik's *Drip Irrigation for Every Landscape and All Climates*. For creative ideas on irrigation in arid regions, including pitcher irrigation, see ECHO's *Amaranth to Zai Holes: Ideas for Growing Food Under Difficult Conditions*, Bill Mollison and Reny Mia Slay's *Introduction to Permaculture*, or any of the xeriscaping guides listed in Part III.

Weeding

If you have done a thorough job of site preparation, there should be few or no perennial weeds remaining in your beds. But there is no way to get rid of the thousands of weed seeds lying dormant in your soils. The use of mulch (see below) or dense groundcovers can prevent these existing seeds, and any new arrivals, from germinating. To my mind, using one or both of these strategies is essential in the perennial vegetable garden. With the exception of root crops, perennial vegetables don't require digging once planted. This means that you won't be turning up hundreds of tiny weed seeds every time you cultivate, as in annual gardening. The drawback of these crops is that if some nasty perennial weeds do survive or sneak in, it can be hard to remove them without disturbing your perennial vegetables.

Every region has its own terrible perennial weeds, usually something that spreads by runners. In my region I have had to adopt a zero-tolerance policy for quack grass (*Agropyron repens*) and bindweed (*Convolvulus* spp.). It is important to keep an eye out for any tiny plants of these species, because if left alone even for a minute they can take over, often intertwining their roots with those of your crops, making for messy removal. Monitoring for these "killer weeds" should become a part of your regular walks in the garden. If your beds are next to wild weedy areas (or aggressive crop plants), you may want to install a rhizome barrier to keep unwanted plants from getting into your beds. Once you have pulled weeds, throw some mulch down immediately to keep anything else from taking advantage of that bare soil spot. Or better yet, pop a low-growing groundcover in so that it fills up the niche the weed was trying to occupy.

Fertilizing

Unlike the ornamental perennial beds you may be familiar with, you will be removing a fair amount of nutrients by harvesting. An annual spring application of compost or well-rotted manure will help to keep your soil in good condition. Have your soil tested annually for the first two years, every other year for the next four to five years, and every third or fourth year thereafter. Rake your mulch back and add amendments as indicated by your soil test. Your plants will also let you know if your fertility is out of balance; see table 7, Diagnosing Nutrient Imbalances, for indicators to watch for. It is often best to amend with a complete fertilizer even if you are only low on one nutrient—it is important to keep nutrient levels balanced in relation to one another.

You may also want to add additional fertilizers every few weeks to boost growth, like liquid fish and seaweed emulsion. Just remember that too much nitrogen makes plants susceptible to pest and disease problems, and lay off the fertilizer by late summer in cold climates, to encourage your plants to get ready to go dormant for winter.

In the long term, compost and slow-release fertilizers are the best bet for plant health, but the quickest way to get nutrients to plants is by foliar feeding. Liquid fertilizers are sprayed directly onto the surface of the leaves, and from there the nutrients are absorbed directly into the plant's circulatory system. Spray in the morning or evening, and make sure to spray the underside of the leaves too. Manure tea and

Table 7: **Diagnosing Nutrient Imbalances**

Major Nutrients	Role	Deficiency Symptoms	Symptoms of Excess
nitrogen (N)	vegetative growth	slow growth, yellow leaves at base, pale green foliage	rich green foliage, little fruit or flower production, aphids
phosphorus (P)	flowering and fruiting	dark bluish leaves, purple stems and veins, late fruit set and low fruit production	limits uptake of boron, iron, and zinc—look for deficiency symptoms
potassium (K)	root growth	young leaves curly, older leaves ashy gray, bronze, or yellow; leaf edges brown, roots stunted	limits uptake of calcium and magnesium—look for deficiency symptoms
Minor Nutrients	**Role**	**Deficiency Symptoms**	**Symptoms of Excess**
calcium (Ca)	water uptake, cell development and division	fruits drop early, wilting, new leaves dark green with yellow edges	rare
magnesium (Mg)	chlorophyll, respiration	brittle, curled leaves, lower leaves turn yellow then brown	rare; will lead to symptoms of potassium deficiency
Micro or Trace Nutrients	**Role**	**Deficiency Symptoms**	**Symptoms of Excess**
boron (B)	cell walls, carbo-hydrate transport	young leaves turn black or purple	yellowing, then turning brown and dying
iron (Fe)	chlorophyll	young leaves with yellow or white patches between veins	bronzing, stunting
zinc (Zn)	plant hardiness, hormones, and enzymes	small leaves with yellow mottling, shortened internodes (distance between leaves)	leaves dark green or yellow

fish emulsion will supply macronutrients, while compost tea or liquid seaweed will help with micronutrient deficiencies.

Not only is foliar feeding a nutritious shot in the arm for your crop, but foliar feeding with compost tea can actually make your plants more resistant to pests and diseases (see Preventing and Controlling Plant Diseases on page 50). It is easy to make your own compost or manure tea. Put a shovelful of compost or manure into a burlap or cloth sack. Soak it in a bucket of water, cover, and let it sit for one to seven days (the longer, the stronger). The resulting "tea" can be used as a liquid fertilizer, or diluted to make a foliar spray.

Nitrogen-fixing perennial companion plants can help to provide for fertility in the long term, as can dynamic accumulators, which "mine" nutrients from the deep soil. See chapter 2, Design Ideas, for more information.

Cultural Practices

These handy techniques help you get the most out of your perennial vegetable garden, by mulching for weed control and soil improvement, hilling up to improve root crop yields, blanching for sweeter flavor of spring shoots, trellising and pruning for best leaf and fruit production, and harvesting and storing crops to maintain freshness and quality.

Mulching

I consider mulch an essential component of the perennial vegetable garden. Mulch prevents the germination of weed seeds, and helps to smother perennial weeds. It prevents erosion and increases soil organic matter as it breaks down. Mulching even helps reduce soil diseases by minimizing the amount of soil splashed on leaves by rain or irrigation. Finally, mulch helps to keep soil moist, and moderates soil temperature, making your plants' roots warmer when it is cold out and cooler when it's hot. Plus it makes your garden more beautiful. Any kind of organic material can be used for mulch, including straw, hay, leaves, wood chips, and more. See what you can find for free or for low cost in your neighborhood, but make sure it is not full of seeds (like some hay), or you'll end up with a weed problem all over again. Lay down a few inches of mulch after planting, and renew annually or as needed.

Hilling up or earthing up

This simple technique can dramatically improve yields of some root crops. You may already earth up your potatoes, for example. All you do is pile some soil around the base of the plant every week or so. The plant keeps on making new tubers from the newly buried portions of the stem. Some gardeners even pile tires on top of their root crops, one at a time, and fill in with soil or compost. This technique does not work for all root crops, and you have to be careful not to smother your plants with too deep a layer of soil. Root crops that are earthed up include aroids, sunchokes, and many of the Andean tubers like oca and mashua.

Blanching

Blanching is the practice of excluding light from the young shoots or leaves of a plant. It results in a paler, more tender, and milder-flavored crop. You can blanch by piling mulch or soil over plants when they are ready to sprout or leaf out (spring in cold climates), although the most elegant way is to use an overturned flowerpot with the hole covered up. Blanched species include sea kale, asparagus, and garlic chives. Blanching also creates a warmer microclimate under the pot or soil, and forces early growth in many crops including rhubarb. See the illustration of a traditional sea kale pot on page 110.

Trellising

Just like their annual relatives, perennial crops in the Bean and Squash families are usually trellised, as are many other perennial vegetables like yams, mashua, and Malabar spinach. These plants are long-lived and often much more robust than their annual counterparts. Thus trellises and other support structures must be stronger and larger—no delicate pea trellises made from twigs and string here! A trellis can be a classic garden trellis, or you can use a tree, shrub, or preexisting fence. Vines can be used to perform other functions in the garden too— like climbing fences to provide privacy screening, or providing a shady hangout under an arbor or edible shade house. For some creative ideas on support structures for living vines, see *Introduction to Permaculture*. Perennial vegetables can even be used to cool your house in summer

Trellis types: (1) Malabar spinach on a fence trellis, (2) pepino dulce in a tomato cage, (3) runner beans on a living wall, (4) chayote on a pergola, (5) Chinese yam on a tipi trellis, and (6) perennial cucumber as a living shade house.

by training them as a living wall (for details see *Planting Green Roofs and Living Walls* by Nigel Dunnett and Nöel Kingsbury).

Pruning

Many perennial leaf crops will produce better when properly pruned. Pruning is also important for maintaining tree and shrub crops at a convenient height for harvest. Of course, you may also want to prune your perennial vegetables to keep them looking nice. *Note:* In the case of leaf crops, pruning and harvesting are often one and the same action. So harvest with a practical and artistic sense, and you will get your work done in half the time!

Essentially, pruning encourages the plant to put on a flush of new growth, resulting in tender new leaves and shoots. Pruning is primarily used with leaf crops (especially woody ones)—the fruit and root crops profiled here need little if any pruning except for aesthetic purposes. *Note:* If you intend to heavily prune, you can plant woody leaf crops much closer together.

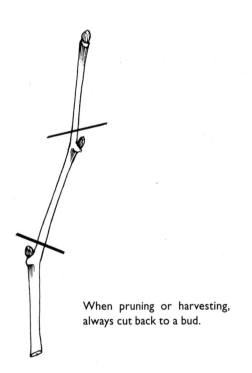

When pruning or harvesting, always cut back to a bud.

Harvest and storage

The challenge with perennial vegetables is to harvest in such a way that the plant will still be perennial afterward. You want your crops to be able to produce for years to come. I offer a few general guidelines here, and more detail in the species profiles.

Greens, shoots, and flowers

To manage these crops as perennials cut the leaves (or other parts) individually, rather than harvesting the whole plant. There are some exceptions to this—see the illustration on coppicing and pollarding, opposite, and review the profiles. Your greens, shoots, and flowers will last longest if harvested in the cool hours of morning or evening. Use them right away, or put in a plastic bag in the refrigerator.

Fruits, flowerbuds, beans, and pods

Harvest these fully ripe for immediate consumption, or a bit green if they will be eaten in a few days. As with greens, harvest in the cool hours of morning or evening. Most fruits profiled here can be left in a cool place on the counter or refrigerated for a week or so—the notable exception being Malabar gourd, which can be stored for years and only gets sweeter. Flowerbuds (like globe artichokes and perennial broccoli) and beans and pods should be put in a plastic bag in the fridge after harvesting.

Roots

Harvesting root crops while maintaining the plant's perennial status can be tricky. The easiest type are air potatoes: Simply wait until ripe and pick off the vine, or let them drop to the ground and pick them up. Colony-forming root crops (sunchokes, for example) are also simple: Just dig what you need and leave the rest to its own devices. Plant/replant root crops (like skirret) are only "sort of" perennial. You dig up the clump, take what you need, and throw a few back in for next year. Generally root crops will store a

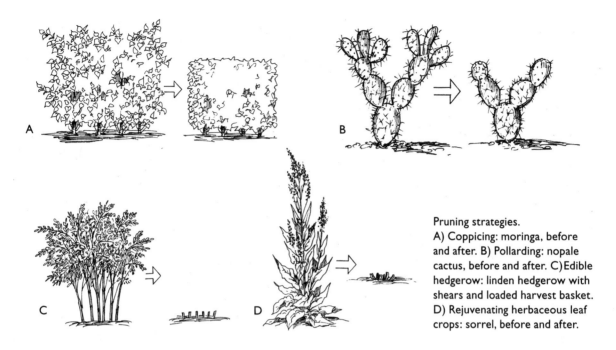

Pruning strategies.
A) Coppicing: moringa, before and after. B) Pollarding: nopale cactus, before and after. C) Edible hedgerow: linden hedgerow with shears and loaded harvest basket. D) Rejuvenating herbaceous leaf crops: sorrel, before and after.

long time in a bag in the fridge, or in a cool place in the basement. There are some exceptions, though; see the individual profiles for details.

Overwintering tender perennials

A range of techniques can enable you to over-winter tender plants in frosty climates. Some information on overwintering techniques is included in the profiles, but my own experience is limited and there is not much written about carrying tropical perennial vegetables through the winter. I encourage you to experiment and share your experiences.

If plants are almost root-hardy in your area, a combination of a good microclimate and 6 to 12 inches of mulch can get them through the winter. In some cases, as long as the roots don't freeze the plant will come back the following year. You can build enclosed leaf piles to protect aboveground plant parts too. Just build a little cage around the plant with stakes and burlap, landscape cloth, or chicken wire, then stuff the cage with dry leaves or straw. For additional protection you can cover with a layer of plastic.

Some tender species can be overwintered as houseplants. Dig up and pot the plants, or take a division or cutting if the plant is too big. Even plants that prefer shade outside will want to be in a window with full sun. Otherwise you should use artificial full-spectrum lights.

Many cold-climate gardeners have dug dahlia bulbs or canna rhizomes and stored them for the winter. The same technique works for many perennial vegetables, including a number of root crops. Storing these crops in a cool, dark, dry place induces a kind of hibernation. Temperatures between 40°F and 45°F are ideal, but anything from 35°F to 50°F is acceptable. Got a basement or garage that doesn't go below freezing? After the tops are killed by frost, dig up the roots. An easy method is to leave the dirt intact, put the tubers in a box or bag in the basement, and cover with plastic. Alternatively, you can wash the roots, let them dry for a few hours, wrap them in newspaper, and store them in a black trash bag. Some gardeners like to wash the roots and then pack in sawdust or peat moss. No doubt there are many other variations.

Check your tubers monthly for rot and shrinkage. Discard any rotten ones, and give them a little spritz with water if they are shriveling.

A very interesting technique I have yet to try is dormant storage. Apparently many tropical plants have evolved the ability to go dormant during prolonged dry or cool spells. As long as the temperature remains above 35°F, and they are in a cool, dark place, many tropical plants will simply take a long nap. For woody plants, dig them up before frost arrives, and pot them up in a sterile potting mix. Their leaves will slowly turn yellow and drop in storage, but don't be alarmed. As for your herbaceous tropical plants, wait for the frost to kill their leaves. Cut back the dead top growth, and pot them up in sterile potting soil. Both woody and herbaceous species should be kept on the dry side. If you stick your finger in the pot and it is dry down to 3 inches deep, give it a bit of water. This should be every two to four weeks. These plants should be gradually reintroduced to sunlight in spring, as they will be very susceptible to sunburn. This technique should be tested with many of the species profiled here, especially those magnificent tropical woody leaf crops. Try maintaining some tropical plants in containers year-round, and use this method for quick and easy winter storage.

To learn more about these and other techniques, read *Palms Won't Grow Here and Other Myths* and *Hot Plants for Cool Climates*.

Managing Pests, Diseases, and Varmints

Every gardener must work to keep other organisms from eating their crops. Compared with annual vegetables, perennials have some pluses and minuses. For example, most vegetables are at their most vulnerable when they are still young and small. Perennials only go through this phase once, and then are more robust and resistant for the rest of their lives. On the other hand, crop rotation, while effective for controlling diseases and some pests of annuals, is not feasible for most perennials, which stay in one spot.

Many perennial vegetables are highly resistant to pests and diseases. Others, however, can be quite susceptible. In most cases resistant varieties have not yet been developed (perhaps an opportunity for the backyard plant breeder).

The following sections offer many suggestions on how to design your garden for minimal pest and disease problems. To learn more about this approach, check out *Edible Forest Gardens* and *Designing and Maintaining Your Edible Landscape Naturally*. See the bibliography in Part III for books that can help you identify and control specific pests and diseases.

Preventing and controlling plant diseases

Annual vegetable gardeners use crop rotation as a central tool to prevent plant diseases. Since rotation is not an option for most perennial vegetables, we must pay extra attention to other techniques to prevent and control diseases. Here are some tips to keep in mind.

Provide optimal growing conditions

Most important is to plant your perennial vegetables where they will be happy. Match your planting area to the crop's sun, soil, and moisture preferences. Well-drained soil is essential to prevent soilborne diseases (except, of course, for those plants that prefer wet soils—see table 3, Perennial Vegetables with Special Tolerances, page 23). If your soils are poorly drained, you may need to make raised beds. Adding lots of organic matter improves drainage and also encourages the growth of beneficial soil organisms that compete with and

An edible hedge of katuk at ECHO offers pea-flavored leaves for the browsing visitor.

even consume soilborne diseases. Maintaining a proper balance of nutrients will keep your plants healthier and better able to resist infection.

Ensure good air circulation

Make sure your plants have plenty of room to breathe. Crowded conditions impede air circulation, which forms a breeding ground for disease. Plant your perennial vegetables at distances that allow them to reach full size without brushing up against their neighbors. Pruning can also help to allow better airflow within and between plants. In the words of "contrary farmer" Gene Logsden, "Sunshine is the best fungicide."

Plant in diverse polycultures

Diversify your garden to make diseases' lives a little harder. Mix up your garden in polycultures of different species instead of large blocks of the same plant. Diseases can spread very quickly when susceptible plants are growing next to each other. Consider growing multiple varieties of the same species. Remember that vegetatively propagated perennials of the same variety are actually clones of one other, and have the exact same susceptibilities to diseases.

Select resistant species and varieties

There are disease-resistant varieties of many annual vegetables, but not so many available for perennials. The good news is that many perennial vegetables have few disease problems at all, and even the perennial vegetables that are closely related to annual crops are often more disease-resistant than their cousins.

Beware of viruses

Viral diseases can be particularly devastating, as there is no known cure, and viruses spread when you propagate vegetatively (and sometimes by seed). Nursery laboratories can use techniques like plant tissue culture to propagate virus-free material from infected plants. Seek out virus-free plant material when shopping for plants. Virus-affected plants should be removed and destroyed.

Solarize to decontaminate suspect soils

Consider solarizing your beds before planting (see the article on Plant-Parasitic Nematodes, page 58), especially if the garden has had disease problems in the past. Solarization can destroy many soilborne disease organisms. Make sure to inoculate afterward with compost, compost tea, or commercial inoculants to populate the soil with "good guys," microorganisms that will prevent the return of disease.

Inoculate with beneficial organisms

Speaking of inoculants, you can purchase potting soils that have been inoculated with a wide range of disease-fighting organisms. You can start your plants in this medium, and toss a little into the planting hole to give your plants a little head start. See the Sources of Gardening Supplies and Materials section in Part III for sources of inoculated potting mix and other disease-control products.

Prevent wet foliage with sensible irrigation

Many diseases need water to spread. Your irrigation practices can make a big difference. Always water in the morning so that your plants have a chance to dry completely before the cooler, disease-friendly temperatures of night. Drip or soaker irrigation is highly recommended, as they water without getting leaves wet. Make sure never to walk through the garden when plants are wet, whether from rain, morning dew, or irrigation.

Use good garden sanitation practices

There are a number of basic garden sanitation practices that can keep your garden disease-free. Wash your hands and tools after working with any diseased plant material. It is a good idea to sterilize pruning and propagation tools between each plant you are working with. Just keep a spray bottle with an alcohol or 5 percent bleach solution handy and give your tools a quick squirt before moving on.

Compost your garden debris to prevent diseases from using it to breed or overwinter, especially debris from disease-susceptible groups like brassicas and solanaceous crops. Make sure not to allow fruit to remain on the vine too long after ripening, as it will become a home base for diseases. Also remove and compost weeds, which can harbor additional diseases that can spread to your crops. Brush the dirt off your tools at the end of the day, and don't leave used plastic pots and trays around. You can wash them in a 5 percent bleach solution and use them again next year.

Don't compost any plants or plant parts that are diseased, as some diseases can multiply in your compost pile. Instead, burn diseased material or put it in a plastic bag and put it in the trash. This is one of the few good uses for a landfill! Wash your hands and sterilize all of your tools that might have come into contact with diseased plants.

Give your perennial vegetables an immune booster
Good soil and preferred growing conditions will offer your plants a healthy start. Give their immune systems an additional boost by spraying liquid seaweed or compost tea. These sprays can help your plants produce protective chemicals, and compost tea can actually inoculate your plants' leaves with beneficial fungi and bacteria, which will fight off infections. See Fertilizing on page 44 for instructions on making compost tea.

Control diseases with least toxic sprays
Finally, if your plants do develop disease problems, there are some minimally toxic products that can help to control some fungal and bacterial diseases. A baking soda spray can be made by mixing 1 tablespoon of baking soda,

Plant/Replant Perennials

A few perennial root crops, known as plant/replant perennials, can be rotated throughout the garden to minimize the buildup of diseases in the soil. These are non-colony-forming root crops, which means you could just harvest the whole batch of roots each year and replant those that you don't eat somewhere else. You probably already grow potatoes and garlic, two classic plant/replant perennials. *Note:* When growing tropical perennials in cold climates, since you have to replant each spring, you may as well consider them all plant/replant perennials and rotate them to minimize disease problems.

Below is list of plant/replant perennials.

aroids	oca
arracacha	potato
cassava	skirret
chufa	ulluco
mashua	yacon
multiplier onions	yams

1 quart of water, and a few drops of dish soap. Recent studies have found milk (diluted with water) to be effective against powdery mildew and other diseases. Some organic fungicides are commercially available. Copper sprays can be effective against fungi, but large amounts can stunt or damage your crops. Sulfur sprays also fight fungi, but kill beneficial soil fungi and earthworms, and can damage plants if used on hot days above 85°F. These materials and more can be ordered from the sources listed in Sources of Gardening Supplies and Materials in Part III.

Learn to identify, prevent, and control the diseases that affect your crops
Get to know the diseases that may affect your crops before they show up in your garden. If you know what to watch out for, you can nip potential problems in the bud. Table 8 reviews the most common plant diseases affecting perennial vegetables, and their symptoms, prevention strategies, and controls. For more information, consult the books on plant pest and disease control listed in Part III.

Table 8: **Common Diseases of Perennial Vegetables**

Diseases	Affected Crops	Symptoms	Prevention	Control
anthracnose (*Colletotrichum, Gloeosporium, Glomerella, Marssonina & Sphaceloma*)	ground cherry, pepino, perennial beans, rhubarb, other Solanaceae, many perennial crops	spots or lesions on foliage, pink spore mass	good air circulation, garden sanitation	remove and destroy affected material, apply baking soda spray or copper fungicides
bacterial wilt (*Erwinia* and *Ralstonia* spp.)	ground cherry, pepino, perennial beans, other Solanaceae, Cucurbitaceae	rapid wilting, stringy ooze	resistant varieties	remove and destroy affected plants
botrytis (*Botrytis* spp.)	globe artichoke, many perennial crops	velvety mold	good air circulation, good drainage, garden sanitation	remove and destroy affected material, apply baking soda spray
root rots (inc. *Aphanomyces, Fusarium, Pellicularia, Phoma, Phytophthora, Pythium, Rhizoctonia*)	aroids, asparagus, saltbush, many perennial crops	general decline, wilting, yellowing, rotting roots	good air circulation, good drainage	remove and destroy affected plants
powdery mildew (*Erysiphe, Sphaerotheca,* others)	chayote, globe artichoke, winged bean, wolfberry, many perennial crops	white powdery growth	good air circulation, garden sanitation	remove and destroy affected material, apply baking soda spray or milk spray
viruses (many)	arracacha, cassava, chaya, ground cherry, papaya, pepino, oca, ulluco, watercress, other Solanaceae, many perennial crops	yellowing, distorted or stunted growth	control insects like aphids and leaf hoppers that spread viruses, purchase virus-free plants, garden sanitation	remove and destroy affected plants: no cure for plant viruses

Pests of perennial vegetables

If you have been following the site preparation and plant care recommendations outlined above you are already ahead of the game as far as pests go. Plants growing in fertile soil, with their preferred light, moisture, and climate conditions, are much better able to resist pests.

So just by building nice beds and treating your plants well you have taken an important step.

Use resistant varieties when available

Using resistant species and varieties can save you a lot of trouble. Many perennial vegetables have few pest problems, especially the less

"domesticated" ones. Among the more susceptible species there are sometimes varieties that are
more resistant to pests. However, most perennial vegetables have not yet received enough
attention from plant breeders and gardeners for
such varieties to be identified.

Create a welcoming environment for beneficial organisms

Serious pest outbreaks are rare in wild ecosystems. This is because birds, bats, toads, spiders,
and beneficial insects consume pests before they
get out of control. We can take some simple
steps to welcome these helpful animals into our
gardens. Most important is to avoid spraying to
control pests whenever possible. Even organic
sprays are devastating to beneficial insects—
they often kill the insects that were invisibly
working, about to make your problem go away.

Beneficial organisms like to have certain
kinds of habitat around. Most important is to
have a garden with diverse layers and kinds of
vegetation: trees, vines, shrubs, grassy places,
and groundcovers. You can also make extra
habitat by putting up birdhouses and bat boxes.
Many beneficial animals and insects like to have
wild places in the garden or nearby, like thickets
or viney tangles, and evergreen plants for year-
round cover. Mulch, rotting wood or stumps,
and dried hollow flower stalks are important overwintering places for many beneficial
insects, and provide habitat for bug-hunting
toads, lizards, shrews, and snakes.

Many beneficial organisms enjoy plant foods
as well as those tasty pests. Many insect-eating
birds also enjoy berries. Plant some native fruiting shrubs to keep them happy. Many beneficial insects enjoy sipping nectar as they cruise
your garden looking for pests to eat or lay their
eggs in. Try to have something flowering in
your garden in every season. Some plant families are especially good at attracting the right
insects, notably anything in the Celery family
(Apiaceae), and any daisy-like plants from the
Aster family (Asteraceae). See page 15 for a list
of perennial vegetables that attract beneficial
insects.

Water is essential for almost all beneficial
organisms. Rocks, twigs, or aquatic plants will
provide a perch for birds and insects to use
while they drink. This means that your edible
water garden not only grows you food, but also
helps to control pests in your whole garden! A
little pond will soon be home base to dragonflies, which are harmless to humans but devastating to pests.

Diverse gardens have fewer pest problems

Mix it up with different species and different
varieties of each species you grow. In doing this,
pests have to work harder to find their favorite plants, and as a result they can't multiply
exponentially. Imagine it from a pest's point of
view—a long row of artichokes is like a huge
feast. But a few artichokes here and there, mixed
with strange plants teeming with predators that
want to eat you, means that your dinner is going
to be a lot more difficult.

Watch closely, but don't leap to respond too quickly

Try to get out in the garden every day, or at
least weekly. Take a good look at your plants.
Are they looking healthy? Any signs of chewing?
Yellow leaves? Obvious aphids, or beetles crawl-
ing on the leaves? If you do see pest damage,
don't jump too quickly. Remember that beneficial insects might already be taking care of the
problem. Keep an eye out for ladybug larvae,
and look for mummified aphids with wasp
larvae inside. The insect identification guides
in Part III's Reccommended Reading can help.
Keep in mind also that a plant can lose up to 20
percent of its leaves without affecting production—as long as the leaves themselves are not
the crop!

Use cultural practices to prevent pest problems

Good sanitation when dealing with diseases is

important. For instance, removing and destroying plant parts infested with scale and leaf miners can keep them from spreading. Floating row covers are light sheets of fabric that cover your crops and present a physical barrier to pests. Row covers are especially useful in the spring against pests like flea beetles.

Begin with nontoxic controls

If you do have a pest problem, start with a non-toxic control. Handpick or knock insects into a bucket of soapy water. Try washing them off the plants with a jet of water from a hose. Squish aphids between your fingers. This kind of basic control is often quite effective.

For some pests, there are nontoxic (to us) solutions that target the pest and have little impact on beneficial insects. These include Bt:

This tomato hornworm has been parasitized by a mini-wasp. When the little white eggs on its back hatch, the tiny wasp larvae burrow inside the hornworm and eat it from the inside out. When they are finished they hatch and fly away looking for new prey. See the text for steps you can take to encourage beneficial insects like mini-wasps in your garden.

a bacterium with strains that control caterpillars, Colorado potato beetle larvae, and some other pests; beneficial nematodes, which can be sprayed on soil or plants to control flea beetles, leaf miners, pest nematodes, and other pests; and milky spore disease, which will kill Japanese beetle grubs in your lawn for 15 to 20 years. Surround is a new clay-based powder that is sprayed onto foliage and fruit, apparently making the plant just an unpleasant place for pests to hang out, without causing pests or beneficial insects any harm. Pests just take their business elsewhere. Surround is being found effective on more pests all the time; it is currently known to be effective against a range of pests, including such difficult buggers as flea beetles and tarnished plant bug.

Try low-toxicity pesticides if necessary

If you still have a problem, you can try some less toxic pesticides. Remember that even the mildest of these controls will impact populations of beneficial insects, often creating more pest control problems for you down the road. Some formulations are easy to make at home. For instance, mix a little dish soap with hot sauce and garlic in a blender then spray the mixture on infected plants to kill a number of pest types. Insecticidal soaps and botanical pesticides like neem, pyrethrum, and rotenone are effective, but they take out beneficial insects too. Diatomaceous earth, a fine powder with sharp edges to cut soft-bodied insects and slugs, is also effective. Consult table 9 below or the books listed in Recommended Reading in Part III for more information.

Varmints

A wide range of mammalian creatures raid gardens throughout North America. You probably already know which ones are likely to be a problem in your area. The best way to prevent damage from varmints is to keep them out of your garden in the first place with a good fence.

Table 9: **Pests of Perennial Vegetables**

Pests	Affected Crops	Signs of Damage	Treatments
aphids	asparagus, globe artichoke, many perennial crops	distorted new growth, sticky "honeydew," sometimes cottony masses; can spread diseases between plants	row covers, garlic spray, insecticidal soap, Surround; often if left untreated, wild beneficial insects devour them
caterpillars (including tomato hornworm, cabbage moth, and many more)	globe artichoke, ground cherry, pepino, perennial brassicas, sea kale, sissoo spinach, other Solanaceae, many perennial crops	ragged holes in leaves, can devour plants rapidly	row covers, handpick, Bt spray, rotenone, pyrethrum, neem, Surround
European corn borer	perennial beans, sea beets, Solanaceae, others	small holes in stems and fruit, with sawdust castings	remove and destroy affected plants; Bt spray, rotenone
flea beetles	watercress, other brassicas, some Solanaceae	tiny holes in leaves	spring row covers, diatomaceous earth, beneficial nematodes, pepper/garlic spray, rotenone, pyrethrum, Surround
Japanese beetle	many perennial crops	skeletonized leaves	handpick, pheromone traps, beneficial nematodes, milky spore disease, rotenone, pyrethrum, neem, Surround
leaf hoppers	breadfruit, many perennial crops	pale disfigured leaves, honeydew with black mold, leaf drop	spring row covers, soap spray, diatomaceous earth, rotenone, pyrethrum, neem
leaf miners	sea beet, sorrels	tunnels in leaves or stems	row covers, remove and destroy affected leaves, beneficial nematodes, neem
nematodes	aroids, arracacha, banana, chayote, daylily, edible hibiscus, groundnut, Malabar spinach, nopale cactus, oca, plantain, sweet potato, winged bean, yams, many perennial crops	see article Plant-Parasitic Nematodes, page 58	see article Plant-Parasitic Nematodes
scales	clumping bamboos, many perennial crops	yellowing, honeydew with black mold, scale insects on stems and foliage	soap spray, horticultural oil, alcohol swab; remove and destroy infested plant parts
slugs and snails	katuk, sissoo spinach, sorrels, many perennial crops	ragged holes, often near base of plant, slime trails	beer traps, garlic spray, diatomaceous earth
spider mites	arracacha, chayote, clumping bamboos	yellow dry leaves, fine webbing	soap spray, horticultural oil, garlic spray
striped cucumber beetles	chayote, perennial beans, Solanaceae, many perennial crops	herbivory plus bacterial wilt (beetles transmit wilt)	row covers, handpick; hot pepper/garlic spray, rotenone, pyrethrum, beneficial nematodes, Surround
tarnished plant bug	many perennial crops	malformed or dwarfed plant parts; blackened terminal shoots	row covers, insecticidal soap, beneficial nematodes, rotenone, pyrethrum, Surround
thrips	banana, plantain, many perennial crops	dried, scarred, silvery leaves	soap spray, diatomaceous earth, garlic spray, horticultural oil, rotenone, neem
whiteflies	many perennial crops	yellowing, honeydew with black mold	soap spray, garlic/pepper spray

Plant-Parasitic Nematodes

Nematodes are tiny worm-like organisms that are abundant in most soils. Most are beneficial or neutral as far as gardens are concerned, but a small group is among the most feared of pests, the plant-parasitic nematodes. Most plant-parasitic nematodes are root-feeders (including root-knot, cyst, sting, and root-lesion nematodes). They are the most common pest affecting perennial vegetables, particularly dangerous in warm climates and sandy soils (hello, southern United States).

Symptoms may include stunted or dwarfed growth; yellowing; daytime wilting; distorted growth of leaves, stems, roots, or flowers; and galls or knotty growths on roots. In addition to the direct damage they inflict, disease fungi and bacteria colonize the wounds caused by nematode feeding. Nematodes can also spread viruses between plants. Once a plant is seriously infected by nematodes, there is nothing you can do but remove and destroy or throw away the plant and immediately surrounding soils. The focus therefore needs to be on prevention.

In healthy soils with high organic matter, a range of beneficial fungi and other organisms keep plant-parasitic nematodes under control. Building organic matter content through compost and mulching is thus an essential preventive measure. Crop rotation is great for annuals, but of little use with perennials. The exception is plant/replant perennials (see page 53), which should be rotated by botanical family and not return to the same spot for several years. A point in our favor is that tillage and soil disturbance increase nematode populations, so perennials have an advantage (except for root crops). Garden sanitation is also important. Make sure any new plants you are bringing into the garden look healthy, and clean your tools when you have been working in suspect areas.

If you have reason to suspect that your planting site may have nematodes, there are several steps you can take to get rid of them. Some plant species suppress or kill off nematode populations. Planting dense cover crops of these species (occupying the entire planting area) for a full season before planting your perennial vegetables helps make a clean slate. Nematode-killing cover crops include cereal rye, barley, sudan grass, castor beans, and sesame. French and African marigolds (*Tagetes patula* and *T. minuta*, respectively) are especially effective. Breeders have selected the cultivars 'Nema-Gone', 'Single Gold', and 'Nema-Gold' as particularly effective.

Some brassicas, especially rapeseed (also called canola, *Brassica napus*), are also highly effective, especially the cultivar 'Humus'. *Note:* The perennial root crop mashua (profiled on page 193) is also nematocidal.

Another preplanting technique is solarization. In warm, sunny climates, you can sterilize your soil by turning your soil into a greenhouse. Spread a large sheet of clear plastic over the area you want to treat. Bury the edges with soil to keep cool air from getting inside. After six to eight weeks of sunny weather the job should be done. If you solarize immediately after turning under a rapeseed cover crop, the fumes from the decomposing brassica combined with intense heat are as effective as methyl bromide, an incredibly toxic (and now illegal) soil fumigant.

After solarizing and/or cover cropping, amend the soil with plenty of compost. You may also want to add additional amendments and inoculants. Chitin, made from crab shells, will increase the effectiveness of beneficial fungi that feed on nematodes. Beneficial fungi inoculants are also commercially available and can be added to your soil periodically. Other nematocidal products include a type of Bt (similar to the organic pesticide that controls caterpillars), and beneficial types of nematodes that eat their troublesome kin.

This sounds like a lot of work, but remember, you only get one chance. Then you can keep improving your soil organic matter, to build a nematode-resistant soil ecosystem for the long term. Just keep an eye out for symptoms, and cull any infected plants quickly. Nematocidal cover crop seed, soil amendments, and inoculants are available from garden supply companies listed in Part III.

A cover crop of nematocidal marigolds will fumigate your soil. PHOTO COURTESY OF SEEDS OF CHANGE/ SCOTT VLAUN.

Siting your garden close to the home, or wherever human scents are strongest, will also help. The presence of dogs (and for some varmints, cats) will also scare away many hungry mammals.

Fencing

A good fence is your best defense against varmints. The type of fence depends on the sort of animals you are dealing with. Physical barriers can prevent feeding damage. These include wire mesh or plastic tree tubes to prevent bark feeding by deer and mice, and underground wire mesh surrounding prized root crops to prevent feeding by gophers.

Trapping, shooting, and other nasty tricks

If varmints are eating your vegetables, the best revenge is to invite them to dinner—as the main course! While shooting varmints is traditional and effective in rural areas, many of us live in populous neighborhoods, where discharging firearms is a bad idea.

How else can you kill or remove problem animals from your garden? Commercially available gas cartridges dropped into groundhog holes give the message that they are not welcome. You can purchase baits that poison mice and voles but are relatively safe to use around pets. Many traps are available for small and mid-sized varmints, some that kill and some that trap live. Remember, if you choose live trapping you are going to have a terrified animal to handle and move to a safe location. Check your local regulations before transporting and releasing wild animals.

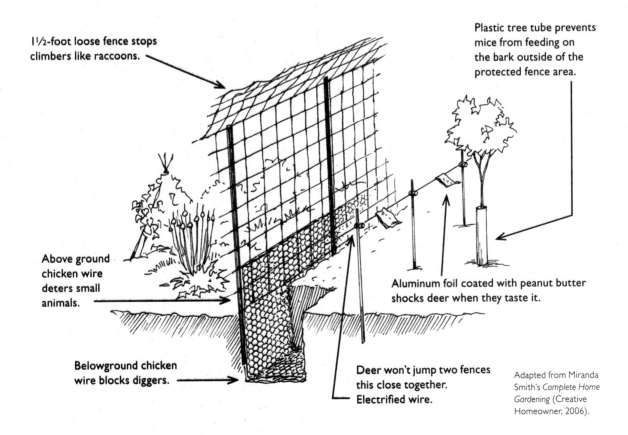

1½-foot loose fence stops climbers like raccoons.

Plastic tree tube prevents mice from feeding on the bark outside of the protected fence area.

Above ground chicken wire deters small animals.

Belowground chicken wire blocks diggers.

Aluminum foil coated with peanut butter shocks deer when they taste it.

Deer won't jump two fences this close together. Electrified wire.

Adapted from Miranda Smith's *Complete Home Gardening* (Creative Homeowner, 2006).

Table 10: **Varmints of Perennial Vegetables**

Animal	Crops Affected	Fence Type	Controls
deer	leaves, fruit, and stems of many perennial crops, including woody crops	6 feet or taller; overhang helps; electrified also useful	dogs, repellents (moderate effectiveness), shooting
gophers	root and tuber crops	underground, ¾-inch mesh or smaller	cats, traps
mice and voles	root and tuber crops, seedlings, tree bark in winter	n/a	cats, traps, tree guards, poison baits
rabbits	many crops	underground 10 inches, above ground 3–4 feet; 1-inch mesh or smaller	dogs, cats, traps, shooting
raccoons	many crops	underground 10 inches, electric useful, also "floppy" top portion (see illustration)	dogs, cats, traps, shooting
woodchucks (groundhogs)	many crops	underground 10–12 inches deep, above ground 4 feet; plus an electric wire on top prevents climbing	dogs, traps, shooting, commercial gas cartridges

The Edible Water Garden

In many parts of the world aquatic vegetables are important aspects of gardening. Here in North America water gardens are almost exclusively ornamental—though in fact many water gardeners are growing edible species and don't even know it.

The edible water garden combines food production with the tremendous satisfaction and tranquility of water gardens. Edible water gardens are easy to maintain and can produce a range of root and leaf crops, like watercress, taro, and lotus root. In my water garden, the edible greens are mild-flavored all summer long and make up the bulk of my summer salads. Nothing brings a garden to vibrant life like a water feature. Water brings a range of beautiful and beneficial wildlife to the garden: dragonflies, frogs, birds, and more. You can even set up a water garden on paved, compacted, or contaminated soils.

The edible water garden is easy to care for—there are few weed problems, and you certainly don't need to irrigate! Aquatic vegetables are delicious, with unique flavors, and can be extremely productive. Many are outstanding ornamentals. They don't need to be expensive; in fact, a very basic kiddie pool can be transformed into an abundant food oasis. Pick up a water gardening book and a couple of catalogs and give it a try this year. I bet you will fall in love with it just as I did.

There are three basic options for water gardens described as follows:

Artificial ponds

Kiddie pools are the easiest way to get started. Keep in mind that different water crops like to grow at different depths. Either get a few pools of different sizes, or put some rocks in your pool to boost pots to the right height. You

Edible water garden featuring water lotus, arrowhead, and water chestnut. Also note wild rice. This beautiful and productive garden was grown on a concrete porch in a $10 kiddie pool.

can also buy prefabricated pools, which usually come with shelves for different pot depths, or buy a plastic pond liner and excavate your own custom pond shape.

Although ordinary weeds will not bother your water garden, algae can be a problem. There are two main strategies to controlling algae in artificial ponds. The first is to shade it out. A good guideline is to shade 60 percent of the pond's surface with the leaves of floating or emergent vegetation. The second strategy is to keep the water as clear and sterile as possible. Mud, decaying organic matter, and dissolved nutrients from plant pots make food for algae. Submerged aquatic plants use up the nutrients without causing your aquatic food plants

to get slimy. See below for suggested edible submerged aquatic species. *Note:* Algicides and alga-suppressing dyes are not appropriate for use in edible water gardens, although you may want to experiment with barley straw bundles, which are toxic to algae but presumably not to us.

Artificial ponds can become breeding havens for mosquitoes. I buy a few cheap goldfish every year, which consume mosquito larvae and other aquatic organisms. You can also purchase an organic mosquito killer (similar to the Bt used on caterpillars) from aquatic garden supply catalogs.

Plants in artificial water gardens are usually grown in pots, as bare soil and muddy bottoms

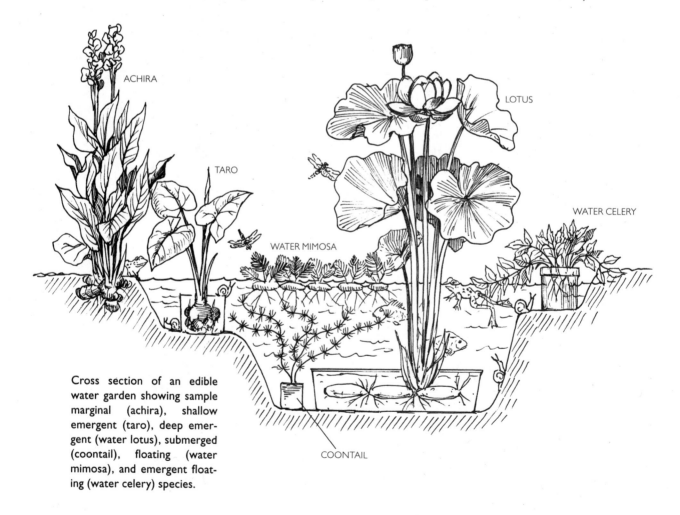

Cross section of an edible water garden showing sample marginal (achira), shallow emergent (taro), deep emergent (water lotus), submerged (coontail), floating (water mimosa), and emergent floating (water celery) species.

breed algae. It turns out that wide, shallow pots are ideal for most aquatic food crops (see table 11 below for specific recommendations by species). A layer of pea gravel on top of the pot will keep soil from dissolving into the water. Soil should be a mix of clay or heavy soil and compost. You can add organic fertilizers like bone- and blood meal and greensand, or slow-release chemical fertilizers. Although I am usually organic, I confess I add a few of the commercially available fertilizer tablets every couple of weeks to maintain vigorous growth. Fertilizer is especially important for leaf crops that are being heavily harvested—remember, the soil in the little pot is all they have. Most water garden plants are repotted annually. With root crops just divide and repot after harvest.

Natural ponds

If you are fortunate enough to be able to garden in a natural pond, lake, or stream, you can plant aquatic vegetables and allow them to form natural colonies. Arrowhead is a great candidate. You may also want to try the native wild rice (*Zizania aquatica*), a self-seeding annual with gourmet grains. Unfortunately, waterways make it very easy for nonnative plants to escape from cultivation and become problematic. For this reason I would discourage wild cultivation of nonnative aquatic plants unless the body of water is quite isolated.

Water quality is also an issue in natural edible water gardens. Make sure to have your water tested for chemical and biological toxins. In Europe the liver fluke (a parasite) can cause illness in people who consume wild-grown watercress. All plants harvested from natural bodies of water should also be thoroughly cooked.

Aquaponic systems

The future of intensive urban food production may be aquaponics. These integrated systems produce fish and aquatic vegetables. The fish are grown in tanks, and the manure-rich wastewater is pumped into tanks or troughs. Floating plants like watercress and water celery filter out the nutrients using their dense root systems. This cleans the water, which can then be pumped back into the fish tanks after a bit of additional filtration. Vegetarian fish varieties like tilapia and grass carp are ideal for these systems, since they can be fed garden weeds or excess aquatic vegetables. To learn more about this fascinating area of gardening, check out the books listed in the bibliography in Part III.

Classes of Aquatic Perennial Vegetables

Almost all of the cultivated aquatic vegetables are from Asia, probably because farmers there were already growing rice in flooded fields. The following are the primary types of aquatic perennial vegetables:

Emergent aquatics

These plants grow underwater but send leaves up above the surface. Most are grown for edible roots, corms, or tubers. Some of the aroids are also good leaf and stem crops. Water chestnut, taro, and violet-stem taro prefer fairly shallow water, ideally about 3–4 inches of depth above the top of the pot. Water lotus and arrowhead grow somewhat deeper, up to 2 feet deep. Cattails (*Typha* spp.) are worthy of inclusion as well: While not especially delicious, these native perennials are known as the supermarket of the swamps because so many parts are edible. In my own water garden I also enjoy the emergent aquatic culinary herbs licorice flag (*Acorus gramineus*) and tsi (*Houttuynia cordata*).

Floating aquatics

These plants float on the surface of the water. They are beautiful, and provide shade to prevent algal infestation. Water mimosa is a unique and beautiful perennial vegetable, which has its own flotation devices that look like a series of marshmallows impaled on a stick. Water

Table 11: **Aquatic Perennial Vegetables**

Species	Water Depth	Ideal Pot Type	Propagation Technique	Food Use
arrowhead	deep emergent (6 inches–2 feet)	wide, shallow	tuber	nutty tubers
Chinese arrowhead	deep emergent (6 inches–2 feet)	wide, shallow	tuber	nutty tubers
taro	shallow emergent (3—4 inches)	wide, shallow	corm	starchy sweet roots, cooked leaves
violet-stem taro	shallow emergent (3—4 inches)	wide, shallow	corm	cooked leaves and stems
water celery	emergent floater	small pot, partial floater	cuttings	leaves like celery
water chestnut	shallow emergent (3—4 inches)	wide, shallow	corm	sweet crisp corms
watercress	emergent floater	small pot, partial floater	cuttings	pungent, delicious leaves
water lotus	deep emergent (1—2 feet)	wide, shallow	root	crisp large roots
water mimosa	floater	none, or small	cuttings	cabbage-flavored leaves
water spinach	emergent floater	small pot, partial floater	cuttings	like spinach

mimosa can be grown as a free-floating plant, and fixes its own nitrogen. You can anchor one end in a pot or muddy bank to provide even greater fertility for faster growth. Other edible floating aquatics (not profiled in this book) include duckweeds (*Lemna* spp.) and water meal (*Wolffia* spp.). For those interested in exploring aquatic food production, Asian water meal (*Wolffia globosa*) is a cultivated crop in Southeast Asia. It is reported to contain 20 to 40 percent protein and to taste like sweet cabbage. The tiny Southeast U.S. native *Azolla* is a floating fern that forms dense mats discouraging mosquitoes. *Azolla* also fixes nitrogen and grows aggressively, although you can harvest regularly and use it as nitrogen-rich mulch.

Emergent floaters

This group contains the best aquatic greens—water spinach, water celery, and watercress. All three have a similar growth habit. They can grow as floating aquatic mats, and/or root in muddy banks, pots, or soil. My favorite way to grow them is to set some plants or cuttings in a 1-gallon pot, and leave the top inch of the pot sticking out of the water. This keeps algae

from forming on those tasty greens. You can just stick the cuttings in dirt and plant right away; nothing is easier than propagating these plants. They will grow upright and can be easily harvested, while excess growth will spread across the surface of the water. Make sure to place the pots close to the edge of the pond for ease of harvest. All three are used as biological filters in aquaculture due to their dense floating root systems and ability to convert dissolved nutrients into rapid vegetative growth.

Marginal plants

Many perennial vegetables tolerate or enjoy wet soils. They can be grown at pond edges or in pots with the bottom few inches submerged. Achira, chufa, and ostrich fern are examples. See the table of wet-loving plants on page 23 for more information. *Note:* Many of the plants listed above will also thrive in this situation.

The water garden should also contain the following group of primarily functional species:

Submerged aquatics

These plants grow primarily underwater, and

help prevent algae by using up dissolved nutrients. A number are listed as having edible greens, although I can't vouch for their palatability. As submerged aquatics are especially likely to naturalize, I will recommend a few species that are both native to most of North America and listed as edible: coontail (*Ceratophyllum demersum*), whorl-leaved water milfoil (*Myriophyllum verticillatum*), and sago pondweed (*Stuckenia pectinatus*). Also edible is the Northeast-native eelgrass (*Vallisneria americana*).

Propagation

Almost all familiar vegetables are grown from seed. They come up quickly, and with little trouble, as the result of centuries of unconscious selection for fast, reliable germination by gardeners and farmers. This is rarely the case for perennial vegetables. Most are propagated vegetatively, through division or cuttings, and those grown from seed are often slower to germinate. Some seeds require special treatments. The species profiles tell you which propagation techniques will be most successful for each crop.

Readers who are unfamiliar with these techniques will find them easy to learn and rewarding to practice. Once you have the hang of it you can give plants to your friends and neighbors, offer them through seed and plant exchanges, and even help some progressive nurseries get on the perennial vegetable bandwagon!

Growing from seed

Unlike their annual cousins, many perennial vegetables are difficult to germinate. In fact, some species cannot be grown from seed at all; they either make sterile seeds or do not produce any at all. When it is possible, growing from seed has many benefits. It is inexpensive, and it allows you to grow large numbers of plants. It results in each plant being genetically unique, a diversity that can produce new and tasty varieties. Seedlings also vary in disease and pest resistance, which means your crop will not succumb uniformly to infestation or infection. The disadvantage is that certain desirable traits may not be passed on to offspring. For example, good skirret varieties have tasty, tender roots. But their seedlings may revert to having woody cores inside each root. Ultimately, you may not have a choice; some perennial vegetables are quite rare, and seed may be the only way to acquire a particular species. Hopefully this situation will change as these species gain greater visibility.

Growing perennial vegetables from seed may require patience. While some, like perennial brassicas, germinate as quickly as garden annuals, others may take a few weeks to sprout. Keep them moist but not too wet while you are waiting. They may also require special treatments, explained below. Don't be intimidated—seeds are designed to grow. And remember, you only have to do this once! See the notes under Propagation in each profile to determine if the techniques listed below are necessary. Unless otherwise noted, plant outside after all danger of frost is past.

Cold moist stratification

Mix the seeds with a moistened, sterile medium (like sterile potting mix, peat, or vermiculite) and refrigerate for 30 to 60 days or the period specified in the profile. This simulates the experience of spending a winter outside in the soil. These plants can also be fall-sown in climates with long enough winters. If seed also requires scarification, do it *before* stratifying.

Scarification

These seeds need you to simulate being in the stomach acids of an animal, which the plant relies on to disperse its seeds. Try rubbing seeds lightly between sheets of sandpaper, or soak overnight in cold water and then dip briefly in 160°F water. Larger seeds can be nicked with a knife or filed just enough to cut through the seed coat.

Seed saving with perennial vegetables

For most seed-producing perennial vegetables, saving seed is as easy as collecting and storing it. Many perennial vegetables have no named varieties or wild relatives, and thus there is no need for screening, isolation distances, and other common seed-saving techniques. Even in the case of those crops that do have multiple varieties, as long as you are growing only one variety and there are no neighboring plantings or wild plants of the same species, you need not use precautions. There are a few species that do require special measures, which are covered in the profiles. See Carol Deppe's *Breed Your Own Vegetable Varieties* and Suzanne Ashworth's *Seed to Seed* to learn about techniques for seed saving, as well as for more information on perennial vegetable seed-saving needs.

Vegetative propagation

Many perennial vegetables can only be propagated vegetatively. The benefit is that the new plant will be genetically identical, and share the characteristics of the original plant. Some vegetative techniques end up with productive plants much more quickly than growing from seed. Plus vegetative propagation is a fascinating and enjoyable art. The disadvantages: All plants will be clones of the original, and thus with the same exact susceptibilities to pests and diseases. It is also easy to propagate diseases along with plants; make sure to propagate only from healthy, virus-free stock. Sterilizing your tools with 10 percent bleach solution or alcohol between each plant is also important to prevent transmission of diseases.

Division

Division is the easiest way to propagate perennials. The technique depends a bit on the type of plant. For most root crops, just harvest a tuber

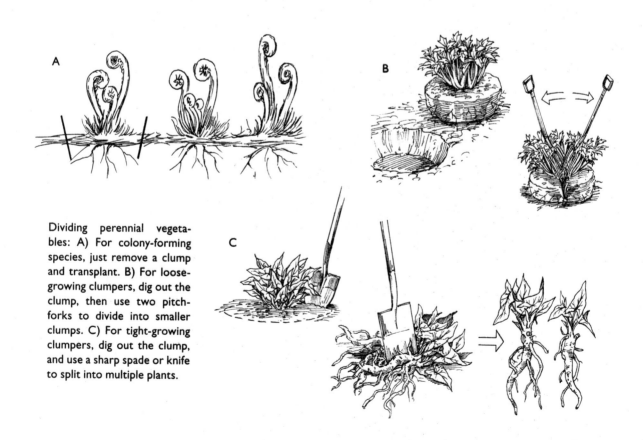

Dividing perennial vegetables: A) For colony-forming species, just remove a clump and transplant. B) For loose-growing clumpers, dig out the clump, then use two pitchforks to divide into smaller clumps. C) For tight-growing clumpers, dig out the clump, and use a sharp spade or knife to split into multiple plants.

and plant it out elsewhere. Pretty simple! Colony-forming crops are also easy: Just dig up a clump and plant it somewhere else. Many root crops and colony-forming perennial vegetables will actually yield better if thinned like this on a regular basis. For clumping species, dig up a clump and brush away the soil so you can see the roots. Using hand tools, divide the clump into separate plants. A trowel is fine for loosely clumping plants, but you will need a sharp spade or knife for tight clumps. You can also use the "double-fork" technique (see illustration opposite) for large tight clumps. Replant your original, and plant out the others or pot some up if you are going to give them away or plant them later.

The best time for division is early spring, when leaves are just a few inches high. If you don't have the luxury of dividing at the perfect season, cut back the foliage by one-half to two-thirds to keep the plant from dehydrating while it is growing new roots. If you are propagating a leaf crop, make sure to cook up this free harvest. Make sure that each division has plenty of roots and at least three "eyes" (dormant buds). Larger clumps come back into production the quickest, but you can divide into 1- or 2-inch plugs if there are enough eyes and roots.

Layering

The stems of some plants form roots when in contact with the soil. With a bit of patience, these crops are very easy to propagate. Simply bend a stem to the ground and gently pin it there with a rock or a wire staple. Bury it with soil or compost, and cover with mulch. A year later you can cut the connection with the mother plant and dig up your new plant.

Softwood cuttings

With some perennial vegetables you can just take a cutting and put it in a glass of water. In a week you will have plenty of roots and can plant right away. These species include water celery, water spinach, watercress, and sweet

Layering is a great propagation technique. Bend a branch to the ground, and secure it with a stone or a wire hoop. One year later, separate from the parent plant. You can also use serpentine layering to create multiple layers from a single plant.

potato, though it is worth trying with others. Unfortunately taking cuttings from most perennial vegetables takes a bit more work.

Softwood cuttings are taken from the green growing stems. The top 3–6 inches of a branch are best. Take softwood cuttings from healthy, vigorous plants in spring, before they start to flower, if possible. The ideal cutting is rigid enough to stand up on its own, but flexible enough to bend a good bit.

Before taking cuttings, and between each plant, sterilize your tools with alcohol or a 10 percent bleach solution. Prepare your cuttings by cutting just below the leaf nodes (see the illustration on page 68). Remove the bottom leaves. For species with larger leaves, cut them down to 1 square inch. Ideally, take cuttings in the morning, on a cloudy and humid day.

Most species root better if dipped in a synthetic rooting hormone. This encourages cells in the nodes and cut surface to start rooting. In *Native Trees, Shrubs, and Vines*, William

Cullina describes how you can make a homemade rooting hormone with willow branches. Cut ten 2- to 3-foot-long willow branches after the leaves have dropped in fall. Chop the stems in 2-inch segments, and put them in a pot. Pour a gallon of warm water over them. Soak for one to two days. This hormone is good for softwood cuttings, and can be stored in your refrigerator for several years!

Prepare pots or trays filled with moistened, sterile potting medium (you can make your own by mixing perlite and peat). Poke holes in the medium with a pencil, and stick your cuttings in. Bury them an inch or so deep, with at least one node, preferably two above the soil surface. Stick your cuttings far enough apart that their leaves are not touching one another. Lightly firm the soil around each cutting.

Now comes the hard part. You need to provide your cuttings with a warm, humid environment for the next several weeks. An easy method is to stick your cuttings in a pot, and place the top half of a clear soda bottle on top. Leave the cap off to allow for ventilation. You can also use some sticks to prop up a plastic bag over your pots or trays. Make sure the plastic does not touch the leaves of your cuttings. If you use a plastic bag, open it daily to allow fresh air inside. Put your pots or trays in a sunny window, or place under grow lights on a 16-hour timer.

After a week to 10 days, lightly tug on your cuttings. If you feel some resistance, they are growing some roots. Congratulations! The hard part is over. Remove your plastic bag or soda bottle. Lightly fertilize. Transplant out when your cuttings have started to grow new leaves, and have developed decent root systems.

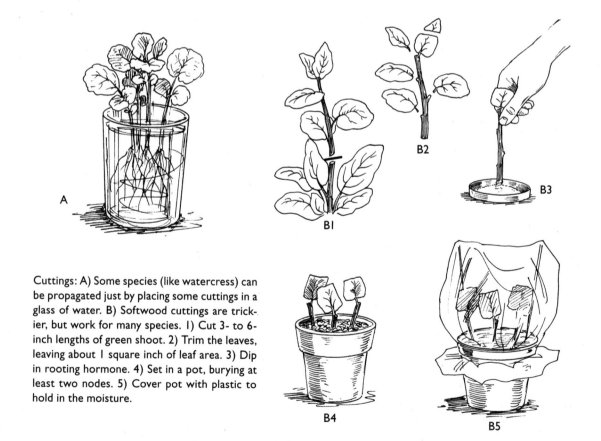

Cuttings: A) Some species (like watercress) can be propagated just by placing some cuttings in a glass of water. B) Softwood cuttings are trickier, but work for many species. 1) Cut 3- to 6-inch lengths of green shoot. 2) Trim the leaves, leaving about 1 square inch of leaf area. 3) Dip in rooting hormone. 4) Set in a pot, burying at least two nodes. 5) Cover pot with plastic to hold in the moisture.

Hardwood cuttings

This technique can be used to propagate woody plants: trees, shrubs, and woody vines. Hardwood cuttings are much slower to take than softwoods, but don't have the same complicated heat and humidity requirements. Cuttings are best taken when plants are dormant (as in the fall, after leaf-drop in cold climates). If this is not possible, remove all leaves from your cutting. You want to get wood from the most recent year's growth, with at least three nodes. Cut the bottom of your cutting at an angle, but leave the top flat, so you can tell which way is up later on (see the illustration). You will need to use a stronger type of synthetic rooting hormone. In the old days, hardwood cuttings were buried upside down over winter, with a grain seed stuck in a crack in the bottom of the cutting. The spring sun warmed the basal ends of the cuttings more quickly since they were buried upside down, and induced the seed to germinate. When the seed sprouted it gave off hormones that induced rooting in the cuttings.

As with softwood cuttings, stick hardwood cuttings into sterile medium. Bury at least three nodes if possible, but leave at least one above the soil surface. Place your pots or trays in a place where the soil won't freeze, and keep the medium moist. In cold climates they will root slowly over winter and on into spring, but in warmer areas it can happen quite a bit faster. When they start to put out leaves, give them a tug and check for roots. Transplant when they have reasonable leaves and strong roots.

Backyard Breeding

Many gardeners are intimidated by the idea of plant breeding. It seems like something best left to professionals with advanced degrees. Unfortunately, professional plant breeders are not working on perennial vegetables. Their

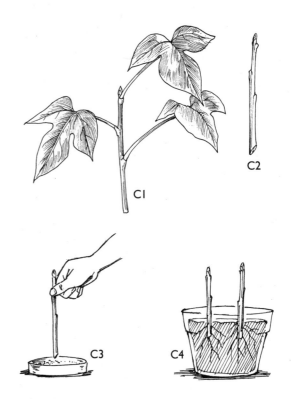

C) Hardwood cuttings. 1) Cut the top portion of a hardened shoot. 2) Remove leaves (if dormant); cut bottom at an angle so you remember which is down. 3) Dip in rooting hormone. 4) Pot up your cuttings.

focus is largely determined by the large corporations that fund their research, which means most of their work is dedicated to agronomic crops like wheat, potatoes, and soybeans. If we want to develop improved perennial vegetables we are going to need to do it ourselves.

Thank goodness for Carol Deppe. Her book *Breed Your Own Vegetable Varieties* puts the knowledge of amateur plant breeding in your hands. Deppe is a perennial vegetable fan, and even writes about domesticating wild edibles! It turns out that breeding is often no more complicated than seed saving, which is already practiced by many gardeners. There are several breeding and crop improvement practices that perennial vegetable enthusiasts may want to consider. Breeding perennial vegetables is especially easy because once you have a plant with characteristics you like, it can be propagated vegetatively. This enables you to skip several of the steps that are necessary to produce new varieties of annuals that will come "true to type" from seed. Techniques to consider include:

- **Screening of existing varieties.** The traits you are looking for may already exist in currently available varieties. For instance, the flavor of the edible leaves of sweet potatoes varies from unpleasant to delicious among different varieties. Simply growing out a number of named varieties and sampling them might give you the results you are looking for. In the case of sweet potatoes, we know that there are varieties grown in Asia and Africa just for their leaves. Importing these varieties would save a lot of unnecessary breeding work.

- **Selection of superior seedlings.** If you start with a relatively unimproved crop, just planting out a large number of seeds, preferably from several sources, will often give you what you are looking for. Most seedlings of skirret have roots with a fibrous core, making them unpleasant to eat. But within any group of skirret seedlings, even from the same parent plant, there is much variation in fibrousness. All you have to do is plant a bunch of skirret seed and taste the roots to see which ones are the best. Then you can vegetatively propagate the plants and share them with your friends! You could make a major contribution to many of the less well-known crops profiled here just by growing out a hundred seeds and dividing or taking cuttings from the tastiest plants.

- **Making deliberate crosses within a species.** You can cross any two varieties within a particular species. Perhaps you are interested in perennial lima beans. The variety '7 Year' lima is vigorous and long-lived in dry climates, but suffers from disease problems in moister climates. You could, however, cross '7 Year' lima with a more disease-resistant lima variety. The act of making crosses is not that complicated: Essentially, you replace a honeybee and do the pollination yourself, while preventing the plant from pollinating itself. Then you just grow out the seedlings for a generation or two and (in this case) see which plants are both perennial and disease-resistant. Deppe's book tells you all about how to do this.
- **Making wide crosses between related species.** Often, closely related species (within the same genus) can be crossed to create interesting hybrids. Good king Henry (*Chenopodium bonus-henricus*) is usually grown for the leaves and shoots, but it does have small edible broccoli-like flowerbuds. Huauzontle (*C. nuttalliae*), a related annual species in the same genus, is grown in Mexico for its large broccoli-like heads. You could try crossing these two species to develop a new crop, a perennial "chenopodial broccoli." Sometimes species from two closely related genera can even be crossed successfully. Again, please refer to Carol Deppe's fine book for the details.

It must be admitted that the tropics have a far better palette of perennial vegetables to work with than the frost-prone areas of the world. For tropical backyard breeders, selecting disease-resistant varieties of the perennial vegetables they already have could occupy much of their time. For those of us outside the tropics, let's do the selection and breeding work to catch up with the rest of the world! Many of the best tropical perennial vegetables were once bitter or even had stinging hairs. The dedicated work of generations of farmers and gardeners brought them to the place they are today. Should we ask less of ourselves? In a decade or so we could have perennial sunflower-seed-bearing sunchokes, saltbush shrubs with magenta leaves, and perhaps even a hardy hybrid hibiscus with delicious edible leaves. How can we resist?

To this end, each of the profiles in Part II has suggestions for backyard breeding. Be sure to pick up a copy of Carol Deppe's fine book and see what contribution you can make to the future of perennial vegetables!

Part II

Species Profiles

Using This Book

Use Caution When Sampling New Food Plants for the First Time

Some caution is in order when trying new foods for the first time. You can never be entirely certain how your body is going to react.

First, make sure to prepare the food properly. Some vegetables are toxic when raw, but quite healthy to eat when sufficiently cooked. Also make sure you are eating the proper part of the plant. For example, rhubarb stalks must be cooked before eating. In addition, the leaves and roots are extremely toxic and should never be eaten.

You can never know if you are going to be allergic to a new food. Even such ordinary foods as corn, soybeans, and peanuts can cause serious allergies in some people. When trying a new food plant it is prudent to proceed slowly, particularly if you are already prone to food allergies. It is always best to start by tasting a small amount of any new vegetable. Try some and see how you feel over the next 12 to 24 hours. If all is well, try a larger amount. On the third try eat all you like.

Some new foods can cause digestive upset. For example, if you are not used to eating foods containing inulin (like sunchokes, yacon, and camass), you could end up with a bad case of gas if you eat too much.

Of course, in all likelihood you are going to have a fantastic experience eating the vegetables profiled here. People all over the world have eaten all of these species for centuries. Just use a bit of common sense when cooking new plants for yourself, or when serving them to your friends who have never tried them before.

Papaya is not just a luscious fruit—in many parts of the world the unripe fruit is an important vegetable.

Understanding Latin Names

As you will see in the profiles, many plants have multiple common names, which can be confusing. Each plant has only one correct Latin (botanical) name, which helps botanists from around the world share a common language. Each Latin name has two parts, a genus and a species. The genus (plural *genera*) is capitalized, and indicates a related group of plants. For example, all cultivated onions and alliums are in the genus *Allium*. All of the cultivated *Allium* species share certain traits: a strong onion aroma, bulbs, and that beautiful blue-green foliage. A species is a more "specific" group within a genus, which does not cross with other species under normal circumstances. The species name is in lowercase letters and follows the genus. For example, *Allium sativum* is garlic, as distinguished from *A. ampeloprasum* (leeks) and *A. cepa* (onions). If a genus is listed multiple times, the genus is abbreviated after the first mention.

A family is a collection of related genera. Often you can see common traits within a family. The Squash family, or Cucurbitaceae, contains the genera *Cucurbita* (squashes and pumpkins), *Citrullus* (watermelons), and *Cucumis* (melons and cucumbers). All of these familiar garden annuals are vining crops with large edible fruits. In many cases members of a botanical family have similar cultural requirements, flavors, growth habits, or pests and diseases.

How to Read the Profiles

Part II of the book features profiles of over 100 perennial vegetables. Each follows the same format, allowing you to quickly find the information you need.

The plants are grouped together in their botanical family. Families are listed in alphabetical order; within families they are again in alphabetical order by genus and species. While this arrangement may not be familiar to some readers, seeing a plant in the context of related species can help to create a broader context.

The best species receive major profiles (see the box on page 77 for an explanation of the format). Less relevant species receive minor profiles, which are just a few paragraphs to give a general overview.

Family Name

Synonyms
- Latin synonyms
- Common synonyms

Aspects
- Form (tree, herb, etc.)
- Sun or shade
- Moisture

Each profile includes a map showing the approximate range of the crop as a perennial in pink, and, if applicable, the range as an annual in yellow.

General Overview, History, and Ecology: This section of the profiles gives the big idea. What makes this crop an excellent perennial vegetable? Where is it grown, and how is it used?

Crop Description: This is a brief description of the form and habit of the plant.

Climate: This section lists where the plant can be grown, and whether it can be grown outside of that range as an annual or by other means. *Note:* All zones listed are USDA zones.

Tolerances and Preferences: This lists the soil, sunlight, and water requirements of the crop.

Naturalization Status: This tells you if and where the species might naturalize.

Pest, Disease, and Weed Problems: Lists any particular problems you might encounter. This section does not usually say how to handle these pests and diseases. For that information you will have to turn to the general discussion of Managing Pests, Diseases, and Varmints, which begins on page 50, or to the references listed in Part III.

Propagation and Planting: How to grow the crop from seed, cuttings, or division.

Other Cultivation Information: Anything else you should know, such as information about trellising, earthing up, or pruning.

Harvest and Storage: How and when to pick, dig, or otherwise harvest the crop, with information on storage where appropriate.

Uses: What parts are eaten, tips for cooking, and any cautions if necessary.

Related Species and Breeding Potential: Similar species you might want to experiment with, and ideas for backyard breeding to develop interesting new varieties or even entirely new hybrid crops!

Onward

I hope you enjoy reading these profiles as much as I have enjoyed writing them. These are remarkable plants. With luck you will find many species that inspire you to plant them in your garden. May some of them someday become old friends.

With good examples in our gardens, we can demonstrate the great promise of perennial vegetables, which is now just a gleam in our eyes. More nurseries and seed companies will start to catch on, and perhaps we just might change the face of gardening for the better.

Alismataceae: The Water-Plantain Family

Sagittaria spp. · Arrowhead

Synonyms
- Duck potato
- Wapato
- Kuwai
- Chee koo

Aspects
- Running herb
- Edible tubers
- Full sun
- Aquatic to wet soil

General Overview, History, and Ecology: The tubers of this aquatic species are an important food crop in Asia, particularly in Japan. The many native species were once a staple of Native Americans throughout much of what is now the United States and Canada, where they are now popular ornamentals in water gardens. This crop is productive, delicious, and easy to grow. The roasted tubers have a savory, nutty, rich flavor. Arrowhead is an outstanding candidate for water gardens, both as a container plant and a colony-forming root crop for naturalizing in larger ponds.

There are several techniques that can be used to grow arrowhead. Plants can be naturalized in ponds and riverbanks if you are fortunate enough to have an unpolluted pond or river where you can garden. The plants will colonize readily. Arrowhead can also be grown as a potted plant in water gardens—use a wide, shallow pot for best results. Tubers are much more easily harvested in pots—in muddy ponds they often form at quite a distance from the parent plant. Potted arrowheads must be harvested and thinned or repotted annually. In Asia arrowhead tubers are produced in paddy culture like rice: Sprouted corms are planted in fields, which are then flooded with flowing water just a few inches deep.

S. latifolia (Arrowhead, Duck potato, Wapato). This species is a native wild edible found almost everywhere in the United States and Canada where there is fresh water. There are a number of other native edible species, which are similar to one another in appearance and often hybridize. Wild arrowhead grows from wet, muddy banks into quite deep water.

S. graminea (Chinese arrowhead, Kuwai, Chee Koo). This species has been cultivated in Asia for centuries. It is sometimes available in Asian grocery stores. There are apparently two types: an aquatic form and an upland form that prefers moist soils. This species is not nearly as cold-hardy as *S. latifolia*. Tubers that do not freeze will overwinter—and even in quite cold areas muddy pond bottoms often will not freeze. Unlike our native species, the tubers can be harvested all year round. It is sometimes known as *S. sinensis*.

The tubers of an arrowhead have a rich, nutty flavor.

Crop Description: Arrowheads are herbs with large, arrow-shaped leaves about 1–3 feet tall. Plants spread by rhizomes to form large colonies. Arrowheads are grown as ornamentals for their striking foliage and pretty white flowers. The tubers are egg-sized or smaller, and have a cream-white or purple color.

Climate: The native species is extremely hardy, and can grow virtually anywhere in the United States or Canada. The Asian species is more or less tropical and should be protected from freezing.

Tolerances and Preferences: Arrowheads can be grown in wet soils or as fully aquatic plants. They should be in full sun.

Naturalization Status: *Sagittaria latifolia* is native throughout the continental United States and Canada. *S. graminea* is Asian and has not naturalized here, although it certainly could in warmer areas.

Pest, Disease, and Weed Problems: Muskrats can be serious pests of arrowheads that have been naturalized in ponds or rivers, as can waterfowl to a lesser degree. If they become a problem for you, you can trap and remove the muskrats or switch to cultivation in artificial ponds.

Propagation and Planting: Arrowhead is easily grown from tubers. Seed takes two to six weeks to germinate and should ideally be used fresh. You can sometimes find tropical arrowhead tubers at Asian markets. Arrowhead plants should be spaced 4–5 feet apart in ponds, or put one to three tubers in a large pot.

Other Techniques: Arrowheads are classic emergent aquatics. See the section on edible water gardens on page 60 for details on producing emergent aquatic vegetables in water gardens.

Harvest and Storage: Tubers of the Asian species can be dug year-round. Native arrowheads should be harvested after the foliage dies back. Harvesting from naturalized colonies can be a challenge. A traditional Native American harvesting technique was for women to wade deep in the cold water in fall and loosen the tubers from the mud

---

Roasted Arrowhead
with Sunchokes and Watercress

1 pound arrowhead tubers
1 pound sunchoke tubers
Olive oil
Chili flakes
1 bunch watercress

Chop large sunchoke tubers and arrowhead tubers into 1-inch pieces—many arrowhead tubers are already just the right size. Mix tubers with olive oil and a pinch of chili flakes. Bake mixture in a covered dish at 425°F until soft (about 45 minutes), then stir and bake uncovered 5–10 minutes more to brown. Chop, add watercress, and serve. Nutty and sweet!
Serves 5.

---

with their toes. Other accounts claim that women felt for the tubers with their toes and then used sticks to loosen them. You can use a rake, hoe, or hooked pitchfork for same purpose. Follow the roots out from the base of the plant to find the tubers on their rhizomes. For ease of harvest I recommend container-grown plants.

Uses: Arrowhead tubers have a nutty, slightly earthy flavor. They can be cooked like potatoes and are quite delicious when roasted with sunchokes and olive oil and tossed with fresh watercress.

Related Species and Breeding Potential: There are millions of wild arrowhead plants in North America. A bit of wild collecting could help to identify individuals with larger tubers. Backyard breeders should focus on developing larger tubers spaced more closely together. Selecting for a richer purple color would also be nice. Attempts to hybridize the two primary species would also be interesting.

Alliaceae: The Onion Family

Allium cepa aggregatum · Multiplier Onions

Synonyms
- Shallot
- Potato onion
- Mother onion
- Nest onion

Aspects
- Clumping herb
- Edible bulbs
- Edible greens
- Full sun
- Moist, well-drained soil

General Overview, History, and Ecology: These perennial bulb-forming onions are widely adaptable and easily grown crops. There are two kinds of multiplier onions, the potato onions and the shallots. Both types form clumps of multiple bulbs and are usually divided every year. The spring greens of both types are a tasty vegetable. Both species are extremely hardy and easy to grow. Multiplier onions descended from the common onion (*Allium cepa*) that was domesticated thousands of years ago in central Eurasia, perhaps in Afghanistan or Iran. At some point the multiplier onions diverged, selected as a plant/replant variant on the familiar onion theme.

Single bulbs are planted and form a large cluster of bulbs. These are divided annually and replanted. Bulbs are usually moved to a new location to avoid buildup of onion diseases in the soil. On a small scale, it would be very interesting to experiment with growing these plants as perennials by leaving them in the ground for several years.

Potato onions used to be an important cultivated onion in many parts of the United States. While their bulbs are smaller than ordinary biennial onions, their flavor is excellent and their storage qualities are superior. I use them just like ordinary white onions and find them indistinguishable (besides the personal satisfaction of knowing that I am cooking with perennials). Yellow and white varieties are available. Potato onions have a strange life cycle. If small bulbs are planted, they yield one or two larger bulbs. When larger bulbs are planted they yield 10–12 smaller bulbs. For this reason a mix of sizes should be planted each year. These onions are among the most productive of vegetables. Some varieties can produce bulbs up to 4 inches across under ideal conditions.

Shallots are a popular onion worldwide, and one of the best choices for growing in tropical climates. Their mild flavor is somewhere between red onion and garlic, and is preferred in gourmet cooking because it is more delicate than ordinary onions. Shallots are important in many fine cuisines of the world, from France to Southeast Asia. Some varieties of shallots produce seed.

Crop Description: Both types of multiplier onions are clump-forming perennials closely resembling ordinary garden onions. They form clumps 12–18 inches high and 6–12 inches wide.

Climate: Plants are hardy to at least Zone 5. They can be grown in colder climates by storing bulbs indoors and planting them out in spring. The shallot is widely grown in the tropics, but the multiplier onion is probably not as well suited to the tropics. Between potato onions and shallots, you should be able to grow one species or another in virtually any climate as long as they receive enough water.

Tolerances and Preferences: Both types are heavy feeders, requiring a rich, well-drained soil for best results. Plants should not be allowed to dry out, as this will substantially lower yields.

Naturalization Status: Seed-forming shallot varieties may naturalize, though the other multiplier onion types will not.

Pest, Disease, and Weed Problems: Multiplier onions are resistant to some onion pests, including the larvae of the onion fly. Like all alliums, their tall, thin leaves cast little shade and do not suppress the growth of weeds, necessitating the use of a hoe, mulch, or perhaps a groundcover like white clover.

Propagation and Planting: As described above, potato onions are grown exclusively from the division of bulbs. Smaller bulbs yield a few large ones, and large bulbs yield a great number of smaller bulbs. Plant some of both each year. Shallots are grown similarly, but some varieties can also be grown from seed. For seed-saving purposes, shallots must be isolated from other flowering shallot varieties, Egyptian (walking) onions, and biennial bulb onions by a mile of distance, or a screen cage or other insect barrier. Plant 6–8 inches apart.

Harvest and Storage: Plants are harvested when the tops die down, just like ordinary onions. For storage, brush off the worst of the dirt and cure whole clumps in a warm, dry, dark place for one or two months. Then separate the bulbs and store them in a cool, dry place.

Uses: Potato onions are used like ordinary garden onions. Shallots have a more delicate flavor and are ideal for many kinds of gourmet cooking. The young greens of both species can be used like scallions.

Related Species and Breeding Potential: Potato onions rarely flower and thus have little hope for breeding. Since multiplier onions are in the same species as ordinary biennial onions and walking onions, the flowering types of shallot could potentially be crossed with any of a wide range of onion types.

Potato onions are highly productive. The smaller bulbs are used for propagation.

Allium tricoccum · Ramps

Synonyms
- Wild leek

Aspects
- Colony-forming herb
- Edible greens
- Part to full shade
- Moist to wet soil

General Overview, History, and Ecology: This eastern North American native onion is one of the most promising and underutilized perennial vegetable crops for cold climates. Ramps are one of the few shade-loving vegetables really worth growing. Ramps, also known as wild leeks, resemble lily-of-the-valley, with broad leaves. They can be found in the wild in great colonies, often carpeting the forest floor for miles. Ramps come up early in spring, before the trees or shrubs in the moist deciduous forests they favor have leafed out. The leaves reach about 10 inches long and then die back, followed by pretty white flowers. In this way ramps have evolved to utilize the brief period when there is good light to be had on the forest floor.

My favorite part of the ramp is the leaves, which are much larger and wider than most onions. They are also more tender, with a rich, somewhat pungent flavor. When cooked they become more mild, and are truly a gourmet delicacy. The small bulbs are also eaten, with a flavor between garlic and onion.

Every year in the mountains of the southeastern United States, ramp festivals celebrate the brief season of this delectable wild edible. For several years I hosted my own ramp festivals, featuring many delicious traditional recipes, like ramp green omelets and ramps fried with bacon. Even Martha Stewart has taken an interest in ramps, and they have become popular at gourmet restaurants. Unfortunately, the formerly abundant wild stands of ramps are at risk of damage from overharvesting. This is further impetus for establishing one's own patch of ramps, and indeed for reestablishing them in any eastern moist deciduous forest that does not already have them. Areas that were cleared for agriculture and regrown as forest are unlikely to have ramps, since in the wild they travel very slowly. We can assist them to recolonize many suitable habitats, while providing ourselves, and our neighbors, with a lifetime of pungent harvests.

While few people raise their own ramps, it is quite easy to do so. A pioneer in ramp cultivation is Glenn Facemire of G&N Ramp Farm in Richwood, West Virginia, who has written several booklets on the subject. In fact, in my experience growing ramps is easier than it has any right to be. They can even be transplanted when in full leaf. As long as you have moist soil with good organic matter and a shady (deciduous) spot, you should be fine. I have been promoting ramp cultivation for many years, and I won't stop until they are much more widely known and grown.

Though ramps are native to eastern North America, it is possible that they could naturalize anywhere with deciduous forests and chilly winters. They may be used as an ornamental bulb—their foliage resembles lily-of-the-valley (*Convallaria majalis*), although it is short-lived and the naked flowers appear later in the year.

Crop Description: Ramps are herbaceous perennials 6–12 inches high that only leaf out for a short period of time in the spring. They grow in small clumps, and spread over many years by dropping seed to form huge colonies.

Climate: Ramps will grow from roughly Zone 4 to 8. They are well suited to most of the eastern United States and southeastern Canada, and are worth trying in the Pacific Northwest as well, as far north as coastal Alaska, corresponding to the cold temperate and cool maritime climate zones used in this book.

Tolerances and Preferences: Ramps grow in deciduous shade. They require rich soil, preferably woodland humus. Mulching with leaves works well. Soil can be fairly acidic. In the wild they require moist to wet soils (in fact I often see them just uphill a bit from skunk cabbage), but under cultivation ramps can grow in soils of ordinary moisture.

Ramp Omelets

4 ramps
6 eggs
Olive oil or butter

Trim the bulbs and lower white portions off the ramps (save them to use like garlic or cook with bacon—mmm!). Whisk eggs and pour half into a warm saucepan with olive oil or melted butter. Lay coarsely chopped ramp greens over the eggs as they begin to cook and fold over half of the eggs so ramp greens are inside. Cook until golden brown on outside. Fantastic flavor! I also like to include additional fillings like gorgonzola or feta cheese, walnuts, sliced apples, and/or bacon.
Serves 2.

Naturalization Status: Native to eastern and central North America, ramps could naturalize in deciduous forests elsewhere.

Pest, Disease, and Weed Problems: I am not aware of ramps having any notable pests besides overzealous wild harvesters.

Propagation and Planting: The easiest way to propagate ramps is through division. Bulbs form nice clumps and can be easily divided. This should ideally be done when they are dormant, but, remarkably, they survive fairly well even if transplanted when they are fully leafed out. Ramps are also grown from seed, though this is more complicated. Seed can be sown in the fall and covered with a light coating of leaves. Seedlings will come up over the next two years. Otherwise seed can be cold-stratified (see Propagation on page 65) for 90 days and then planted. Set out ramp bulbs on a spacing of 12–18 inches.

Harvest and Storage: Many people dig up the whole plants, leaving just a few from each clump. I sometimes just cut one leaf from each plant, but I have found that their shelf life is much greater when plants are dug whole.

Uses: Ramp leaves can be used like leeks or scallions, although their shape and texture makes them far superior for use as a green. The bulbs are used like garlic or onions. Whole plants can also be roasted or fried. They are unsurpassed for use in omelets, and taste great in virtually every recipe I have ever tried.

Related Species and Breeding Potential: Some ramps have red mid-ribs, which is particularly attractive. Ramps could potentially be crossed with any number of alliums. Personally I am content with their current level of perfection.

Allium spp. • Perennial Onions

Synonyms
- See below

Aspects
- Clumping herbs
- Edible greens
- Edible bulbs
- Light variable; see below
- Moist, well-drained soil

There are a great number of useful perennial *Allium* species. Here I highlight a few of the best and most tested. Perennial onions can provide edible scallions, greens, bulbs, flowers, and topsets (tiny bulbs that grow on top of the stems). They are generally easy to care for, and most are suited to a wide range of climates. All of those listed here are of Eurasian origin. I have not included species whose use is as culinary herbs rather than vegetables (e.g., chives and garlic). There is lots of potential for crossing the various *Allium* species to develop interesting new perennial vegetables.

These species are bulb-forming perennials. Most are upright and form small clumps. Since their growth is upright, this allows for lots of sunlight for weeds or intercrops. Most prefer full sun and good soil.

Propagation varies by type. These species tend to be less susceptible to pests and diseases than ordinary garden onions, but don't be too lazy. Weeds are often a problem; mulch or a good low intercrop like white clover can help to suppress them.

All of these species either have naturalized or could conceivably do so, although none have done so aggressively.

A. ampeloprasum (Perennial Sweet Leek, Salad Leek, Leek). This perennial Eurasian species has been cultivated since ancient times, and has given rise to the biennial garden leek, elephant garlic, and other cultivated culinary herbs and vegetables. Many perennial subspecies and varieties exist with edible leaves and bulbs. The salad leek or perennial sweet leek was an important vegetable in ancient Egypt, and is still grown as a perennial leaf crop today in North Africa. Perennial leek types include 'Tarée Irani', a salad leek type from Iran, 'Poireau Perpétual' from the Mediterranean, 'Prei Anak' from Indonesia, and 'Kurrat' from Egypt. *Note:* Some varieties of ordinary biennial leek produce small bulbils called leek pearls that will cause the plants to form clumps over time if undisturbed. Plant geek extraordinaire Craig Hepworth reports that they form a large clump and can be grown for years, supporting perennial harvests. Elephant garlic can also be allowed to grow as a perennial. The salad leek is tolerant of hot and dry conditions.

A. cepa proliferum (Walking Onion, Egyptian Onion, Topset Onion). Walking onions are prolific and easy to grow. Instead of flowering they produce small bulbs on top of their stalks. When they mature, these stalks fall over, planting new bulbs for the following year. Thus the plants "walk" around the garden. The sprouting bulbs in spring make fine scallions and are produced in abundance. The topsets can be eaten, but are difficult to peel because they tend to be small. However, when still immature the bulbils can be used without peeling. Walking onions are hardy in Zones 4–10, and evergreen in many climates. Walking onions are one of the earliest and latest sources of edible greens in cold-climate gardens. This species is often so successful in gardens that people complain of having too much, so don't hold back on harvesting.

A. fistulosum (Welsh Onion, Scallion). This plant, commonly grown as an annual scallion, is also a perennial. Welsh onions will form a clump, which can be divided in spring for scallions. Replant a few and you will have another clump for next year.

Like walking onions, they are hardy to Zones 4–10 and evergreen in mild climates. The hollow leaves of this and other species can be stuffed with cottage cheese or other fillings for a tasty snack at most times of the year.

A. tuberosum (Garlic Chives). While usually grown here as a culinary herb, garlic chives are an important vegetable in China, where plants are blanched and harvested at 6–8 inches high. Two or three cuttings a year can be made of the mild-flavored yellow blanched shoots. Of course you can also just cut the greens as you need them. Flower stalks and flowers are also edible. In warm areas garlic chives produce leaves all year long. They are usually propagated by dividing clumps. Garlic chive seed quickly loses viability, so use seed no older than those from the previous season. This is one of the best onions for the tropics and subtropics.

A. ursinum (Ramson). This species is the European version of ramps. It is a spring woodland ephemeral, leafing out in early spring and soon disappearing. The large, broad, un-*Allium*- like leaves are eaten, and have a strong garlic flavor. Plants form large colonies in deciduous shade, growing in ordinary to wet soils. This species is probably only hardy to Zone 8, and is worth trying in the Pacific Northwest, where it has the potential to naturalize.

Amaranthaceae: The Amaranth Family

Alternanthera sissoo • Sissoo Spinach

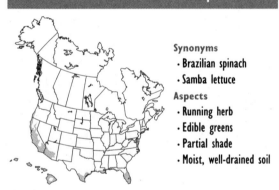

Synonyms
- Brazilian spinach
- Samba lettuce

Aspects
- Running herb
- Edible greens
- Partial shade
- Moist, well-drained soil

This species is a perfect edible groundcover for tropical polyculture systems. Sissoo spinach, originally from Brazil, is a low (1 foot high) groundcover that roots at the nodes and spreads indefinitely. It forms a dense enough cover to suppress the germination of weeds. It prefers partial shade, actually having many fewer pest problems at 50 percent shade. The leaves are a mild cooking green. Some cultivars are slightly bitter. Like many greens, sissoo spinach contains oxalic acid, and if you are going to consume large quantities they should be cooked (see the article on page 120). Sissoo spinach does not set viable seed and is reportedly not invasive. Plant some in the shade of your clumping bamboos and moringas today!

Sissoo spinach tolerates a wide range of soil pH, but needs high nitrogen, organic matter, and plenty of water. The foliage turns yellow when it needs nitrogen, and changes back to green quickly once it is added. Sissoo spinach could be grown as an annual in hot-summer areas by bringing in cuttings as winter houseplants. Plants are propagated with softwood cuttings. In addition to truly tropical Hawaii and South Florida, sissoo spinach is worth trying in the hot and humid Gulf Coast, and mild subtropical Southern California. In these areas, try throwing a blanket over your plants on the occasional frosty night. Cultivated varieties are seedless and do not escape from the garden to naturalize. Plants are vulnerable to leaf-eating caterpillars and slugs.

Apiaceae: The Celery Family

Arracacia xanthorhiza • Arracacha

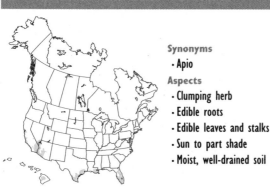

Synonyms
- Apio

Aspects
- Clumping herb
- Edible roots
- Edible leaves and stalks
- Sun to part shade
- Moist, well-drained soil

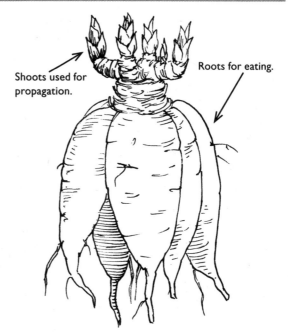

Shoots used for propagation.

Roots for eating.

Arracacha roots.

General Overview, History, and Ecology: This root crop was described by the great plant explorer David Fairchild as being "much superior to carrots." Arracacha roots are mild, savory, and filling. They contain flavors of carrot, celery, parsnip, and even cabbage and roasted chestnut. One plant can yield up to 6 pounds of roots.

Although it is a bit picky about where it will grow, arracacha is suitable for warm, long-season parts of the United States, and it has been grown successfully in central Florida and parts of California. It is cultivated in much of South and Central America, and we will probably be seeing more of the roots in grocery stores in coming years. Such a good-flavored vegetable can only be held back for so long.

If permitted to flower, arracacha would attract beneficial insects.

Crop Description: Arracacha resembles a large clump of celery, 3–5 feet tall and wide. The roots grow like large, very thick clusters of carrots, with flesh ranging from white to yellow to purple.

Climate: Arracacha requires a long growing season, 10–14 months depending on the variety, climate, and growing conditions. Smaller yields can be achieved in shorter periods, but roots do not usually size up until the advent of short days in fall (some day-length-neutral varieties do exist). This rules out growing arracacha in most of the United States and Canada without serious season extension. It is well suited to much of Zone 9 and warmer, and is being grown successfully as far north as San Francisco on the West Coast. Foliage is killed by frost. Although it hails from the cool upland tropics, arracacha can also tolerate the sweltering heat of South Florida, although according to some sources it cannot grow in true tropical lowlands.

Tolerances and Preferences: Arracacha will grow in full sun or partial shade. It is popular with South American farmers because it requires so few inputs to produce a good crop. It prefers well-drained soils, and plenty of phosphorus.

Naturalization Status: Arracacha has naturalized in Puerto Rico and could conceivably do so in warmer climates of North America.

Pest, Disease, and Weed Problems: Plants are sometimes attacked by spider mites and nematodes. Since they are vegetatively propagated, viruses can be a problem. Try to plant virus-free stock.

Propagation and Planting: Arracacha's large edible roots are not used for propagation. Instead, the shoots that emerge from the crown are used. Remove the shoots from the crown, and slash

"Lost Crops of the Incas"

Arracacha is one of many remarkable perennial crops domesticated in the Andean mountain range of South America. Twelve Andean crops are profiled in this book. While some Andean crops, like the potato, have been adopted around the world, others have never been adopted outside the region—some have become virtually extinct even in the Andes. Because they are adapted to the high-altitude tropics, some are not well suited to growing on the mainland United States and Canada, but many amateur and professional plant enthusiasts are working to introduce Andean food plants and determine how and where they can be grown here. For a fascinating review of the subject, check out *Lost Crops of the Incas* (see Recommended Reading in Part III). Other Andean-origin crops profiled in this book are the root crops ulluco, yacon, mashua, oca, and the edible canna achira; lima beans and the tree bean basul; the babaco papaya (suitable for California); Malabar gourd; and tomato relatives goldenberry and pepino dulce.

Levisticum officinale • Lovage

Aspects
- Clumping herb
- Edible greens and stalks
- Sun to part shade
- Moist, well-drained soil

them a few times with a knife. Leave them to sit for a few days, then plant. Arracacha should be planted about 3 feet apart.

Other Cultivation Information: Cut back flower stems to make the plant devote its energy to root production. Arracacha is usually grown as a plant/replant perennial. When grown in this fashion the original planted root becomes woody and the fresh side roots are eaten. When left in the ground too long roots can become fibrous and tough, so only the newer roots from perennial plants can be eaten. Intriguingly, however, plants will live for many years if undisturbed. Adventurous gardeners may want to experiment with techniques for growing arracacha as a true perennial.

Harvest and Storage: Arracacha roots store very poorly. They should be harvested as needed.

Uses: Arracacha roots should be cooked. They are particularly delicious in soups, but are used in any of the ways root crops are cooked. The stems and young leaves are also used, like celery. The roots are high in vitamin A.

Related Species and Breeding Potential: Importing day-length-neutral and short-season varieties should be a priority. Arracacha is limited by its short shelf life, and breeding work to rectify this situation has been recommended.

Lovage is essentially a gigantic perennial celery. It has long been grown as a perennial vegetable in Europe. Every year I look forward to making lovage-sorrel soup from the young shoots in early spring. These young leaves and stems have a strongly aromatic celery flavor that is usually too intense to eat raw, but works fantastically well in soups. Later growth is much too strongly flavored to eat. Some gardeners blanch lovage in the

The tender spring growth of Lovage.
PHOTO BY JONATHAN BATES.

> ### *Recipe: Lovage-Sorrel Soup*
>
> 6 cups rich chicken stock
> 3 medium potatoes
> 3 cloves garlic
> 1 butternut squash or other winter squash
> 10–12 8-inch lovage shoots
> 1 pound fresh sorrel leaves (same
>   amount as a 1-pound bag of spinach)
> Salt, black pepper, and chili flakes to taste
>
> Boil chicken stock and 3 cups of water. Add
> chopped potatoes and minced or crushed
> garlic. Peel the squash, remove the seeds,
> and chop into 1- to 2-inch chunks. Add
> squash a few minutes after potatoes. Simmer
> for about 15 minutes, or until the vegeta-
> bles begin to get soft. Chop lovage as you
> would celery and cook for 5 more minutes.
> Stir in chopped sorrel and remove from
> heat. Season with salt, black pepper, and
> chili flakes. Using blanched lovage shoots will
> make for a milder flavor. Serve with hearty
> toasted bread and butter.
> Serves 4.

spring for a milder flavor that is enjoyable even raw. A great advantage of lovage is that the greens are ready very early in the garden, sometimes pushing up through the last of the snow here in Massachusetts. Apparently the traditional way to drink a Bloody Mary is through the hollow stalks of lovage, used as a straw. The seeds are used as a flavoring, much like celery or dill seeds, and the roots are also edible.

Lovage plants can grow 6 feet tall or more. After flowering, the tall stalks often fall down, crush-ing nearby plants. Cutting back the flower stalks when seed is setting will prevent this. Lovage is hardy in Zones 4–8. It is also worth grow-ing because it attracts beneficial insects to its large yellow umbel-shaped flower heads. Lovage will grow in full sun or part shade. It grows in ordinary garden soils. Lovage has naturalized in some areas of the United States and Canada. Propagation is best done from division of fully dormant plants. Lovage can also be grown from

seed, which germinates best from fresh seed harvested in the fall. Seed can also be kept fresh and viable in a refrigerator.

Oenanthe javanica • Water Celery

Synonyms
- *Oenanthe stolonifera,*
- Water dropwort
- Nase

Aspects
- Running herb
- Edible greens and stalks
- Sun to part Shade
- Aquatic to moist soil

General Overview, History, and Ecology: This aquatic vegetable is cultivated in much of Asia, and is popular in Hawaii, but it has been largely over-looked on mainland United States and in Canada. This is quite a shame, as it is easily grown and tasty. The raw leaves and stems of water celery have a strong flavor somewhere between parsley and celery, which becomes milder with cooking. In Asian cuisines it is used in soups, salads, and numerous other dishes. Water celery can be grown in water gardens but it will also thrive in moist soils, where it can spread rapidly. The dwarf vari-ety 'Flamingo' has beautiful variegated foliage of green, white, and pink. 'Flamingo' is less aggres-sively spreading than the species form and makes a beautiful edible groundcover, although to my taste the flavor is not nearly as good for eating raw.

There seems to be a debate as to the hardi-ness of this species. Some catalogs list it as fully tropical, while others claim hardiness as far north as Zone 4! Apparently hardiness varies among different cultivars—although both the variety 'Flamingo' and some green varieties have overwin-tered successfully in Zone 6 in Massachusetts, including in my own garden. Water celery can also certainly be effectively grown as an annual virtually anywhere. In the hot, humid tropics it is grown as a cool-season crop.

Water celery is an aggressive grower; in water gardens it grows very vigorously. This plant could

Water celery is very tasty and can thrive floating on water, in a pot in a water garden, in wet soils, or even in ordinary garden soils, as well as in full sun or part shade!

easily escape into natural bodies of water, so be careful. Like watercress, it will root in pots but will also spread horizontally across the surface of the water, forming a mass of roots as it goes. Grow it as an emergent floater as described in the water garden section (page 60). It is often used in biological filtration systems due to its densely branching roots.

Like most members of this family, the flowers of water celery are excellent for attracting beneficial insects. *Note:* There are some deadly poisonous species in the genus *Oenanthe*, so make sure you are getting the right species!

Crop Description: Water celery is a running perennial about 2–4 feet high, spreading indefinitely. The branches root as they spread across soil or water, forming dense colonies.

Climate: Apparently can be grown as a perennial from the tropics through the cold temperate zones, and possibly farther. Mine actually puts out new shoots underneath the snow, which I snack on during winter thaws and in early spring.

Tolerances and Preferences: Water celery grows in sun to part shade, in moist garden soils or as a floating mat in water gardens. Drier soils and heavier shade may serve to slow its growth without killing it.

Naturalization Status: While water celery is not reported to have naturalized, it certainly has the potential to do so.

Pest, Disease, and Weed Problems: None in my experience, and most books describe it as having few pest problems.

Propagation and Planting: Water celery is easily propagated from cuttings. Stems will often already have formed adventitious roots, and can be potted or planted out immediately. The plant sets small amounts of seed, which should be sown when fresh. You can probably buy a bunch of it at an Asian market, root the cuttings in a glass of water, and plant them out just as you would with watercress. For planting in soil, space at 18–24 inches apart, to fill in over one year's time.

Harvest and Storage: Best used fresh; like most greens, water celery will not store for a long period.

Uses: Used as a fresh greens in salads or in cooked dishes. I grow it in a pond near my kitchen door and often run out to clip some to add to soups or other dishes.

Related Species and Breeding Potential: Some related species are very poisonous. Breeding within the species should begin with screening already developed varieties for flavor, productivity, hardiness, and less aggressive growth.

Sium sisarum • Skirret

Synonyms
- Suikerwortel

Aspects
- Clumping herb
- Edible roots
- Sun to part shade
- Moist, well-drained soil

General Overview, History, and Ecology: According to the classic reference *Sturtevant's Notes on Edible Plants*, skirret roots are "esteemed when boiled as among the sweetest, whitest, and most pleasant of roots." The name comes from the Dutch *suikerwortel* meaning "sugar root." Skirret roots were once an important vegetable in European and American gardens, and they remain impor-

Skirret is a low-maintenance root crop with few pest problems. The roots have a potato-parsnip flavor.

tant in their native northeastern Asia. Its importance in North America and Europe faded as it was discarded in favor of the potato, which had arrived from Andean South America.

Skirret roots look like a cluster of pencil-thick white carrots. I had always read that skirret roots have a fibrous or woody core, and I assumed that this trait was responsible for the plant's falling out of favor. However, when I cooked up my first harvest of skirret roots I was surprised to find no woody core whatsoever; instead, it was like a tender blend of parsnip and potato. I have found several possible explanations. First, I clearly lucked into a superior variety—better than any I had heard of. But it also turns out that first-year seed-grown plants have woodier root cores, though their roots are a bit thicker. I grew out some seedlings as an experiment, and they did have larger, woodier roots. Had I had a larger garden at the time, I would have grown the seedlings out for a second year and sampled them, although seedling skirret plants are usually inferior to their parents. Thus, the optimal way to grow skirret is to get hold of a good nonwoody clone and propagate it vegetatively. This is one perennial crop that is often grown as an annual, but clearly is better when grown as a perennial.

Skirret fills the niche for cold climates that its cousin arracacha does in warmer regions. Each year clumps multiply into easily separated plants, making division and harvest easy. Clumps can be dug and easily divided, just by tugging the stems apart. Replant some and eat the rest! To my mind, the minor amount of extra work in cleaning and prepping the roots to cook is offset by the fact that plants seem to grow with very little care. The small white flowers are very attractive to beneficial insects, highly ornamental, and have a long bloom time.

Crop Description: Skirret is a clump-forming herb that grows about 4 feet high. It produces a large number of flowers in umbels that resemble those of Queen Anne's lace (wild carrot). After flowering the stems often lie down on the ground, smothering their neighbors a bit.

Climate: Skirret is a plant for cold and temperate climates. It is hardy to at least Zone 4 and probably a good bit colder. I imagine it would not like long, intensely hot summers of the humid South, but it is worth trying anywhere with a half decent winter. It thrives in the mild Zone 9 maritime climate of Cornwall, England.

Tolerances and Preferences: Skirret grows the largest, sweetest, least fibrous roots in rich moist soils. In my gardens it has only produced good yields in the best soils. Addition of fertilizers will also boost flavor and yields. Skirret is productive in full sun or light shade. The plant likes plenty of moisture; in fact, its wild ancestor grows on muddy streambanks.

Naturalization Status: Skirret has not naturalized in the United States or Canada.

Pest, Disease, and Weed Problems: Skirret is quite resistant to pests and diseases. Its flowers attract beneficial insects that will help to control pests throughout your garden.

Propagation and Planting: Skirret is extremely easy to divide—clumps come apart very easily, forming separate plants. Just dig up a clump, gently tug the plants apart, harvest some for eating, and replant others in the original hole, setting out some new plants elsewhere (skirret is a classic plant/replant perennial). Though the quality can be inferior to the parent plant, skirret can be easily grown from seed; however, it can take a few weeks to germinate and grows slowly at first. Transplant seedlings or replants out about 2 feet apart.

Harvest and Storage: Skirret roots are harvested in the fall, as they become sweeter after the foliage is killed by frost. Apparently they store well if given the same care as carrots.

Uses: Skirret is a versatile root crop. It can be eaten raw, boiled, roasted, baked, in soups, or mashed. I have simply boiled it and enjoyed it as a side dish. When I have more plants I look forward to eating large quantities of it mashed with butter. It is no wonder that this sweet and filling root was an important staple for so long. The fact that skirret has a cluster of thin white roots makes it a bit intimidating to clean, but a few minutes of scrubbing with a brush is satisfactory. However, cooking with first-year plants and varieties with woodier cores is challenging: The flesh needs to be scraped away from the woody core before eating, and as the roots are fairly small this can be a major drawback.

Related Species and Breeding Potential: Identifying or developing varieties free of woody root cores should be a priority. The plants I purchased from Perennial Pleasures (see Sources of Plants and Seeds in Part III) were perfect. Skirret also has a wild native relative with edible roots. The water parsnip (*Sium suave*) is an aquatic wild edible. Unfortunately, it is very difficult to distinguish water parsnip from the deadly water hemlock (*Cicuta maculata*), and so I recommend that only experienced botanists experiment with this plant.

Araceae: The Aroid Family

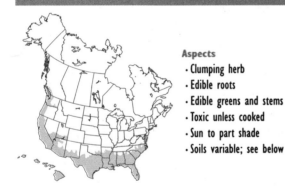

Xanthosoma and **Colocasia** spp. • Edible Aroids

Aspects
- Clumping herb
- Edible roots
- Edible greens and stems
- Toxic unless cooked
- Sun to part shade
- Soils variable; see below

General Overview, History, and Ecology: This group of closely related crops is no stranger to Hawaiian gardeners! Grown there for centuries, taro (one of the common aroids) was brought in the first canoes to settle the islands. Aroids are also familiar to water gardeners and ornamental gardeners as "elephant ear." The leaves are shaped like enormous arrowheads with long stalks. Aroids were domesticated in both the New and Old Worlds: taro (*Colocasia esculenta*) originally in Southeast Asia, and the similar and closely related tannier and other *Xanthosoma* species in northeastern South America and the Caribbean.

Taro and tannier are premier tropical starchy plant/replant root crops, and some varieties are also grown as leaf and stem crops. As leaf crops aroids are excellent tropical perennial vegetables. It is not well known, however, that many taro varieties are hardy to Zone 7, although in short-season climates they are better suited to leaf than root production. Aroids produce two types of edible roots: large single corms, and multiple smaller cormels that grow from the central corm.

C. esculenta (Taro, Cocoyam, Eddo, Dasheen). Taro is an ancient tropical Asian root crop, and an important global staple. Taro roots are the basis of the classic Hawaiian dish poi. There are numerous varieties, with many differences including a range of colors like red, amber, lilac, white, and gray. The cooked leaves and petioles are also eaten. There are two broad classes of taro. Eddoes have a large corm and many cormels. Dasheen has a smaller corm and multiple cormels. Dasheen likes wet or flooded conditions, while eddoes dislike flooding but will tolerate waterlogged soils. Surprisingly, many taro varieties are hardy without protection in the warmer portions of USDA Zone 7.

Aroids (including tannier, shown here) make a dramatic statement in the edible landscape. Some aroids are surprisingly hardy, to Zone 7 or beyond with protection.

C. esculenta ('Celery Stem' Taro, 'Zuiki' Taro). This variety is cultivated for its edible leafstalks, which are eaten like celery. These stems can actually be eaten raw due to low oxalate content. They have a sweet flavor and a unique, spongy texture. The stems are cooked, or peeled and used raw in salads. The young leaves are also edible but should be cooked for 10–20 minutes. The unfurling leaves are cooked like asparagus. The corms of this variety are not usually eaten. 'Celery Stem' Taro is more tolerant of dry soils than most types. It makes its best growth and largest leaves in partial shade. This variety is highly resistant to pests and diseases, including viruses and nematodes.

X. brasiliense (Belembe, Tahitian Taro, Tannier Spinach). Tropical crop expert Dr. Frank Martin considers belembe one of the best leaf crops for the tropics. It is only grown for the leaves and stems, since the corms are small and essentially inedible. Belembe was domesticated in the Amazon and is now widely grown throughout the tropics. Compared with other aroids, it has very low calcium oxalate content, although leaves should still be cooked before eating. Leaves and stems are often treated as separate vegetables, with the stems cut into small ½-inch sections so they cook thoroughly—just like you would cook chard or bok choi. If overcooked it becomes mushy, so the stems should be cooked separately since they take longer to cook than the leaves. Do not consume the cooking water. The lower parts of the leafstalks are too tough to eat.

Belembe has an excellent flavor and is a very popular vegetable where it has been introduced. In the tropics it will produce leaves year-round. Plants should be divided regularly to keep them vigorous. They will grow in full sun to light shade.

X. saggitifolium (Tannier, Yautia, Malanga). This species is the major New World aroid root crop, domesticated in the Amazon. Unlike taro, tannier does not like being flooded, though waterlogged soil is fine. Tannier also tolerates more shade than taro, making it better suited to intercropping with fruit trees. Only the cormels of tannier are eaten, as the corms are usually too fibrous. The leaves and leafstalks are also eaten. Many varieties are hardy to Zone 8. You can leave the corm in place when harvesting if you are careful, to ensure additional future cormel harvests.

X. violaceum (Woo Chai, Violet-Stem Taro, Primrose Malanga). This species is smaller than other edible aroids, with 5- to 7-inch leaves on 1-foot stalks. Leaves, stems, and cormels are edible. The leafstalks, mid-ribs, and veins are a beautiful violet color. This species is a fine edible water garden plant, with the soil line submerged 3–6 inches below the water level.

Crop Description: Edible aroids are clumping herbaceous perennials with large arrow-shaped leaves. Most species profiled here grow 3–6 feet high and form clumps of equivalent width. The large, arrowhead-shaped leaves give a dramatic tropical look to the landscape.

Climate: Aroids are excellent tropical and subtropical leaf and root crops. Aroids like warm, but not hot, weather, growing best between 70°F and 80°F. They won't grow at all when temperatures go below 60°F. With sufficient moisture they can be grown throughout the tropical lowlands and uplands, as well as much of the hot and humid Southeast, arid hot Southwest, and Mediterranean mild subtropical California. Many taro varieties are hardy in the warmer parts of USDA Zone 7 without protection—and it is worth trying to grow it with mulch into Zone 6. However, a long season is necessary to ripen the corms and cormels. In short seasons it will take two years to ripen corms and cormels.

Calcium Oxalate

All aroids contain varying amounts of a toxic chemical called calcium oxalate. The crystals of calcium oxalate can cause intense burning and itching in your mouth, throat, and digestive tract. Calcium oxalate is rendered harmless by sufficient cooking. The amount of this chemical varies greatly among different cultivars. Do not eat wild or ornamental varieties, as they are likely to contain excessive amounts. Some cultivated varieties, like 'Celery Stem' taro, have very small amounts of calcium oxalate, so low that certain parts of the plant can even be eaten raw. It is easy to test and see if aroid leaves, stems, or roots have been cooked thoroughly. Just chew on a small amount. If you get a scratchy feeling in the back of your throat, it's not done yet! Usually leaves should be cooked for at least 10 minutes, and corms and cormels until soft. You should wash your hands after handling the plants, as the juice can cause skin and eye irritation. Calcium oxalate is also found in other edible plants of this family, like the fruit of the delicious monster vine (*Monstera deliciosa*) and the roots of the minor perennial root crop konjak (*Amorphophallus konjak*).

Thus, in many areas aroids are probably only worth growing as leaf crops.

Tolerances and Preferences: Aroids thrive in conditions considered too poorly drained for most crops. Some aroids thrive in flooded culture, or are grown as water plants. All require flooded, wet, or very moist soils. They can tolerate quite acid soils. All will grow in full sun or partial shade, with *Xanthosoma* species being more shade-tolerant. In the edible water garden aroids can be grown as marginal or emergent crops.

Naturalization Status: Aroids have naturalized in some portions of the tropical and subtropical United States.

Pest, Disease, and Weed Problems: Aroids can be affected by many disease problems. Taro grown in flooded paddies is especially vulnerable to diseases. Tannier is resistant to many of these diseases; this is part of the reason for its popularity. Nematodes are also a problem. Fortunately, insects are not much of a problem, probably because the calcium oxalate poisons them!

Propagation and Planting: Aroids are propagated by division. Corms and cormels can be planted. Make sure there are at least three or four buds per cormel. Only the top part of the corm is needed; the remainder can be eaten. Trim back most of the leaves from nondormant cormels before planting. Plant aroids 2–3 feet apart.

Other Cultivation Information: Corms are often earthed up for better yields.

Harvest and Storage: Taro is grown as a plant/replant perennial. Tannier cormels can be carefully removed, leaving the corm in place for perennial harvests. In the tropics, corms and cormels are harvested after most of the older leaves have died back. This can be from 6 to 15 months, depending on variety and cultivation technique.

Uses: Edible aroid corms and cormels can be used in all the ways potatoes can, including baking, boiling, and frying. Corms and cormels must be thoroughly cooked to remove toxic calcium oxalate (raw aroids cause burning and itching in the mouth from this chemical). Aroid roots are high in carbohydrates and low in protein and vitamins. The large leaves and leafstalks of aroids can also be eaten. The young leaves are cooked, and larger ones are stuffed like cabbage. The leafstalks are used like celery and have a somewhat okra-like texture. Leaves and stems of most varieties must be cooked for 10–20 minutes to remove calcium oxalate.

Related Species and Breeding Potential: Aroids are difficult to breed because they rarely flower. Seedlings are not true to type, and often have high calcium oxalate content. More northern growers should screen existing varieties for early cormel ripening and hardiness. Screening existing varieties to find those with low acridity in leaves and stems is also important.

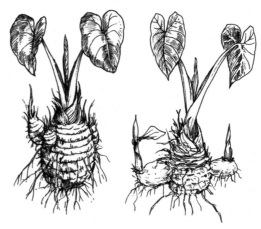

Corms and cormels of taro and tannier.

Araliaceae: The Spikenard Family

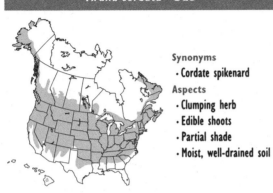

Aralia cordata • Udo

Synonyms
- Cordate spikenard

Aspects
- Clumping herb
- Edible shoots
- Partial shade
- Moist, well-drained soil

Udo grows up to 10 feet high and has striking flowers.

This perennial vegetable is a popular cultivated crop in Japan, used somewhat like asparagus. Udo is a striking large perennial growing 4–8 feet tall and 3–4 feet wide, with large compound leaves and enormous beautiful heads of small white flowers (these flowers attract beneficial insects). The shoots are blanched by piling up soil or leaves, and are harvested at 18 inches in height (although some sources indicate they can be eaten up to 5 feet tall). The shoots have a crisp texture and a lemon-fennel flavor. The drawback is that, before using them, they must be processed to remove an unpleasant turpentine flavor. I have not eaten udo myself, but processing techniques in the literature include: boiling in salted water; slicing and soaking in cold water; and soaking in water with vinegar. After treatment they can be used raw or cooked, much like asparagus. The roots can also be cooked and eaten. Several named varieties have been developed in Japan.

Udo prefers part shade, and needs moisture. It can tolerate poor soils as long as they are moist. Udo is hardy in Zones 3–8. The tender spring growth is vulnerable to frosts and should be protected. Propagation by division is easy when the plants are dormant. Growing from seed is more difficult. Seed must be cold-stratified for three to five months. After stratification it will take one to four months to germinate. Alternatively, seed can be sown outdoors in the fall and allowed to stratify naturally, as long as your winters are suffi-ciently long and cold. Udo sets crops of inedible berries, and it is possible that it could naturalize through being spread by birds, although to date it has not naturalized in North America.

While the processing issue sounds like a bit of a hassle, udo is a very easy crop to grow and a beautiful ornamental, providing many years of crops, and it is certainly worth experimenting with in cold- and temperate-climate gardens.

Asteraceae: The Aster Family

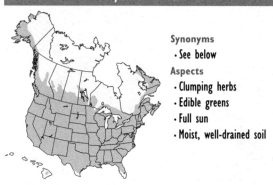

Cicorium intybus and **Taraxacum officinale** •
Chicory and Dandelion

Synonyms
· See below
Aspects
· Clumping herbs
· Edible greens
· Full sun
· Moist, well-drained soil

General Overview, History, and Ecology: Chicories and dandelions are popular vegetables in Europe but have never caught on in the same way in the United States and Canada. The rich, nutty, and slightly bitter flavor of their leaves is a fantastic addition to gourmet mesclun salads, and is tasty in many cooked dishes as well. Both chicory and dandelion are highly nutritious as well. The odds are that you already have one or both of these species growing as weeds in your garden or nearby. Take a cue from nature, and cultivate their improved relatives.

C. intybus (Chicory, Italian Dandelion). The ancestral wild chicories include both biennial and perennial individuals. Naturalized wild chicories can be seen flowering along many roadsides in the United States and Canada, with pretty blue flowers on tall stalks. Some cultivated chicories are annuals or biennials. Perennial types tend to be leaf rather than heading types, and most resemble dandelions or lettuces. Perennial heading varieties will usually only form tight heads the first year. Some seem to be more strongly perennial than others. Often only certain seedlings of a variety will be perennial. Like most greens, the leaves become more bitter when flowering. In the second year and thereafter plants will flower earlier, although cutting back the flower stalks can prolong the length of the harvest. Perennial varieties include the following:

- 'Cerolio', with tight dark rosettes.
- 'Dentarella', or 'Italian Dandelion', with green leaves resembling a large dandelion.
- 'Grumolo' is small with green leaves.
- 'Italo Rossico', or 'Red Rib Dandelion', resembling a very attractive dandelion with deep red mid-ribs. I spoke to one gardener with a plant that had produced greens for 10 years!
- 'Puntarella', bred for its thick, succulent, contorted stems.
- 'Rossa di Treviso', with long leaves turning red with cold weather. Plants for a Future in Cornwall, United Kingdom, find this their most productive perennial cultivar.
- 'Rossa di Verona' is similar to the above, with smaller leaves.
- 'Spadona', with long rounded leaves like elongated spinach.

No doubt there are many more perennial varieties. Experimentation to determine the best perennial production methods should proceed hand in hand with work to breed varieties that produce well as perennials. An easy backyard experiment would be to order as many varieties as you can find, including the great variety available from European sources, and see which turn out to perennialize. Chicory is sometimes sold as Italian dandelion.

T. officinale (Dandelion, French Dandelion). Dandelions are one of the most popular wild edibles in the United States and Canada but are rarely cultivated. In spring their nutty, bitter flavor heralds the taste of summer to come. Unlike chicories, dandelions are all reliably perennial, as you no doubt know already from your garden and lawn. Wild, weedy dandelions have spread all over the country. Personally I think their leaves are at their best if they are blanched first with mulch. Improved varieties have larger leaves with reduced bitterness. Whether you grow wild or improved types, you can be guaranteed that the plants will be low-maintenance! The flowers are sometimes battered and used to make fritters.

Climate: Both species are hardy from extremely cold Zone 3 through the hot humid South.

Tolerances and Preferences: The wild relatives of chicory and dandelion are weeds thriving in virtually any soil. For tasty and tender leaves, they should be grown in good garden soil. You will be surprised how big dandelions can get when they are treated with a bit of TLC. Both plants will grow in either full sun or light shade.

Naturalization Status: Both species have thoroughly naturalized in the United States and Canada—you may as well plant them, as they are here to stay anyway!

Pest, Disease, and Weed Problems: Neither species has much in the way or pest or disease problems. Both can themselves become weeds. Don't let them go to seed if you want to keep your garden free of seedlings.

Propagation and Planting: Both species are easily grown from seed. When plants are large enough they can be divided. Plant on 12-inch centers if growing them as perennials.

Other Cultivation Information: Blanching greatly improves the flavor of both species. Both chicory and dandelion have deep taproots and accumulate minerals from the subsoil. As their leaves decompose, they enrich the soil for surrounding plants.

Harvest and Storage: Leaves are harvested from plants before they flower. Stalks can be cut back to prolong the harvest season.

Uses: The leaves of both species are used raw in salads and cooked in many dishes. Their strong flavor can be overcome by mixing them with other species. The roots of both species are also roasted to make coffee-like beverages.

Related Species and Breeding Potential: Inventorying existing varieties for success as perennials would be a good place to start. Eventually varieties that perform excellently as perennials should be found or developed. Reducing bitterness could help both species become more acceptable to American and Canadian palates. Chicory is related to the biennial cultivated edible *C. endive*, which includes radicchio and endive.

The nutty, somewhat bitter leaves of chicory are important in Italian cuisine.

Chicory with White Beans
This recipe is nutty, bitter, rich, and savory.

1 small red onion
Olive oil
1 15-oz. can white or cannelini beans
1 bunch (10–12 leaves) chicory
1 tablespoon red cooking wine
Pinch of salt
Pinch of tarragon and thyme
Fresh Parmesan or Romano cheese to taste

Chop onion and sauté in olive oil. Add beans and chopped chicory, sauté on low heat for 10 minutes. Add red wine, salt, tarragon, and thyme. Add fresh-grated Parmesan or Romano and serve with garlic bread. I like to use 'Red Rib' chicory for this recipe.
Serves 2.

Cynara scolymus · Globe Artichoke

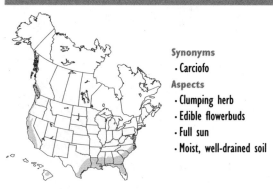

Synonyms
- Carciofo

Aspects
- Clumping herb
- Edible flowerbuds
- Full sun
- Moist, well-drained soil

General Overview, History, and Ecology: Ancient Egyptians enjoyed this perennial thistle relative 6,000 years ago. A large herb with silvery foliage, the plants make a striking component of edible landscapes. If allowed to flower they sport huge 7-inch thistle-like flowers. Each plant produces multiple heads, with the largest ones on the central stems and a number of smaller heads as well.

Surely any fan of globe artichokes would be excited to grow their own. Until recently, artichokes were primarily grown in California, particularly in coastal areas, the Central Valley, and interior Southern California. These areas feature the ideal climate for artichoke production: cool summers and mild winters. Californian artichokes thrive as perennials and will crop for 5–10 years. Hotter summers make for smaller yields of tougher buds, and winters colder than Zone 7 or 8 (depending on the variety) will kill the plants.

Recently techniques have been popularized that permit artichokes to be grown as annuals outside of this region, and new varieties are being developed with wider adaptability. You have probably only tasted 'Green Globe'—this variety is mono-cropped on a massive scale in California. There are other varieties with interesting characteristics that might be worth experimenting with, such as 'Purple Sicilian', which is extra heat-tolerant and has small, purple heads that can be eaten raw when young.

Crop Description: Artichokes are large herbs growing up to 6 feet tall and 6–8 feet wide. They have feathery silver foliage and beautiful thistle-like flowers if buds are not harvested.

Climate: Intensely hot summers impact the eating quality of the flowerbuds with most varieties. In areas with hot summers artichokes should be grown in partial shade. Light frost will disfigure flowerbuds, but the insides are still fine to eat. Hard frost will ruin them.

Artichokes prefer Mediterranean climates with mild summers and cool winters. If your climate isn't like this, however, don't give up hope. Recently developed varieties permit cultivation of artichokes as annuals in northeastern summers, while varieties like 'Purple Sicilian' offer gardeners in the sweltering heat of the Gulf Coast and Florida an opportunity to grow them too.

To grow artichokes as an annual in cold-winter climates, you need to fool the plants into thinking they are in their second year. Use a variety especially selected for this like 'Imperial Star'. Start seeds indoors a good eight weeks before the last frost date. Pot them up when they are a few inches tall and put them somewhere where they will have 60°F to 70°F days and 50°F to 60°F nights. Transplant them out to the garden after danger of frost is over. At this point they still need at least 250 hours of temperatures below 50°F in order to start making flowerbuds. All this work fools the plants into thinking they have experienced a mild Mediterranean winter and it is time to start making flowers.

Tolerances and Preferences: Artichokes should be grown in rich, well-drained soil. They are tolerant of salt spray and somewhat salty soils. Grow artichokes in full sun unless you are in an area with intensely hot summers. They require consistent moisture in order to yield well.

Naturalization Status: Artichokes have naturalized in California and Arizona.

Pest, Disease, and Weed Problems: In California artichokes can experience heavy losses from the artichoke plume moth, which bores into the leaves, stems, and even the buds themselves. Affected plant parts should be removed and destroyed. This pest can cause losses of 50 percent or more, but can be controlled with Bt, pheromone traps, and beneficial nematode products. Various other insects, including caterpillars and aphids, can cause damage. Artichokes are also affected by a plethora of pathogens, including botrytis, powdery mildew, crown rot, and more.

Propagation and Planting: Most artichoke varieties are not true to seed and must be propagated by division of suckers. Some varieties can be easily grown from seed. Space globe artichokes 3–4 feet apart.

Other Cultivation Information: In Southern California it never gets cold enough to induce dormancy and trigger another round of fruiting. After the plants have finished the season's production, cut them back to the ground and let them dry out for a few weeks without irrigation. When fall arrives they will pick right back up again. In colder areas cut the plants to the ground before frost and mulch them.

Harvest and Storage: Harvest artichokes when the buds reach their maximum size, just before the bracts (the large scales that you eat) start to open. Each plant can produce 10 or more buds in a year in optimal climates. If stored in a cool, moist place buds can last for up to a month.

Uses: Although artichokes are not very nutritious, their flavor makes them very popular. Whole flowerbuds are boiled. Scrape the tender bases of the bracts with your teeth, and then remove the hairy fibers (the choke) and eat the whole delectable base of the bud (the heart). You can also boil small buds and eat them whole. The peeled flower stems can also be eaten. The leaf mid-ribs can be cooked much like bitter celery (similar to the related cardoon).

Related Species and Breeding Potential: Good work is being done on developing artichokes for hot climates and for growing as annuals. It would be interesting to cross artichokes with the closely related cardoon (a leaf crop) and grow out a bunch of seed to see what you get. To develop hardy perennial artichokes (and cardoons), try crossing with the hardy perennial silver thistle (*Carlina acaulis*), whose flowerbuds are used as a cold-hardy substitute for artichoke. This species, native to the Alps, is hardy to Zone 4 and is a member of the same thistle "subtribe" of the Aster family along with artichokes and cardoon.

Gynura crepioides • Okinawa Spinach

Synonyms
• Hung tsoi

Aspects
• Running herb
• Edible greens
• Sun to part shade
• Moist, well-drained soil

General Overview, History, and Ecology: Okinawa spinach is a low-maintenance, fast-growing perennial leaf crop. While believed to have been domesticated in Indonesia or elsewhere in Southeast Asia, it is sold commercially in parts of tropical Asia. Jay Ram says in the *Tropical Perennial Vegetable* series that it is "one of the easiest and least complicated tropical vegetables that can be grown." It is also a good candidate for growing as an annual in hot-summer areas.

Okinawa spinach is also outstanding in tropical and "tropicalesque" edible landscapes. It is an attractive evergreen ornamental shrubby ground-cover, with vibrant purple undersides to the leaves and pretty orange flowers. The leaves have a nutty, almost piney taste, and their purple color makes quite a striking addition to salads, although their flavor is a bit strong to be the sole ingredient of a salad.

Crop Description: Okinawa spinach is a low, spreading herb or shrub growing up to 4 feet high, though it is usually much lower.

Climate: Okinawa spinach is a tropical vegetable that is killed to the ground by a hard frost. It thrives in hot and humid conditions. In frost-free areas it can produce year-round. It is worth trying as a dieback perennial in warmer parts of the hot and humid South, arid hot Southwest, and warmer parts of California. If you live somewhere with hot summers and cold winters you could plant some out and just take a few cuttings indoors for the winter as houseplants, replanting them outside in spring. Growth is much slower in cooler seasons.

Tolerances and Preferences: Okinawa spinach will grow in full sun or light shade, and is sometimes grown as an edible understory for tropical fruit trees. This plant will tolerate virtually any soil, although it prefers well-drained, rich soils. It is more productive when kept fertilized. It is also somewhat drought-tolerant.

Naturalization Status: Okinawa spinach has not naturalized in North America. Cultivated forms are sterile.

Pest, Disease, and Weed Problems: Few pests or diseases bother Okinawa spinach. It forms a dense groundcover that suppresses weeds.

Propagation and Planting: Okinawa spinach is easy to grow from cuttings. They will root in about a week. First harvest begins in about one month. Plant at a 12- to 18-inch distance.

Other Cultivation Information: This plant will spread quickly in hot weather, and may require harvest or trimming to keep it in place.

Harvest and Storage: The leaves and top 4 inches of the shoot tips are harvested. As mentioned above, the more you cut, the more tender new shoots and leaves are produced.

Uses: The leaves and tender shoots of Okinawa spinach can be eaten raw or cooked, although older, tougher leaves should be cooked. Okinawa spinach can be mucilaginous when cooked, although not when used raw. For the best texture, steam rather than boil leaves and stems. Otherwise, mix with other vegetables when cooking if you want to minimize this mucilaginous quality.

Okinawa spinach is a reliable leaf crop for tropical and subtropical gardens.

Remember that this texture is prized in tropical Asia, particularly for thickening sauces. The purple pigment in the leaves and shoots imparts a red dye to other foods it is cooked with. The raw leaves are beautiful in salads or as a garnish.

Related Species and Breeding Potential: Cultivated forms are sterile and already fantastic, so this is a case where breeding work is difficult and not particularly important.

Helianthus tuberosus • Sunchoke

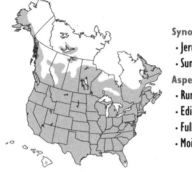

Synonyms
- Jerusalem artichoke
- Sunroot

Aspects
- Running herb
- Edible tubers
- Full sun
- Moist, well-drained soil

General Overview, History, and Ecology: Sunchokes are native to eastern North America. They were cultivated by many groups of Native Americans, who selected the wild forms with the largest tubers. The plants grow 6–12 feet tall and have attractive small sunflower-like flowers in the late fall. Sunchokes produce enormous yields of tubers, as much as four times the yield of potatoes. The tubers are crisp and sweet. Their size and shape vary, with some forms as large as a medium-sized potato. Some varieties have smooth tubers; others are knobby and harder to clean. Tuber color ranges from white or yellow to red and purple.

Sunchoke tubers are sweet and good to eat raw. When cooked, especially when baked, they become even sweeter. They can be used as any root crop, except that when fried they become somewhat mushy. I particularly like them mashed with potatoes, or used in soups. For those unaccustomed to eating them they can cause a bit of gas (see the article on inulin, opposite, for more information).

Sunchokes are famous for their aggressive and persistent behavior in the garden. If not kept in

The tubers of the sunchoke cultivar 'Dwarf Sunray' grow in a tight cluster at the base of the plant and do not spread as far as other sunchokes.

Inulin

Inulin is a type of starch used to store energy in the roots of many members of the Aster family, as well as a few non-related species like camass. Inulin can cause gas because it is not digestible by humans, and it has no effect on blood sugar levels. For many years it appeared that sunchokes were not a great food plant for this reason, although they were known as a good vegetable and sweet treat for diabetics and dieters.

However, recent research has discovered that inulin can significantly increase the body's ability to absorb calcium, making sunchokes a newly trendy "nutraceutical" food. This increased calcium-uptake ability can significantly increase bone density and help fight osteoporosis. Inulin also increases populations of beneficial microbes in the digestive tract, and may help prevent colon cancer.

So, while perhaps not a good source of sugars, inulin-rich roots certainly prove that eating your vegetables is good for you! Inulin-containing perennial crops profiled in this book include sunchokes, yacon, chicory root, and camass.

check, they will spread over time to form large colonies. Their tall and dense growth makes them a poor companion for most vegetables. Once planted, they can be very difficult to get rid of, as any piece of tuber that remains will resprout. So plant them where they can stay and have room to grow. They are easiest to remove in midsummer when the tubers are at their smallest.

Note: Sunchokes are also known as Jerusalem artichokes. This name is confusing since they are neither artichokes nor from Jerusalem. Apparently this is a corruption of the Italian *girasole*, for the related sunflower. The name *sunchoke* is being used by farmers trying to market tubers in a less confusing fashion.

I have recently started growing 'Dwarf Sunray', a variety of sunchoke better suited to my small garden. This variety grows only 6 feet high (half the size of my previous selection), and has tubers clustered close to the base of the stem for easier harvest and reduced weediness. As an added bonus, it flowers much earlier (August instead of October here) and it has attractive flowers and dark purple stems. Finally, since it is shorter, it is less prone to lodging (blowing over in strong winds), which can be a problem with taller varieties on windy sites.

Crop Description: Sunchokes are extremely tall herbs, growing as high as 12 feet and spreading to form large colonies.

Climate: Sunchokes are extremely cold-hardy, with-standing temperatures in Zone 2. They can be grown as perennials anywhere that there is some frost. In the tropics they can be grown as annuals, but they are less sweet without a bit of frost.

Tolerances and Preferences: Sunchokes will grow in full sun or light shade, and will produce best in good soil with sufficient water. Once they get over 6–8 feet tall they become vulnerable to being blown over by strong winds.

Naturalization Status: Domesticated from a species native to eastern and central United States and Canada, and naturalized outside of that range. Sunchokes were grown outside of their native range by Native American farmers and have persisted in the wild for centuries.

Pest, Disease, and Weed Problems: The only pests worth mentioning are mice and voles. These little rodents love the tubers and can unwittingly trans-plant them all over your garden. In bad years they may decimate your tubers during the winter, but in the spring every little corner of a tuber they left behind will sprout and grow.

Propagation and Planting: Propagation is by tubers or pieces of tubers. Any piece with an eye on it will produce a good yield of tubers. Plant your tubers 1–3 feet apart, or harvest most of the tubers and throw back a few on equivalent spac-ing. If you don't keep harvesting and "thinning the herd" every year the plants will decrease in productivity in a few years. Some sunchokes are sterile, while others apparently produce viable seed. Plants should start easily from seed.

Other Cultivation Information: Sunchokes can be earthed up for even higher yields. Plants produce best if all or most of the tubers are harvested every year. If you are on a windy site you can pinch back the tops when they reach 2–3 feet tall to make them wider and bushier instead of tall.

Harvest and Storage: Tubers store best in the ground. You can dig some and store them in the fridge for a few days. They will last longer if you leave dirt on them until just before cooking.

Uses: The flavor of sunchoke tubers is at its best after a hard frost. After a cold winter you can dig them up in spring for a super-sweet treat. Sunchokes can be used in almost any root crop recipe. Their sweetness is especially good when they are roasted. Mashed sunchokes are also excellent. Raw tubers can be sliced into salads. If you are going to eat a lot of them, be advised that digestibility is best when they are cooked.

Related Species and Breeding Potential: Sunchokes are in the same genus as annual seed-bearing sunflowers (*Helianthus annuus*), and the two plants can be and have been crossed. The tiny seeds of sunchoke are also edible. A great backyard experiment would be to develop a perennial seed sunflower. There are many other perennial sunflowers with edible roots; some are smaller and less vigorous, and perhaps they could be used to develop less aggressive sunchokes.

Fuki can form enormous colonies in wet shade.

Petasites japonicus · Fuki

Synonyms
- Sweet coltsfoot
- Giant butterburr

Aspects
- Running herb
- Edible leafstalks
- Part to full shade
- Moist to wet soils

This unusual vegetable grows in dense colonies, which can cover large areas. A native of eastern Asia, giant butterburr is native to moist woods near streams. It is cultivated in Japan for its edible leafstalks, which are somewhat like rhubarb, but not sour. This is one enormous vegetable—leaves can be up to 16 inches wide, held 3–4 feet high on the edible leafstalks. The somewhat bitter flowerbuds, which appear early in spring and are almost the size of artichokes, are also eaten. Fuki grows in dense colonies, which spread by aggressive rhizomes. It is not a good companion plant for any but the largest and toughest herbs! Fuki grows wonderfully as an understory companion to trees, however. The variety 'Giganteus' is even larger, with 4-foot leaves held 5–6 feet above the ground. Its leaves are so large that they are used by Japanese children as umbrellas. Some people say that 'Giganteus' is a better variety than the species form as an edible vegetable; others claim the reverse is true.

I had long been skeptical of fuki as a vegetable, but as part of researching this book I felt obligated to try eating it. I cut the young stalks in spring, when they were already 2 feet or more long. Following written directions, I cut them into 6-inch segments and boiled them for 10 minutes, dipped them in cold water for a minute, and peeled off the outer fibrous skin. This process was much easier than I had thought, and removed most of the medicinal smell that had scared me. Much to my surprise the taste experience was quite nice, like eating a slightly gelatinous celery with a bit of a medicine taste. Sounds strange, but it was quite good, although perhaps not for everybody. Even better was the next day when I added some of my leftover fuki to chicken soup and found it was delicious—in fact I kept adding more to my soup. I look forward to eating more fuki next spring. Apparently in Japan the stalks are also often fried in sesame oil.

This dense groundcover outcompetes everything else its own size or smaller. It requires lots of moisture so the leaves won't droop. In fact its preference for wet shade is unusual in a vegetable. The large leaves, especially of the giant variety, lend a tropical look to the landscape. Fuki is hardy in Zones 4–9. It has naturalized a bit in Canada and certainly could do so elsewhere.

In addition to being a root crop, scorzonera has lettuce-like edible leaves. PHOTOGRAPH COURTESY OF S. J. KAYS.

Scorzonera hispanica • Scorzonera

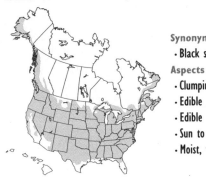

Synonyms
- Black salsify

Aspects
- Clumping herb
- Edible greens
- Edible roots
- Sun to part shade
- Moist, well-drained soil

Scorzonera is usually grown as a root crop. However, it produces only a single taproot so it cannot be grown as a perennial root crop—once you harvest it, it's gone! Scorzonera also has edible leaves, which Carol Deppe, in *Breed Your Own Vegetable Varieties*, says taste almost indistinguishable from lettuce. Perennial leaf crops that are good to eat raw are somewhat rare, particularly for cold climates. Deppe and her friend Dan Borman are working on developing scorzonera as a new leaf crop. With their work, and hopefully the work of other backyard breeders, we may soon have a new, truly excellent perennial leaf crop.

Scorzonera is easy to grow. It is hardy at least to Zone 4, and can probably be grown southward through Zone 8 or 9. It provides greens throughout most of the mild Pacific Northwest winters. Simon Hickmott of Future Foods Nursery in

England recommends blanching the greens. Plants are propagated by seed, and produce roots in 100–120 days. The carrot-like roots remain of high quality for years, so you can harvest after several years of growth if you like. Wait to peel them until after cooking, as the roots are delicate and will "bleed."

Scorzonera is often lumped together with the similar root crop salsify (*Tragopogon porrifolius*). Both have carrot-like roots, but scorzonera is a perennial with black skin on the roots, while salsify is biennial with white roots.

Smallianthus sonchifolia • Yacon

Synonyms
- *Polymnia sonchifolia*
- Bolivian sunroot

Aspects
- Clumping herb
- Edible tubers
- Moist, well-drained soils

General Overview, History, and Ecology: Yacon is one of the few Andean root crops that is not day-length-sensitive and has a short enough growing season that is can be grown in much of the United States and the warmer parts of Canada (at least as an annual). While it is a root crop, yacon is eaten more like a fruit, as its tubers are sweet

The yield of one yacon plant grown in an unheated greenhouse in Massachusetts.

and crisp like an apple. It is grown throughout much of South America, where it is eaten fresh and used as the basis for snack foods and even used to make sugar. Yacon has become popular on the West Coast of the United States recently, where it is quite well adapted. It can be found in more and more catalogs and seems destined for greater popularity. The flavor of the roots has been described as "fresh apple with a hint of watermelon." Inferior varieties have a bit of a piney taste. Plants bear large clusters of tubers up to the size of sweet potatoes, and have white, yellow, purple, or orange flesh.

Like sunchoke, yacon is a relative of sunflower, though not as close. Unlike sunchoke, it does not spread aggressively. The flowers attract beneficial insects.

Crop Description: Yacon is a clump-forming perennial growing about 6 feet tall. It has little daisy-like flowers.

Climate: Frost will kill the foliage, but the tubers will survive as long as the ground does not freeze. It takes about six to seven months of growing season to grow good-sized tubers. Yacon is grown year-round in the tropics, but it can be grown as an annual in areas with long enough hot summers. It thrives in hot, humid weather. Yacon has been successfully grown as an annual as far north as coastal Oregon on the West Coast and Virginia in the East. In my experience Massachusetts has too short a season outside, although in my unheated greenhouse I had a good yield.

Tolerances and Preferences: Yacon prefers full sun or part shade and rich, well-drained soil.

Naturalization Status: This crop has not naturalized in the United States or Canada and is unlikely to.

Pest, Disease, and Weed Problems: Yacon has few pest or disease problems to speak of.

Propagation and Planting: Yacon is propagated by replanting the smaller tubers with shoots that form at the base of the clump—larger tubers are not usually used for propagation. It can also be grown from stem cuttings. Clumps can also be divided. Plant at 3-foot spacing.

Harvest and Storage: When the tops die back after flowering it is time to dig them up! Dig carefully, because the tubers are fragile. Tubers can be stored in a cool dry place for months.

Uses: The tubers are eaten raw like apples, although some varieties are less flavorful than others. They can be also baked or used in any recipe that calls for root crops. Their starch is in the form of inulin (see the sunchoke entry, page 98, for more information), although they do not seem to cause as much indigestion to the uninitiated as sunchoke does. Yields of yacon tubers can be very high. The stems and young leaves can also be eaten.

Related Species and Breeding Potential: Yacon varieties vary greatly in flavor, demonstrating room for interesting breeding work. Yacon used to be classed in the genus *Polymnia*. Adventurous backyard breeders could try crossing yacon with the eastern native nonedible species *P. canadensis* and *P. uvedalia*, for increased hardiness. It would also be useful to have shorter-season varieties. More adventurous yet: a wide cross with sunchoke for a hardy, colony-forming hybrid.

Basellaceae: The Malabar Spinach Family

Basella alba • Malabar Spinach

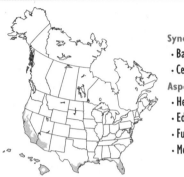

Synonyms
- Basella rubra
- Ceylon spinach

Aspects
- Herbaceous vine
- Edible greens
- Full sun
- Moist, well-drained soil

General Overview, History, and Ecology: This succulent vine is a popular vegetable throughout tropical Asia. It is believed to have originated in India or Indonesia. Malabar spinach is also grown as an annual heat-loving spinach substitute in much of the United States and Canada. It is an attractive ornamental, worthy of growing for its heart-shaped leaves and vigorous vines. The leaves have a mild flavor and a very mucilaginous texture. They are excellent in sauces, which they thicken nicely, but personally I find them a less desirable for salads. Malabar spinach is often divided into two species: the green-leaved variety (*B. alba*), and the very attractive red or purple type (*B. rubra*), though the red is really just a variety of *B. alba*.

Malabar spinach is a remarkably heat-loving vegetable. Young plants will sit and do nothing until a heat wave comes. Then they explode into growth, producing a tremendous abundance of greens. When trellised and pruned with frequent harvesting one or two plants could feed a small army. Even in short summers a few plants can produce far more than you can eat as long as there is enough heat.

Crop Description: A perennial vine with succulent, round to heart-shaped leaves. In the tropics it can reach up to 12 feet in height; as an annual it is much smaller.

Climate: The vines are fully tropical and are killed by frost. They will produce year-round in the warm tropics or heated greenhouses. Malabar spinach can be grown as an annual even in climates with short growing seasons, as long as there is a period of high temperatures. It makes a good container plant, and is worth experimenting with as an indoor overwintered edible houseplant.

Tolerances and Preferences: Malabar spinach likes full sun and rich soils, with plenty of nitrogen and water.

Naturalization Status: Malabar spinach has naturalized in Hawaii.

Pest, Disease, and Weed Problems: Malabar spinach is highly sensitive to nematodes. Grow it as a container plant with sterile purchased potting soil if nematodes are a serious problem in your area. It is also susceptible to a fungus (*Cercospora beticola*) that eats holes in the leaves. Remove affected leaves, and remember that this fungus also attacks beets (and presumably chard and sea beets), so you may want to keep these plants separated in your garden and/or crop rotation plan.

Propagation and Planting: Malabar spinach is easily grown from seed (sow 1 inch deep) or cuttings. Direct-seed or transplant after danger of frost in frost-prone climates. For germination, nighttime temperatures must be no lower than 60°F. Space plants 2–3 feet apart.

Other Cultivation Information: The most important cultural consideration is to provide a trellis or something for the vines to climb on. Otherwise they sprawl on the ground, making a tangled mess

Malabar spinach is a climbing leaf crop that makes a beautiful ornamental. PHOTO BY CRAIG HEPWORTH.

that is difficult to harvest. Untrellised plants also get dirt and grit in their crinkled leaves, requiring more washing.

Harvest and Storage: Frequent harvesting of shoot tips for food will stimulate increased production of new growth—good luck keeping up! You can also pinch off the flowers to increase leaf production.

Uses: The young leaves and the top 6 inch of shoots can be eaten raw or cooked, while older leaves must be cooked. All have a mild flavor and a mucilaginous texture.

Leaves and shoots are used like spinach or chard. They are nutritious, with high levels of vitamins A and C, as well as calcium and iron. The red variety is beautiful when used raw in salads, but when cooked loses its color and becomes pale. Use the green variety for cooking. Malabar spinach is an important leaf vegetable in South Asian cooking.

Related Species and Breeding Potential: This vegetable would be more popular here if less mucilaginous varieties could be selected.

Ullucus tuberosus • Ulluco

Synonyms
- Papa lisa
- Melloco

Aspects
- Herbaceous vine
- Edible tubers
- Edible leaves
- Full sun
- Moist, well-drained soil

For centuries ulluco has been grown in the Andean highlands. It has recently been undergoing a renaissance, and the brightly colored tubers can be found in many urban markets in South America. These egg- to fist-sized tubers come in many beautiful bright colors, including yellow, pink, green, red, and purple, with some striped or splotched. The tubers have a crisp texture and a nutty taste, and can store for up to a year in a cool, dark place. The leaves are also edible, and are similar in texture and use to its family relative Malabar spinach.

Ulluco is a fantastic crop, which is unfortunately best grown in cool tropical climates (e.g. upland Hawaii), though it can be grown as an annual in the Pacific Northwest. It suffers from day-length restrictions, dislike of heat, and the need for a long growing season. The plants will not set tubers until the short days of fall. They then require five to nine months to mature. Researchers are working to find or breed varieties that can at least be grown as annuals outside the tropics, but at the time of this writing they have not done so.

Ulluco can yield well in poor soils. It has few pests or diseases to speak of. Most plants are infected with viruses, which lower production, but virus-free selections are becoming available. Propagation is by tubers or pieces of tubers, and by stem cuttings. Plants should be earthed up like potatoes.

The tubers of the ulluco come in many bright colors. PHOTOGRAPH COURTESY OF S. J. KAYS.

Brassicaceae: The Cabbage Family

Brassica oleracea · Perennial Brassicas

Synonyms
- See below

Aspects
- Clumping herbs or shrubs
- Edible leaves
- Edible flowerbuds
- Full sun
- Moist, well-drained soil

General Overview, History, and Ecology: Almost everyone who has ever grown a vegetable has grown brassicas, and with good reason: This outstanding group of plants contains many of our most beloved vegetables, such easy-care, cold-tolerant plants as broccoli, cabbage, cauliflower, kale, and collards. Medical research is discovering anti-cancer properties and other health benefits of including brassicas as a regular part of one's diet. As surprising as it is to discover, there are a number of perennial brassica varieties. They are among the best perennial vegetables, and their familiar appearance and flavors make them much more easily accepted than some more unfamiliar crops. Imagine growing a grove of 9-foot-tall purple 'Tree Collards' or harvesting leaves year-round from a 6-foot-tall bush kale. Strange as it sounds, these vegetables exist and should no longer be neglected! Anyone living in the Pacific Northwest should make it a high priority to acquire some of these plants right away.

Unfortunately for the rest of us, perennial brassicas seem to be somewhat picky about where they like to grow. When I first read Robert Hart's *Forest Gardening* I was very excited to discover that he grew perennial kales and broccolis in his garden. Over the years I struggled to get my hands on seeds or plant material for this holy grail of perennial vegetables. I grew several varieties, including 'Dorbenton Perennial' kale, an inferior type of tree collards, 'Western Front' kale,

and '9 Star Perennial' broccoli. None did well in my Massachusetts winters, and I was forced to conclude that the currently available varieties are just not well suited to my climate. Most of the varieties listed here are only hardy to Zone 8 or 9, and prefer mild climates. They are also unlikely to thrive in intense heat (except for tropical tree kale and gai lon).

Fortunately for those of us outside of the cool temperate Northwest, there are heat- and cold-tolerant brassicas that can serve as parents of breeding efforts to develop more widely adapted perennial varieties. There are heat-loving greens like collard greens and Ethiopian kale (*B. carinata*). And many kales are extremely cold-hardy, overwintering here in Massachusetts and even colder climes.

But we do not just have to breed brassicas for heat or cold resistance. The wild perennial *Brassica oleracea* is the ancestor of a remarkable range of crops, all of which can be crossed with one another. These include common garden vegetables like kale, collards, cauliflower, cabbage, brussels sprouts, and kohlrabi. Many of these have been crossed to form strange biennial vegetables like big-stem broccoli (broccoli crossed

'Tree Collards' is productive and delicious. PHOTO BY BROCK DOLMAN.

with kohlrabi) and Dalmeny sprouts (cabbage crossed with brussels sprouts), which features a cabbage head on top of a tall stalk of brussels sprouts! By crossing perennial brassicas with their many cousins, a virtually limitless menagerie of perennial vegetables could be developed. That's not to mention crosses with closely related *Brassica* species like mustard greens and bok choi. Brassica breeding can be intimidating, but much benefit could be gained simply from planting a number of perennial or perennial and annual forms together, letting them cross, and saving the seed. Who knows what you might turn up with? (*Note:* Most brassicas flower early in their second year, including some perennial types I have grown. Other perennials flower rarely or never.)

It is apparently possible to perennialize ordinarily biennial brassicas. According to Patrick Whitefield, author of *How to Make a Forest Garden*, certain brassicas including kales, cabbages, and sprouting broccoli can be cut back and harvested, leaving a stalk to resprout. Whitefield observes that this seems to work best in shady areas.

B. oleracea (Wild Cabbage). This mother of them all, wild cabbage is itself a short-lived perennial (of three to five years). Many parts can be eaten, primarily the leaves and small broccoli-like flowerbuds. The leaves have a flavor somewhat stronger and more bitter than cultivated brassicas. Wild cabbage grows on the seacoasts of Europe. It is more resistant to pests and diseases than its progeny. Strangely, such an important source of breeding material is virtually impossible to come by in North America. In fact the USDA germplasm collection, which is supposed to maintain wild relatives of crop plants for breeding purposes, does not have it! Importing seeds should be a high priority.

B. o. acephala ('Western Front' Perennial Kale). This is a variety recently bred by the remarkable Tim Peters of Peters Seed and Research. In his Pacific Northwest conditions, about 50 percent of seedlings become perennial and live for up to five years. Once you identify a perennial plant you can propagate it by cuttings. The plants are very resilient survivors for him; in my garden very few plants have overwintered, though it self-sows nicely. This variety is extremely productive and delicious. 'Western Front' strongly resembles 'Red Russian' kale, one of my favorites. The flavor is mild, creamy, and nutty. Peters also offers other interesting perennial brassicas, perennial grains, and many other fascinating and useful new vegetable varieties (see Sources of Plants and Seeds in Part III).

B. o. acephala ('Tree Collards', 'Walking Stick Kale'). This vegetable is an heirloom variety or cluster of similar varieties that seems to have been developed in the mild climates of the British Jersey islands. In old drawings they resemble palm trees, with a long straight stalk and a flush of collardlike leaves on top. In that mild climate they could grow up to 20 feet tall and live for many years. The varieties I know of currently are shorter (more like 6–12 feet) and tend to branch. Tree collards were originally developed as a fodder crop for livestock, and temporarily became a cash crop for the production of walking sticks, made by treating the tall, straight stalks. I obtained seed a few years ago and was unimpressed by the rubbery texture and strong cabbage flavor of the leaves. The plants did not survive my winters. However, I recently obtained a plant of a superior variety from Sascha DuBrul of the Bay Area Seed Interchange Library (BASIL), an urban "seed library" in Berkeley, California. Sascha tells me that this variety, which has purple leaves in cool weather, is grown by urban gardeners in Oakland. It is perennial there and propagated exclusively by cuttings. It tastes fantastic. Ken Fern of Plants for a Future considers tree collards the best of the perennial brassicas. His system for managing the plants is to cut back the tops to encourage branching, and every few years to cut the whole plant back to about 1 foot tall. They usually recover and resprout vigorously. Tree collards can be grown from seed or cuttings. Most plants will flower if permitted to. It is possible that tree collards might be able to be grown in hot-summer areas.

B. o. acephala (Tropical Tree Kale). This is closely related to and may be identical to tree collards. Although rare, several sources including Jay Ram, author of the *Tropical Perennial Vegetable* series, recommend it as an excellent perennial leaf crop for the tropics. Plants grow up to about 4 feet tall and then sometimes fall over. When they land their stems root and send up new shoots. In this manner they can "walk" around the garden like walking onions (though this is not necessarily the most efficient way to grow them). The leaves are of good but not excellent flavor (perhaps the delicious purple tree collard should be tried in the tropics?). Plants produce larger, more tender leaves in partial shade. They are propagated by cuttings or by removing sprouts from the base or from fallen and rooted plants. They do not set seed. Plants are resistant to nematodes but otherwise have typical brassica pest and disease problems.

B. o. alboglabra (Gai Lon, Chinese Broccoli). This Asian brassica is believed to be a descendant of seed brought to Asia long ago by Portuguese traders. The upper 9 inches of the thick, succulent stem, leaves, and flowerbuds are harvested when the first flowers begin to open. The flavor is like a nutty mix of asparagus and broccoli—this is really a remarkably good vegetable. Each plant gives multiple harvests. Gai lon is a popular vegetable in Southeast Asia, where it is grown in the cooler seasons of the year. It is frequently referred to as a perennial grown as an annual, but no one seems to know what happens if you grow it as a perennial. It seems likely that a perennial production system could be worked out.

B. o. botrytis (Perennial Broccoli). The only variety of perennial broccoli I know of is '9 Star', although there are or have been others. Perennial broccoli is botanically a cauliflower, although you would not guess it from looking it. It grows like a sprouting-type broccoli, with multiple small heads. The flavor is good, but their small size is a bit of a hassle. The real problem with perennial broccoli is that all of the heads have to be harvested, or at least prevented from going to seed, because the entire plant will die once it sets seed. Apparently plants have lived up to five years, with three being more typical. I found the leaves are also quite good for cooking, but apparently this can rob the plant of the energy it needs to remain perennial. Certainly the perennial broccoli is an interesting, though high-maintenance, vegetable. Breeding work could surely improve the size of the broccoli heads.

Pests and Diseases of the Brassica Family

While many generalist pests and diseases (like aphids and powdery mildew) afflict brassicas, some species specialize in consuming members of this important crop family. Here are a few brassica specialists you might have to deal with in your garden.

Cabbage maggots are the larvae of a fly species that dig brown, slimy tunnels in brassica stems and eat the roots. Cabbage maggots are vectors for several plant diseases. Watch for small white eggs on plant bases in spring—row covers can prevent egg-laying. Diatomaceous earth, a neutral pH, and beneficial nematodes can help control this pest. Rotate your perennial brassicas through the garden over time. Also avoid cold, wet microclimates.

Caterpillars, including cabbage looper, diamondback moth, and imported cabbageworm, can be problematic. Look for ragged holes in leaves. Prevent egg-laying with row covers or Surround (a kaolin clay sprayed on leaves), handpick, or control with Bt, rotenone, pyrethrum, or neem sprays.

Clubroot is a dreaded brassica root disease. Prevention starts with bringing the soil pH up to 6.8 or higher. Rotate crops when possible, and avoid cold, wet microclimates.

Flea beetles can make thousands of tiny pinholes in brassica leaves—especially watercress and sylvetta arugula among the perennials. They are most active in spring, when row covers are very effective. Surround is effective, and pyrethrin sprays can control severe infestations.

In general, the use of floating row covers (with all edges sealed to prevent insect access) is a good idea, along with rotating at least at the end of the life cycle of your perennial brassicas. Avoiding cold, wet spots and bringing the pH up to 7 or higher also seem like good practices. In areas where cabbage maggot is a problem, use of beneficial nematodes is an excellent idea as annual rotation to avoid this pest won't be possible.

B. o. ramosa (Branching Bush Kales). This is the true queen of perennial brassicas. Bush kale is probably one of the earliest domesticated forms of *B. oleracea*. Pliny described what is thought to be this plant as 'Tritian Kale' in AD 70, and at that point it had lost its ability to flower, which indicates that it had already had a long history of cultivation. Bush kales grow as evergreen shrub-like herbs in mild climates, with some varieties growing up to 9 feet tall in the mild temperate climate of the Netherlands. Most varieties never flower, and others do so only rarely. They do not die after flowering. Plants are multi-stemmed and bushy, with stems traveling horizontally on the ground before ascending. They often root where they touch the ground. I have grown the variety 'Dorbenton', which has a delicious nutty taste even raw (apparently distinct from the variety named 'Daubenton' which is said to have poor flavor). Apparently in mild climates like the south of Britain the leaves can be eaten year-round. Plants are somewhat pest-resistant and can grow in light shade. Some varieties have purple leaves.

One has to ask, why is this remarkable plant not more widely grown and available? In fact it seems to be a vanishing heirloom. One reason is that in the European Union it is actually illegal to sell seeds of varieties not on an approved list. All the plants on the list are of course developed for commercial production, and this variety certainly does not fit into annual production schemes. With luck this magnificent vegetable of ancient and noble lineage will someday be widely grown again. Meanwhile it is up to enthusiastic gardeners to keep the plants going. I have no confirmation that bush kales are hardy past Zone 9; in fact, my own hard-won plant was sadly lost in a winter where deep snow kept the ground from freezing all winter, which should have been an ideal situation. Next time I will take some cuttings and bring them inside!

The fact that so few of the varieties described above are available though nurseries and seed companies is simply astounding.

Crop Description: Perennial brassicas resemble their biennial brethren. They are herbaceous perennials, although some forms become somewhat woody and can grow unbelievably tall.

Climate: As mentioned above, most of these varieties prefer cool temperate climates with the gentle winters of Zone 8 or 9. However, that does not mean they shouldn't be tried where you live! With protection from winds and intense heat or cold, you may be able to expand their range quite a bit. It seems likely that some could be grown as dieback perennials in colder areas as well. Some are much more adaptable than others, such as 'Western Front', which is a bit hardier than most, and tropical tree kale and gai lon, which love heat. Tree collards are worth trialing in hot-summer areas.

Tolerances and Preferences: These plants are just like the brassicas you already know and love—they are heavy feeders and love rich soil with plenty of organic matter.

Naturalization Status: Wouldn't it be great if they did? None of these varieties is known to naturalize, but various *Brassica oleracea* types have naturalized in areas throughout the country.

Pest, Disease, and Weed Problems: Perennial brassicas are susceptible to all the usual pests and diseases of brassicas (see Pest and Diseases of the Brassica Family on page 107). The cabbage moth is particularly bothersome. The other challenge of growing perennial brassicas is that you cannot rotate your crops, at least not as frequently. Try to provide your plants with well-drained soils that have not been used to grow brassicas for many years.

Propagation and Planting: Those types that set seed can be easily grown just like ordinary biennial brassicas. All can also be grown from cuttings, which take quite easily. Cuttings should be from ¼ inch to 1 inch wide and 4–6 inches long. Bury about ½ of the cutting in soil. They will root in four to six weeks or sooner. Plant out perennial brassicas on a wider spacing than ordinary types, as they tend to spread out a bit more. Perhaps 2–4 feet between plants is appropriate, depending on the variety.

Harvest and Storage: Harvest individual leaves or buds rather than whole plants. Otherwise harvest is just the same as with ordinary brassicas.

Uses: These crops are used exactly like their biennial relatives. Enjoy!

Related Species and Breeding Potential: As mentioned above, these plants will cross with one another and any other *B. oleracea*. Other interesting crosses could include the heat-loving Ethiopian kale (*B. carinata*), mustard greens (*B. juncea*), and the incredible diversity of vegetables in *B. rapa*, including Chinese cabbage, broccoli raab, tatsoi, and mizuna. Seed saving and breeding in brassica species is somewhat complicated; refer to *Seed to Seed* and *Breed Your Own Vegetable Varieties* for recommendations. Fortunately, perennials are unlikely to cross with wild brassicas like mustards, which are all in different species.

Bunias orientalis • Turkish Rocket

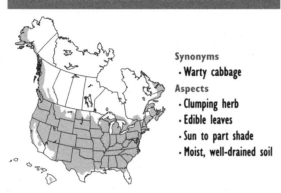

Synonyms
- Warty cabbage

Aspects
- Clumping herb
- Edible leaves
- Sun to part shade
- Moist, well-drained soil

The flower clusters of Turskish rocket have the nutty mustard flavor of broccoli raab.

Here is a truly low-maintenance perennial. Turkish rocket, also known by the unflattering name of warty cabbage, resembles an enormous woolly dandelion until it flowers, when it becomes clear that it is a brassica after all. The young leaves are edible, with a pungent, hot flavor like mustard greens. I eat them up to about 10 inches long. If you keep removing the older leaves and flower stalks, the plants will apparently crop all season long. I mostly eat it in the spring and fall, as an addition to mixed cooked greens. In early spring the leaves can be eaten raw and have a nice mild heat. The large leaves have a very strong flavor even when cooked, although some people enjoy them this way. Even better, the flowerbuds look and taste like broccoli raab (a nutty, pungent, mustardy broccoli flavor). Established Turkish rocket plants produce a truly enormous number of these mini-broccolis.

Turkish rocket thrives in Mediterranean, cool temperate, and cold climates. It is a popular vegetable in the former Soviet Union. It is very hardy, at least to Zone 4, though not a good choice for tropical areas. Turkish rocket is somewhat drought-tolerant, and grows in full sun or light shade. The plants form clumps with multiple growing heads, and spread to several feet across. If you dig them up and leave any bit of root in the ground it will come right back, so think before you decide where to plant it. Plants are very tough—I have seen them holding their own against the very pernicious goutweed (*Aegopodium podagraria*). Some companies sell ordinary annual arugula seed under this name—in fact I once did

so mistakenly when I ran my own company. Some seed wholesalers apparently don't know the difference. Turkish rocket seed is large and bumpy, the size of whole black peppercorns. Arugula seed is tiny, the size of mustard seed, and smooth.

I personally like having such a survivor in my garden, and enjoy adding it to cooked green dishes, but there is lots of room for breeding to select for plants with a milder, improved flavor.

Crambe maritima • Sea Kale

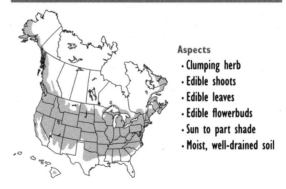

Aspects
- Clumping herb
- Edible shoots
- Edible leaves
- Edible flowerbuds
- Sun to part shade
- Moist, well-drained soil

General Overview, History, and Ecology: Sea kale is one of the few perennial vegetables that have been domesticated in Europe. The plants, resembling large silvery gray cabbages, grow wild on the seacoasts of Europe, where they have been harvested since ancient times. Sea kale was not brought into cultivation until the late 1700s, when it became quite the rage. Since then the crop has lapsed into minor-vegetable status.

Sea kale is a perennial brassica used like collards, asparagus, and broccoli.

The main crop of sea kale is the spring shoots. In the wild these shoots are blanched by layers of rock, which cover the plants on beaches. Under cultivation, upside-down flowerpots or mulch are used to keep light from reaching the shoots and ruining their flavor. Blanched shoots are cut at 6–9 inches and have a hazelnut flavor with a slight bitterness. They are used like asparagus. Plants can provide good harvests for up to 10 years.

Carol Deppe, author of *Breed Your Own Vegetable Varieties*, suggests that the edible flowerbuds are worthy of developing into a perennial broccoli. They resemble 1-inch broccoli heads and have very good flavor. The flowers themselves are beautiful and have a strong honey fragrance. The leaves of first- and second-year plants can also be eaten, and taste like collards. In the late fall, after flowering is completed, the leaves of more mature plants can also be eaten.

Here we have a mild-mannered perennial vegetable for cold and temperate climates, with multiple edible uses. Its potential as a perennial broccoli may someday eclipse its use for edible shoots.

Crop Description: Sea kale is a clump-forming perennial growing about 3 feet high and wide. The gray-blue foliage reminds one of true kale (*Brassica oleracea*), but the flowers are white and produced in large masses. It is sometimes grown as an ornamental.

Climate: Sea kale is hardy to Zone 4 or colder, and also succeeds in Mediterranean climates. It will grow in the South to about Zone 8 on the East Coast, and should prosper in the cooler summers of the West Coast. Plants should be mulched in cold climates.

Tolerances and Preferences: Sea kale thrives in a rich, fertile soil. Not surprisingly for a coastal plant, it loves seaweed as a fertilizer. Plants perform best for shoot production in full sun.

Naturalization Status: Sea kale has naturalized on the West Coast of North America.

Pest, Disease, and Weed Problems: I have had some problems with cabbage moth, but less than on my true *Brassica* species. The plant is not noted for having pest problems.

Propagation and Planting: Sea kale is easily propagated by division. Plants can also be multiplied by using root cuttings. Cut root sections ¼–½ inch thick and 4–6 inches wide. Plant them right-side up and they should succeed just fine—in my own garden, every time I transplant sea kale a few roots are left behind and they always sprout. Sea kale can also be grown from seed. Seed viability deteriorates rapidly after the first year. I have had best luck removing the shell from seeds before planting. Apparently fresh seed germinates well.

Other Cultivation Information: Like asparagus, sea kale is slow to grow the first and second year, and should not be harvested until the third year.

Harvest and Storage: Blanched shoots are cut at 6–9 inches. They have a purple color, except for the pale shoots of the 'Lily White' variety.

Uses: The roots can be used raw or cooked, usually boiled or steamed like asparagus and served with butter. The flowerbuds are used like regular broccoli, and the leaves of nonflowering plants can be eaten like collards.

Traditional sea kale pot used for blanching.

Related Species and Breeding Potential: Breeding for larger broccoli-like flower heads seems to be the most interesting direction. Crosses could also be tried with the similarly used *Crambe cordifolia*, *C. orientalis*, and *C. tatarica*.

Diplotaxis muralis and D. tenuifolia • Sylvetta Arugula

Aspects
- Shrub
- Edible leaves
- Sun to part shade
- Moist to dry soil

Imagine an arugula shrub that can provide greens year-round in mild climates. Two species of wild, perennial relatives of arugula are known as "sylvetta." Both have been collected from the wild for ages, and are recently becoming more popular as ingredients in gourmet salad mixes. The plants resemble lavender bushes, with a woody stem providing year-round arugula leaves. The flavor of the young leaves has a stronger bite than ordinary annual arugula (*Eruca vesicaria*). Many gardeners and chefs prefer the sharper flavor of sylvetta. The older leaves become too strong to eat raw, but can be cooked.

Sylvetta arugula, a cultivated shrub with edible leaves. PHOTO COURTESY OF SEEDS OF CHANGE/SCOTT VLAUN.

Sylvetta is a wild shrub in the Mediterranean area, and thrives in areas with hot summers and cool winters. They are also adapted to cool maritime areas and possibly other climates. Certainly they should be adapted to most of the West Coast, and are worth trialing elsewhere. Sylvetta is hardy in coastal British Columbia and Seattle, and is rated at Zone 7. Soils must be well drained, but otherwise the plants can thrive in quite poor soils. They will grow in full sun to part shade. Plants self-seed freely and can become weedy. The primary difference between these two species is that *D. muralis* has a lower, more mat-like growth and milder flavor than *D. tenuifolia*. *Note:* The related *D. ericoides*, also sold as sylvetta arugula, is an annual.

Nasturtium officinale • Watercress

Synonyms
- *Rorippa nasturtium-aquatica*

Aspects
- Running herb
- Edible leaves
- Sun to part shade
- Aquatic to moist soil

General Overview, History, and Ecology: This delectable vegetable can be grown in almost any climate, from bitter cold to the humid tropics. Originally from Europe, it now grows wild around the world. The flavor is excellent whether eaten fresh or cooked, and watercress is used in many dishes as a vegetable or as a garnish. The leaves are high in vitamins A, B, and C, as well as iron and calcium. Commercial beds of watercress can live for 10 years or more, but plants also self-seed readily. I grow watercress in my water garden and love being able to harvest some to eat fresh along with my dinner.

Watercress grows best in shallow, slowly running fresh water that is free from contamination. Some roots will anchor the stems to the streambed, but most of the nutrients are received

Watercress is pungent and nutritious, excellent in soups and salads.

from the roots that grow from the floating stems. A stream near a farm where I worked in Colorado was filled with delicious watercress that had been planted and naturalized there many years before, and all you had to do was harvest it.

Fortunately, since few of us have such conditions in our gardens, watercress can be grown in many other ways. In my water garden (a large kiddie pool), I pot up watercress cuttings in pots of soil with gravel on top to keep the soil in place. I have tried different water levels and find I prefer having the top lip of the pot about an inch above the waterline, to keep algae off the stems. In the winter I transplant some to an unheated greenhouse with row covers for additional protection. The flavor of winter-grown watercress is much milder and sweeter, and the texture more succulent.

Watercress can also be grown as a houseplant or outdoor container plant by planting it in pots of soil and placing the pots in saucers of water that are kept full so the soil remains wet. Watercress will also grow just fine in ordinary soil as long as it is moist enough, as in my winter greenhouse.

Crop Description: Watercress is a low-growing herb that spreads by runners at roots along the stems.

Climate: Watercress is incredibly versatile, growing from Zone 2 through the tropics. In my experience, when grown outdoors, watercress leaves are killed by frost. Strangely enough, inside the greenhouse they appear to handle routine freez-

ing temperatures just fine. Commercial producers raise the water level or use screens to push the plants underwater when frost threatens. I am not certain whether watercress functions as a self-seeding annual or a true perennial at either extreme end of its range.

Tolerances and Preferences: Watercress requires moisture, whether simply a consistently moist soil or growing in 6 inches of water. In naturally flowing water it can derive most of its nutrients from the water, but otherwise it needs to be in good fertile soil. Plants will grow in full sun or partial shade.

Naturalization Status: Watercress has naturalized throughout North America.

Pest, Disease, and Weed Problems: Flea beetles can be a serious problem. Submerging plants for a few days will help. A mosaic virus that looks like yellow spots on the leaves can also be problematic. Remove affected plants. Watercress itself can become a weed, and has naturalized in many parts of the world.

Propagation and Planting: Watercress is easily grown from cuttings. Most branches already have roots on them. I usually just purchase a bunch at the grocery store and put them in a glass of water for a few days until the roots are well developed and then plant them out. If they are going in a water garden, you could probably just pot up the cuttings and stick them in the water. Plants also grow quickly from the tiny seeds sown on moist soil.

Other Cultivation Information: Watercress is easily grown in artificial ponds. I would caution against growing it in naturally occurring bodies of water. For one thing, it naturalizes, and this may be a concern for you. More immediately, watercress can pass along many kinds of illness when grown in contaminated water, most notably the liver fluke parasite. Liver fluke can be found in water that runs off from areas where livestock graze, particularly sheep. Chemical contaminants in water can also make naturalized plants unsafe to eat.

Harvest and Storage: Like many greens, watercress has a poor shelf life and is best used fresh. Plants harvested in cooler seasons have a much milder flavor. Once plants flower the flavor becomes exceedingly pungent.

Uses: Watercress can be used fresh in salads and also makes an excellent cooked vegetable. The fresh leaves make a fantastic topping for soups and stews.

Related Species and Breeding Potential: Watercress has been hybridized with the related *N. microphyllum* to create 'Brown Cress', with darker brownish purple leaves. The foliage of brown cress is less affected by frosts. Plants must be propagated vegetatively. Watercress has many close relatives in its own and other genera, including cultivated minor vegetables like the perennial upland cuckoo-flower (*Cardamine* spp.), annual garden cress (*Lepidium*), and native cresses of the genus *Rorippa*. An interesting project would be to develop an upland (more dry-tolerant) running groundcover with edible leaves, probably by crossing with a *Cardamine* species.

Cactaceae: The Cactus Family

Opuntia spp. • Nopale Cactus

Aspects
- Tree-like cactus
- Edible pads
- Full sun
- Extremely well-drained soil

General Overview, History, and Ecology: Throughout the warm, dry regions of the world, cactus pads are a popular vegetable. In Mexico, where they were first domesticated 9,000 years ago, edible cactus pads are three times as widely grown as carrots. The sweet fruits of some *Opuntia* cacti, known as tunas, are also important commercially.

The pads of most prickly pear cacti (a subset of the genus *Opuntia*) are edible, but covered in intense spines, making them challenging to use. "Spineless" varieties of several species are cultivated for the edible pads, known as nopales. There are two kinds of spines to worry about, however. Spineless varieties can be entirely free of the large, visible spines. But at the base of each spine, or where each spine would normally be, is a warty bump. In ordinary cacti these bumps have tiny hairs called glochids. If you come in contact with glochids they can cause itching and irritation for days. Even spineless varieties have some glochids. Proper harvesting and handling, along with simple cleaning procedures (described below), will safely remove all glochids in about the time it takes to peel a cucumber.

Nopale pads taste similar to green beans with a hint of asparagus and lemon flavors. They somehow manage to be both crisp and quite mucilaginous, and are reminiscent of okra in texture and color. Nopales are important components of Mexican and southwestern cuisine. They are truly at their best when served with eggs and salsa. Nopale pads have the added bonus of lowering levels of LDL, the "bad cholesterol."

Species cultivated for spineless nopales include *O. ficus-indica*, *O. robusta*, and *O. streptacantha*. All are hardy to roughly Zone 8, making nopales a great vegetable for the arid Southwest and much of California. Of course, the great benefit of nopale cacti is that they can be grown in extremely arid environments, although they can also be grown in humid areas. They are perhaps the finest perennial vegetable for American deserts, and along with moringa, perennial beans, and chaya can provide a suite of low-maintenance, drought-resistant vegetables for the edible xeriscape.

Many *Opuntia* species have naturalized around the world, quite aggressively in some areas. In parts of Australia they are considered a noxious weed. Here in North America there are native *Opuntias* in almost every state and province. These spiny cacti are incredibly hardy, some growing north into Alberta and Manitoba. They offer the potential of breeding hardy spineless nopales for a wide range of climates.

Spineless nopale cactus is a great perennial vegetable for warm, arid areas.

Crop Description: Spineless nopales are produced on several species of tree-like cactus, growing 12–18 feet high, although they are usually pruned lower for ease of harvest.

Climate: Nopale cacti are creatures of the arid Southwest and Mexico. They are at home in deserts and love heat, although they are hardy through Zone 8. Nopales can, however, be grown even in the intense humidity of the Southeast as long as they are grown in extremely well-drained soils. They are more susceptible to diseases in humid climates.

Tolerances and Preferences: Nopales should be grown in full sun. They require very well-drained soils. They will produce best when fertilized with well-rotted manure, and, surprisingly, when irrigated with supplemental water from time to time.

Naturalization Status: These crops are native to the American Southwest, Mexico, and Central America. They have naturalized in arid climates around the world, including Australia, South Africa, and the Mediterranean, and are considered extremely problematic weeds in some areas.

Pest, Disease, and Weed Problems: Nopales can be affected by nematodes. In some areas of the Southwest they may need fencing to protect them from javelinas (wild pig relatives similar to peccaries). In humid climates they are susceptible to rotting diseases.

Propagation and Planting: Propagating nopales is easy. Just pick some pads (or buy them at the grocery store) and store them in dry shade for two to four weeks. Then bury them halfway in the ground or in pots and they will take root. You can often find rooting pads at the base of existing plants, which have been knocked down by wind and taken root. Nopales can also be grown from seed if you are patient with their slow germination, but they are not true to seed and the resulting plants will have plenty of spines and glochids. Planting distance is variable and depends on how tall you plan to let them grow—space at 10–12 feet for full size, or 5–8 feet if coppicing.

Other Cultivation Information: Coppicing or low pruning of nopales makes for easier harvests, and encourages them to send up lots of new fresh growth.

Harvest and Storage: Use thick leather gloves or tongs to hold pads while you harvest them. Use a knife to cut them at their narrowest point if they won't come off easily.

There are several techniques used to remove spines and glochids. Elizabeth Schneider recommends a technique in her excellent *Vegetables from Amaranth to Zucchini.* "Wearing rubber gloves, scrub pads with a vegetable brush under running water to knock off some of the stickers and the 'eyes' to which they attach. With a swivel peeler, zip off those that remain then shave the rim of each pad and trim any dry or fibrous areas (this takes no more time than peeling a cucumber). Rinse thoroughly to remove any prickles and some of the sticky stuff."

Hardier folk can rub most of the spines and glochids off with thick leather gloves. Then singe the pads over a flame and scrape the remaining glochids off with a knife. Make sure to rinse them well and double-check for spines and glochids.

Uses: There are numerous recipes for nopales in Mexican and southwestern cookbooks. Think of them as somewhere between green beans and okra. As mentioned above, nopales go exceedingly well with eggs.

The flowers and fruits are also edible. Nopale fruits, called tunas or sabras, are commercially grown, although the spineless forms are not noted for their exceptional-quality fruit.

Related Species and Breeding Potential: Ideally, forms of nopale could be developed that are entirely free of glochids as well as spines. It would also be nice to develop a spineless cactus with world-class fruit. Hardier spineless forms could be developed by crossing with northern cacti such as the beavertail cactus (*O. basilaris*), which is hardy to Zone 6. Beavertail cactus also makes large, but spiny, nopales. The beavertail variety 'Aurea' is hardy to Zone 5. Other hardy *Opuntias* tend to be smaller and make less ideal breeding stock. This year I purchased a spineless hybrid (*Opuntia x ellisiana*), which is claimed to be hardy in Zone 6—we will see how it survives the Massachusetts winter.

Cannaceae: The Canna Family

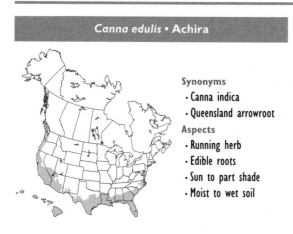

Canna edulis • Achira

Synonyms
- Canna indica
- Queensland arrowroot

Aspects
- Running herb
- Edible roots
- Sun to part shade
- Moist to wet soil

General Overview, History, and Ecology: This ancient Andean crop is surely one of the world's finest edible landscaping plants. The 6- to 10-foot plants are very similar to ornamental cannas, although the flowers are a bit less showy. They are also an excellent perennial root crop, vigorously forming large colonies in wet and marginal soils not suitable to most crops. Achira is cultivated in the tropical Americas, Southeast Asia, and Australia.

Hardy to Zone 8 or thereabouts, achira is well suited to the warmer parts of the United States. But gardeners elsewhere are already quite familiar with techniques for growing cannas outside of their range.

In the warm tropics, roots are harvested 6–10 months after planting. Achira is often managed as a large perennial colony, with harvests removing most but not all plants and allowing regrowth. In colder areas roots are harvested when plants are killed by frost. In short-season areas it may require two summer seasons to produce a good harvest. Rhizomes can weigh up to 50 pounds, although at that stage they become somewhat woody. The root rhizomes are thick, with white, red, or violet flesh. When baked they become sweet and transparent, with a somewhat mucilaginous texture. After a few weeks of storage roots become even sweeter, and are baked as a dessert. The young leaves and shoots are also edible. Achira is also grown as a starch producer. It produces the world's largest-known starch grains, which are so large they can be seen by the naked eye. This starch is easily digested and used for many purposes.

Surely a crop that combines great beauty, productivity, and edibility, and is similar to widely grown ornamentals has excellent potential to become a popular new crop in the warmer parts of the United States and Canada.

Note: It turns out that ornamental cannas also have excellent edible roots, although they are quite a bit smaller (in my climate, they are similar in yield and size to potatoes). According to Jaime Iglesias, garden projects coordinator of Nuestras Raíces in Holyoke, Massachusetts, ornamental canna roots (called maracas) are commonly eaten in the mountains of Puerto Rico. When I baked some I was stunned by how tasty and filling they were. It is hard to believe that thousands of gardeners are missing out on this productive and enjoyable food crop in their own backyards!

Crop Description: Achira resembles ornamental cannas, growing 6–10 feet tall, with green foliage with red and purple splotches. Plants spread to form colonies.

Climate: Though native to the cool upland tropics, achira can grow in cool or hot climates. It has roughly the same hardiness as ordinary cannas, to about Zone 8 without protection. Foliage is killed down to the ground by hard frost. Just like ordinary cannas, achira can be overwintered farther north with a good location and mulching. Rhizomes can also be brought inside and stored just like ordinary ornamental cannas; just dig up the roots and put them in a box in a cool dark place—they don't even need to be packed in peat moss.

Tolerances and Preferences: Achira requires a consistently moist soil, and will tolerate poorly drained soils. It cannot grow in droughty soils, but will grow well in soils of marginal quality. It will grow in full sun or partial shade, and in the tropics is quite tolerant of shade.

Naturalization Status: Closely related *Canna* species have naturalized in the southeastern United States.

Pest, Disease, and Weed Problems: There are few pests or diseases affecting achira. Once plants are established they usually outcompete and shade out weeds.

Propagation and Planting: Achira is propagated vegetatively. Divide rhizomes, leaving tops with at least two buds. Clumps can be easily dug from established colonies. It can be grown from seed but the quality is variable and usually poor. Plant rhizome segments 18–24 inches apart.

Other Cultivation Information: Plants can be earthed up like potatoes as the season progresses to increase yields.

Harvest and Storage: Younger rhizomes should be used, before they become too woody.

Uses: The roots can be eaten raw or cooked. When cooked they become translucent and sweet, even sweeter after a few weeks of storage. Roots are high in potassium and carbohydrates. The young shoots are edible and relatively high in protein. The younger leaves are used to wrap tamales.

Related Species and Breeding Potential: Work should be undertaken to develop magnificent ornamental edible varieties of this premier edible landscaping plant. Ornamental canna varieties should also be screened for their quality as food plants.

Achira roots are sweet enough to eat. PHOTOGRAPH COURTESY OF S. J. KAYS.

Achira has highly ornamental leaves and flowers.

Caricaceae: The Papaya Family

Carica spp. • Papaya

Synonyms
- Paw paw
- Lechoza
- Mamao

Aspects
- Trees
- Edible fruit
- Edible leaves and flowers
- Sun to part shade
- Moist, well-drained soil

Papaya at ECHO.

Papayas are well known as one of the finest fruits of the tropics. Their mild, sweet melon-like flesh sprinkled with lime juice is luscious and nourishing. Unripe papayas, of full size but still firm and green, are an excellent vegetable. Green fruits, once they are peeled and deseeded, can be used in many ways. The most famous is to grate or julienne the flesh and add a spicy chili and lime sauce to make green papaya salad, popular throughout Southeast Asia. Green papayas can also be boiled, baked, pickled, and used in numerous other ways. The crisp texture is reminiscent of chayote, and vaguely like cucumber or firm summer squash. The fruits of both species profiled here can be huge, of football size or larger.

Papaya trees are short-lived but incredibly productive. *Carica papaya* can produce as much as 300 pounds of fruit in a year! Both species profiled here like full sun and rich soils. The main challenges to papaya production are several viruses, which can injure or kill plants. These viruses have made papaya production difficult in many areas of the tropics, including Hawaii. Conventional breeding efforts have failed to develop resistant varieties with high-quality fruit. In recent years a genetically engineered papaya resistant to mosaic virus has been developed and widely introduced in Hawaii. While resistant to the virus, it turns out to be unusually susceptible to the papaya black spot fungus, necessitating massive spraying of chemicals on commercial papaya fields. Papayas in gardens and mixed planting are less susceptible than those in monocultures, although the virus continues to be a problem for growers of all scales in all the papaya-growing regions of the United States. As with any plant virus, infected plants should be removed and destroyed.

Papayas are tropical or subtropical trees. They bear quickly after planting, sometimes maturing in six to nine months. Fruit to be used as vegetables has a shorter season as well. Some gardeners and farmers are experimenting with growing papayas as annuals with season extension as far north as southern Georgia.

C. papaya (Papaya, Paw Paw). This is the widespread and commonly cultivated tropical papaya, originally from Central America. This species loves heat. The Hawaiian lowlands and South Florida are ideal climates. Prolonged exposure to 32°F temperatures kills plants to the ground. Papaya pollination can be confusing. Some plants have all female flowers, some all male, and some have perfect (hermaphrodite) flowers. Some even switch genders during periods with high temperatures. Papayas can be propagated vegetatively, but are also grown from seed. Predicting the gender of seedlings can be tricky. For more information consult a reference on tropical fruits like Julia Morton's *Fruits of Warm Climates* or your local tropical fruit enthusiast society. The flowers and young leaves of papaya can also be eaten, and have a slightly bitter flavor. *Note:* The common name *paw paw* is also shared with a hardy fruit, the unrelated *Asimina triloba*.

C. pentaphylla (Babaco, Mountain Papaya). The babaco is a naturally occurring hybrid between two wild papaya species growing high in the cool tropical mountains of Ecuador. The trees are dwarfed, growing only 6 feet tall, and produce large, five-sided, seedless fruits. They are self-pollinating. Babaco prefers cooler temperatures than the common papaya, and is able to survive temperatures down to 28°F. Babaco survives the cool, wet winters of coastal Southern California far better than *C. papaya*, even growing as far north as San Francisco with a protected location. Despite virus problems, babacos are a good choice

---

Eric's Spicy Papaya Salad

This spicy salad is a great introduction to the vegetable uses of the papaya. It is delicious served with cubed grilled swordfish, fresh watercress, and avocado.

    1 semi-ripe papaya
    1 small purple cabbage
    A 1-inch piece of fresh ginger
    A small bunch of scallions
    A small bunch of cilantro
    Roasted peanuts
    Juice of 2 limes
    Hot sauce or chili paste
    Tamari or fish sauce
    Umeboshi or raspberry vinegar

Select a papaya that is full-sized but not yet ripe. (A ripe papaya has a little give when you press it, like a melon or avocado, and often a golden color coming through the green of the skin.) It should be green or green and orange inside, though you can use a fully ripe papaya too. Cut the papaya in half, scoop out the seeds, and peel the skin. Chop into bite-sized chunks. Add shredded cabbage, grated fresh ginger, chopped scallions and cilantro, and peanuts. The sauce should be hot and tangy. I use the juice of 2 limes, 1 tablespoon of chili paste, and ½ cup each of tamari and umeboshi vinegar.
Serves 4.

---

for upland Hawaiian gardens. High temperatures and humidity damage the fruits. The enormous fruits are eaten green but apparently only cooked, unlike common papayas, and are also eaten ripe, with a sweet unique flavor all their own. Babaco papayas make fantastic container plants.

Chenopodiaceae: The Goosefoot Family

Atriplex halimus • Saltbush

Aspects
- Shrub
- Edible greens
- Full sun
- Dry to moist soil

General Overview, History, and Ecology: One of the moments that really changed my life in terms of understanding the potential of perennial vegetables was the day I grazed on the leaves of this beautiful shrub at Plants for a Future (PFAF) in Cornwall, England. To see a hedge of this beautiful silvery gray shrub producing copious quantities of edible greens virtually year-round, and to just stand there and stuff the tasty, salty leaves into my mouth, was a remarkable experience.

This North African shrub is drought-resistant, extremely tolerant of wind, and even thrives in salty soils and ocean salt spray. Reports differ greatly as to its quality as a vegetable. Apparently the flavor is not good in its wild condition, but with just a bit of TLC and sufficient water, it becomes a truly fantastic woody shrub vegetable, although it could be that PFAF simply has a remarkably superior variety.

Unlike most good tree and shrub vegetables, which are tropical, this salty spinach bush is likely to succeed in much of the western United States and maritime western Canada. It is hardy to Zone 7 or 8, and thrives in both the arid regions of North Africa (to the edge of the Sahara) and the cool temperate coasts of southern England. I strongly urge western gardeners to acquire some and start planting it out. It is a fantastic low-maintenance vegetable and an attractive plant for the landscape as well.

Crop Description: Saltbush is an evergreen shrub with gray-green leaves, growing up to 6 feet high by 9 feet wide. It forms dense clumps and does not spread by runners.

Climate: Saltbush is adapted to Mediterranean and warm to cool temperate climates, experiencing dieback in temperatures below approximately 14°F.

Tolerances and Preferences: Unlike many vegetables, the soil should not be too good. In fact, chemical fertilizers should be avoided as the leaves can accumulate nitrates. Saltbush likes light to moderate soils, which must be well drained. It can tolerate very alkaline and saline soils. It tolerates intense wind and maritime exposure. Saltbush needs full sun.

Naturalization Status: This species of saltbush has not naturalized in the United States or Canada.

Pest, Disease, and Weed Problems: In wet winters saltbush is susceptible to rot problems if it is in rich or poorly drained soils. Otherwise it has few pest or disease problems.

Propagation and Planting: Cuttings are very effective, both of the half-ripe wood and of the hardwood, and are the preferred method of propagation.

The author grazing on saltbrush at PFAF in England in 1997. It was hard to tear me away from that salty spinach: like pretzels in a shrub! PHOTO BY DAVE JACKE.

Oxalic Acid

Oxalic acid is found in many crops, including members of the goosefoot, mountain sorrel, and smartweed families. This includes such common crops as spinach, beets, and chard. Many plant books feature stern warnings that oxalic acid can strip the body of calcium (sort of an "anti-inulin"; see article on page 99). These books recommend eating only small amounts of oxalic-acid-containing plants. However, this is another chemical that has gotten a bad rap.

Oxalic acid is responsible for the delicious sour taste of these vegetables. It can in fact prevent the body from absorbing some of the calcium you eat, which is a bad thing. But it turns out that you would have to eat very large quantities of it, and over an extended period of time, to experience any trouble. In most cases foods with high oxalate levels also have very high calcium, evening out any problems. Cooking also minimizes the effects of oxalic acid. So unless you are going to eat 5 pounds of saltbush or sorrel leaves raw every week for months, you are in the clear.

Profiled perennial vegetables with oxalic acid include saltbush, sea beet, good king Henry, oca (in the genus *Oxalis*, named for this chemical), sorrels, rhubarb, pokeweed, and sissoo spinach. *Note:* It is not oxalates that make pokeweed and rhubarb leaves poisonous.

Saltbush rarely sets seeds. Presoak the seeds before planting. They will germinate in one to three weeks. Give saltbush room to spread—remember that a single bush can be 9 feet wide.

Harvest and Storage: The top 5 inches of shoots are harvested and eaten. Cut 10- to 12-inch branches and strip off the leaves, but don't leave stripped branches on the shrub, as they will not grow leaves and will become vulnerable to disease. Leaves can be harvested all year long, but will not grow during winter so they should be harvested sparingly during that time.

Uses: Saltbush can be eaten raw or cooked in any way that spinach is used, although it is a bit saltier in flavor. I found it to be one of the best greens for snacking that I have ever had, perhaps because I am fond of salty pretzels. It retains a good texture even when steamed. Avoid consuming excessive amounts raw frequently for long periods, as the leaves contain some oxalic acid (see the article above).

Related Species and Breeding Potential: First it should be determined if saltbush in England tastes better because of a superior variety or simply because of moister growing conditions. If certain strains are in fact superior they should be propagated and made widely available. Saltbush could be crossed with hardier but less tasty edible natives like *Atriplex canescens* to develop hardier strains. Even more interesting might be to cross it with its annual relatives that are cultivated for edible greens, such as orach (*A. hortensis*). There are even magenta-colored varieties of orach—how about a mixed hedgerow of silvery gray and bright magenta salty spinach bushes?

Beta vulgaris maritima • Sea Beet

Synonyms
- Beta perennis
- Wild spinach

Aspects
- Clumping herb
- Edible greens
- Full sun
- Moist, well-drained soil

Sea beets are the wild ancestor of beets, chard, and the lesser-known fodder and sugar beets. Here is another example of a European wild perennial becoming annual or biennial through domestication. Sea beets grow on the beaches of Europe and the Mediterranean, where they remain popular wild edibles. The young leaves are quite delicious, with much of the flavor and texture of chard. By crossing sea beets with their domesticated offspring, backyard breeders have the opportunity to develop perennial chards and beet greens.

Sea beets are herbaceous perennials with leathery leaves. They form clumps that eventually reach 3 feet across, and when they flower they get about 3 feet high. They prefer good garden soil with plenty of moisture. Their preferred climate is cool temperate, and my suspicion is that this is where their flavor is best. Here in Massachusetts their flavor is at its best in the cool of spring and fall—hot weather seems to make them more bitter. Apparently on the west coast of Britain they are evergreen and can be harvested year-round. They are hardy to at least Zone 6 or 7 in my trials. Sea beets are probably a fantastic choice for coastal Northern California and the Pacific Northwest up into the milder areas of Alaska, where summers and winters are relatively mild. I transplanted a clump into my unheated greenhouse and was rewarded with truly delicious greens, with a delightful mild flavor, through March and April.

At least here in my climate, when planted outdoors their flavor quickly becomes unpleasant once the plants are flowering. Richard Mabey, author of the British wild-food bible *Food for Free*, says that the leaves of flowering plants are good to eat. That has certainly not been the case in Massachusetts—in fact they can cause some throat irritation. Try cutting back the flower stalks to prolong their season. New, tender, tasty leaves are produced again in fall. Like chard, the leaves contain oxalic acid and should not be eaten raw in great excess for long periods.

Plants grow easily from seed. They should not be harvested much in their first year of growth. With the plants I have grown, the centers of clumps die after flowering, but they produce numerous offshoots that continue the life of the plant. These offshoots can also be used for propagating new plants.

Sea beets seem to be susceptible to many of the pests and diseases of beets and chard, though they may perhaps be more resistant. In my observation, leaf miners and stink bugs have been particularly bothersome. Some strains are annual or biennial, but most are perennial.

Sea beets have become a weed in fields of sugar beet. Because sugar beet is bred originally from sea beets, the sea beets have been able to mimic it in fields. These weedy forms are not recommended as a source of planting material—try to get plants originally from a wild source.

Aspiring breeders need look no farther than the domesticated relatives of this feral vegetable. Breeding for roots like beets is out of the question, since the plants only form one taproot. But find your favorite beet greens and chards and start crossing! The chard variety 'Perpetual Spinach' has good flavor all season long, and would be a good candidate. Cold-climate gardeners, what chards overwinter best in your region? We can develop sea beets for hardiness, disease

resistance, size of leaves (the leaves are more spinach-sized than chard-sized), and of course color. Most sea beets are plain green, perhaps with a bit of pink. Chards and beet greens come in a wide range of leaf and vein foliage—green to red to deep red-black leaf foliage, and veins and petioles including white, green, yellow, orange, red, and screaming magenta. Try crossing with the almost black 'Bulls Blood' leaf beet, or the fluorescent yellows, oranges, and pinks of 'Bright Lights' chard. Breeding for later flowering should also be a priority. *Note:* Wild populations of sea beets are currently threatened by the introduction of genetically engineered sugar beets, with which wild individuals easily (and frequently) interbreed—all the more reason to get wild material into the hands of gardeners for preservation and improvement.

Chenopodium bonus-henricus • Good King Henry

Synonyms
- Fat hen
- Lincolnshire asparagus

Aspects
- Clumping herb
- Edible shoots
- Edible greens
- Edible flowerbuds
- Sun to part shade
- Moist, well-drained soil

General Overview, History, and Ecology: Good king Henry is a traditional European vegetable. It is primarily grown for its edible asparagus-like shoots, but is also has edible leaves, flowerbuds, and seeds. Perhaps what is most remarkable about this plant is its potential to be the basis for breeding a wide range of new perennial leaf crops, from spinach to broccoli to grain. Good king Henry is a reliable, low-maintenance spinach relative adapted to most of the United States and Canada. It has been cultivated in Europe in the past as a cooking green and for its shoots, known as Lincolnshire asparagus, as well as for its edible seeds as a grain crop. Its ease of growing and its tolerance of partial

Good king Henry is a versatile plant, with edible
shoots, leaves, flowerbeds, and seeds.

shade make it a fine choice for the perennial
vegetable garden.

The shoots were once a very popular vegetable in England. If given a rich soil with plenty of
compost or rotted manure, it can produce shoots
20 days before asparagus and continue to do so
until several weeks after the asparagus harvest is
over. That's a season of over three months! The
leaves are eaten as a fine cooking green, although
their flavor is a bit bitter and they are best mixed
with other greens.

Crop Description: An established good king Henry
plant resembles a large spinach plant. It also
appears similar to its cousin lamb's-quarters
(*Chenopodium album*), a common annual weed and
popular wild edible.

Climate: Good king Henry is hardy in Zones 3–
9. With a good location and plenty of mulch it
might even be hardier. Its leaves are up early in
the spring and persist late into the fall.

Tolerances and Preferences: It thrives in full sun or
partial shade and is not picky about soils, although
it is not particularly drought-tolerant. It probably
prefers partial shade in areas with hot summers.

Naturalization Status: Good king Henry has naturalized in parts of the United States and Canada,
though not aggressively so.

Pest, Disease, and Weed Problems: It does not seem
to have many pest or disease problems.

Propagation and Planting: Good king Henry grows
quite easily from seed, taking a few weeks to
germinate but then coming up strong. Division
of established plants is also fairly easy. In fact,
it grows so well in Europe that it can be somewhat weedy when allowed to go to seed, and it
has naturalized a bit in some parts of the United
States. You might want to deadhead plants before
they set seed. In my garden spreading a layer of
mulch below plants has prevented seedlings from
becoming established. Good king Henry seedlings will seem small and weak the first year. Take
heart: By the second year they will have become
well established and will grow well enough to
make you feel like you are a great gardener. Plant
them 18–24 inches apart.

Other Cultivation Information: Hold off on harvesting the leaves for the first year while plants get
established. Plants will need replacing after about
five years, which is easily done by division at that
time. Shoots are sometimes blanched to make
them sweeter, by piling leaves or straw around the
plants.

Harvest and Storage: The shoots are harvested just
like asparagus. If the skin is tough it can be easily
peeled off from the bottom upward.

Uses: Good king Henry is related to spinach, beets,
and chard, and like them contains oxalic acid,
which is destroyed by cooking. Shoots are eaten
like asparagus when they are about 8 inches high.
The leaves are eaten cooked, and are usually mixed
with other greens. When eaten raw they have
an unpleasant, bitter taste. Patrick Whitefield,
author of *How to Make a Forest Garden*, says, "when
added to stews, stir-frys and other mixed dishes
the sharpness is lost and they add a rich, savory
flavor to the food." Unlike most greens their
flavor is not diminished by flowering; in fact the
leaves are often larger and more succulent after
flowering. The tender young flower clusters are
eaten somewhat like broccoli. Seed is cooked as a
grain, but should be soaked overnight to remove
its mildly toxic saponins (saponins are a soapy
compound also present in quinoa).

Related Species and Breeding Potential: It may be
that by simply planting out 50 seedlings you
could discover a variety with better-flavored
leaves for eating raw, or perhaps one that has
large edible flower clusters, or abundant seeds.

The seeds of good king Henry available in the United States and Canada are from a small number of selections brought over from Europe (where it is native). There is presumably much greater variation among European populations. Ordering seeds from multiple European sources should provide much greater genetic variability, with a correspondingly greater chance of finding seedlings with interesting and desirable traits.

Good king Henry also has many annual edible relatives with which it might be crossed to develop interesting new perennials. By crossing good king Henry with various *Chenopodium* species, new perennial vegetables could be created with edible leaves, grain, shoots, and broccoli-like flower clusters. Since so many of good king Henry's parts are edible, as are those of these relatives, breeding can be taken in many direction without fear of losing edibility.

Quinoa (*Chenopodium quinoa*) is a cultivated grain crop (technically a "pseudo-cereal" because it is not a grass) from the Andes. Good king Henry has edible seeds and has even been cultivated for them in the past. Perhaps a cross could result in a moderately productive perennial *Chenopodium* grain crop.

Several *Chenopodium* species have varieties cultivated for their edible leaves. Lamb's-quarters or fat hen (*C. album*) is a tasty wild edible with edible leaves, which have a much better flavor when eaten raw than good king Henry. Several improved varieties are available. Crossing with improved lamb's-quarters might greatly improve the flavor of good king Henry. Several relatives with edible leaves have magenta or pink leaf color, including 'Magenta' (*C. album*). The 'Magentaspreen' lamb's-quarter is *C. giganteum*. Why not breed perennial greens with magenta leaves?

Finally, there is even a species of *Chenopodium* that is grown as a "chenopodial broccoli." Huauzontle (*C. nuttalliae*) is annual native from the southwestern United States through Central America. It is cultivated for its large flower clusters, which are used like broccoli. Some varieties are bright magenta. Huauzontle is served in many fine Mexican restaurants. This could be crossed with good king Henry to develop a perennial broccoli-type crop.

Clearly this humble crop has tremendous potential. Perhaps someday in the future gardeners will look back on good king Henry as the ancestor of a full range of perennial food crops, much like wild cabbage has given birth to a whole suite of vegetables including broccoli, kale, cabbage, brussels sprouts, and other crops.

Convolvulaceae: The Morning Glory Family

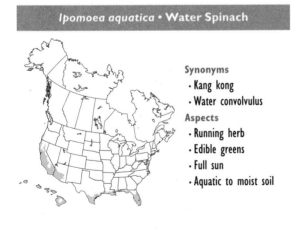

Ipomoea aquatica • Water Spinach

Synonyms
- Kang kong
- Water convolvulus

Aspects
- Running herb
- Edible greens
- Full sun
- Aquatic to moist soil

General Overview, History, and Ecology: Water spinach is an important leafy vegetable throughout tropical Asia. The leaves and young shoots have a mild, slightly nutty spinach flavor. There are two strains of water spinach. The aquatic form, called pak quat or white-stem water spinach, has arrowhead-shaped leaves. It runs aggressively and roots at the nodes wherever it comes in contact with water or moist soil. The upland form, known as ching quat or green-stem water spinach, has narrower leaves and grows in an upright, less aggressive form. Water spinach is perennial in the tropics but is often grown as an annual, particularly the upland form.

Water spinach is a highly productive leaf crop with weedy potential in tropical waterways. PHOTO BY JENNIFER HASHLEY.

Unfortunately, the aquatic form spreads so quickly that it can become a major pest in bodies of water. On farms in Massachusetts water spinach stems can grow 9 feet long in a growing season, rooting all along the stem. In the tropics plants grow with lightning speed. Most of our aquatic ecosystems are so disturbed by agricultural runoff, dredging, channel modification, and other human activities that they are highly vulnerable to colonization by aggressive species. Water spinach can grow so vigorously as to clog channels and make them impassable to boats. For this reason it is banned as a noxious weed in the United States, though many states offer permits because of its importance as a crop for Asian growers and markets. Water spinach is perfectly legal in Canada and quite unlikely to naturalize there.

Despite its weedy potential, there are ways to grow this crop responsibly. First, it seems unlikely that it can survive winters outside of the tropical or subtropical parts of North America. Though it could conceivably self-seed in colder areas, it is not reported to have enough time to flower in a New England growing season. Second, upland strains are much less aggressive, and would be a great candidate for cultivation as a perennial in our warmer areas. Finally, it seems that growing aquatic types in artificial water gardens far from natural bodies of water should be quite safe.

Crop Description: Water spinach is an herbaceous perennial growing about 2–3 feet high. In aquatic gardens it apparently behaves similar to water celery and watercress, floating on the surface and producing numerous roots.

Climate: This crop is fully tropical and is killed by frost, though it makes a fine annual anywhere with a hot summer.

Tolerances and Preferences: Water spinach grows in full sun and requires plenty of moisture. It can be grown in moist or wet soil or as an emergent floater in a water garden.

Naturalization Status: Water spinach has naturalized in Hawaii, Florida, and California. It has been declared a noxious weed in the United States.

Pest, Disease, and Weed Problems: Water spinach shares many pests and diseases with sweet potato. Those that affect sweet potato leaves (often ignored by sweet potato growers) are more problematic with water spinach, including aphids, flea beetles, and the sweet potato weevil. Tarnished plant bugs can also be problematic.

Propagation and Planting: Water spinach is extremely easy to grow from cuttings. Some home gardeners simply buy it at an Asian grocery and stick it in water—it roots very effectively. Even more effective is to pot up cuttings and place in the pot in an artificial pond. Aquatic water spinach grown in this fashion is incredibly productive. Plants can also be grown from seed, although a germination rate of 60 percent is not unusual. Some gardeners plant several cuttings to a pot in water gardens—keep in mind the plants will spread across the surface of your pond if you do not harvest frequently. For upland varieties, allow perhaps 6–12 inches of space between plants.

Harvest and Storage: Water spinach is a typical leaf crop and should not be allowed to wilt: Harvest in the cool morning hours and bag and refrigerate promptly. If grown in a water garden, keep the lip of pots above the waterline to prevent algae, just as you would with watercress or water celery.

Uses: The leaves and tender stalks of water spinach are a world-class vegetable, and can be used raw or cooked in any way you would ordinary spinach.

Related Species and Breeding Potential: Crossing upland water spinach with sweet potato might yield a very interesting and slightly hardier new perennial leaf crop. Perhaps such a hybrid would be far less invasive.

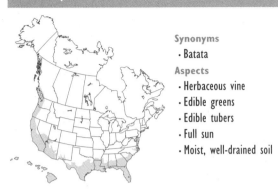

Ipomoea batatas • Sweet Potato

Synonyms
- Batata

Aspects
- Herbaceous vine
- Edible greens
- Edible tubers
- Full sun
- Moist, well-drained soil

General Overview, History, and Ecology: Though the roots are a familiar food in North America, most U.S. and Canadian gardeners are unaware that sweet potato leaves are an important crop in many parts of the world. Not all varieties have good flavor, but some varieties are grown just for leaf production in the Philippines, parts of tropical Africa, and elsewhere. The high protein content of the cooked leaves makes up for the lower protein of the tubers. Sweet potatoes are one of the most important crops in the world, having spread almost everywhere from their native Amazon region.

Sweet potatoes are a great perennial groundcover, and overwinter without protection at the Zone 8/9 border, indicating that they could be grown as perennials through Zone 8 (if not colder) with some protection. Perennial groundcovers with edible leaves should be highly sought after as edible landscaping species and as understories in polycultures. At ECHO I saw sweet potato thriving as the groundcover companion for many species, including trellised winged bean, pigeon pea, bananas, and mangoes. At least in the subtropics they seem to yield very well in the light shade of these polycultures.

Of course sweet potatoes are also an excellent root crop. Apparently, though, when grown as perennials they are somewhat annoying. They form a nice set of roots where they are originally planted, but then they also root where the vines touch the soil and make more tubers. This can make finding tubers to harvest somewhat challenging, as it is very difficult to determine where they are. By cutting back the tangled vines, it is possible to follow the thickest stems to discover the hidden bounty. Personally, as a cold-climate gardener I don't have much sympathy for people who complain that there are too many pesky sweet potato roots everywhere in their garden. But we must heed the experience of subtropical perennial vegetable enthusiasts and conclude that, as root crops, sweet potatoes are imperfect perennial vegetables—though the roots can certainly be seen as a major added bonus to their role as an edible-leaved groundcover.

There are many varieties of sweet potatoes available. Seed Savers Exchange, for instance, lists 50 varieties. It should be a priority for perennial vegetable enthusiasts from warm climates to start screening cultivars for the quality of their greens. There are ornamental varieties with beautiful colored foliage. While I don't like their flavor, many of my friends think they are very good.

Note: In the United States, yams and sweet potatoes have been confused. What we call yams in the United States are actually sweet potatoes. True yams are in the genus *Dioscorea* (see page 138).

Crop Description: Sweet potatoes are vigorous herbaceous vines. They do not climb, but sprawl over the ground.

Climate: Sweet potatoes thrive in hot, humid climates, but they are hardy perennials in at least

In addition to edible roots, this cultivar of sweet potato is grown for its edible leaves. It also makes a beautiful groundcover.

the warmer parts of Zone 8. It can't really be too hot for sweet potatoes. Short-season varieties like 'Beauregard' can be grown as annual root crops in cold climates as long as there is a long enough hot summer, and could be grown as an annual leaf crop in almost any climate. With protection they might be able to be overwintered in Zone 7 or possibly even colder areas. Black plastic mulch gives additional heat for growing as an annual in colder climates.

Tolerances and Preferences: Sweet potatoes should be grown in full sun in shorter-season areas, but will handle partial shade in the tropics and subtropics. Soils should be moist and well drained but do not have to be rich. The plants will produce well in poor soils. Too much nitrogen makes them focus on leaves instead of roots, which is fine if you want to grow them as a leaf crop. By their fourth or fifth month of growth they become somewhat drought-tolerant.

Naturalization Status: Sweet potato has naturalized in various regions of the United States.

Pest, Disease, and Weed Problems: The sweet potato weevil can be a serious problem, eating the leaves and stems and burrowing into the roots. It can be controlled with rotenone, pyrethrum, or neem. When sweet potatoes are grown as a leaf crop, many pests (including flea beetles and tarnished plant bugs) that attack the leaves and are usually considered minor suddenly become something to worry about. Nematodes can cause damage. Several diseases are also problematic, although resistant varieties are available.

Propagation and Planting: In the United States and Canada, many gardeners buy rooted cuttings, or slips, every year. You can also take your own stem cuttings. They should be 12–18 inches long. You don't need to remove the leaves. Tie the cuttings up in bundles and put them in a shady place for a few days, keeping them moist. Then they should be planted or potted up with the bottom two-thirds of the cutting buried. Sprouting tubers can also often be found in grocery stores. Sweet potatoes can be raised from seed, although these seedlings will produce plants that will not necessarily resemble or be nearly as good as their parent strain. Many varieties do not flower or set seed without special treatment.

Harvest and Storage: Tubers can be stored for two to eight weeks in cool temperatures. By curing them they can last up to a year. To cure roots, store them for four or five days at 90°F–95°F and 80–90 percent humidity in a greenhouse or sunroom. Then store in a cool dry place as you would potatoes. Roots can be stored over winter and replanted in cold-climate areas.

Uses: The top 3–4 inches of the shoot tip and attached young leaves are cooked. They are at their best in the second and third month of growth (each season where plants are perennial). These should be cooked for 15–20 minutes. They should not be eaten raw. The roots are familiar to us all as one of the finest-flavored vegetables in the world.

Related Species and Breeding Potential: A great many interesting varieties are available through Seed Savers Exchange and other sources, which should be trialed for leaf quality. Although it would require a bit of tricky breeding work, crossing sweet potato with water spinach (definitely a superior leaf crop) could create a fantastic new perennial leaf crop groundcover. Breeding for increased hardiness is possible as well. Two native species, *I. leptophylla* and *I. pandurata*, are quite hardy and have somewhat edible (and enormous) roots. Neither has edible leaves, and breeding for a hardy perennial leaf crop should proceed cautiously, as there are many poisonous plants in this family.

Cucurbitaceae: The Squash Family

Coccinia grandis • 'Sterile Perennial' Cucumber

Synonyms
- *C. cordifolia*
- *C. indica*
- Ivy gourd
- Scarlet gourd
- Tindora

Aspects
- Woody vine
- Edible fruit
- Edible leaves
- Sun to part shade
- Moist, well-drained soil

General Overview, History, and Ecology: This perennial cucurbit is cultivated in Asia and Africa for its miniature cucumber-like fruits. These 1- to 2-inch fruits are borne in great abundance, and in the tropics are available year-round. They have a crisp, almost crunchy texture and a delightful lemon-cucumber taste. Perennial cucumber is also one of the few cucurbits whose leaves can be eaten raw. Like the fruits, fresh greens are available to eat year-round in the tropics. These characteristics make it a very valuable food plant for tropical and subtropical areas.

The bad news is that perennial cucumber is an incredibly weedy plant. It spreads very aggressively by seed, presumably dispersed by birds. The vines also root where they come into contact with the ground, and can spread rapidly in this fashion as well. Perennial cucumber has become a very serious weed problem in much of tropical Asia and the Pacific islands, including Hawaii, where it is considered a noxious weed. It has naturalized to some degree in the southeastern United States as well.

Fortunately, there is a sterile variety, which produces fruits without viable seed, and is also much less aggressive about spreading vegetatively. This variety is the only type that will be profiled here, and is probably the only type that that can be responsibly grown here. Even so, it should be managed in "quarantine" on a trellis or fence surrounded by a mowed strip or other bare perimeter. The sterile cultivar is less aggressive than most, and will not send long, searching tendrils from the trellis to find new victims. Nonetheless, site the trellis so the plant is not close to any trees, which the vines will smother if given the opportunity. Keep an eye on any woody stems that root at the base of the trellis. In this fashion they can make a nice living fence, or even be grown over a dome frame to create an edible shade house.

This species is an interesting case. As a perennial vegetable providing both fruit and greens it presents great opportunities. Unfortunately this promise is greatly dimmed by its extremely invasive tendencies, both in the garden and in the surrounding ecosystems. Thoughtful and cautious use of the sterile variety in the warmer parts of the United States may provide an interesting and productive new vegetable.

Crop Description: Perennial cucumber is a very large vine, which can live for many years and becomes woody. It generally resembles a large squash or cucumber vine with ivy-like leaves.

Climate: Perennial cucumber thrives in the hot, humid tropics, although it will tolerate drier conditions and is found as a weed at least as far north as Atlanta. It will sprout back from the

Perennial cucumber has edible leaves and fruit. Here a fruit is forming on the sterile variety. PHOTO BY JAY RAM.

roots as long as the ground does not freeze. It is likely that it can be grown in all of Florida, the Gulf Coast, and much of Southern California. Like so many tropical perennials, in hot-summer areas it could be planted outside and a cutting or tuber taken in for winter. Perennial cucumber grows excessively well in Hawaii. Even the sterile variety will spread aggressively by tip layering (rooting wherever it touches the soil) if not managed properly.

Tolerances and Preferences: As long as soils are well drained perennial cucumber is not picky, although it will prosper in soils high in organic matter. It grows in sun to part shade. In partial shade it grows larger leaves.

Naturalization Status: A noxious weed in Hawaii and naturalized in the southeastern United States, even the sterile variety can spread quite quickly through vegetative means.

Pest, Disease, and Weed Problems: Perennial cucumber is generally resistant to pests and diseases, although apparently some diseases can spread from it to cucurbits and papayas. As mentioned above, seeded forms are extremely weedy. Even the sterile form should be carefully managed (as described below) to ensure that it does not spread by rooting where mature stems touch the ground.

Propagation and Planting: Seed, cuttings, and division of tubers can propagate this species. It also spreads by rooting where vines touch the soil. The sterile variety can only be propagated vegetatively. Cuttings are taken from the woody stems, about 5–10 inches in length, containing at least two nodes. Bury one node and leave the other above the soil surface. Keep cuttings moist and in a warm, sunny place. You can also dig up woody stems that have contacted the ground and rooted under your trellis. Planting distance depends on the type of trellising (see below).

Other Cultivation Information: Sterile perennial cucumber should be grown on a trellis. A single plant can eventually cover a 45-foot length of fence or trellis 6 feet high, but they are usually planted more densely so they fill in quicker.

Harvest and Storage: In the tropics perennial cucumber will produce fruit and fresh new greens all year long.

Uses: The young leaves and top 8 inches of shoot tips are eaten raw or cooked. Older leaves can be cooked. The small young (1–2 inches) fruits are eaten just like tiny, crisp, lemony cucumbers. Mature fruits turn red and become slimy and sour, but are apparently popular in India.

Related Species and Breeding Potential: The most important project, that of finding a sterile and less aggressive variety, has been accomplished. It would be nice if this variety were more widely available commercially. I have been playing around with *Melothria pendula*, an eastern native with small "cucumber berries" that are quite similar to tindora though smaller (and allegedly causing diarrhea in some people).

Cucurbita ficifolia • Malabar Gourd

Synonyms
- Chilacayote
- Malabar melon
- Figleaf gourd
- Zambo

Aspects
- Herbaceous vine
- Edible fruit
- Full sun
- Moist, well-drained soil

General Overview, History, and Ecology: This perennial squash produces enormous fruit and has been cultivated in Latin America for thousands of years. A single plant can produce up to 100 cantaloupe- to watermelon-sized fruits. Fruits of some varieties can weight up to 20 pounds, although others are much smaller. The fruit has incredible keeping qualities, remaining in good quality for up to two years without refrigeration! I wish I could say the flavor of the flesh is fantastic, but it sounds as though it is just okay. It is usually sweetened and used as a dessert, but can also be cooked like an ordinary winter squash. Young fruits are used like zucchini, and the cooked leaves are eaten as well.

It is a short-lived perennial in frost-free areas but can be grown as an annual in areas with long growing seasons, including coastal California,

Malabar gourd, or chilacayote, can grow larger than a watermelon.

where it is very successful. Malabar gourd is also used as rootstock for grafted, intensively grown greenhouse cucumbers. Established outdoor perennial plants could offer a tremendous energy boost to annual cucumbers, squash, and possibly other cucurbits grafted onto them. Imagine a cucumber seedling inheriting the vitality of a squash that can cover 600 square feet!

Crop Description: Malabar gourds are extremely vigorous squash vines. A single runner can be up to 30 feet long.

Climate: Malabar gourd is successfully grown in southern England and the central California coast. It seems to be able to tolerate light frosts, and prefers cool climates. It apparently flowers when days are short, making it a poor choice for areas with early frosts in fall.

Tolerances and Preferences: Malabar gourd likes plenty of water and prefers good soil, although it is not terribly picky.

Naturalization Status: This species is naturalizing in coastal California.

Pest, Disease, and Weed Problems: Malabar gourd is quite resistant to pests and diseases—one reason it is used as a rootstock for greenhouse cucumbers. As a very vigorous grower, the issue is not so much what will weeds do to it as what will it do to the weeds (and the other crops or desirable plants nearby).

Propagation and Planting: Malabar ground is grown from seed just like ordinary squash. Plant 6 feet apart or farther.

Other Cultivation Information: It would be best to have at least two plants for best pollination, although Malabar gourd can self-pollinate to some degree.

Harvest and Storage: Fruits can be picked young, like zucchini. In England fruits are not considered ripe until the leaves are killed back by frost. Storage of fruits is truly remarkable—they can be stored for two years or more in a dry place and they get sweeter as they age. This is due to the very hard, thick rind, which is so tough it sometimes requires an ax to open it!

Uses: When young (and already up to the size of a football) the fruits are eaten like zucchini. Some varieties mature to enormous size. All have an extremely hard rind when mature. When cracked open, the flesh detaches easily, exposing a large quantity of edible white flesh and nutritious seeds. This flesh can be cooked like winter squash or boiled as a potato-like vegetable, but the favored use is to cook the flesh with milk, cinnamon, and sugar to make a delicious dessert. The variety 'Alcayota' is like a spaghetti squash, and is commercially cultivated for its thick, easily separated noodle-like strands of flesh. Malabar gourd seeds are tasty, like pumpkin seeds, but have a shell, which is difficult to remove. Like cultivated squashes, the young leaves and tips of shoots can be eaten as a cooked vegetable (many readers may be unaware that pumpkin greens are a major vegetable in some parts of the world).

Related Species and Breeding Potential: Malabar gourds seeds are hard to come by north of Mexico. Some Californian should work on acquiring some different varieties and running trials on them for flavor and productivity. Work should be done to breed and select more flavorful varieties. Certainly attempts to widely cross this species with annual squash to create perennial summer and winter squash are worth trying. Perhaps it could be crossed with the hardy (and horrible-tasting) *Cucurbita foetidissima* to increase its northern range.

Momordica charantia • Bitter Melon

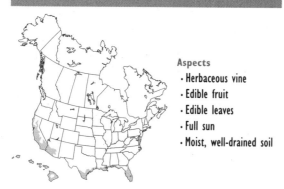

Aspects
- Herbaceous vine
- Edible fruit
- Edible leaves
- Full sun
- Moist, well-drained soil

Bitter melon definitely lives up to its name. Bitter vegetables and herbs have an important place in many cuisines, like chicories and endives in Mediterranean cooking. The immature fruits of bitter melon are very popular in tropical Asia. Although they might be an acquired taste for many gardeners in the United States and Canada, they are worth getting accustomed to. Their intense bitterness is offset by a nutty, rich summer squash flavor and a great texture. The unripe fruits, up to about 8 inches, are halved and the seeds and fiber removed. They are then usually soaked or boiled in salt water to remove some of the bitterness, and used in various dishes. They are frequently stuffed, for which they are perfectly built. Some less bitter varieties are available, notably some of the white-fleshed types.

Bitter melon is excellent when stuffed with rice and meat.

Bitter melons are grown much like cucumbers, and often trellised. They are perennial in the tropics, but are easy to grow as annuals elsewhere. Some varieties can fruit in as little as 65 days from seed. They prefer rich, well-drained soil and plenty of water. Bitter melons will fruit in full sun or light shade. Bitter melon has naturalized in many parts of the tropics and subtropics, as well as Hawaii and some areas of the eastern and southern United States.

Sechium edule • Chayote

Synonyms
- Mirliton
- Chook
- Vegetable pear
- Pimpinella

Aspects
- Woody vine
- Edible fruit
- Edible leaves
- Edible roots
- Full sun
- Moist, well-drained soil

General Overview, History, and Ecology: Chayote is an outstanding perennial vegetable. The versatile fruits are used in a wide range of dishes and are popular throughout much of the world. This remarkable plant also features nutritious greens and tasty edible roots! Chayote was domesticated in southern Mexico and Central America, where it continues to be an important commercial and home garden crop. It is now grown throughout much of the humid tropical and subtropical areas of the world.

The fruits are roughly the size and shape of a pear. Commercial varieties are light green, although cultivated forms range from white to dark green, in a range of shapes and sizes. Some varieties even have soft edible thorns on the fruit. Fruits can be used raw like zucchini or cucumbers, or cooked like potatoes. They are crisp and crunchy, with a pleasant, mild flavor. One plant can produce 100 fruits in a year, and when well watered and fertilized as many as 300! They will produce much less in less than ideal climates. Chayote fruits continuously in the tropics. Vines

Chayote is a long-lived perennial cucurbit vine with zucchini-like fruit, plus edible leaves and tubers. PHOTO BY JUDY DOLMACH.

are usually most productive for the first three years, and sometimes up to eight.

The young leaves and shoot tips (the top 10 inches) are used as cooking greens, with a mild celery/cabbage flavor. This is the most nutritious part of the plant. The tubers, known as chinchayote or chinta, are cooked like potatoes. These tubers are similar nutritionally to potatoes and have an excellent flavor.

Chayote can be grown in the warmer areas of the southern United States and Southern California, and of course in Hawaii. With protection it can be grown a bit farther north, and northerners who really want to fruit chayotes in their gardens can use a new low-tech but high-maintenance technique (described at right) to grow it as an annual almost anywhere you can grow squash.

In the tropics vines can grow up to 100 feet, but when grown as an annual or where it is killed back by frost it grows a somewhat less vigorous 30 feet or so in a year. Each plant produces multiple shoots. Chayote has a reputation as an aggressive sprawler; in fact it is used in Australia to smother unwanted weedy plants. Don't plant chayote close to any delicate plants or slow-moving pets you care about!

Crop Description: Chayote is a perennial vine with leaves resembling those of cucumber.

Climate: Chayote is grown commercially in tropical and subtropical areas around the world. In the United States it is grown in Hawaii, and on the mainland in southern Florida, Louisiana, Mississippi, southern Oklahoma, and Southern California. In these areas it is an excellent candidate for the perennial vegetable garden, and should be more widely grown.

The picture elsewhere is a bit bleaker. Reports differ on its hardiness. Plants are killed to the ground by hard frosts, but the roots can survive Zone 8 winters if well mulched. Some growers in northern Louisiana cut back the frost-killed plants, mulch them, cover them with a basket, and then put more mulch leaves or hay on top. Growers in colder areas could also bring in tubers for the winter and plant them out again in spring. Some varieties dislike long periods with hot nights and will abort fruit. Temperatures below 55°F will damage fruits.

The real challenge with chayote is day length. It blooms in the short days of August and September in San Diego and Los Angeles. In Panama it blooms and fruits throughout the year. Chayote could be grown as an annual or even a well-mulched perennial in a much greater range of the United States and even coastal western Canada if it weren't for the day-length problem. When days are longer than 10 hours it puts most of its energy into vegetative growth and neglects fruit and tuber production.

Extending the Range of Chayote and Other Day-Length-Sensitive Plants

If your heart is really set on growing chayote outside of its ideal range, researchers have worked out a technique for those who are very serious about wanting to fruit chayotes. This technique might be workable for other day-length-sensitive vegetables like oca, ulluco, and mashua. In an article in the journal *Economic Botany* titled "Developmental and Nutritional Aspects of Chayote," the authors report their technique for fruiting chayote in Virginia. Plants are started in a greenhouse to get a head start. Once they are planted outside and have been growing for a total of six to eight weeks, a frame is built over the plants and covered by a dark cloth, which shades the plants. They remove the shade after sunrise each morning, and put it back on after eight hours. This fools the plant into thinking that it is in Mexico at fruiting season and it starts to flower. Once little fruits have formed, the cloth can be removed and fruits will develop normally. It takes four to six weeks of doing this for fruits to form, and another month until they are harvestable. This technique can be used to simulate whatever day length is required for fruit or tuber formation in a range of crops.

> ### *Chilacayote with Cinnamon*
> Thanks to Marikler Girón Ramirez and her mother, Flora Elma Ramirez for this traditional Guatemalan recipe. You can buy lime stone at your local Mexican or Central American grocery.
>
> 1 watermelon-sized chilacayote
> 1 tablespoon powdered lime stone
> 1 pound brown sugar
> 2 cinnamon sticks
> 2 cups water
> ½ teaspoon salt
>
> Clean and dice the chilacayote. Then place it in a large bowl, add the lime stone, and cover with water. Leave it overnight. The following day, take it out of the lime stone water. Place sugar, cinnamon, water, and salt in a saucepan and bring to a boil. Add the chilacayote and keep at a gentle boil until it looks transparent and the syrup is sticky. It takes about 5 hours. Serve warm or cold as candy.
> Serves 10.

That is fine if you only want to grow it as greens, but fruits and tubers begin to be produced only when days are less than 10 hours long. While fruits only take a month or so from flowering, and are at their best for eating when somewhat unripe, in most of the United States and Canada that means plants won't start to fruit until it is too late in the season and plants are killed by frost. In northern greenhouses chayote flowers in late fall but does not produce well.

Tolerances and Preferences: Chayote likes full sun, lots of space, and lots of water. It likes to have rich soil, and it is particularly important that it be well drained to prevent root diseases. Like other cucurbits it likes to be fed additional compost or well-rotted manure during the growing season.

Naturalization Status: Chayote has naturalized in Hawaii and Louisiana.

Pest, Disease, and Weed Problems: Nematodes can be a serious problem for chayote. Cucumber beetles are also problematic, especially with unmulched plants. Mildew and mites are also sometimes problems. In its native range in Mexico and Central America there are many more pests and diseases, but outside of that area fewer pests are reported.

Propagation and Planting: Whole fruits are planted in the garden or in pots. They are buried on their side, with a third to a fourth of the fruit above the surface. You can purchase fruits in many grocery stores—some will even have already started to sprout.

Chayote can also be grown from cuttings. Older stems are cut into 8-inch lengths, and kept moist and shaded while getting established. Plants are usually planted in mounds 15 feet apart.

Other Cultivation Information: Chayote should be supported by a trellis, fence, outbuilding, or unpopular tree. Remember, it can grow 30 feet in a season, and much more in the tropics.

Be careful when harvesting or working around the plants, since contact with the foliage may cause a rash on sensitive skin.

Harvest and Storage: The fruit is challenging to store because it tends to start sprouting. In fact, sometimes it starts sprouting while it is still on the vine! Storing fruit at 45°F–50°F will minimize sprouting and avoid chilling damage.

Tubers must be eaten in the first one or two years after planting, or they become woody. At this point, you can remove the large storage roots and leave the feeder roots behind to keep growing. This must be done very carefully; you must avoid damaging the plant if want it to come back. If you are growing chayote as an annual you should definitely harvest this extra crop.

Uses: The versatile fruits can be used like zucchini, or cooked like potatoes (even to make french fries!). Fruits can be mixed with lime juice and substituted for apples in pies. They are also used fresh in salads like crunchy cucumbers. Chayote fruits are usually used when immature, at 4–6 inches. The soft seed inside immature fruits is totally edible, and not ordinarily noticeable. Later, the fruits become tougher and the seeds must be cooked to eat them. Fully mature fruits are used like potatoes. Sprouted young fruits can be eaten.

Young leaves and shoots to 10 inches long are

cooked. The tendrils are very fibrous and should be removed before cooking. Newly emerging shoots are eaten like asparagus. The roots are cooked just like potatoes.

Related Species and Breeding Potential: Chayote has a great diversity of fruit types, but only a very limited range is grown commercially. Certainly existing strains should be evaluated to see if there are any day-length-neutral types, and, if not, this trait should be bred for this trait. This versatile and productive crop would have a much wider audience as a result!

Cyperaceae: The Sedge Family

Cyperus esculentus var. sativa • Chufa

Synonyms
- Tiger nut
- Earth almond
- Yellow nutsedge

Aspects
- Clumping herb
- Edible tubers
- Full sun
- Moist to wet soil

The small but abundant tubers of chufa.

Yellow nutsedge, the ancestor of chufa, is one of the world's worst weeds. It spreads by seed and aggressive rhizomes, and also persists by small tubers. Nutsedge is found throughout the world and especially likes poorly drained soils. But several thousand years ago someone started domesticating it for those edible tubers. By 2400 BC it was a popular enough crop to be buried with Egyptian pharaohs in their tombs. This cultivated variety (known as variety *sativa*) is not weedy, rarely forms seed, and does not spread by aggressive rhizomes. Today it is a popular crop in northern Africa and the Mediterranean, especially the Valencia region of Spain, where the tubers are used to make a popular vanilla-almond-flavored milky drink called horchata. Chufa is also widely grown in the South of the United States as a wildlife plant.

Chufa is a clump-forming sedge, resembling a tufty clumping grass. Apparently, if left alone for a few years it spreads very slowly to form a clump.

Chufa prefers full sun but will tolerate partial shade. It tolerates wet feet and poorly drained soils. While it will grow in virtually any soil, it produces the largest tubers and highest yields in sandy soils. Unlike the weedy form, chufa is frost-sensitive. Tops are killed by frost, and tubers are killed by frozen ground. It is generally considered hardy to Zone 8.

Much more research has been done on how to kill (weedy) chufa than how to grow it. Tubers propagate chufa plants. Some growers have trouble with long dormancy periods. Apparently the best technique is to dry the tubers somewhat (to about 60 percent of their original weight). Dry tubers I received from the J. L. Hudson Seed Company sprouted in about two weeks. True chufa seed is rarely set and germinates poorly. Scarifying seed with acid has improved germination, or you could try rubbing it with sandpaper.

Mice love the tubers and can be a problem. There are few insect pests or diseases to be concerned with. Chufa will grow as a water garden plant with just the bottom inch or two of the pot submerged.

The tubers are small, up to ¾ inch in size. A single plant can yield over 100 tubers. They are too hard to eat more than a few raw. They become somewhat softer if soaked for a few days or cooked. Chufa tubers are also a source of high-quality edible oil similar to olive oil. Drying the tubers is easy in hot, dry climates: Just leave them out in dry shaded place. In humid climates you could try to use a home-scale food dehydrator. The tubers are rather small and difficult to clean without specialized equipment.

There are a number of named varieties in Valencia. Many other species of *Cyperus* have edible tubers, notably *C. rotundus*. Breeding is difficult due to the rarity of producing viable seed. Perhaps chufa could be crossed with wild, weedy yellow nutsedge to produce a hardier chufa, perhaps even (dare I say it) one that forms larger colonies.

Horchata

2 pounds dried chufa tubers
2 gallons water
1 cinnamon stick
2 pounds white sugar

Soak 2 pounds of dried chufa tubers for 12 hours. Rinse them several times until the water is clear. Blend the tubers with a little water or use a very sturdy food processor (even soaked tubers are pretty hard). Add 2 gallons of water and a cinnamon stick and refrigerate for a few hours. Stir in 2 pounds of white sugar until dissolved. Strain through a cheesecloth several times. Serve cold or frozen as ice cream.
Serves 10.

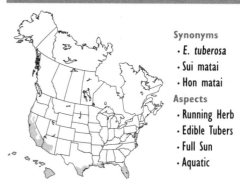

Eleocharis dulcis • Water Chestnut

Synonyms
- *E. tuberosa*
- Sui matai
- Hon matai

Aspects
- Running Herb
- Edible Tubers
- Full Sun
- Aquatic

General Overview, History, and Ecology: Most gardeners in the United States and Canada have only eaten canned water chestnuts. The real, fresh roots, called corms, have a far better, nutty flavor and a fantastic crisp texture. Water chestnuts are very easy to grow and produce well. They are very well suited to water gardens. Water chestnuts originally hail from tropical Asia and West Africa, but hardy native relatives (some with edible corms) offer intriguing breeding potential.

Water chestnut is a grass-like member of the Sedge family, with 2- to 4-foot thin, hollow leaves, somewhat resembling enormous chives. The edible "nuts" are actually corms (tuber-like structures), which form at the base of each clump. Water chestnut spreads by rhizomes to form a colony of numerous small clumps, each with a corm at the base. A single plant can produce over 2 pounds of chestnuts.

This species should not be confused with the water caltrop or singhara ling nut (*Trapa natans*), which is also called water chestnut. Water caltrop is also edible but is a very aggressive weed of aquatic ecosystems.

Crop Description: Water chestnut grows in large, grass-like clumps.

Climate: Water chestnut is a tropical plant. If the corms are protected from freezing, it can remain outside. Otherwise tubers should be stored indoors for the winter and replanted outside in spring. It needs a six- or seven-month growing season, although smaller corms can be harvested a bit earlier if you have a short season. I tried to grow water chestnuts in my Massachusetts garden for several years, but never achieved full-sized mature corms, even with some season extension.

Tolerances and Preferences: Water chestnut is an aquatic plant, and requires wet soil or actual submersion in up to 5 inches of water. It should be grown in full sun.

Naturalization Status: Water chestnut has naturalized in Georgia.

Pest, Disease, and Weed Problems: Water chestnut reportedly has few pest and disease problems in the United States.

Propagation and Planting: Corms are planted and quickly multiply by sending out rhizomes. They can multiply quite impressively in a growing season—give them 1- to 2-inch spacing to allow plenty of room to grow. Water chestnut is rarely grown from seed, as it takes two years from seed to harvest.

Other Cultivation Information: Plants can be grown in pots in water gardens. The soil level of the pots should be 3–5 inches below the surface of the water. This technique can produce large amounts of corms in a small area. In tropical and subtropical areas they could be grown in artificial ponds, where they could be managed as perennials, leaving some corms each year to fill in the gaps left by those harvested. It is probably not a good idea to plant water chestnut in natural bodies of water, as it does spread rather rapidly and also sets viable seed.

Dr. Martin Price of ECHO suggests a novel form of hydroponic cultivation. Pack a kiddie pool tightly with pine needles. Work in some good fertilizer and dolomitic lime, transplant sprouted corms into the pool, and add water. After the foliage turns brown, the whole root mass can be removed in one piece. The chestnuts will all be at the bottom and can be easily harvested.

Water chestnuts are also commercially grown in paddy culture similarly to rice.

Harvest and Storage: Corms are ready to harvest two to three weeks after the foliage turns brown or is killed by frost. To store corms over the winter for later consumption or replanting, keep them in a cool, moist, dark place; they can last up to six

Crisp and sweet, water chestnuts are easily grown in water gardens.

months! Peeled chestnuts can be kept in water in the refrigerator for several weeks.

Uses: The roughly walnut-sized corms have a tough skin that should be peeled. The delicious flesh inside can be eaten raw in salads or on its own. Water chestnuts can be cooked (as they often are in stir-fries), but should be added toward the end of cooking so they remain crisp.

Related Species and Breeding Potential: There is hope for breeding hardy perennial water chestnuts, since some *Eleocharis* species are hardy to Zone 3 and lower, including many plants native to the United States and Canada, some of which have edible corms. The crop itself needs little breeding work, already being delicious and productive, and storing well.

Dioscoreaceae: The Yam Family

Dioscorea bulbifera • Air Potato

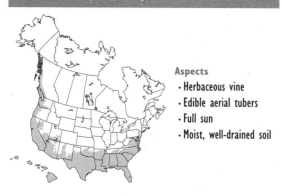

Aspects
- Herbaceous vine
- Edible aerial tubers
- Full sun
- Moist, well-drained soil

General Overview, History, and Ecology: Imagine walking out to your garden to harvest some root crops to roast up for dinner. You don't need to bring a shovel—the tubers you will be harvesting grow on trellised vines like starchy fruits, and with a twist of the wrist they can be picked and popped in your basket and brought inside. Along the vines of air potato, tubers form at the leaf axils, where the base of the leaf emerges from the stem of the vine. Air potatoes are an important garden crop in much of the world's tropics and subtropics, but they are rarely grown commercially. This is largely because they spread their yield over a period of four or five months, making them a bad choice for commercial farming, but an ideal garden plant. Their overall annual yields can be enormous: Some varieties can yield 17,000 pounds per acre, higher than the global average yield for potatoes! Using intensive growing practices, this could double, actually beating the U.S. potato yield as well. Keep in mind that this is all without any need to plow or dig the soil at all, although labor is still needed for trellising and frequent harvests, and the operation is less suited to mechanization than potatoes. Tropical vegetable expert Dr. Frank Martin writes in *Tropical Yams and Their Potential*, "the potential of *D. bulbifera* is undoubtedly in the home garden, where its health and vigor commend it for growth . . . The best Asian varieties of *D. bulbifera* merit collection, trial, and widespread distribution. Because of their potentially high yields, they should be magnificent producers of edible flesh and starch." Some varieties also form underground edible tubers.

Air potatoes seem to have been independently domesticated in Asia and Africa. The Asian varieties are round and have mild-tasting flesh, while those of African origin have sharp angles (making for more difficult preparation for eating) and varying degrees of bitterness. Individual aerial tubers of some Asian varieties can reach up to 2 pounds, with excellent yields for the vines overall. To my knowledge, these superior varieties have not yet been introduced to the United States.

Crop Description: Air potato is a vine growing 45 feet tall or higher. It loses its leaves every year, even in the tropics. The heart-shaped leaves are quite attractive, which has led to the poisonous varieties being used as ornamentals, facilitating their escape into the wild. Tubers grow in the leaf axils.

Climate: Air potato thrives in humid tropical and subtropical areas. It is hardy through Zones 7 or 8, and worth trying in much of the United States and coastal western Canada. It is apparently less likely to naturalize outside of the humid tropics and subtropics.

Tolerances and Preferences: Air potato tolerates many soils, but prefers good drainage. It loves organic matter in the soil. Some varieties require a long rainy season (or lots of irrigation in drier areas).

Naturalization Status: Air potato has naturalized in Florida, the Gulf Coast, and Hawaii. It is classed as a noxious weed in Florida and Alabama, where you need a permit to grow it. The edible types are reported to be less aggressive.

Pest, Disease, and Weed Problems: There are very few important pest problems. Some leaf spotting can occur late in the season, but this is usually just before the leaves drop anyway.

Propagation and Planting: Aerial tubers propagate air potato. These can be cut into smaller pieces, given a few days to heal up, and planted. Plants can also be grown from true seed, which germinates fairly well in cultivation.

Air Potato: An Ecological Conundrum?

Air potato is a unique perennial crop. Most perennial starch crops are roots that require digging. Digging to harvest root crops causes soil disturbance, and interrupts the natural soil-building process of the slow accumulation of leaves and other materials on the soil surface. Leaving soil undisturbed is one of the most important ecological benefits of perennial vegetables. Of course, not digging is good for the gardener's back as well as for the soil! Breadfruit, green bananas, and plantains also produce starchy "no-dig" staples, but air potato can be grown much farther north and has a superior storage life. I am not aware of any other crop with such potential.

However, mention air potato to many people in the southern United States and they bristle. Wild forms of air potato are grown as ornamentals. They have poisonous tubers and have aggressively naturalized in Florida and the Gulf Coast region (indeed, they can be found throughout the humid tropical and subtropical areas of the world). These vines grow 50 feet or more into trees, frequently smothering the preexisting vegetation. In fact, air potato has been declared a noxious weed in several states.

Edible types are reported to be much less aggressive. This may be because the tubers of edible types are consumed by wildlife when they fall to the forest floor, unlike the tubers of the ornamental poisonous types, which carpet the ground uneaten beneath the vines. Every air potato that is eaten by animals (or people) is one less that will start a new plant. If it turns out that edible air potatoes do in fact rapidly naturalize in areas where the wild forms do not yet exist, perhaps they should not be grown—but where the poison types are already rampant, there is certainly nothing to lose!

The issue of air potato invasiveness also begs the question of balancing the ecological benefits of developing a new form of perennial no-dig agriculture versus the concern of introducing new species to the environment. This crop has tremendous potential as a staple in a truly sustainable agriculture. To that end I propose a research agenda for citizen gardeners, nurseries, and interested university and government researchers:

1. Import superior clones of edible air potato.
2. Compare their aggressiveness and palatability to wildlife with naturalized poison types.
3. Experiment with methods for quarantined growing to minimize escape—such as growing on trellises in the middle of wide-open mowed areas with no trees in easy reach of sprawling vines.
4. Determine productivity under U.S. growing conditions.

If the best edible types (or some strains of them) show little tendency to escape, they should be widely planted and promoted. If they are somewhat aggressive, the water grows a bit murkier. Surely techniques can be developed to allow for productive harvests without allowing escape into new areas. And certainly in areas where air potato is already fully established, adding the weaker edible types cannot add to the problem, as they will be unable to compete in the wild.

Those criticizing the air potato would do well to wonder where their starches are coming from now, and consider the costs of fossil fuel use, pesticides, and loss of topsoil that go into grain and potato production. These "invisible costs" must be balanced against the potential role of naturalized edible air potato in the ecosystem. The dialogue on the pros and cons of planting nonnative species could be moved forward with a few good demonstrations (with permits where necessary) of the productive and sustainable starch production power of this remarkable crop—will you take up the challenge?

Air potato on "quarantined" trellis with mowed borders so it cannot escape into adjacent ecosystems.

The unique and remarkable air potato may be the world's only root crop that is picked like apples!

Other Cultivation Information: Air potato vines are enormous, and require something to grow on, be it trellises or trees. They will swamp trees less than 40 feet tall. A 6-foot-high trellis will allow for easy harvest, although ripe tubers fall to the ground eventually anyway.

Harvest and Storage: Aerial tubers can be picked like apples—when ripe, they will easily twist off. They can also be picked up off the ground, since they fall when they are ripe. Aerial tubers can be ready to harvest in as little as three months after planting. The harvest season can last four to five months. Immature potatoes can be picked but are less tasty. Air potatoes store well in a cool, dry, dark place. Underground tubers can be harvested when the foliage dies back.

Uses: The aerial tubers can weigh up to 2 pounds, although they are usually more apple-sized. The yellow flesh has a good texture, although not quite as rich a flavor as some related cultivated yams. According to Dr. Martin, the best varieties have soft, succulent flesh, and nice sweetness. Air potato tubers are cooked like any root crop. Remember that wild forms are poisonous and bitter. *Note:* In this case yellow flesh does not indicate the presence of beta-carotene (vitamin A).

Related Species and Breeding Potential: The agenda for air potato should be twofold: to introduce the best varieties, which have not yet been grown in the United States; and to work to breed hardier types, probably by crossing with *D. batatas* or *D. japonica*. Reduced weediness is also desirable. *Note:* Many other *Dioscorea* species have varieties that produce air potatoes (usually much smaller), including the tropical *D. alata*.

Dioscorea spp. · Yams

Synonyms
- See below

Aspects
- Herbaceous vines
- Edible tubers
- Full sun
- Moist, well-drained soil

Here in the United States and Canada, we are quite confused about the difference between yams and sweet potatoes. What we often call yams are actually sweet potatoes (*Ipomoea batatas*, see page 125). True *Dioscorea* yams tend to have white or yellow flesh and a more floury texture than sweet potatoes, and are not related to them. In the tropics, yams are a critically important staple food. In fact, they were domesticated independently in Southeast Asia, Africa, and South America. This is a huge genus of root crops with worldwide importance (about 60 species are used for edible tubers), yet yams have been largely neglected in the United States and Canada—perhaps because they are thought to be purely tropical. In fact many species are well adapted to the United States and even the more densely populated parts of Canada. It is only a matter of time until yams are more widely grown here, as new waves of immigrants who farmed in the tropics want to grow crops that are used in their cuisine. Everyone else should get on the bandwagon too!

Some types of yams produce multiple tubers,

enabling production as perennials. Others form large single tubers, but the top third can be removed and replanted—and yam tubers can be quite enormous, with some edible types weighing up to 20 pounds. Some species also produce yields of aerial tubers in their leaf axils like air potatoes.

No matter where you live, you can probably grow some species of yam. Gardeners in the tropical regions, plus the Gulf Coast, southern Texas, the low desert around Phoenix, and most of California have the mild winters and 10-month growing season necessary to grow some tropical and subtropical yams (with protection in Zone 8). The rest of us can grow Chinese yam and jinenjo, which are popular vegetables in Japan and China. Intriguing easier-to-harvest new varieties of Chinese yam may soon be available for your garden, perhaps priming an explosion of interest in the worldwide staple, which has been largely neglected here.

D. alata (White Yam, Greater Asiatic Yam, Ñame). This is a major cultivated tropical yam and one of the most important food crops in the world. There are a great many varieties with widely variable characteristics. The tubers can be truly enormous, up to 20 pounds. Some varieties also have multiple tubers per plant, making this a good choice for a tropical perennial root crop. Of course, perennialize single-tuber varieties by cutting off and replanting fist-sized chunks. Tubers start to form when day length shortens. Many varieties need a 10-month growing season, some up to 11. Some varieties have a vibrant purple tuber color, which is gorgeous when cooked. Some varieties form aerial tubers up to 2 inches by 4 inches. White yams are fully tropical, not tolerating frost while in leaf, but their roots will survive winter as long as the ground does not freeze. In my area tubers of this species can be purchased in grocery stores under the name ñames. It has naturalized in the warm southeastern United States.

D. batatas, D. opposita (Chinese Mountain Yam, Cinnamon Vine). This species is grown as a minor ornamental in the temperate and cold parts of the country. Meanwhile, in Japan 100,000 tons are produced annually for food production! It seems that we are missing out on a great opportunity.

There are several types, of which only one seems to be available here, known in Japanese as *nagaimo*. This type has long tubers that grow as single taproots growing straight down to 3–4 feet deep, making harvest a challenge. Roots are usually harvested after two to three years. The top portion of the root can be replanted after harvest. This type is least easily grown as a perennial.

The type known as *ichoimo* has multiple fan-shaped tubers, while *yamatoimo* produces multiple round tubers (this latter type was formerly sold here as *D. decaisneana*). Some *yamatoimo* varieties are not hardy.

Chinese yam does form aerial tubers, generally rather tiny, though sometimes in great quantity. There may be varieties with larger air potatoes.

The flowers have a strong and quite delightful cinnamon smell. Tubers of both *ichoimo* and *yamatoimo* store well, and may be available at Japanese grocery stores. This species has naturalized in much of the eastern and central United States.

D. esculenta (Asiatic Lesser Yam). This yam is not well known outside of tropical Asia, but it is a good choice for cultivation in the warmer parts of the United States. The somewhat thorny vines produce good yields of up to 20 round or heart-

The beautiful foliage of *Dioscorea alata*, the white yam.

shaped tubers. No aerial tubers are formed. This species has a 10-month growing season, meaning it can be grown as an annual as far north in California as the northern Central Valley, and perhaps as a perennial, with frost protection and a good microclimate.

D. japonica (Japanese Yam, Jinenjo, *Yama Na Imo*). This hardy species is very popular in Japan. The roots are productive and have a delectable flavor. The spring shoots are also eaten, like asparagus. It is as hardy to Zone 4 as *D. batatas*, but produces a cluster of sweet-potato-like roots at the base of the vines, rather than a difficult-to-harvest deep taproot like the types of *D. batatas* available here. This species is currently much less available than *D. batatas* and to make matters worse, I suspect that much of what is sold as *D. japonica* is actually mislabeled *D. batatas* or *D. opposita*. Jinenjo produces small aerial tubers. Jinenjo tubers might be available at Japanese grocery stores.

D. trifida (Cush Cush Yam). This is the major species of yam domesticated in South America, probably originating in what is now Guyana and Surinam in the tropical northeast of the continent. It produces large numbers of small tubers, and is considered to be adapted to warm temperate climates as long as they have a 10-month growing season. It is probably killed when the ground is frozen like other tropical yams. Cush cush yam is worthy of growing in the warmer parts of the United States. This species does not produce aerial tubers.

Crop Description: The species mentioned here are all herbaceous perennial twining vines. They die back in cold or dry seasons. Several species are cultivated as ornamentals for their attractive foliage.

Climate: See the individual species descriptions. Tropical yam species do not start to form tubers until days become shorter. Most of the tropical species listed here have 10-month growing seasons, which enables them to be grown either as annuals or as protected perennials in much of California and the coastal Southeast.

Tolerances and Preferences: All *Dioscorea* yams prefer deep, well-drained soils. They require higher fertility than most other root crops.

Naturalization Status: See the individual species descriptions.

Pest, Disease, and Weed Problems: When young, the plants do not cast much shade and do not compete well with weeds. Nematodes are often a problem, as are some insects and viruses. In Florida diseases often attack the leaves in fall, before the plants would naturally die back, but this does not seem to affect tuber yields.

Propagation and Planting: The easiest way to grow yams is to cut a fist-sized piece from a tuber and wait for it to sprout. Yams follow their own internal timer for sprouting, although cooler storage temperatures can slow them down. For the tropical species, which can be found in stores, you can buy a tuber, cut off a chunk to plant, and eat the rest. Many Asian and Latin grocery stores sell *D. alata*. Yams are rarely propagated by true seed, which tends to produce inferior tubers when seed is viable at all. Small tubers and aerial tubers (sometimes called bulbils) are planted. Cuttings are also used for some species.

Other Cultivation Information: All of the species listed here should be trellised for best production. Yams are often mounded to provide a deep, loose space for tubers to form.

Harvest and Storage: Tubers are dug when the foliage dies back, in cold or dry seasons. For those types with multiple tubers, some tubers can be left in the ground after harvest. This is also the best way to store yams. Otherwise tubers should be stored in a dry place. Once they start to sprout they spoil quickly. For types that form aerial tubers, just pick the bulbils like fruits, or gather them when they fall on the ground.

Uses: Tubers are sometimes enormous. They are boiled, fried, or baked, much like potatoes. The texture is more mealy or floury, with a mild flavor. Nutritionally, yams are high in starch and low in protein, although not as low as cassava.

Related Species and Breeding Potential: As mentioned above, there are at least 60 edible species. Numerous varieties exist of the cultivated types. Initial work should focus on obtaining interesting varieties, which have already been developed due to the hard work of small farmers over the last several thousand years. Certainly, for those of us in cold climates, obtaining good varieties of the hardy species is a priority.

Dryopteridaceae: The Wood-Fern Family

Matteuccia struthiopteris • Ostrich Fern

Synonyms
- *Matteuccia pensylvanica*
- *Onoclea struthiopteris*
- Fiddlehead fern

Aspects
- Running herb
- Edible shoots
- Part to full shade
- Moist to wet soil

General Overview, History, and Ecology: Every spring on the East Coast, from New England to New Brunswick, foragers go hunting along riverbanks and in floodplain forests for the shoots of this native fern, known as fiddleheads because their spiral shape looks like the head of a violin. These foragers harvest large quantities to sell to restaurants and supermarkets, where they bring a good price. Strangely, while many people grow this fern as an ornamental few home gardeners seem to grow it for fiddleheads.

In the wild, ostrich fern is found primarily in floodplain forests and riverbanks, but under cultivation it succeeds in a variety of moist, shady conditions. In fact, it is often so successful as to outcompete neighboring plants of similar size. It can even hold its own against the lower-growing but pernicious bishop's weed (*Aegopodium podagraria*).

The fiddleheads are ready for harvest in early spring. Ostrich ferns have a short edible harvest season, but serve the rest of the year as magnificent ornamentals. In ideal situations they can grow up to 6 feet high, and they can spread to carpet a wide area as a low-maintenance groundcover. This is a great example of a low-maintenance, edible native plant that for some reason is neglected as a naturalized crop plant.

Crop Description: Large, beautiful ferns up to 6 feet tall, these plants spread by rhizomes to form large colonies.

Climate: Ostrich ferns grow from the extremely cold Zone 2 through Zone 8.

Tolerances and Preferences: Ostrich ferns prefer part or full shade, although they can survive in full sun if they are in consistently moist soil. They prefer a fairly acid soil in the wild, but will survive in a wide range of garden soils.

Naturalization Status: This species has not naturalized outside of its native range.

Pest, Disease, and Weed Problems: Pests or diseases do not particularly trouble ostrich ferns.

Propagation and Planting: Division usually propagates these ferns. If you live in a cool temperate climate chances are you probably know someone who has plenty of extra plants they could dig up for you. They can also be grown from spores—if you would like to do so consult a book on fern growing, as the procedure is somewhat complicated. Plant 2–4 feet apart and allow them to fill in the gaps.

Harvest and Storage: Pick fiddleheads when they are still tightly curled in the crown of the fern in spring. They are still okay to harvest when they are a few inches tall, but they rapidly become tough and unpalatable.

Uses: Fiddleheads must be cooked for at least 10 minutes. They are eaten steamed, boiled, pickled, or served in omelets. They have a crisp texture

Fiddleheads emerging in spring.

and a nutty, wild flavor. Fiddleheads are often seen for sale in markets in New England in the springtime. They are even available frozen and canned!

Related Species and Breeding Potential: The fiddleheads of many ferns are eaten, but those of ostrich fern are considered the safest and most palatable eating. Bracken fern (*Pteridium aquilinium*) has recently been linked to stomach cancer and probably should be avoided. It would be interesting to see if there are ostrich ferns with superior flavor or productivity.

Euphorbiaceae: The Spurge Family

Cnidoscolus chayamansa • Chaya

Synonyms
- Spinach tree
- Mayan spinach

Aspects
- Shrub
- Edible leaves
- Full sun
- Dry to moist soil

General Overview, History, and Ecology: Throughout Mexico and Central America, this productive and nutritious woody leaf crop is an important vegetable. It grows wild from the Yucatan peninsula to the southern tip of Texas. Chaya bushes love heat, are drought-tolerant, and can sprout back from the roots following a frost, making this crop ideal for the hot, dry areas of the Southwest. Phoenix, take note! Chaya also can grow in hot, humid areas, and it is quite successful in Florida. The shrubs are hardy and robust, thriving in difficult conditions.

Chaya is a favorite perennial vegetable of Dr. Martin Price of ECHO. He says it has a finer texture than many leafy vegetables, and is convenient to use because the leaves are large, and, unlike many greens, do not reduce much in size when cooked.

This widely adaptable vegetable crop does have some drawbacks. Most types have stinging hairs like nettles, although 'Stingless' varieties are available. You should definitely only grow the 'Stingless' varieties. The other major drawback is that the leaves have cyanide in them. Many plants use cyanide to keep animals from eating them—for example, almonds have some cyanide in them. However, cooking the leaves for three minutes completely deactivates the cyanide, rendering it harmless. The leaves, once cooked, are very nutritious, being especially high in protein, calcium, iron, and vitamins A and C.

Crop Description: Chaya is a shrub growing up to 15 feet but usually kept smaller by pruning and harvesting. It has large, attractive maple-like leaves.

Climate: Chaya is tropical, but can shrug off light frosts. It is killed to the ground by hard frosts but quickly grows back, making it a good choice for a dieback perennial for the warmer parts of the United States. Stingless chaya would make a good container plant for colder areas. It loves heat and grows much more slowly in cold or cool temperatures.

Tolerances and Preferences: Chaya is fairly drought-tolerant, and according to most sources it does not like wet feet. It will grow in almost any soil. That

Chaya is a shrub with delicious edible leaves (which must be cooked before eating).

said, it produces more and tastier leaves when it is grown in fertile soil with plenty of moisture. It does need some supplemental nitrogen, but is mostly low-input. It will appreciate interplanting with nitrogen-fixing trees or an occasional top-dressing of compost or well-rotted manure.

Naturalization Status: Chaya is native to the southern tip of Texas (and south through Central America) but has not naturalized elsewhere in North America.

Pest, Disease, and Weed Problems: Chaya has very few pest problems, presumably due to the cyanide in the leaves. However, it has had some virus problems in Florida. Make sure to get virus-free stock, because starting with virus-free cuttings is the best means of prevention.

Propagation and Planting: As it rarely sets seed and is a clump-former, chaya is not at all an invasive threat. It is usually propagated from cuttings. Those taken from older wood are most successful. Cuttings should be 6–24 inches long and kept somewhat dry, as they are susceptible to rotting diseases at this stage.

Harvest and Storage: Most gardeners like to keep chaya at a good height for harvesting. Pick the leaves and shoots frequently or cut back to 2 feet or so and let it grow back—in hot weather this will happen quickly. The stinging varieties have an intense sting and are not recommended for planting. Avoid getting chaya sap on you when harvesting, as it can irritate the skin. If for some reason you are growing the stinging type, use gloves to harvest. Stinging types lose their sting when cooked, like stinging nettle.

Uses: The leaves are delicious and a good candidate for cooking since they do not shrink much. They are nutritious and have a good texture (not at all slimy, unlike many tropical perennial leaf crops). Most important is to remember that chaya must be cooked at least three minutes to turn the poison into gas. You can then eat the leaves and the water or sauce they were cooked in. A brief stir-frying is not enough to remove the cyanide—they really must be thoroughly cooked. Frying and boiling are the usual methods, but it can be cooked any way you would cook spinach. Chaya should never be eaten raw, although some people reportedly do so.

Related Species and Breeding Potential: Chaya could be crossed with hardier *Cnidoscolus* species (see below). Thankfully, nonstinging varieties are available. Breeding for reduced cyanide content would be nice.

Cnidoscolus spp. • Spurge Nettle, Bull Nettle

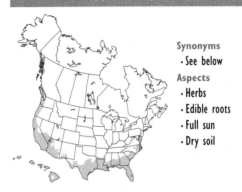

Synonyms
- See below

Aspects
- Herbs
- Edible roots
- Full sun
- Dry soil

These North American relatives of chaya are wild edibles with edible roots and terribly stinging leaves. Both produce large yields of sweet-potato-sized or larger roots, often buried deeply in sand. Little cultivation information is available because of the severity of the stinging leaves. Perhaps these species could be crossed with stingless chaya cultivars to develop new drought-tolerant root crops. The sting of these species is worse than that of ordinary nettles (*Urtica* spp.). *Note:* A few people have extreme allergic reactions to the stings of these plants. Be extremely cautious about introducing these plants to your garden or neighborhood. There are a number of other edible species in the genus, some of which are cultivated.

C. palmeri (Bull Nettle, Tread-Softly, Mala Mujer, Ortiguilla). This species is native to Baja California and the Mexican state of Sonora, and was once a staple of the Seri Indians. The roots can be harvested year-round. Wendy Hodgson describes the roots as "crisp and succulent" in *Food Plants of the Sonoran Desert*. They are probably only hardy to Zone 9. Adapted to desert life, it is worth trying in the warmer areas of Southern California and the hot, arid Southwest.

C. stimulosus (Spurge Nettle, Tread-Softly). This species produces excellent edible tubers. These roots grow up to 2 feet in size and are of excellent flavor. It is native to the southeastern United

States, in sandy areas, notably in dunes where tubers can be dug from the side of the dune without the harvester coming into contact with the stinging leaves. It could presumably be grown throughout the Southeast and elsewhere in Zone 8 as well, in well-drained or excessively well-drained soils.

Manihot esculenta • Cassava

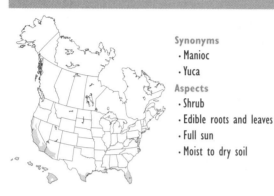

Synonyms
- Manioc
- Yuca

Aspects
- Shrub
- Edible roots and leaves
- Full sun
- Moist to dry soil

Cassava is an important world staple, and could be grown much more widely in the United States.
PHOTO BY CRAIG HEPWORTH.

General Overview, History, and Ecology: This root crop is a staple throughout the tropical world. Cassava was domesticated as much as 10,000 years ago somewhere in tropical Latin America, and was widespread through South and Central America and the Caribbean by 3,000 years ago. Cassava is processed into many products, like tapioca and flour for delicious *casabe* bread. The roots are large—longer but thinner than sweet potatoes, with dark woody bark and light flesh. When cooked, their flavor is sweet, bland, and slightly buttery. While filling, they are low in protein (2–3 percent) and most vitamins and minerals. The low protein is offset by the higher protein content (7 percent) of the cooked leaves, which are a popular vegetable in much of tropical West Africa.

Like the closely related leaf crop chaya, cassava roots and leaves have toxic cyanide content. In most cultivated varieties cooking deactivates cyanide. Certain "bitter" types are still grown in parts of Brazil and tropical Africa, by small farmers who know how to process roots to remove the toxicity and leave a delicious almond flavor. I would discourage readers from growing these varieties unless you have personal experience or a knowledgeable mentor to teach you the proper processing techniques.

Cassava roots are at their best yield and edibility between 9 and 12 months after planting. Smaller roots can be harvested sooner, and larger, woody roots (used for starch extraction) can be harvested later. The life of the shrub can be extended by carefully harvesting only a few roots at a time, leaving the remainder alive and intact. Some African cultivars reportedly yield in as little as three months' time: Importation of these varieties should be a priority for North American tropical crop enthusiasts. As a leaf crop it can be grown as a perennial for several years.

Crop Description: Cassava is a shrub that can grow up to 16 feet high, although it is usually shorter.

Climate: Cassava is a crop for the tropics and subtropics. It usually requires a nine-month growing season, although some short-season varieties exist.

Tolerances and Preferences: Cassava will grow in poor soils, and is somewhat drought-tolerant.

Naturalization Status: Cassava has naturalized in Hawaii and the Gulf states.

Pest, Disease, and Weed Problems: Cassava is susceptible to viral diseases—make sure to plant virus-free cuttings. The cyanide in uncooked roots and leaves discourages most insect pests, though you may have problems with scales and spider mites. Fungal blights can also be a problem (see page 50 for recommendations).

Propagation and Planting: Cassava is grown from stem cuttings. These should be used while fresh, within a few days of cutting. Whole cut branches can be kept viable in a shady place for up to three months.

Harvest and Storage: Most so-called root crops are actually tubers or corms—storage organs designed for long life and future growth. Cassava roots are actually roots and they continue breathing after harvest, giving them a shelf life of just a few days. Dig roots only as needed and use within a few days after harvest, or coat with wax for longer storage. Cassava roots also freeze well. Cassava leaves should be used or bagged and refrigerated quickly, like most leaf crops. Leaf harvest begins 50–70 days after planting.

Uses: Cassava leaves and roots should always be cooked to remove the cyanide. The roots can be cooked like any other root crop, and are particularly good mashed with butter. Cassava is often served with a garlic citrus sauce. The leaves are used like any cooked spinach.

Related Species and Breeding Potential: Farmers and researchers in the tropical world have developed many varieties. Importation of short-season varieties would be a boon to gardeners in warmer North American climates. *Manihot* is a large genus filled with edible (but often also toxic) species. A few species are considerably hardier, like *M. grahamii* (edibility unknown to me), which survives as a dieback perennial in Zone 7b. Experiments crossing cassava with various relatives should proceed with great caution, as many are extremely poisonous.

Sauropus androgynous • Katuk

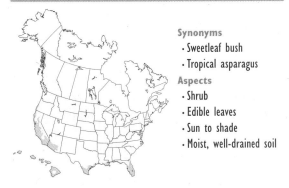

Synonyms
- Sweetleaf bush
- Tropical asparagus

Aspects
- Shrub
- Edible leaves
- Sun to shade
- Moist, well-drained soil

General Overview, History, and Ecology: In the sweltering heat of tropical Malaysia, Indonesia, and India, the katuk shrub is a common sight in gardens. It is little known elsewhere in the world, but with luck it will be widely considered as one of the finest perennial leaf crops for the tropics. Tropical vegetable expert Dr. Frank Martin rates katuk highly, due to its year-round production, flavor, yields, and nutrition. The flavor of katuk leaves resembles a mild blend of green peas and peanut.

Giving katuk plenty of water and manure or rich compost, along with a bit of shade, will create extra-long, tender shoots for eating. These are now marketed as tropical asparagus, and are becoming a commercial crop in Hawaii.

Katuk is well suited to growing in the shade of fruit and nut trees like coconuts, papayas, and breadfruit. In fact it produces its best crops in partial shade. It has potential as a dieback perennial in the warmest parts of the continental United States, where it might be grown in the shade of avocados and citrus, and in the company of pomegranates.

Note: At one time consumption of large amounts of raw katuk juice was a weight loss fad in Japan. This caused lung damage and limb pain in some people. While it has been a staple vegetable in its native range for centuries, katuk should not be juiced and should probably not be eaten in excessive quantities frequently.

Crop Description: Katuk is a lanky shrub, which grows up to 12 feet high but is usually kept trimmed to 3–6 feet.

Climate: Katuk is ideal for the hot, humid tropics, originating as a tropical rain forest understory species. It is killed to the ground by frost, but will resprout if the ground does not freeze. Like many of the tropical plants mentioned here, it is worth trying with protection in South Florida, the Gulf Coast, and coastal Southern California. It is a great crop for lowland Hawaii. Katuk is also worth trying as a container plant.

Tolerances and Preferences: Katuk prefers light shade, but grows in full sun or shade too. The plants should have a rich soil with high organic matter, so use lots of compost. It prefers mulch and likes good drainage. Katuk plants grown in consistently moist soils will yield better, more tender leaves.

Naturalization Status: Katuk has not naturalized here.

Katuk is a shrub with leaves that taste like pea-nuts and green peas. Also see the photo of a katuk hedge on page 51.

Pest, Disease, and Weed Problems: Diseases and insects are seldom a problem. During "chilly" winters in Florida it goes dormant, and is sometimes attacked by some pests and diseases while in that state. Slugs can be a problem with small cuttings and seedlings.

Propagation and Planting: Propagation is by seeds or cuttings. Seed may take several months to germi-nate, and only fresh seeds should be used, as they are not viable for long. Katuk takes well from cuttings.

Other Cultivation Information: Katuk grows too tall and falls over if not cut back. Regular pruning or harvesting keeps it at a more manageable size and also keeps greens in easy reach for harvest. Katuk is often grown as a hedge; plant shrubs at 4-inch spacing for this purpose.

Harvest and Storage: Katuk greens and shoots are cut and used fresh. Like most greens they do not last long once cut. Young leaves can be harvested year-round.

Uses: The leaves and young shoots of katuk have a strong nutty or pea-like flavor. These can be eaten raw in moderation, but older leaves should be cooked. Steamed katuk is particularly good. Katuk contains 6–10 percent protein and is high in vitamins A and C. Tender "tropical asparagus" shoots are especially flavorful. Apparently the flowers and fruits are also edible.

Related Species and Breeding Potential: It seems that katuk is already a fine vegetable and in little need of breeding work. In Asia many varieties are available, with variable leaf color and plant habit.

Fabaceae: The Pea Family

Apios americana • Groundnut

Synonyms
- Potato bean

Aspects
- Climbing herb
- Edible tubers
- Sun to part shade
- Moist to wet soil

General Overview, History, and Ecology: Groundnut is a wild edible native to eastern North America, often found with its vines sprawling in thickets and areas with moist or wet soils. The tubers were an important staple of many Native American groups in the region. Apparently Native people would transplant tubers into suitable habitats near their settlements, where the plants would naturalize and be managed in semi-cultivated stands. Groundnut was probably carried far outside of its native range in this fashion. Without groundnut tubers, early European colonists in New England would probably not have survived their first few winters. Like many minor and wild crops, groundnuts were introduced to France and cultivated there for a time but did not catch on. In the past decade, researchers at Louisiana State University and Southwest Louisiana University have collected plants from all over eastern North America. They crossed the best of these plants and developed improved varieties with larger, easier-to-harvest tubers. Some of their variet-

The tubers of groundnut are high in protein, and grow like walnuts on a string.

ies can yield 8 pounds in a single long Louisiana growing season. The groundnut seems poised to become an important new vegetable crop.

The tubers of groundnut are unusual. They grow like walnuts on a string, often with 6 inches or more between tubers. The tubers may be situated some significant distance from the crown of the plant. Tubers of wild plants grow as large as an egg. The improved varieties have tubers that grow closer together, and sometimes they are fused into a single larger tuber. These tubers contain 16 percent protein—three times that of potatoes. When cooked their flavor is like a mildly earthy, nutty potato, although they are admittedly somewhat dry and mealy if not prepared properly.

Groundnuts take a few years to become established. In cold, short-season climates they require two or even three years to achieve a good yield. However, once they get going the vines become very vigorous, swamping nearby shrubs and growing in thick tangles. They fix nitrogen, which provides them with the energy to outcompete less vigorous plants. The easiest way to grow groundnuts is to naturalize them in a suitable area, just as Native Americans have for centuries. Find an area with moist or even wet soil and plant the tubers near something they can climb on, like some wild shrubs. Give them a few years' time and then come dig tubers from part of the patch every fall. Alternatively, plants can be grown on a trellis. Trellis production is especially useful in the humid South, where tubers mature much more rapidly.

Crop Description: Groundnuts are herbaceous vines growing 4–8 feet tall.

Climate: Groundnuts will grow in hot, humid areas but not in the true tropics. They apparently require some winter chilling. They are extremely cold-hardy as well, being hardy to Zone 3.

Tolerances and Preferences: Groundnuts will grow in full sun or partial shade. They produce best in rich soils, although they do fix nitrogen and can grow in poor soils. Soils should be moist, and can be fairly wet, but must be well drained. Plants will tolerate quite acidic soils—wild groundnuts are a major weed in highly acidic cranberry bogs.

Naturalization Status: Native to the eastern and central United States and Canada, groundnuts have not naturalized elsewhere.

Pest, Disease, and Weed Problems: Groundnuts can have minor problems with nematodes in the Deep South.

Propagation and Planting: Division propagates most groundnuts. Transplant an entire string of tubers or cut them into individual tubers. If the strings are cut at any time other than the fall, the tubers will go dormant for a season. Plants can also be grown from cuttings. Growing groundnuts from seed is challenging, as many plants do not set viable seed. If you do get seed, be prepared for slow germination (10 to 30 days). Pinch back seedlings and young cuttings so they don't twine all over one another. Plant groundnuts 1 foot apart.

Other Cultivation Information: Plants need a trellis, a shrub to climb on, or plenty of room to sprawl on the ground.

Harvest and Storage: Tubers can be harvested year-round. They store best in the ground. They can also be stored indoors in plastic bags in a moist, dark place. If they are allowed to dry out they will die. They can remain viable for a surprisingly long time in a plastic bag in the fridge.

Uses: Groundnut tubers for eating must be cooked. LSU breeders describe their flavor as one somewhere between potato and boiled peanut, with a texture that is mealier then potatoes (closer to *Dioscorea* yams to my taste). They can be used in any way you would use a potato.

Related Species and Breeding Potential: The breeding goal of LSU researchers was plants with higher yields, larger tubers, and tubers closer together on the rhizome. After crosses from diverse plants, they found some with edible nontuberous roots, some with fused tubers, some with both tubers and roots, and some with just inedible rhizomes. The wide variation in wild plants offers much breeding promise. Surprisingly, some traits are not passed on vegetatively—plants grown from tubers with close spacing on the rhizome are often not as closely spaced. There are two other species with edible tubers, *A. priceana* and *A. fortunei*. Eurasia has a similar species with smaller tubers, the earthnut pea (*Lathyrus tuberosus*). The yields are smaller and the vines less aggressive. According to Ken Fern of Plants for a Future, earthnut pea is worthy of improvement through breeding. In my experience, though, earthnut pea is currently not worth growing as anything more than a novelty vegetable.

Erythrina edulis • Basul

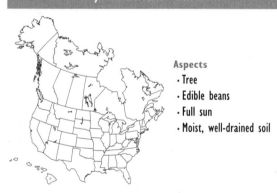

Aspects
- Tree
- Edible beans
- Full sun
- Moist, well-drained soil

This remarkable tree can produce up to 500 pounds of protein-rich beans every year. It is a fantastic perennial vegetable, but unfortunately prefers a cool tropical climate in which to grow. Thus, in all of the United States and Canada it will probably only find ideal conditions in upland Hawaii. However, in Ecuador it tolerates a bit of frost, and grows in hotter lowland areas too, so adventurous gardeners should give it a try in Southern California and even Florida and see what happens. Basul is only semi-domesticated, but is being developed as an improved crop by scientists in Colombia and elsewhere. With breeding work, and within the limited climate it is suited for, it could become a major perennial protein staple crop.

Basul bears very large bean pods, up to a foot long, with beans over an inch across inside. The beans are cooked and served as a side dish or used in other ways. They should always be cooked—if boiled, for at least 45 minutes, or thoroughly fried. Think of them as lima beans that grow on a tree, as they are used the same way. The flowers are also edible.

Trees are easily propagated by seed, cuttings, or just cutting thick branches and sticking them in the ground. They are very thorny and make a good living fence. The trees fix nitrogen and are fast growing. Basul trees cannot tolerate heavy or frequent frosts. They are not picky about soil but prefer full sun. Basul has great potential as an edible nitrogen-fixing tree for polyculture systems in the upland tropics.

There are more heat-tolerant *Erythrina* species, but many are poisonous and none have edible seeds. Proceed in breeding with caution!

Lablab purpureus • Hyacinth Bean

Synonyms
- Dolichos lablab
- Lablab bean
- Chicharo

Aspects
- Climbing herb
- Edible pods and beans
- Edible greens and flowers
- Edible tubers
- Full sun
- Moist to dry soil

Many gardeners have grown hyacinth beans as ornamentals for their beautiful flowers and attractive pods. But lablab beans are also a fine food plant, and have been cultivated for centuries. It is believed these plants were introduced to Africa from Southeast Asia in the eighth century. The young pods are eaten, and have a sweet flavor like green peas. The ripe seeds can be cooked as dry beans. The flowers, young leaves, and tubers

Hyacinth beans are an outstanding choice for the edible landscape.

are also edible. While sometimes the pods are a bit fibrous for my taste and have minor toxicity problems, this crop is incredibly productive even in my Massachusetts garden and is worthy of further breeding work.

Not all hyacinth beans are perennial. Annual strains are known as variety 'Typica', while perennials are 'Lignosa'. Many forms from Northeast Africa are perennial. Even perennial types are short-lived, usually having a productive life of about three years. Hyacinth beans are grown like pole beans. Build a large trellis because they can grow up to 18 feet tall!

Plants are killed by frost, but could be tried with protection in the warmer areas of the United States. Hyacinth beans love heat and humidity, but also tolerate drought. They will bear well in full sun or light shade. This species has naturalized in Hawaii and the eastern United States.

Some references treat hyacinth bean as a toxic plant, though it has been grown as a food for millennia. The dry seeds contain toxins that are deactivated by cooking. The pods also should be thoroughly cooked. Several sources recommend discarding the cooking water or even boiling in several changes of water.

Neptunia oleracea • Water Mimosa

Synonyms
- Pakkrachet

Aspects
- Aquatic floating herb
- Edible leaves
- Full sun to part shade
- Aquatic to wet soil

Picture a bunch of marshmallows skewered on the same stick, with feathery leaves that close up when lightly touched. Water mimosa is an aquatic plant that produces its own flotation devices, which truly resemble marshmallows. Pink nodules for nitrogen fixation adorn the roots between the marshmallow segments. The leaves are typical of sensitive-plant-type mimosas, beautiful and delicate. They are also delicious, with a nutty cabbage flavor, and can be eaten raw or cooked. This most unusual vegetable is cultivated in Southeast Asia, and grown here occasionally as an ornamental water garden plant.

Water mimosa grows exceedingly well in my water garden. Apparently it will thrive in a short season as long as there is enough heat. It is high

Surely one of the most unique vegetables, water mimosa provides its own flotation devices so it can float on top of your edible water garden.

in protein, easy to grow, productive, beautiful, and a great conversation starter in the garden.

This crop is tropical (hardy in Zone 9) but can be overwintered indoors in an aquarium. Water mimosa can occasionally be found for sale in Asian markets, and this material could be purchased for planting.

Water mimosa is grown as an emergent floater (see page 64). Plants can be anchored and rooted in a pot, or they can float freely. It apparently also will grow in wet soils. This crop needs full sun to part shade. Water mimosa is propagated quite easily by dividing the plants at the nodes—although it can also be grown from seed if you can acquire any.

Though water mimosa has not naturalized in the United States or Canada, it is apparently very aggressive in tropical waterways. Grow it with caution in areas with minimal frost.

There is a species in the same genus native to the southeastern United States, which is not reported to be edible but could have interesting breeding potential.

Phaseolus spp. · Perennial Beans

Synonyms
- *P. coccineus*—Scarlet runner bean, runner bean
- *P. lunatus*—Lima bean
- *P. polyanthus*—Cache bean, botil

Aspects
- Climbing herbs
- Edible pods and beans
- Full sun
- Soils variable; see below

General Overview, History, and Ecology: The annual common bean (*Phaseolus vulgaris*) is among the most important food crops in the world. It is the source of most of the green beans we eat, as well as kidney beans, black beans, and many other dry beans. The common bean was domesticated as many as six different times in different areas of Central and South America, where many other species of *Phaseolus* were also domesticated, including several perennials. While not especially

hardy, they are fine candidates for cultivation in warm areas of the Southeast and West Coast. All can be grown as annuals as well.

I didn't actually believe lima beans were perennial until I viewed the '7 Year' lima variety at ECHO in Florida. ECHO received this variety from Zimbabwe, where it has been selected for performance in arid climates. It grows as a dense vining groundcover, and is very productive. Apparently in Zimbabwe it is usually trellised onto the roofs of houses to keep the foliage from being eaten by goats. They were largely defoliated by diseases when I viewed the plants after an unusually wet summer, but apparently they spring right back from that sort of damage and are a long-lived, resilient perennial food crop. '7 Year' lima would be a fantastic candidate for the warmer areas of Texas, the Southwest, and inland Southern California.

I have also read accounts of runner beans living for 20 years or more in England. So, believe it or not, there really are perennial beans! They play an important role in the perennial vegetable garden as one of the few really good sources of protein. And they can be crossed with one another, with annual common beans, and with hardy edible perennial relatives! Congratulations to those gardeners living where these beans can be grown as perennials. For the rest of us, there is an opportunity for backyard breeders to develop some important new crops.

P. coccineus (Runner Bean, Scarlet Runner Bean). Runner beans are largely grown as ornamentals in the United States and Canada. In Britain, however, they are the most popular species grown for green beans. Their tubers can survive soil temperatures down to 23°F, making them slightly hardier than the other perennial beans. After the first year they produce earlier in the season, but with less heavy production. Plants in Britain have been known to live 20 years and longer. Green beans can be produced in a very short season, but to produce dry beans you will need from 115 to 120 frost-free days. They can produce reasonably well in partial shade. Generally runner beans have few pest problems compared with common beans (*P. vulgaris*), although they are vulnerable to slugs in spring. In addition to the use of the young pods as green beans, runner beans are also used like shell beans (the green seeds are eaten cooked and fresh), and they make a good dry bean for cooking. The flowers, young leaves, and tubers are also edible when cooked. Climbing varieties of runner bean are perennial, and bush types are annual.

P. lunatus (Lima Bean). Traces of lima beans that are 8,000 years old have been found in Peru, attesting to the history of use of this tasty bean. Like runner beans, the climbing types are perennial, and bush forms are annual. Climbers are also more productive. Perennial types usually have a productive life of about four years. The young pods are used like green beans. The fresh green seeds are the most commonly used part in the United States and Canada. The dry beans are also edible. All of these parts must be cooked before being eaten.

P. polyanthus (Cache Bean, Botil). This species is little known outside of Mexico and Central America. Cache bean plants will live for two to four years. Cache bean is primarily grown for the green seeds (like lima beans, edamame, or butter beans) but also are edible as a dry bean. This species naturally hybridizes with *P. vulgaris* and *P. coccineus.*

Crop Description: All three species are herbaceous perennial vines, although there are some annual bush varieties of lima and runner beans. After the first year they send multiple shoots from a clump, with vines growing as much as 15 feet long.

Climate: These three species share some traits in

A sampling of the many diverse varieties of runner beans. PHOTO BY BROCK DOLMAN.

common. All are hardy to roughly Zone 9, and with mulch and a protective microclimate are worth trying in Zone 8 or even 7. All should be inoculated with standard legume inoculants before planting to make sure they will be able to fix nitrogen. The tubers of runner beans can be brought in and stored over the winter in colder climates. You could try bringing in root crowns of the other species as well. They can also all be grown as annuals in cold climates.

Tolerances and Preferences: Perennial beans prefer a rich garden soil, sufficient moisture, and full sun or light shade.

Naturalization Status: Scarlet runner and lima beans have naturalized in the eastern and southeastern United States. Cache beans are not reported in the United States or Canada.

Pest, Disease, and Weed Problems: The pests and diseases that attack common beans also attack these species, although perennial beans are generally more resistant. Mexican bean beetles, for instance, can be problematic; control by hand-picking or spray neem, rotenone, or pyrethrum.

Propagation and Planting: All three species are easily grown from seed. Propagate runner beans by dividing tubers—it is likely the others can be propagated by division as well.

Other Cultivation Information: All three species are essentially grown like annual pole beans. They should be trellised or given something to climb on.

Harvest and Storage: If you keep picking the green beans they will keep bearing heavily. Otherwise the pods will dry out and produce mature dry beans.

Uses: Perennial beans contribute important protein to the perennial vegetable garden. They can be used in all the same ways you would used common beans, including any recipe for green beans, shell beans, or dry beans. See individual species for more information.

Related Species and Breeding Potential: These perennial beans are all good crops just as they are. All cross with one another and with *P. vulgaris*, the common or kidney bean. Gardeners in the tropics, subtropics, and mild West Coast areas might want to breed for flavor, productivity, and adaptation to local conditions.

As for those of us in colder climates, what we

need are hardy perennial beans. The 'White Dutch' runner bean offered in the Seed Savers Exchange catalog is said to be hardier than most types. There may be other hardy varieties of any of these three species. The East Coast native *P. polystachios* is hardy in the wild to at least Zone 6 and already has edible, if tiny, beans and pods. Attempts to hybridize it with the species listed here should be a priority for backyard breeders in colder areas.

Gardeners in the arid Southwest might want to cross with the wild native perennial edible *P. metcalfei* or annual cultivated tepary beans (*P. acutifolius*) to develop a highly drought-tolerant perennial bean. The '7 Year' lima would be a particularly good choice for this.

Psophocarpus tetragonobolus • Winged Bean

Synonyms
- Goa bean
- Asbin
- Ku-bemya

Aspects
- Climbing herb
- Edible pods and beans
- Edible greens and flowers
- Edible tubers
- Full sun
- Moist, well-drained soil

General Overview, History, and Ecology: Winged bean is a remarkable vegetable. The pods, beans, young leaves and shoots, flowers and flowerbuds, and tuberous roots are all edible. Probably domesticated in tropical Africa or Asia, they are a very important home garden vegetable throughout tropical Asia, Africa, and the Caribbean. Although winged beans are tropical, the recent availability of 'Day Length Neutral' varieties permits them to be widely grown as annuals.

The young pods are eaten like green beans, and are both productive and delicious. They are larger than green beans, and are tender and good up to about 8 inches in length. As the name implies, they have four "wings," or flanges, running down their length. A bit later the unripe seeds can be used like lima beans. The dried seeds are quite versatile, and nutritionally are similar to soybeans, but

are small and are not produced in great quantity. They are roasted, like peanuts, or used to make bean milk, tofu, and tempeh.

The young leaves (the top three sets of leaflets on a shoot) are cooked as greens. Unlike many other beans, these greens do not constitute a minor crop but are actually quite good in their own right. In smaller quantities they can be eaten raw, but too many raw leaves can cause dizziness, nausea, and flatulence—so it's probably best to cook them! The flowers are also edible, and actually taste something like sweet mushrooms.

The tuberous roots are another important crop, and can be eaten fresh or cooked. They contain 20–25 percent protein. Some varieties do not form tubers.

The vigorous vines are among the world's most effective nitrogen-fixers. Anyone in the tropics should certainly plant a few winged beans in their garden to enjoy the multiple benefits of this extremely useful crop. Northern gardeners can now enjoy experimenting with 'Day Length Neutral' varieties as annuals.

Crop Description: Winged bean is a perennial climbing legume, resembling annual pole beans. They reach about 12 feet in height. Plants die back to the ground annually, and are considered short-lived perennials.

Climate: Winged bean is a crop of the hot, humid tropics. Foliage is killed by frost, but as long as the roots do not freeze the plant will resprout. Most varieties are at their northern limit in South Florida due to day-length restrictions, although 'Day Length Neutral' varieties are available. I have tried to grow the day-length-neutral selections several times in Massachusetts, and have gotten poor yields (unlike lablab beans, which sprawl like kudzu!). It may be that with season extension and pampering they would produce well here, but my hunch is that they are better suited to longer, warmer summers.

Tolerances and Preferences: Winged beans thrive in a variety of soils, but are somewhat drought-sensitive. Grow them in full sun.

Naturalization Status: Winged beans have not naturalized in the United States or Canada.

Pest, Disease, and Weed Problems: Winged beans have few insect pest problems. However, nema-

The remarkable winged bean has edible pods, seeds, flowers, leaves, and roots!

in order for them to germinate. They should be scraped or nicked with a knife, rubbed with sandpaper, or rubbed on a rough surface like cement or bricks. They can then be soaked overnight or planted right away. If they have not sprouted within a week or two, dig them up, scratch them harder, and try again.

Other Cultivation Information: To grow winged beans for pod or leaf production, plants should be trellised. For continual heavy pod production you should top-dress with aged manure or fertilizer every two to three weeks.

If your main goal is the edible tubers, do not trellis the plants; instead, let them sprawl on the ground. For best tuber production flowers should be removed by hand.

Harvest and Storage: Plants will produce edible pods in about 60 days, but require 180 frost-free days to ripen seed. Leaving tubers out to dry for a few days after harvest makes them easier to peel.

Uses: The young pods (8 inches) are used like green beans. After that stage, they can be used as shell beans, and the dry beans are also used. The cooked young leaves can be eaten, as well as the mushroom-flavored flowers. Winged bean tubers are used like potatoes. Once you plant winged beans you probably won't have to go to the grocery store for a while!

Related Species and Breeding Potential: Winged bean is already a fantastic perennial vegetable for the tropics. Day-length-neutral selections are available and expand its growing range northward. Little is left for breeders to do but make tastier and more disease-resistant types. It would also be worthwhile to breed for better dry bean production.

Note: An annual legume with pods that resemble winged bean is grown in Europe. This species, known as asparagus pea (*Lotus tetragonobolus*), should not be confused with winged bean.

todes can be a serious problem. Many fungal diseases can be problematic too, including leaf spot and powdery mildew.

Propagation and Planting: Winged beans are grown from seed. Germination is somewhat tricky. The seeds have a tough coat that needs to be scarified

Lamiaceae: The Mint Family

Stachys affinis • Chinese Artichoke

Synonyms
- *Stachys sieboldii*
- Japanese artichoke
- Crosnes
- Choro-gi

Aspects
- Running herb
- Edible tubers
- Full sun to part shade
- Rich, well-drained soil

General Overview, History, and Ecology: Chinese artichoke is a mint relative that can spread to form large colonies. When you dig up the tangled "turf" of fuzzy leaves and stems, you find little (1–2 inch) white tubers like alien seashells, ready to be picked out of the ground. On closer inspection they have an unfortunate resemblance to fat, segmented grubs. Their flavor and texture are thankfully not grub-like. In fact, Chinese artichoke tubers have a delightful crisp texture and a mildly sweet flavor. Chinese artichokes were domesticated in Japan and China, and became popular in France, where they are still grown as a minor root crop.

While they can persist without care as a dense groundcover for years, Chinese artichokes produce their highest yields if harvested annually. Just leave a few or replant them with 8-inch spacing between the tubers. They can be quite productive when grown in this fashion. Think carefully before you plant them, because they are likely to come back for years even if you swear you dug them all out.

Crop Description: Chinese artichokes are running perennials, forming a 12- to 18-inch high carpet.

Climate: Chinese artichokes can be grown from Zone 5 (or colder) through Zone 9, and can handle intense summer heat. They can also be grown in the tropics as a cool-season annual.

Tolerances and Preferences: Chinese artichokes will grow in full sun or light shade. They grow best in rich garden soils.

Naturalization Status: At the present time Chinese artichokes have only naturalized in the state of New York.

Pest, Disease, and Weed Problems: Chinese artichoke is quite resistant to most pests and diseases, and can hold its own even against quack grass (*Agropyron repens*). Sometimes mice and voles develop a taste for the tubers.

Propagation and Planting: Propagation is usually by division or by planting tubers. Apparently the plants can also be grown from seed. Set out plants 8 inches apart.

Harvest and Storage: In cold climates, dig up the tubers when the plants are killed back by frost. Otherwise allow five to seven months for them to mature.

Roasted Root Vegetables

This flexible recipe can be used with virtually any of the root crops profiled in this book, including Chinese artichoke, oca, arrowhead, sunchoke, yacon, achira or canna tubers, sweet potato, yams, groundnuts, mashua, and potatoes. You can also add other fruits and vegetables like carrots, parsnips, rutabaga, turnips, whole garlic cloves, quartered onions, big chunks of winter squash, and fat quince slices.

    4 pounds root crops in 1-inch cubes
    Olive oil
    Rosemary
    Chili flakes

Simply cut the root crops to roughly 1-inch chunks (quicker-cooking species like onions can be in larger chunks). Add olive oil and spices, and stir until all roots are lightly coated in oil. Put in a layer no deeper than 2–3 inches in large baking dishes and cover with tinfoil. Bake at 425°F for about 1 hour (until tender). Then remove tinfoil and stir, and return to oven for about 5 to 10 minutes until golden brown. Serve warm. Serves 8.

Uses: The raw tubers make a pleasant snack. They can be cooked in a variety of ways, but don't cook them for too long or they will lose their crisp texture, which is their best feature.

Related Species and Breeding Potential: Selecting for larger tubers would help make this vegetable more popular and easier to harvest and process. There are also many native edible *Stachys* species, including *S. palustris*, *S. floridanum*, and *S. hyssopifolia*. These might be used to develop hybrids that are especially well adapted to local conditions.

Note: The Livingstone potato (*Plectranthus esculentus*) and Sudan potato (*P. rotundifolius*) are also perennial Mint family root crops. Both are ancient domesticates from tropical Africa, very low-maintenance tropical crops, and unfortunately in danger of being lost. The Livingstone potato is 13 percent protein! They are very difficult for gardeners in the United States and

The edible tubers of Chinese artichoke are crisp and sweet.

Canada to acquire, but would be a worthy challenge to import. Getting them in cultivation here could help preserve this important legacy for the future.

Liliaceae: The Lily Family

Asparagus officinalis • Asparagus

Aspects
- Clumping herb
- Edible shoots
- Full sun
- Moist, well-drained soil

General Overview, History, and Ecology: Ah, the most famous perennial vegetable of all. Every spring we remember the taste of real, fresh asparagus from the garden. The flavor deteriorates rapidly after harvesting, and, like sweet corn, this is a vegetable truly worth growing in your garden because spears from the supermarket will never be as good.

There is a reason why so many plant descriptions in this book say, "used like asparagus."

Asparagus is the archetypal example of a plant with edible shoots. Native throughout much of Eurasia, asparagus has been cultivated for at least 2,000 years. No doubt it was used as a wild edible long before that, as the naturalized wild seedlings are still used here today.

Asparagus is the model of what other perennial vegetables could become with proper breeding and good care. Although growing the highest-quality spears requires some labor, and plants are subject to problems from pests, weed, and diseases, asparagus shoots fresh-cut from the garden and cooked up are one of the most sublime vegetables on the planet. Mature plantings yield for 10 to 15 years or longer, and each year's harvest can last about two months.

Modern asparagus varieties are male hybrids, which live longer and yield better. An additional benefit of male plants is that they do not produce seeds. Female asparagus will make for a weed problem of little asparagus seedlings in your garden and your neighborhood.

In addition to the traditional delicious green varieties, there are also several beautiful purple

Asparagus is the classic perennial vegetable—long lived, productive, and delicious.

varieties. White asparagus is not a particular variety but the result of blanching. It is not necessary to blanch asparagus, but if you want even more tender white spears, cover the plants with soil or mulch, or set up temporary black plastic polytunnels.

Crop Description: Mature asparagus plants have feathery foliage. The tops of the plants are often referred to as *ferns*. Female plants produce small, hard red berries.

Climate: Asparagus is extremely hardy, growing north to Zone 3. It will grow quite far south as well. Asparagus requires an annual rest period, either from cold or drought. The hot, humid areas of central and South Florida, the Gulf Coast, and southeastern Texas are all too hot and humid for asparagus, but it can be grown in tropical and subtropical areas as long as there is a substantial dry season to induce dormancy.

Tolerances and Preferences: Asparagus is a weed that has naturalized in many areas of the United States and Canada. It grows wild along roadsides and in other disturbed areas, but for best production plants should be babied. Provide your asparagus with rich, well-drained soil. Plants should receive annual applications of compost or well-rotted manure. Soils should be kept close to pH 7. Use lime if necessary. Asparagus should be well watered all season long, including after shoot season is over.

Naturalization Status: Asparagus has naturalized in much of North America.

Pest, Disease, and Weed Problems: Asparagus has trouble with all three. The asparagus beetle and spotted asparagus beetle can cause serious damage, as can the asparagus aphid. Row covers and rotenone can prevent beetle damage. Many diseases affect asparagus, including rotting and wilting from *Fusarium*, as well as asparagus rust and needle blight, which defoliate the plants. Disease problems can be minimized by planting resistant varieties and by removing all foliage in the fall after it dies back. Weed problems can be severe as well, because the feathery foliage of the "ferns" casts little shade. If you have female plants, the seedlings themselves can become quite weedy. A good layer of mulch helps both kinds of weed problems.

Propagation and Planting: Most gardeners buy asparagus crowns. Plants can also be grown from seed. Allow four to five weeks for germination. Seed-grown plans will include males and females. You may want to eventually rogue out the females, because they will produce weedy seedlings. The females will be the ones that produce red berries in the fall.

Other Cultivation Information: Planting asparagus properly is time consuming, but doing it right will give you great benefits down the road. Remember that asparagus plants can yield for 10 to 15 years or more. Prepare the soil well and amend richly with compost or well-rotted manure. Make sure the pH is close to 7. Then plant the crowns 6–8 inches deep. Fill in above them with about 2 inches of soil. As the shoots grow, add more soil, making sure not to bury the shoot tips. The first season, don't harvest any shoots. You can pick a bit the second season, and more the third. Only pick the largest shoots from young plants.

Asparagus plants should not be crowded too close together. They should be set at least 8–14 inches apart within rows, with the rows spaced 3–5 feet apart. Overcrowding causes lower yields and thinner spears.

Harvest and Storage: To harvest asparagus, cut or snap spears off by hand at ground level. Asparagus does not store well, and is at its best when brought right from the garden to the kitchen.

Uses: Asparagus is, well, used like asparagus. Shoots can be eaten raw or cooked in a variety of ways, particularly steaming and boiling. Fresh boiled asparagus with butter is about as good as a vegetable gets.

Related Species and Breeding Potential: Disease and insect resistance are key areas to focus breeding. Because asparagus is such an important commercial crop, professional breeders have done excellent work to develop new varieties.

Asphodeline lutea • Yellow Asphodel

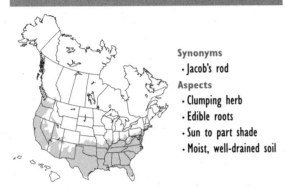

Synonyms
- Jacob's rod

Aspects
- Clumping herb
- Edible roots
- Sun to part shade
- Moist, well-drained soil

This species, currently a popular ornamental, was a cultivated root crop of the ancient Greeks. Apparently they loved to mash the cooked roots up with figs. In fact it has multiple edible uses, making it an ideal edible landscaping plant. Dig under the clumps and you will find clusters of edible roots, the size of a child's finger but borne abundantly. Ken Fern, author of *Plants for a Future*, says they have a "pleasant, nutty flavor" when cooked. Roots can be harvested any time of the year, but are at their best when plants are dormant. The flowers are also edible and very sweet. Finally, the young shoots are eaten like asparagus, and have a good flavor although they smell bad when they are cooking.

Yellow asphodel grows in clumps up to 3 feet across. It grows well in Mediterranean and cool temperate climates and can also be grown elsewhere, between Zones 6 and 9. It will grow in full sun to part shade, and requires well-drained soil. Propagate plants by division, but be careful, as it is easy to damage the roots. Yellow asphodel can also be grown from seed, which takes one to three months to germinate. This species has not naturalized in the United States or Canada.

Camassia spp. • Camass

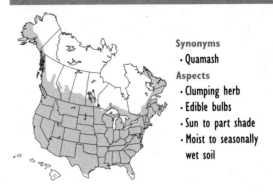

Synonyms
- Quamash

Aspects
- Clumping herb
- Edible bulbs
- Sun to part shade
- Moist to seasonally wet soil

General Overview, History, and Ecology: Before the introduction of grazing agriculture to the mountainous region of the West, camass grew in such enormous colonies that when their blue flowers were in bloom they were sometimes mistaken for lakes. The edible bulbs of camass were a crucial staple for many western Native peoples; in fact wars were sometimes fought over the rights to harvest from certain areas. Most camass bulbs are small, about 1 inch across, but they grow in large numbers and large amounts can be easily harvested. Some varieties and species have bulbs two or three times as large. The flavor of the bulbs has been compared to such disparate flavors as winter squash, figs, molasses, licorice, and baked pears.

Today camass is growing in popularity as an ornamental bulb, but very few people still use it as a food. One reason for this is the amount of work required to prepare the roots properly for eating. Like sunchokes and many other root crops, the bulbs contain large quantities of inulin, which cannot be digested in its raw state. Although inulin is valued for increasing calcium absorption, it can also cause a bad case of gas. Historically, camass bulbs were steam-cooked in huge pits for up to 72 hours. This method produces dark, sweet bulbs. Most gardeners will have neither the thousands of bulbs required or the desire to dig a pit 3 feet deep and 10 feet wide in which to bake their camass. John Kallas reports in his *Wild Food Adventurer* magazine on his attempts to use different techniques to cook camass.

Camass bulbs were once an important staple for native people of the Northwest.

According to Kallas, properly cooking camass requires high temperatures for a long period of time. When ready, the bulbs should taste like mildly sweet winter squash, should not be gummy or stick to your teeth, and should not cause flatulence. Kallas found that baking and microwaving were not feasible without constantly adding more water to keep the bulbs moist. The best method was to cook the bulbs in a pressure cooker at 257°F for nine hours. I am indebted to Kallas for his reports on his experiments with camass and many other wild edible species.

Camass will form large colonies over time. Bulbs can now be purchased wholesale for very reasonable prices, giving the opportunity for a good head start on a colony. This is another case of a vegetable that is very easy to grow but that takes some extra work in the kitchen.

Camass has also suffered from fear of its poisonous cousin, death camass (*Zigadenus* spp.). Death camass is one of the rare North American plants that are deadly poisonous if enough is eaten. In the wild, the two species often grow together, and they are very hard to tell apart. This makes wild harvesting very dangerous when the plants are not flowering. Ordering bulbs from a large bulb company will ensure that you are receiving nursery-propagated, completely safe camass bulbs. You might want to avoid sources that sell wild-harvested bulbs. If you want to be really certain, you can grow only blue-flowered varieties of camass (some camass varieties have white flowers), as death camass has only white flowers.

C. cusickii (Cusick's Camass). Cusick's camass is restricted to mountains in Oregon in the wild. The species is notable because the bulbs are two to three times as large as those of *C. quamash*. This species is hardy in Zones 5–8.

C. leichtlinii (Leichtlin's Camass). This widespread western species is found from British Columbia south to the Sierras. It is easily grown and common in the nursery trade. Leichtlin's camass is hardy in Zones 4–8.

C. quamash, *C. esculenta* (Common Camass, Quamash). The common camass grows widely and was the species most utilized by Native peoples. Like *C. leichtlinii* it is available from many bulb companies. Common camass is hardy in Zones 4–8, but some gardeners have had trouble growing it in cold areas in eastern North America.

C. scillioides (Wild Hyacinth). This is the eastern native camass, growing in open woods and prairies as far east as Pennsylvania and Georgia. Form *Petersenii* has 2-inch bulbs, twice the normal size. Wild hyacinth is hardy in Zones 3–9.

Crop Description: Camass is a bulb-forming plant similar to ornamental onions and other bulbs. They produce spikes of beautiful blue to white flowers. After flowering, plants die back until the next year.

Climate: Camass plants can be grown in cold and temperate climates. They are one of the few perennial vegetables that really thrive in cold mountain regions. The western species are well adapted to mountainous areas as well as the Pacific Northwest and the Central Valley of California. *C. scillioides* will better tolerate the humid heat of the Southeast.

Tolerances and Preferences: Camass is somewhat picky about conditions. For optimal growth, soils should be wet in spring but dry out in summer.

Naturalization Status: Camass species are native

throughout most of the United States and Canada.

Pest, Disease, and Weed Problems: Camass has few pest or disease problems.

Propagation and Planting: Camass can be divided just like any ordinary ornamental bulb. Over time plants will spread to form colonies. Sow seeds outdoors in the fall, or cold, moist stratify them for three months. Seedlings grow very slowly, and take four to five years to bloom and reach harvestable size.

Other Cultivation Information: Camass bulbs are grown much like daffodils and other bulbs. They are quite beautiful and are a great bulb for edible landscaping.

Harvest and Storage: Bulbs can be stored in a cool dry place.

Uses: Once prepared, camass bulbs can be used as a sweet food similar to cooked winter squash or mashed potatoes. Bulbs have also been used in pies, and boiled down to make molasses-like syrup. Raw bulbs can be eaten in small quantities. The cooked roots were traditionally sun-dried and stored for the winter.

Members of the Lewis and Clark expedition lived largely on these dried camass roots for an extended period. The first few days were pretty rough on their digestive systems, but after a while they acclimated, and came to be very fond of camass. Let their experience be a lesson to us—start with small amounts of camass and work up your tolerance slowly. Follow John Kallas's recommendations on preparing camass with a pressure cooker, as described above.

Related Species and Breeding Potential: Several species and varieties of camass have unusually large bulbs. Increasing the availability of these strains should be a priority. Crossing these strains with one another could result in large-bulbed hybrids. Breeding for increased digestibility and decreased cooking time would also be desirable. Famous plant breeder Luther Burbank worked on camass breeding and was very enthusiastic about its potential as a food and ornamental crop (although he was also known to exaggerate his claims to sell more plants). If any of his breeding material is still available, it would be a great place to start.

Hemerocallis spp. • Daylily

Synonyms
- Jin zhen cai

Aspects
- Running herbs
- Edible flowers and flowerbuds
- Edible tubers
- Sun to part shade
- Moist, well-drained soil

Daylilies are the quintessential low-maintenance perennial. They thrive on neglect; in fact they have naturalized throughout much of the United States and Canada along roadsides and other areas with frequent disturbance and poor soils. Hundreds or thousands of named varieties, mostly hybrids, are available. While these are grown as ornamentals, in China the daylily is an important vegetable. The flowers and flowerbuds are the main use of daylilies. The flowerbuds are used like green beans, with a crisp texture and the unique flavor shared by all parts of the daylily. The buds can be dried for storage by stringing them up with a needle and thread in a dark, dry place. After a week to 10 days, pack them in airtight containers. Dried buds are known as golden needles and are used in many Chinese dishes. The flowers themselves can be used in salads, as garnishes, or battered and fried. Daylilies can produce large

The edible buds of daylily. PHOTO BY NEIL SODERSTROM.

numbers of flowers and buds every day over a month or more, providing lots of time to test recipes. In China the 'Flore Peno' variety of *H. fulva* is the type most cultivated for flowerbud production.

Other parts of daylilies can also be used as minor vegetables. In spring the young leaves can be cooked, tasting something like creamed onions. Don't eat too much—apparently over-consumption can be mildly toxic. The tubers are also edible, although admittedly not a fantastic vegetable. All the tubers I have seen are the size of a large garlic clove, although apparently they can be a good bit larger. They have a very strong flavor of daylily, and are cooked like potatoes. They can cause digestive upset and flatulence. Breeding for increased tuber size, flavor, and digestibility would be a worthy goal, as daylilies produce large numbers of tubers.

Daylilies will grow in poor soils, as well as those with somewhat dry or wet tendencies. They will thrive in sun or partial shade. Nematodes can be problematic. Varieties are available that thrive in Zones 2–10, although most individual varieties have a smaller range. Check with your local nursery or garden center for varieties that will thrive in your climate. Edible species include *H. fulva* and the slightly smaller *H. lilio-asphodelus*, though the vast majority of daylilies available are hybrids.

Giant Solomon's seal is an eastern native with shoots that really do taste like asparagus.

Polygonatum biflorum var. commutatum • Giant Solomon's Seal

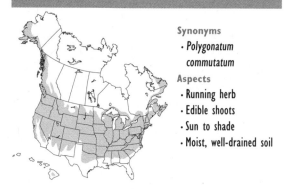

Synonyms
- *Polygonatum commutatum*

Aspects
- Running herb
- Edible shoots
- Sun to shade
- Moist, well-drained soil

This eastern wild edible is a giant form of a common woodland wildflower. Ordinary Solomon's seal (*P. biflorum*) is a lovely colony-forming herb reaching about 18 inches tall. The giant variety can reach an astounding 7 feet tall in ideal conditions, and is often easily 4–5 feet tall (this is due to polyploid chromosomes). Plants put up a number of tall, arching stems with beautiful white flowers dangling beneath, and are truly striking ornamentals. The spring shoots of all Solomon's seals are edible, but those of the smaller type are much smaller and thinner. Giant Solomon's seal has large, thick shoots that look and taste very similar to asparagus. They differ in that they have a cluster of folded leaves at the top of the shoot, and the stalks are thinner than asparagus. Their flavor is quite good—though the leaf cluster at the top can be bitter, in my experience—and they are a great candidate for breeding to develop a great new perennial vegetable crop. Joe Hollis of Mountain Gardens likes giant Solomon's seal better than asparagus, because of the flavor and because it is so much easier to grow.

Giant Solomon's seal spreads by runners to form a colony. It tends to send roots in different directions, forming clumps here and there. In full sun clumps are dense, but in the shade they are diffuse and can be easily interplanted with other species. Plants essentially take care of themselves. They will grow in moist to somewhat dry soils, including quite acidic forest soils. Plants prefer partial shade, but will grow in full sun or full shade as well. This wild edible can be grown in Zones 3–7. Division easily propagates giant Solomon's seal, but to produce from seed is much trickier. Collect the seeds when the fruits are black and ripe. Clean off all the flesh from the seeds and sow them immediately. They will not show leaves above ground for two years. At that time they can be transplanted.

Several related species also have edible, though smaller shoots. These include false Solomon's seal (*Smilacena racemosa*), twisted stalk and rosybells (*Streptopus amplexifolius* and *S. roseus*), and other *Polygonatum* species including *P. biflorum* and *P. odoratum*.

Malvaceae: The Mallow Family

Abelmoschus manihot • Edible Hibiscus

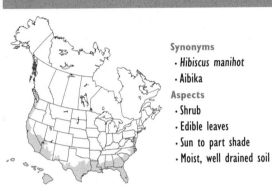

Synonyms
- *Hibiscus manihot*
- Aibika

Aspects
- Shrub
- Edible leaves
- Sun to part shade
- Moist, well drained soil

General Overview, History, and Ecology: Edible hibiscus is a beautiful shrub with large, vivid green edible leaves. It is quite a treat to just pick off a leaf and start chewing, as they have a very nice mild flavor, as long as you enjoy a mucilaginous texture—this species is closely related to okra (*A. esculentus*)! I found them quite enjoyable. Dr. Martin Price of ECHO, who thinks this is one of the best perennial vegetables for Florida, recommends eating them like lettuce in a sandwich to minimize the slimy texture. In Florida, where plants will live for years even when cut back by frosts, this species is considered an easy-to-grow "survivor." This plant is an outstanding candidate for tropical and subtropical edible landscapes—in addition to its beautiful foliage it has large, yellow hibiscus-like flowers with red centers.

This species is one of the world's most productive leaf crops, and will yield year-round in the tropics. It was originally domesticated in New Guinea or nearby islands, and was carried in canoes throughout the tropical Pacific, where it remains one of the most important vegetables. Named varieties available here include 'Jade Green' and 'Sunset'—though 'Sunset' is strictly ornamental, with prickly hairs on the leaves. 'Red Zinger' is a good eating variety with extra-large flowers and burgundy-red foliage. 'Red Zinger' is easily grown as an annual from seed virtually anywhere (this variety is not the source of the delicious Celestial Seasonings tea).

Crop Description: Edible hibiscus is a shrub growing up to 12 feet tall, although it is usually kept pruned to 6 feet in cultivation. The leaf shape is highly variable, but generally maple-like. The creamy yellow hibiscus-like flowers are quite beautiful.

Climate: This crop is well adapted to tropical lowlands. It is killed back to the ground by frost but will recover and send up new shoots if the ground does not freeze. It is certainly a good candidate for a woody dieback perennial in the warmer climates—it is rated as root-hardy in Zone 8. Edible hibiscus can be grown as an annual in colder climates, or as an edible container plant.

Tolerances and Preferences: It prefers well-drained soils, and with additional nitrogen will yield more and larger leaves.

Naturalization Status: Has not naturalized in the United States or Canada. Many varieties do not make viable seed at all.

Pest, Disease, and Weed Problems: In the heart of the tropical Pacific where it is a major crop, many pests and diseases affect edible hibiscus. It seems to have left those problems behind, for it has had few pest problems in Florida and Hawaii. In its native range it is grown on mounds or ridges to prevent being ravaged by collar rot. A range of insects attack it, but in Florida nematodes are the primary pest. Fresh cuttings are apparently quite vulnerable to disease: Follow good sanitation practices when taking and caring for cuttings.

Edible hibiscus has gorgeous flowers and highly nutritious leaves.

Propagation and Planting: Propagate edible hibiscus by cuttings, as most varieties do not set seed. Cuttings are taken from the middle or top of stems. Cuttings should have four to eight nodes and be 4–24 inches long. Bury two to six of the nodes. Rooting hormone is usually not necessary. Alternatively, cuttings can also be rooted in water in a shady place. Water should be changed daily, and the cuttings can be planted out once they have rooted. The plant will grow well from seed, when it is available. For perennial plantings allow 3 feet between plants.

Other Cultivation Information: In the Pacific plants are usually grown for one or two years; then cuttings are taken and replanted elsewhere. This is apparently usually because plants begin to succumb to disease or pest pressure at that point. That is not a problem in Florida, where apparently they can live in the same place for years.

Harvest and Storage: The leaves and the top few inches of stem tips are harvested year-round. They wilt easily after harvest, and should probably be put in a plastic bag and refrigerated if you are not going to use them right away.

Uses: Edible hibiscus leaves are probably a bit mucilaginous for the palates of most U.S. and Canadian gardeners, but this texture is very popular in the Pacific islands. They are tender when eaten raw, and more slimy when cooked. They are less slimy when roasted than when boiled. The tender tops are less slimy than the larger leaves. The large leaves are used as a wrapper for cooking other foods, and make a great thickener for sauces. The flavor is rich, and the leaves are very nutritious—according to one study, superior to spinach and Chinese cabbage in almost every way. They are high in vitamins A and C, and moderately rich in protein and fiber.

Related Species and Breeding Potential: Edible hibiscus belongs to the same genus as okra, which itself can be weakly perennial in the tropics. Perhaps tropical perennial okra with edible leaves and pods might be bred. Nontropical folk might want to try a wide cross with the related *Hibiscus rosa-sinensis*, a woody hibiscus with edible young leaves and flowers (neither delicious) hardy to Zone 5. In fact, edible hibiscus is sometimes classed in the genus *Hibiscus*.

Hibiscus acetosella • Cranberry Hibiscus

Synonyms
- False roselle

Aspects
- Shrub
- Edible leaves
- Full sun
- Moist, well-drained soil

General Overview, History, and Ecology: Cranberry hibiscus is a fantastic edible landscaping plant. A short-lived perennial in the tropics and an annual elsewhere, with delicious leaves produced abundantly, I am not certain why everyone is not already growing this resilient, attractive, and functional plant.

It looks similar to a red-leaved Japanese maple, but is actually a woody annual or short-lived perennial. The color of the leaves and stems is a deep maroon, and is variegated in some varieties. I was pleasantly surprised by the delicious tart flavor of the leaves, and how they were not noticeably mucilaginous compared with their relative edible hibiscus. They can be eaten raw, and make a beautiful and tasty addition to salads. The top several inches of the shoots, leaves and all, can be cooked. Left to its own devices, cranberry hibiscus is an annual.

However, with pruning (i.e., harvesting frequently) it can live for several years. In fact, pruned plants are often grown as an edible hedge.

Cranberry hibiscus is a hybrid that originated in tropical Africa, where it remains a popular vegetable. In fact it is grown, and has naturalized, around all the world's tropical regions. While it is only capable of perennializing in the tropics and subtropics, it makes a fine annual in colder climates as long as there is plenty of summer heat. This is a crop that should be grown *much* more widely in the warm regions of the United States.

Note: In Africa the red-leaved form is grown primarily as an ornamental, and the green-leaved forms are grown as vegetables. However, these forms are currently unavailable here.

Crop Description: Cranberry hibiscus is a short-lived perennial or long-lived annual woody plant. Essentially it is quick-growing shrub with deep maroon leaves, red stems, and beautiful small pink hibiscus flowers.

Climate: Cranberry hibiscus is tropical yet can survive a bit of frost. A hard frost will probably kill it to the ground, but this just works like a heavy pruning to rejuvenate the plant. Thus it is a great choice for Zone 9, and even for experimentation in Zone 8 with protection. It loves intense heat, and even as an annual in the North it will grow well in hot summers.

Tolerances and Preferences: Cranberry hibiscus is not particular about soils, although they must be well drained. Like most plants, it will perform best in deep, rich soils.

Naturalization Status: This species has naturalized throughout the world's tropics, and certainly could do so here in any region with a long enough summer for it to set seed. In Massachusetts it doesn't even have time to flower, let alone set seed.

Pest, Disease, and Weed Problems: Cranberry hibiscus is resistant to insect pests and nematodes, but is susceptible to some soilborne diseases, particularly in poorly drained soils.

Propagation and Planting: Cranberry hibiscus is easily grown from seed or cuttings. Set out plants on 3-foot centers unless you are planting a hedge, in which case they should be spaced closer together, about 2 feet apart.

Other Cultivation Information: Plants must be

The deep red foliage of cranberry hibiscus is outstanding in edible landscapes.

harvested or pruned heavily to extend their life span. It is not clear if they must be prevented from setting seed as well (they will not flower until the short days of fall). When grown as an edible hedge, harvest frequently to keep them trimmed to size.

Harvest and Storage: Trim the top several inches of the shoots for cooking, or harvest young leaves for eating fresh. Older leaves can also be cooked.

Uses: Use like a beautiful burgundy-red, slightly tart spinach. The leaves keep their beautiful red color when stir-fried, but not as well when boiled. I enjoy just grazing right from the bush. The flowers are used to make beverages. One recipe, popular in Central and South America, calls for the flowers to be picked after they have closed up at night. They are blended up with lime juice, sugar, and water, creating a silky smooth pink beverage.

Related Species and Breeding Potential: Closely related to the annual roselle (*H. sabdariffa*), grown for its tart flowers, fruits, and calyces (used to give the tart flavor and red color to many drinks, including Red Zinger tea). This species might be crossed with the hardy shrub rose of Sharon (*H. rosa-sinensis*) to create a delicious, hardy edible-leaved hibiscus. There is also potential for crossing with various *Abelmoschus* and *Hibiscus* species, including okra, edible hibiscus, and others. Plant geeks should note that cranberry hibiscus is itself a hybrid and a diploid, an "allotetraploid," which slightly complicates breeding efforts. Another approach might be to graft cranberry hibiscus cuttings onto rose of Sharon bushes in spring.

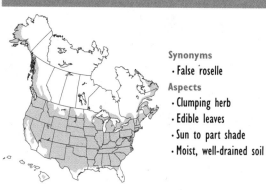

Malva moschata • Musk Mallow

Synonyms
- False roselle

Aspects
- Clumping herb
- Edible leaves
- Sun to part shade
- Moist, well-drained soil

Those of us in cooler climates may well be jealous of those who can grow edible cranberry hibiscus as perennials. Take heart, my fellow frosty gardeners, we also have a perennial vegetable with tasty mucilaginous leaves. In fact, it was by eating the leaves of musk mallow that I came to appreciate mucilaginous vegetables. Their emerald-green hue is so rich you just have to pop it in your mouth. I enjoy them as snacks as I wander in the garden, and find them an excellent cooked green as well, and they are of course great for thickening soups and sauces. Both the leaves and flowers of musk mallow are edible. In mild climates such at the Pacific Northwest it is evergreen, and here in Massachusetts it is among the first greens in spring. Plants can be cut back when they start to flower or after setting seed to produce a new flush of tender growth.

The variety 'Gumbo Leaf' was selected from wild plants by Norwegian seed saver Hiene Refsing, and made available to North American gardeners by Carol Deppe, author of *Breed Your Own Vegetable Varieties*. It seems to be shorter and more resilient than some ornamental types, with less finely dissected leaves.

Musk mallow is hardy from Zone 4 (or colder) to Zone 9. It is a short-lived, clump-forming species that self-sows prolifically. It is grown as an ornamental for its attractive pink or white flowers. Musk mallow will grow in full sun or part shade, and is tolerant of most garden soils as long as they are not too acidic. It has a reputation for being very easy to grow, and that has certainly been true in my garden. Musk mallow is very easy to grow from seed. It can also be propagated vegetatively by rooting the spring side shoots.

Note: Mallows can concentrate harmful quantities of nitrates in soils with excess nitrogen, particularly those that have been treated with chemical fertilizers. The plants will grow just fine without chemical fertilizers, so please avoid them, at least in your mallow patch.

There are many other interesting annual and perennial mallow species to grow and breed with musk mallow. Many have edible leaves, including *M. neglecta*, *M. parviflora*, *M. pusilla*, *M. sylvestris*, and *M. verticilata*.

Meliaceae: The Neem Family

Toona sinensis • Fragrant Spring Tree

Synonyms
- *Cedrella sinensis*
- Toona tree
- Chinese cedar
- Hsiang chun ya

Aspects
- Tree
- Edible leaves
- Full sun
- Moist, well drained soil

Readers from cold climates may be experiencing jealousy over the numerous tropical trees and shrubs with edible leaves. Fortunately there are a few hardy woody leaf crops, including fragrant spring tree, which can grow from the tropics all the way up through Zone 5 or 6. I have seen 40-foot-tall specimens in Philadelphia's Morris Arboretum. The young, tender leaves in spring are a cultivated vegetable in China. A local Chinese restaurant here in Massachusetts grows their own leaves. I ordered their fragrant spring tree leaves cooked with eggs. The flavor was like musky, roasted garlic. To my mind it seems an acquired taste, and that the leaves are best used as a culinary herb. I think it tastes great used instead of garlic in stir-fries. However, it is definitely used as a vegetable like spinach in Chinese cuisine, so I have included it here as a perennial vegetable. The leaves are high in vitamin A. One variety, grown as a vegetable, has beautiful purple leaves in spring. This is probably identical to the ornamental variety 'Flamingo' sold in the nursery trade here.

Fragrant spring tree seeds need to be either cold-stratified for 90 days or sown outdoors in the fall. They can also be grown from 2-inch root cuttings. Plants are tough and have few pest or disease problems. They will sucker and form a colony, and seedlings establish well under the plants as well. For ease of harvest plants can be pruned to a bush height, or managed using coppice or pollard pruning techniques (see page 49).

Fragrant spring tree is one of the few hardy trees with good-quality edible leaves. PHOTO © RAINTREE NURSERY.

Moraceae: The Mulberry Family

Artocarpus altilis • Breadfruit

Synonyms
- Sukun

Aspects
- Tree
- Edible fruit
- Full sun
- Moist, well-drained soil

General Overview, History, and Ecology: Breadfruit is the ultimate perennial staple vegetable—a large potato-like fruit that grows on trees! Originally domesticated in New Guinea or nearby islands, breadfruit trees were carried in canoes thousands of miles east as part of the settlement of Polynesia, one of the great migrations of human history. Today it is an important staple in much of the tropics, particularly on Pacific islands. The vast majority of breadfruit worldwide is grown in home gardens and on subsistence farms. In fact few native-born Americans and Canadians have ever tasted or even seen a breadfruit, although they can occasionally be purchased in Latin and Asian markets here.

Trees will generally produce 25–150 fruits per year. Each fruit weighs 2–8 pounds. They are borne over a four- to six-month period, with early and late varieties extending the season but generally leaving a few months with no harvest. Generally breadfruits bear too much fruit, and too quickly. Often many fruits end up rotting on the ground because they are hard to keep up with.

Breadfruit is an "ultratropical," which, given the territory covered in this book, means it can essentially only be grown in Hawaii and the Florida Keys. Although their range is restricted within the United States and Canada, and they cannot be grown as annuals or even easily with season extension, they are featured here as a major species because of their great importance. Readers from elsewhere can just read and weep, or cling to fantasies of a very wide cross with Osage orange.

Breadfruit is a true perennial staple crop. PHOTO BY JIM WISEMAN.

Crop Description: Breadfruit trees grow up to 85 feet but are often smaller, with very large, glossy, leathery leaves. Trees can be as much as 6 feet wide at the base of the trunk. Leaves are evergreen or deciduous depending on the seasonal distribution of rainfall. The fruits are roughly the size of a cantaloupe or smaller. They are Kermit the Frog green, becoming yellowish when they are fully ripe.

Climate: Breadfruits are adapted to hot, humid tropical lowlands. They prefer temperatures between 60°F and 100°F, and are killed back by temperatures of 42°F or colder. The legendary Julia Morton reports in *Fruits of Warm Climates* that attempts to grow breadfruit on the mainland of Florida have failed: Plants need to be wrapped in plastic to protect them from dehydration in the "frigid" South Florida winters, and even then they will generally persist a few years but never grow. Using the techniques in *Palms Won't Grow Here* for overwintering tender evergreens might be worth a try in southern Florida and maybe even in the San Diego or Phoenix areas, but you will almost certainly need a greenhouse to grow a breadfruit anywhere in the continental United States.

Tolerances and Preferences: Year-round rainfall or substantial irrigation is ideal, with the optimal range being 80–100 inches of water a year. Most varieties need rich, well-drained soil, but some are adapted to the poor calcareous soils of Pacific coral atolls.

Naturalization Status: Breadfruit has been grown in Hawaii for a long time without naturalizing—nor has it (unsurprisingly) naturalized in the mainland United States or Canada.

Pest, Disease, and Weed Problems: Breadfruit trees are relatively free of pest and disease problems. In extremely wet climates, fruits can rot on the tree. Pruning for good airflow helps to prevent this. Otherwise, different pests are problems in different parts of the world. In Hawaii the main pest is the two-spotted leafhopper.

Propagation and Planting: While many breadfruit varieties are seedless, some have large, chestnut-like nuts. These seeds are only viable for a short time, but if planted soon after removal from the fruit will germinate in about two weeks. Seedlings are not genetically identical to the parent.

Propagate most breadfruits by digging suckers. Once you observe new shoots emerging, carefully dig out the area around them and fill in with rich, loose soil. Water and fertilize regularly. When the suckers reach 18 inches tall, use a sharp spade to sever the roots that attach them to the main tree. This can be done in several stages to make sure the sucker is not shocked. Eventually suckers are dug up and transplanted. Alternatively, when suckers reach almost 1 inch in diameter they can be air-layered (see the illustration). Breadfruits should be planted 30–50 feet apart.

Other Cultivation Information: Breadfruit trees require little care once planted. They set fruit without needing pollination from another tree.

Harvest and Storage: Breadfruits are usually picked while at mature size but still green. They last about one week after being picked, or up to 25 days when held at 50°F–60°F.

Uses: Most breadfruits are eaten when at mature size but still green in color, or when just beginning to turn yellow. At this stage they are essentially used like potatoes. The whole fruits are traditionally baked in earth ovens. They can be chopped (discard the core) and boiled, baked, fried, or roasted, like potatoes. Traditionally they are often combined with coconut in many dishes. They are sometimes fermented or dried to preserve their abundant harvests. When still warm from cooking, breadfruits are rich, slightly fibrous, warming, and nourishing. The flavor, texture, and aroma of a good breadfruit combine the best of fresh-baked bread and baked potatoes. They are

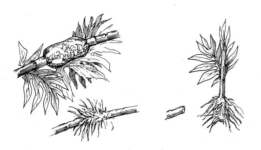

Air-layering breadfruit. Wrap a section of branch and pack with potting soil. When roots emerge from the stem, cut off the branch and pot it up or transplant.

quite delicious, and not at all an acquired taste—I have found that those who have never had them enjoy this vegetable at their first try.

Nutritionally speaking, breadfruits are high in carbohydrates but generally low in protein, fat, and vitamins. They are on par with bananas and sweet potatoes in terms of protein, and higher in protein than cassava. Nutritional content does vary among varieties.

Young fruits, at the 3-inch size, can be cooked, and apparently have the flavor of globe artichokes.

Nuts of seeded varieties are roasted like chestnuts. Ripe fruits are edible, but rather mushy and insipid.

Related Species and Breeding Potential: The hundreds of varieties of breadfruit doubtless already contain many of the traits breeders might desire. A high priority for breeders is to develop a "suite" of varieties with different ripening seasons that, together, would provide year-round production. The young (enormous) fruits of the related jakfruit (*A. heterophyllus*) and several other species are also used as vegetables.

Adventurous breeders might try to cross breadfruit with Osage orange (*Maclura pomifera*), a hardy native of the central United States that is in a different genus within the same family. Osage orange fruits are grapefruit-sized, but are not edible, and such experiments should be undertaken with caution. Connie Barlow's fascinating *Ghosts of Evolution* speculates that Osage orange was once an important food of woolly mammoths, just as wild ancestral breadfruit was originally a food for elephants.

Moringaceae: The Moringa Family

Moringa spp. • Moringa

Synonyms
- Drumstick tree
- Cabbage tree
- Horseradish tree
- Morunga

Aspects
- Tree
- Edible leaves
- Edible pods
- Full sun
- Dry to moist soil

General Overview, History, and Ecology: Although few people in the United States and Canada are familiar with it, moringa is one of the world's most nutritious vegetables. It has been undergoing a surge of popularity in the tropics in recent years, due to its wide adaptability and incredible usefulness. The wood is the only inedible part—leaves, flowers, pods, bark, and roots are all edible in at least one of the species. The seeds can even be used as a low-tech water purifier.

The fresh young leaves and tender stems are used like spinach. When eaten raw, they have a somewhat horseradish-like flavor (both the cooked and dried leaves are mild). The leaves are the most nutritious part of the plant, being high in protein, calcium, iron, vitamin A, and B vitamins. Raw greens have a high vitamin C content. Dried moringa leaf is sometimes known as "mother's best friend" for its important role in the nutrition of pregnant and nursing women and young children in many poverty-stricken areas of the tropics. One- to three-year-old children can get 14 percent of their daily protein needs, as well as 40 percent of calcium, 23 percent of iron,

Moringa is an incredibly nutritious leaf crop that grows on a drought-resistant tree.

and almost 100 percent of vitamin A, from just a single tablespoon of dried leaves!

The pods, or "drumsticks," are also a popular vegetable, especially in South Asia. Very young pods can be cooked and eaten like green beans during the brief period after they reach full size but still have tender skin. Older pods are cooked and split open along the seams. The tender flesh and green seeds are scraped off with the teeth, much like eating globe artichokes. The flavor is like asparagus. Immature seeds are also eaten like shell beans.

Moringa has naturalized in many areas of the tropics, and local people outside of its native range are often not aware of its food potential. Although tender to frost, moringa makes a great dieback perennial and will resprout even as far north as Atlanta. This tree is remarkably versatile and very easy to grow, and should be experimented with throughout the warmer regions of the United States. Moringa can also be grown as an annual in warm-summer areas.

M. oleifera (Drumstick Tree). This species is originally from eastern India, and is now grown throughout tropical Asia, the Pacific islands, and the Caribbean. The leaflets of M. oleifera are less than 1 inch long, about half the size of M. stenopetala leaflets. This species is the more widely cultivated of the two. In addition to edible leaves and pods, the roots of young plants of M. oleifera are used like horseradish—just grate and add vinegar. Root bark should be removed first. Do not eat moringa root sauce in great quantities or great frequency, as it can apparently make some people sick (the same might be said for ordinary horseradish root!). The variety 'PKM-1' has a more bushy growth habit and longer edible pods.

M. stenopetala (Moringa). This species hails from Ethiopia and Kenya in eastern Africa. It is even more drought-tolerant than M. oleifera, and is less adapted to humid climates—it will not set pods in humid areas. Its leaves have a milder flavor than M. oleifera, and older leaves can be used as well. Although the roots are not edible, the bark can be used like horseradish.

Crop Description: Moringa trees grow quickly to 20–45 feet tall, although they are often pruned to a bush form for easier harvesting of the leaves. They have delicate, fern-like leaves and large bean-like pods, making them resemble leguminous trees (to which they are not related).

Climate: Moringa trees tolerate light frosts, but are essentially tropical. However, in northern Florida they vigorously resprout from the roots after freezing, growing multiple shoots 15 feet tall in the next growing season. Clearly moringa can be grown for leaf production as a dieback perennial in the subtropical United States and potentially farther north with protection. It can also be grown as an annual leaf crop anywhere with a long, hot summer. For flower and pod production you must be in the proper tropics.

Tolerances and Preferences: Moringa trees are quite drought-tolerant, but can also be grown in the hot, humid tropics. They grow more slowly in cool temperatures. They prefer full sun but can take some shade. Moringas prefer well-drained soils, although they will grow in anything that is not waterlogged, including quite alkaline soils. Organic matter and good nitrogen are helpful, especially for year-round production.

Naturalization Status: Moringa has naturalized in Florida.

Pest, Disease, and Weed Problems: Moringa has few pest or disease problems. Cuttings can be troubled with rot problems. Otherwise there are a few minor insect and arthropod pests, including termites.

Propagation and Planting: Moringa can be grown from seed or cuttings. Seed takes about two weeks to germinate. Hardwood cuttings should be 18–36 inches long and 2–5 inches thick. Give them a few days to cure in dry shade, then set the bottom third of the cuttings in soil. The soil should be very well drained, as they are susceptible to rotting. Plant trees 15–20 feet apart, or on 3- to 4-foot spacing if they will be coppiced or in climates where they will be frost-killed annually.

Other Cultivation Information: Both species are usually kept trimmed to 3–6 feet high, to make for easier harvest of leaves. When pruned to this height, moringa will keep producing fresh shoots. Often whole branches are harvested to keep trees at the proper height. Moringa trees are often maintained as an edible hedge. For pod production, trees, or at least a few branches, should be allowed to reach a larger size. This can be done even if the rest of the tree is coppiced.

Harvest and Storage: The leaves are easily stripped off the stems. Sometimes whole branches are cut as a simple harvest method (new branches will quickly replace them!). To preserve leaves for later use, dry them in the shade. Remove the stems and grind the leaves in a coffee grinder.

Uses: Leaves can be used raw or cooked, although the mild horseradish flavor of raw leaves means that they are usually cooked. The flowers are edible when cooked.

Young pods are used like green beans as described above.

Dried mature seeds are used to make a cooking oil of good quality. First, roast, mash, and then boil the seeds. Strain out the solids and let the liquid sit overnight. By morning, the oil will have floated to the surface and can be skimmed off.

Related Species and Breeding Potential: ECHO is engaged in breeding and selection work with a number of moringa species and varieties. It may be that certain strains are hardier or better adapted to cultivation as dieback perennials.

Musaceae: The Banana Family

Musa x paradisica • Plantain and Green Banana

Synonyms
- *Musa acuminata*

Aspects
- Tree-like herbs
- Edible fruits
- Edible flowerbuds
- Full sun
- Moist, well-drained soil

General Overview, History, and Ecology: Many readers may be used to thinking of bananas as a fruit. Certainly, ripe bananas are popular around the world. But much of the world's production of bananas is grown for use as a starchy vegetable. And plantains, close cousins of bananas, are a major world staple grown exclusively for use as a versatile vegetable.

Both fruits belong to the same species, some types of which are best for dessert like the bananas we buy in the grocery store, and some for cooking, including the plantains. Many varieties are well suited to both uses. Their wild ancestors still grow from the Philippines to Papua New Guinea. Two wild species with small, seeded fruit hybridized in an ancient tropical forest, and after millennia of selection and breeding we have over 1,000 varieties today.

Plantains and other cooking varieties of bananas are used differently at different stages of ripeness. When the skin is green, they are similar to waxy potatoes (and are used in the same ways), and can be sliced and fried to make the classic dish *tostones*. When their skin turns yellow, the fruit becomes sweeter and more tender. In addition to *tostones*, fruits at this stage are great in soups and stews. When the skin turns black, plantains become creamy and sweet. They are softer, but still hold their shape when cooked. Black plantains can be boiled, baked, and sautéed.

Green bananas and plantains are an important staple crop in much of the world.

Slit their skin and bake them like potatoes. Green dessert and multiple-use banana varieties can be used like green plantains, but ripe bananas have the drawback of turning mushy when cooked. Banana leaves are often used to wrap steamed rice and other foods, and can provide biodegradable disposable plates to eat off.

The artichoke-sized bud that grows at the end of a banana flower stalk is also used as a vegetable. Most banana varieties have rather bitter buds, but 'Saba' and the short-season 'Rajapuri' are especially good for this purpose. To use banana buds, first trim off the tip. Remove the purplish red bracts (they look like big flower petals). Remove and discard all the little white flowers inside each bract; they are horribly bitter. The inner bracts are pale—this is the edible part. Their flavor is bitter with a bit of artichoke and cabbage thrown in. Banana bud bracts should be cooked with other strong flavors to counteract their bitterness.

Bananas and plantains are not actually trees—just very tall herbs without any woody parts. Depending on the variety they can range 6–35 feet tall. The "trunk" is really a pseudo-stem made up of leafy tissue. Bananas and plantains grow from a central clump or "stool" that sends up multiple shoots. Each shoot lives just long enough to flower, fruit, and die. More shoots completing the same life cycle then replace it. Stools have a lifetime of 5–6 years in intense commercial production, but can survive as long as 50 years with gentler treatment.

Now for the big news: We all know that bananas can be grown in the tropics and subtropics. Bananas certainly love warm and hot climates. They are killed to the ground at 28°F, but resprout quite vigorously, meaning they can be grown quite a bit farther north as dieback perennials. The problem has always been that they require 18 months of frost-free growth in order to fruit, so they cannot be grown in consistently frosty areas except as ornamentals. Fortunately, amateur plant geeks in cold climates have been experimenting with pushing the limits of banana production. They have found that by insulating the pseudo-stems, they enable the aboveground banana plant to fruit the following year. Here is the technique, as written in David Francko's *Palms Won't Grow Here and Other Myths*.

"After the first killing frost in autumn, but before even colder weather has a chance to freeze the pseudo stem, cut off all the dead leaves about 1 in. (2.5cm) from the stem. Then carefully tie the stems together with straps or other wide banding material so as not to cut into them. Drive a few posts into the ground in a perimeter about one foot away from the outside edge of the clump and string chicken wire or other material around the posts a little higher than the top of the plant. Fill the entire cage with leaves, straw, or other dry mulching material to cover the entire plant. Some sources recommend covering the entire cage with a tarpaulin or other protective cover to keep the pile dry. Stake or weight the edges down to keep it from blowing away, leaving a crack somewhere in the cover to allow moisture to escape. In the spring, uncover the plant. Although the pseudo stems will be covered with a slimy mess of decomposed material, this will wash off in the first few rains, and in a very short time new leaves will begin growing from the overwintered pseudo stems. In the milder parts of Zone 7 and warmer, with this strategy you should be able to overwinter enough of the first-year growth to allow the banana to complete its life cycle and flower later in the second year."

But wait, there's more. Several banana varieties, including 'Rajapuri', will fruit in 9 months instead of the usual 18. 'Rajapuri' is fully hardy through Zone 8, and has been overwintered in Zone 7 and colder with protection. If you live in Zone 8 (or even the warmer parts of 7), and have nine months of warm temperatures in a year, you may be able to astound your neighbors with fruiting bananas without even protecting the pseudo-stems. 'Rajapuri' is not only hardy and

Coconut Curry with Ripe Plantains, Chayote, Green Mango, Shallots, and Edible Hibiscus

Many tropical vegetables are at their best in coconut curry. Green, unripe mangoes have recently become one of my favorite vegetables. They are hard like a potato, tart and sweet, and a beautiful golden color. This recipe is worth the trouble—it is visually appealing, and will please you with creamy, savory, sweet, sour, and spicy flavors. You can get most of these ingredients at your local Southeast Asian market.

1-inch cube fresh ginger, grated	Tamari or fish sauce to taste
1-inch piece fresh or frozen galangal root, grated	1 tablespoon curry paste (I prefer panang, a mild curry)
5 shallots	2 standard (5.6 oz.) cans coconut milk
5 lime leaves	1 bunch (5–10) edible hibiscus leaves
2 stalks lemongrass	Juice of 3 limes
Peanut oil	Salt, pepper, and chili flakes to taste
2 chayote fruits	1 bunch cilantro
1 green mango	1 cup roasted unsalted peanuts
2 ripe plantains (yellow-black)	

Sauté shredded ginger and galangal, chopped shallots, lime leaves, and lemongrass in peanut oil. Chop chayote and green mango in 1-inch cubes. Chop plantains in ¾-inch rounds without removing skin (each round will have a ring of skin around it). Add all three when shallots begin to get translucent and sauté for 5–10 minutes, till they begin to get softer and show a bit of golden brown around the edges. Splash occasionally with tamari or fish sauce. Meanwhile, use a fork to combine curry paste with ½ cup coconut milk in a dish until smooth. Mix with remaining coconut milk and add to saucepan. Simmer until chayote and plantains are almost soft enough to eat. Then add chopped edible hibiscus, stir, remove from heat, and let sit for 5 minutes. Add lime juice, season to taste with salt, pepper, and chili flakes, and garnish with chopped cilantro and crushed roasted peanuts. It is easy to peel the plantain skin off once it is cooked. Serve with jasmine, basmati, or sticky rice. Adding shrimp in the last 5–10 minutes makes a more protein-rich and savory dish.
Serves 5.

short-season, but has dual-purpose fruit, excellent for cooking when green and also a great dessert banana (plus 'Rajapuri' is among the best bananas for use as an edible flowerbud).

Where plantains can be easily grown, they are certainly an important staple crop for the perennial vegetable garden. Now that we can extend the boundaries of banana production to cities like Charleston, South Carolina, Austin, Texas, and Oakland, California, perhaps they will become known as the new "banana belt"!

Crop Description: Bananas and plantains are tall, tree-like, clump-forming herbs. The enormous leaves can be up to 8 feet long and 2 feet wide. Plants can range 6–30 feet, depending on variety.

Climate: Bananas are tropical and subtropical heat-lovers. They will put on growth at temperatures between 53°F and 100°F. As stated above, the plants will persist as dieback perennials in Zone 8, but unless you have a short-season variety or protect the pseudo-stem you will not get them to fruit.

Tolerances and Preferences: Bananas and plantains are heavy feeders. Give them plenty of composted manure and lots of mulch. Nitrogen and potassium are especially important nutrients to supply. They also need lots of water, although they require well-drained soils. Bananas and plantains grow well in full sun, and can grow in partial shade in the intense sun of the tropics. They should be protected from strong winds, which can shred their leaves. Plantains will tolerate slightly drier and poorer soils than dessert bananas.

Naturalization Status: Bananas and/or plantains have naturalized in Florida, Louisiana, and Hawaii.

Pest, Disease, and Weed Problems: Different pests and diseases are problematic in different areas. The presence of Panama wilt disease is a problem for many Hawaiian plantain and cooking banana varieties. Black leaf streak, bunchy top disease, thrips, and nematodes also affect bananas and plantains in Hawaii. In Florida, Panama disease and nematodes are problematic. In recent years black sigatoka disease has come to South Florida, causing major problems in nonresistant varieties (including 'Rajapuri'). Bananas and plantains in California are free of most problems, although they are susceptible to rotting in cold, wet winter soils. The best solution is to plant varieties resistant to diseases present in your area—there are thousands of varieties to choose from.

Propagation and Planting: Propagate bananas by digging suckers, called pups. You will need to use a sharp shovel or machete to cut through the rhizomes. Remove most of the leaves from a sucker when transplanting. Bananas and plantains are usually planted 8–10 feet apart or more, depending on the size of the variety.

Other Cultivation Information: For best production, prune plantains and bananas, allowing just one pseudo-stem to fruit at a time. You can permit another sucker to start growing once the main stem is about nine months old.

Harvest and Storage: Plantains and bananas grow in large bunches. Cut the stalk when the fruits reach full size but are still green or just starting to turn yellow. Be careful not to bruise the fruit when harvesting. Hang the stalks up in a shady place to ripen.

Uses: Plantains and green bananas are used like root crops in a vast array of recipes. As they ripen, plantains become less potato-like and more tender and sweet, although they still hold their shape when cooked. Plantains are rarely eaten raw. Peeling unripe plantains can be challenging. You might need the help of a knife to start things off. They can also be cut and cooked with the skin on (it is easy to remove after cooking). Green (unripe) bananas are used like plantains. Fresh ripe bananas are eaten as a dessert fruit. The bracts of the flowerbuds are also edible (see above).

Related Species and Breeding Potential: Banana breeding is difficult, as few varieties make viable seeds. There are over 1,000 varieties available to choose from, though, and you can probably find one of them with the traits you are looking for.

Nelumbonaceae: The Lotus Family

Nelumbo nucifera • Water Lotus

Synonyms
- *Nelumbium speciosum*
- Chinese water lotus

Aspects
- Running herb
- Edible roots
- Edible seeds
- Full sun
- Aquatic

General Overview, History, and Ecology: Water lotus has been cultivated for thousands of years in Egypt, India, China, and Japan. Lotus was sacred to the ancient Egyptians, and still is today to Buddhists and Hindus. The edible root-like rhizomes have filled our stomachs as the incredibly beautiful flowers nourished our souls.

Here in the United States and Canada, lotuses are widely grown as ornamentals, but we seem to entirely ignore their potential as a food plant for our gardens. Lotus rhizomes look like a string of fat sausages. When cut in cross section, the air tubes that run through the rhizomes make them look like old-fashioned telephone dials. Lotus "roots" are too hard to eat raw, but when cooked are mild, sweet, and crunchy. They are usually cooked in soups or stews, and can be boiled and added to salads. Their unique appearance and texture make lotus "roots" the centerpiece and conversation starter in any meal. The young unfurling leaves of lotus can also be cooked, and the chestnut-flavored seeds are cooked as well.

Water lotus is one of a number of aquatic vegetables that are neglected by gardeners here for no discernible reason, particularly given the popularity of ornamental water gardening. Water lotus is the deepest-growing of any of the aquatic vegetables, generally planted anywhere from 6 inches to 5 feet underwater. The first leaves in spring will grow flat on the surface like water lily leaves. Next come huge dinner-plate-sized leaves emerging high above the water on long stalks. Finally fist-sized flowerbuds emerge, opening into flowers 9 inches or more across. Few other vegetables can come close to the beauty of water lotus.

Lotuses thrive in the tropics, and are often said to be hardy only to Zone 8, but some varieties are rated for Zone 4. I have collected seed from a 100-year-old planting in Springfield, Massachusetts (Zone 6). It seems that if the plants are well established, and deep enough under water and mud, they survive just fine. This is reportedly because the water does not usually freeze at the bottom of a pond even in quite cold areas, allowing this tropical to grow much farther

Water lotus will undoubtedly be the most beautiful flowering vegetable in your garden.

Lotus roots are segments like a chain of sausages.
PHOTOGRAPH COURTESY OF S. J. KAYS.

north than both nonaquatic perennials and even shallow-growing aquatics.

Growing water lotus as a vegetable is similar to growing it as an ornamental. Although the plants grow (and overwinter) well in the mud at the bottom of a pond, harvesting the rhizomes means groping around in the mud quite a bit. Lotuses can be more easily grown in wide, shallow pots in natural or artificial ponds. Their rhizomes will grow around in a circle, tracing the edge of the pot. They are ready to eat in six to nine months. Container-grown lotuses usually need division and repotting frequently anyway, so harvesting is not harmful. Just save a few segments to replant. Like all aquatics, make sure you are growing them in uncontaminated water.

Note: The genus *Lotus* is completely unrelated to the water lotus; in fact *Lotus* species are legumes including the edible annual asparagus pea (*L. tetragonobolus*).

Crop Description: Water lotuses are large aquatic perennials emerging up to 4–5 feet above the surface of the water.

Climate: Lotuses grow from the tropics through Zone 8, though many varieties can survive winters even in Zone 4 as long as they are growing in mud below the freeze line of a pond. They need six to nine months of warm temperatures to form mature rhizomes. In shorter seasons you will have to wait two years to harvest. I bring my potted lotus into the basement for winter in my Massachusetts garden, since my water garden is a shallow plastic pool.

Tolerances and Preferences: Water lotus is an aquatic plant. The crown of the plant should be placed at least 6 inches under the water's surface. They can grow in up to 5 feet of water, but should be allowed to spread to that depth on their own in mud-bottomed ponds. For best production in containers they should be fertilized monthly.

Naturalization Status: Water lotus has naturalized in the eastern and central United States.

Pest, Disease, and Weed Problems: Water lotus has few pest or disease problems that affect rhizome production, although some insects might chew up the leaves a bit.

Propagation and Planting: Lotus rhizomes are divided when dormant. Make sure to have at least one growing eye per segment. My limited exper-iments with planting store-bought roots failed; too bad, as this would be a great way to acquire varieties cultivated as vegetables. Lotuses can also be grown from seed. Seeds should first be scari-fied: Scratch them with a knife (careful!) or file then soak the seeds in a glass of water for a few days. If they do not swell up, take them out and score them deeper with your knife or file and try again. Once they swell up and sink to the bottom of your glass of water, pot them up and they will germinate over the next few weeks. Lotus seed remains viable for decades.

Other Cultivation Information: For best results, grow lotuses in a round, shallow container 3–4 feet wide. Containers with square or rectangular corners can cause the growing tips to snap off, damaging the plant. In commercial root produc-tion the flowerbuds are removed to focus energy on root production. This seems like an awful shame to me.

Harvest and Storage: Lotus roots should only be harvested when the plants are dormant. Be care-ful, as they are quite delicate. Harvest can take place during ordinary division of container plants.

Uses: Lotus rhizomes are only eaten cooked. They are at their best when boiled. Lotus rhizome is wonderful in soups and stews. They are also quite nice boiled and then served in salads. The unique appearance of cross-section slices is quite attractive.

Young water lotus leaves can be cooked, but are toxic if eaten raw. They are sometimes used to wrap other foods. The seeds are best eaten just before they harden, as they are easier to harvest at this stage. They taste like chestnuts.

Related Species and Breeding Potential: What is most needed is to introduce or make more available the varieties of water lotus grown for their roots. Many ornamental varieties are available, but no nurser-ies in the United States or Canada seem to offer lotuses specifically grown for the roots, though the roots of ornamental types make fine food as well. The eastern native lotus (*N. lutea*) also has edible roots. It has beautiful yellow flowers and is much hardier than the Asian species. It is worthy of growing in its own right, and might also be used to increase the hardiness of Asiatic types.

Oxalidaceae: The Wood-Sorrel Family

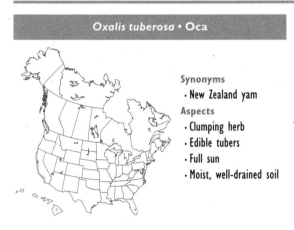

Oxalis tuberosa • Oca

Synonyms
- New Zealand yam

Aspects
- Clumping herb
- Edible tubers
- Full sun
- Moist, well-drained soil

General Overview, History, and Ecology: This crop, virtually unknown in the United States and Canada, is second in importance only to potatoes across vast areas of the South American highlands. It has become a commercial crop in New Zealand and has the potential to become a much more important crop worldwide. In gardens oca can provide high yields in tiny spaces.

Oca's beautiful tubers are shaped like fingerling potatoes and come in bright colors like yellow, orange, red, and purple. They have a crisp, moist, waxy texture, and unlike many root crops make a sweet and tart, almost candy-like snack raw. Flavor varies dramatically among varieties. The varieties I have tasted were mild, sweet, and tart when eaten raw, like a good star fruit. When baked they lived up to their reputation of tasting like potatoes with sour cream already added. Apparently the best way to savor the taste of oca is to steam them until tender and serve them with butter. The sour flavor comes from oxalic acid (named after this genus). If left out in the sun for a few days the tubers lose most of their oxalic acid and become sweeter. Nutritionally, oca is similar to potatoes.

Like so many Andean crops, oca has day-length sensitivity. It does not start to form tubers until days are 12 hours long. After that it needs a good two to three months frost-free to ripen them fully. Oca can probably be grown in San Francisco as a perennial, and as an annual north through much of the Pacific Northwest. Some day-length-neutral varieties apparently exist in Mexico, New Zealand, and the southern part of its range in South America, but these are apparently not available in the United States at the time of writing. Importing day-length-neutral varieties should be a high priority, as this delicious, productive, and attractive root crop will surely find a wide audience for itself here.

Crop Description: Oca grows as a compact perennial, making a mound about 1 foot high. The leaves look like clover.

Climate: Oca is not for tropical lowlands or the hot, humid Southeast. The day-length sensitivity of the varieties available at time of writing makes it poorly suited for areas without long, frost-free autumns. The highlands of Hawaii are perfect, but oca can also be grown in the mild areas of Northern California and the Pacific Northwest. The tops are killed by a hard frost, but the roots can take some freezing, surviving down to soil temperatures of 23°F.

Tolerances and Preferences: Oca prefers full sun but will produce in a wide range of soils, from pH 5.3 to 7.8. It does produce best in light, sandy, fertile soil.

Naturalization Status: Oca has not naturalized in the United States or Canada, and seems unlikely to.

Pest, Disease, and Weed Problems: Few pests and diseases bother oca, though nematodes can be a

Oca tubers come in many beautiful colors and have a delicious sweet, tart flavor.

problem. In hot, humid conditions oca is suscep-tible to rot. Viruses appear to be widespread throughout South America. Tissue culture is being used to create virus-free plants, and is dramatically increasing yields. Oca plants sold through nurseries in the United States and Canada are probably virus-free.

Propagation and Planting: Oca is a plant/replant perennial, grown just like potatoes. Space plants about 12 inches apart.

Other Cultivation Information: Oca is quite easy to grow. Plants are earthed up like potatoes to increase yields.

Harvest and Storage: Tubers should be harvested carefully, as they are delicate. They store extremely well for several months in a cool, dark place.

Uses: Oca tubers can be used raw or cooked like potatoes. The sour leaves are also edible.

Related Species and Breeding Potential: There are many potential avenues for breeding oca. Some day-length-neutral varieties exist, but are not yet available in the United States and Canada. Backyard breeders could develop overwinter-ing ocas by crossing with hardier edible-rooted species like iron cross (*O. deppei*) and violet wood sorrel (*O. violacea*). An even more interesting chal-lenge would be to develop colony-forming oca hybrids by crossing with creeping species like the extremely hardy common wood sorrel (*O. montana*), which carpets the understory of spruce-fir forests in the Great North Woods.

Phytolaccaceae: The Pokeweed Family

Phytolacca americana • Pokeweed

Synonyms
- Poke "salad"

Aspects
- Clumping herb
- Edible shoots
- Sun to part shade
- Moist, well-drained soil

Pokeweed is one of the most popular native wild edibles in the United States, particularly in the Southeast. While it has a long tradition of use as a vegetable, the roots, fruits, seeds, and mature stems and leaves are poisonous. Sufficient quantities can cause diarrhea, vomiting, abdom-inal spasms, convulsions, and even death! The young shoots are boiled in several changes of water to remove the toxins, as described below. As you can imagine, I was not eager to try eating this plant, even though people have been eating the young shoots for hundreds, and probably thou-sands of years. The fear of poisoning, and the

hassle of repeatedly boiling, put me off. When I finally got around to it as part of my research for this book, I was shocked to discover that the hearty, rich flavor left me wanting more! The taste reminded me of a rich, nutty blend of spin-ach and asparagus.

Pokeweed is native to eastern North America, and has naturalized in western North America. It is an herbaceous plant that can grow 4–8 feet, or sometimes even 12 feet tall. It is quite striking, with large, floppy green leaves and bright magenta stalks. In the fall it has dark purple berries. The overall effect is a shockingly loud statement in the ornamental landscape. Pokeweed is a wild and often weedy plant that should be very easy to cultivate. It germinates readily from seed. The huge rootstocks can be divided with a sharp shovel. It should grow in most soils, although it prefers rich, moist condi-tions. Pokeweed grows in sun or partial shade. It will form a clump of multiple stems, and birds are likely to spread the seed all over town.

The consensus among wild-edible enthusiasts seems to be that only the young shoots of poke salad should be eaten, up to about 6–8 inches tall. No portions that have bright pink color should be eaten. Any minor outer layer of pink on stems can be peeled off. Blanching by piling up leaves

Pokeweed shoots can be eaten at this stage, when they do not yet show any pink coloration.

Trichostigma octandrum • Haitian Basket Vine

Synonyms
- *Rivinia octandrum*
- *Trichostigma rivinoides*
- *Villamilla octandra*
- Hoop vine

Aspects
- Woody shrub/vine
- Edible greens
- Sun to part shade
- Moist, well-drained soil

around the plant in spring will keep the pink color (and poison) from developing as quickly. Shoots should be put in water and brought to a boil. Pour off the water and refill with another round of already boiling water. Boil the plants again, and simmer for about five minutes. The pokeweed should then be ready to eat. Time for cooking ranges from 5 to 30 minutes, and different authors recommend boiling up to three times in different changes of water. I found that boiling for 20 minutes left the plants drastically overcooked. It sounds like a lot of work to change the water, and indeed it was a hassle, but remember: This is really all the work you will have to do all year to grow and eat pokeweed once your plants are established. So don't begrudge a few extra minutes to prepare your dinner; once you taste it you won't regret it.

Should you grow pokeweed in your garden? If so, make sure everyone knows that only the shoots should be eaten, and then only cooked as described above. I would be very cautious in planting pokeweed in a garden where young children play, as they are often tempted to eat pretty berries or other plant parts. If you live where this plant is native there is probably some close by that you can use instead. A final caution: Pokeweed can carry viruses that also attack plants in the broadly defined Lily family (including asparagus and onions) and nightshades (like potato, tomato, and eggplant).

In Haiti, where basic human nutrition is a serious issue, basket vine is an important food. According the tropical crop experts at Educational Concerns for Hunger Organization (ECHO), the young leaves of basket vine are an outstanding green vegetable. They can be quickly stripped off the branches. They have a substantial, collard-like texture when cooked. Leaves should be boiled for 10 minutes to remove the bitterness, and the water discarded. Older leaves are too tough to eat. Danny Blank, nursery manager at ECHO, tells a story of a Haitian visitor at ECHO who says he was saved from a life-threatening illness by eating basket vine leaves for several weeks. He wept to see the vines growing in their demonstration garden.

Basket vine is a common native from northern Argentina through the Caribbean. It is even native to South Florida, where it is critically endangered.

Haitian basket vine, little known here though native in Florida, is a productive and nutritious leaf crop.

It is a vine-like bush that can climb 20 feet up into trees or grow as a shrub on its own. When not supported by trees or trellises it grows as a sprawling, tangled mat up to 30 feet wide on the ground. Branches can grow up to 9 feet a year. Basket vine grows in full sun or part shade, and tolerates almost any soil. Plants are propagated by seed or by layering. Often vines will root where the branches touch bare soil, making propaga-tion easy. Basket vine plants will live for several decades. The viney branches are, as the name suggests, used in basketry.

Basket vine is a tropical plant, but worth growing as a dieback leaf crop in subtropical areas such as the warmer parts of Florida, the Gulf Coast, and Southern California. It seems to thrive in western Florida at ECHO. Frosts may kill it back to the roots.

Poaceae: The Grass Family

Bambusa, Dendrocalamus, Gigantochloa, and Nastus spp. • Clumping Bamboos

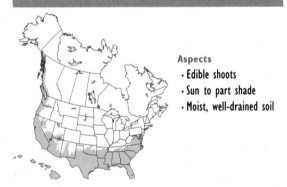

Aspects
- Edible shoots
- Sun to part shade
- Moist, well-drained soil

General Overview, History, and Ecology: Bamboos are among the most useful plants in the world, providing food and a tremendous array of building materials. Unfortunately, in the United States and Canada, bamboos have received a bad reputation for being aggressive spreaders. While many certainly do so (see the following section on running bamboos), there are many genera of bamboos that form clumps and never spread. These include many of the finest edible species. Clumping species tend to have much larger shoots, an easier harvest, and a longer harvest season than runners. Shoots from clumpers can weigh up to 20 pounds! Clumping bamboos are, however, substantially less hardy than running types. Nonetheless, they can be grown in large areas of the United States, with some species in even hardy in coastal British Columbia.

Most people in the United States and Canada have only had canned bamboo shoots, if they have tried them at all. Fresh shoots are vastly superior, and are a major world food, with over a million tons consumed worldwide every year!

Bamboo shoots are primarily used for their crisp, crunchy texture. They assume the flavor of other foods and spices they are cooked with. The shoots are high in vitamins and fiber, low in protein, carbohydrates, and fats. A few species, like *Dendrocalamus asper* and *Nastus elatus*, are even sweet enough to eat raw, especially when bagged or blanched to exclude light from the shoots. Bamboo expert Victor Cusack says in *Bamboo World*, "the 'bag grown' *D. asper* shoots I have eaten taste like a cross between water chestnut and a crisp apple, very fresh, moist, and crunchy; in fact ideal for inclusion in a salad." Clumping bamboos are extremely productive. *D. asper* can produce 60 shoots a year, with 2–3 pounds of edible core on each shoot! Similar yields are also achieved by many clumping bamboos.

An interesting challenge in bamboo shoot production is the phenomenon of bamboo flowering. When a bamboo flowers it uses up tremendous stored energy reserves. In fact, plants often do not survive flowering. All individuals of the same clone (propagated from the same original seedling plant) will flower in the same year, even if it has been 100 years since they last flowered. This has caused the economic ruin of many farmers who had large plantations of the same variety. Bamboos that flower very rarely and then die (setting lots of seed for the next generation) are known as gregarious flowering bamboos. Some species, like *Dendrocalamus laetiflorus*, flower sporadically, mean-

The edible shoots of *Bambusa malingensis*, a clumping bamboo. PHOTO BY CRAIG HEPWORTH.

leaves, and the roots are hardier still. Both culms and roots will resprout.

Crop Description: Clumping bamboos are tree-like grasses, sending up multiple shoots from a tight clump. Even in species that grow over 100 feet tall, clumps are rarely wider than 12 feet across. Bamboos have a unique growth habit: Each shoot, after emerging, reaches full size in about six weeks' time—even if it will be 120 feet tall! They do not leaf out until they reach full size, either. Once planted, clumping bamboos will put out taller shoots each year, until they reach their maximum size in about five years' time.

Climate: The best edible clumping bamboos are limited to tropical and subtropical climates. *Bambusa multiplex* and *B. textilis* are a good bit hardier (see the table below). In colder climates or in less-than-ideal growing conditions they will not attain their maximum height (sometimes this can be desirable).

Tolerances and Preferences: All clumping bamboos tolerate partial shade, and most will grow in full

ing more frequently and with less damage. Thus, if you are serious about growing bamboo shoots, you should plant multiple varieties of the same species, and/or multiple species, to ensure continuous production without losing your crop to seed.

Note: Temperatures given are for leaf hardiness. The culms (woody stems) are hardier than the

Table 12: **Best Edible Shoot Clumping Bamboos**

There are many clumping bamboo species that produce edible shoots. This list highlights some of the best, and also those of lesser quality but better hardiness. *Note:* As these species approach their hardiness limits they will not reach their maximum heights. Consult the American Bamboo Society (see Resources) or your regional bamboo nursery to determine which species are best suited to your area. For example, in Florida, *Dendrocalamus* species do not seem to thrive, while *Bambusa* species grow very well.

Genus	Species	Hardy	Max. Ht.	Notes
Bambusa	burmanica	41°F	50 feet	excellent
	multiplex	10°F	33 feet	somewhat bitter
	oldhamii	15°F	60 feet	excellent
	textilis	5°F	33 feet	somewhat bitter
Dendrocalamus	asper	23°F	100 feet	excellent, eat fresh in salads
	beecheyana	15°F	35 feet	excellent (Bambusa beecheyana)
	brandesii	29°F	128 feet	excellent
	giganteus	31°F	100 feet	excellent
	laetiflorus	25°F	75 feet	excellent
Gigantochloa	atter	32°F	65 feet	excellent
	levis	40°F	65 feet	excellent
	robusta	32°F	65 feet	excellent
Nastus	elatus	31°F	65 feet	excellent, eat fresh in salads

sun. They require well-drained soil. More water will make them grow faster.

Naturalization Status: None of these species has naturalized in the United States or Canada, probably due to their clumping nature and the infrequency of flowering and setting seed.

Pest, Disease, and Weed Problems: After a few years, clumping bamboos are self-mulching, which helps eliminate most weed problems. There are some pest problems from mites, scale insects, and leaf rollers. Leaf rollers can be controlled like other caterpillars, with Bt, pyrethrins, or simply by providing nectar for a diverse population of beneficial insects.

Propagation and Planting: Propagate clumping bamboos most easily by division of clumps. Divided sections should be at least two years old and include a reasonable section of rhizome with good roots. Some species can also be grown from cuttings. Spacing depends on which species you are planting; consult your bamboo nursery or the American Bamboo Society for recommendations.

Other Cultivation Information: To manage a clump for edible shoot production, use the following intensive management practices. Wait two or three years after planting before you start harvesting shoots. The third year, remove the inner shoots, leaving 10–12 culms. Continue to harvest most shoots, removing all culms over three years of age. Try to rotate your cutting so you have an equal number of first-, second-, and third-year culms in the clump, with a total of 8–12 culms in any given year once established. These culms should be fairly evenly distributed throughout the clump. Remove all dead culms. An additional management tip is to avoid fertilizing for one to two months before shoot season, because fertilizing at that time makes shoots less flavorful. In addition, light makes shoots more bitter tasting, so many growers pile leaves around them or carefully cover emerging shoots with a bag filled with straw or leaves to exclude light, similar to the techniques used for blanching asparagus. Consult Victor Cusack's *Bamboo World* for more details on shoot production.

Harvest and Storage: The shoot season can last up to six months. As long as you leave plenty of

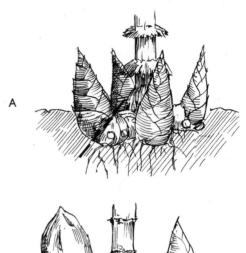

Harvesting clumping bamboos. A) Where to cut. B) Bagged shoot for blanching.

culms with leaves to keep photosynthesis going (see above), you can harvest a great number of shoots from a clump each year. Shoots emerge from the ground, and then pause for a week or two before beginning their explosive growth. This pause period is the ideal time for harvesting clumping bamboos. Using a shovel, ax, or large knife, separate the shoot from the rhizome, trying to cut as close to the rhizome as possible. Shoots have a crisp texture, but rhizomes are very hard, so you should be able to tell where you are cutting. Raw shoots have a shelf life of one to two weeks.

Uses: To prepare shoots, strip off the leafy sheath covering them. This can comprise 50–70 percent of the shoot. With all but the best-tasting species, cut into chunks and boil in salted water for 2–15 minutes. Bitter-tasting species should be boiled in two changes of water. After, boiling, bamboo shoots can be used in stir-fries or other dishes.

Related Species and Breeding Potential: The very rare flowering of most species complicates bamboo breeding. Selection from existing cultivars is the most practical method to determine, for example, the best-flavored, most productive, or hardiest strains of a given species.

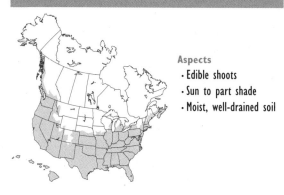

Phyllostachys spp. and other genera • Running Bamboos

Aspects
- Edible shoots
- Sun to part shade
- Moist, well-drained soil

Rhizome Barriers for Aggressive Running Bamboos

There are several methods for controlling the spread of running bamboos. Barriers 3 feet tall can be buried as an underground fence to restrain bamboos. They should be made of concrete, sheet metal, or 60-mil plastic. Ideally they should be fashioned from one continuous piece, as seams are likely escape points for underground runners. Make sure to overlap by 12 inches or more at any seams. Sooner or later these barriers have a tendency to break. See the section on rhizome barriers on page 42 for more information.

You can use a spade to root-prune plants and break rhizomes every year. You can plant in an island surrounded by deep water or a parking lot. A large container placed on top of a large area of concrete is pretty foolproof. You can also use persistent harvesting of shoots to keep plants controlled. Generally, however, placing bamboos where they can run free is your best option, because they will almost inevitably win the war of wills.

In parts of Asia too cold for clumping bamboo shoot production, running bamboos are an important vegetable. These bamboos generally produce vastly smaller shoots than clumpers, but often these have a superior flavor. Many running species produce shoots that are free of bitterness or nearly so, and can be eaten raw. Remember also that bitterness is a desirable quality in many Asian cuisines.

Running bamboos are not well behaved and are not well suited to most gardens. They spread rapidly once established and can quickly take over an area. Unless you like them enough to set aside a sizable area for shoot production and nothing else, you should avoid growing these species. Running bamboos are certainly sublime in the landscape, and have multiple uses such as providing building materials and garden stakes. Here, however, we are solely addressing their use as vegetables.

Running bamboo shoots are at their best when they are still underground, and you can just feel them poking up with the soles of your feet. Some people eat them when they have emerged but are still less than 8 inches high. Running bamboo shoots are very high in protein and have a good flavor. They can be extremely productive. Harvest shoots by pulling or cutting. Their flavor can

be improved by blanching with mulch as they emerge, though it is hard to predict where they will emerge. Once harvested the grassy sheath is removed. Some shoots can be eaten raw, but most should be boiled (5–10 minutes for sweet types, 10–20 minutes with one change of water for bitter types).

Note: The issue of bamboos flowering and dying as discussed under clumping bamboos is also relevant to running species.

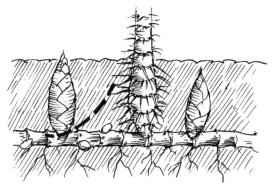

Running bamboos are ideally harvested when the shoot has barely emerged from the soil. Cut underground where the shoot emerges from the main rhizome.

Table 13: **Best Edible Shoot Running Bamboos**

This table lists some of the best runners for shoot production. Plants can survive as dieback perennials quite a bit colder than the leaf hardiness listed. Plants that are routinely killed back by frost will also spread more slowly. *Note:* In colder areas bamboos will not achieve their maximum height.

Genus	Species	Leaf Hardy	Max. Ht.	Notes
Arundinaria	gigantea	−10°F	20 feet	native to eastern United States; somewhat bitter
Phyllostachys	angusta	−3°F	22 feet	excellent
	aureosulcata	−10°F	26 feet	excellent
	dulcis	0°F	40 feet	excellent; can be eaten raw
	flexuosa	−8°F	31 feet	excellent
	heterocycla pubescens	0°F	75 feet	large, somewhat bitter; cultivated
	nidularia	−10°F	33 feet	excellent
	nuda	−10°F	34 feet	excellent; can be eaten raw
	rubromarginata	−5°F	55 feet	excellent
	viridi-glaucescens	−3°F	35 feet	excellent; can be eaten raw
	viridis	0°F	55 feet	excellent
	vivax	−5°F	35 feet	excellent
Qiongzhuea	tumidissinoda	10°F	20 feet	excellent; can be eaten raw
Sasa	kurilensis	0°F	10 feet	excellent
Semiarundinaria	fastuosa	−5°F	35 feet	excellent

Note: Temperatures given are for leaf hardiness. The culms are hardier than the leaves, and the roots are hardier still. Both culms and roots will resprout.

Running bamboos (like these *Phyllostachys* specimens) have delicious shoots and are useful in many ways, but can form undesirably large colonies.

Saccharum edule • Pitpit

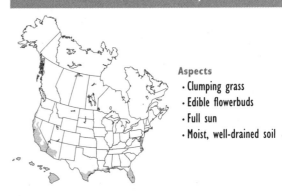

Aspects
- Clumping grass
- Edible flowerbuds
- Full sun
- Moist, well-drained soil

This mutant form of sugarcane is an ancient and popular vegetable in its homeland of New Guinea, but little known outside of Southeast and Pacific Asia. Pitpit is a tall grass growing 6–10 feet high. What distinguishes it from sugarcane is that the flowerbuds never open. Instead they form a banana-sized vegetable wrapped in a leafy sheath. This flowerbud is a nutritious vegetable, high in vitamins and protein. It has been compared to cauliflower as far as its texture and uses, but not its flavor. Some people think it is delicious, while others find it tasteless. Pitpit can be used raw or cooked.

Pitpit forms a clump that spreads slowly by rhizomes. It can prosper in poor soils. Plants thrive in the hot, humid tropics, but are worth trying through Zones 8 and 9 as dieback perennials. They should presumably be hardy anywhere

sugarcane can be grown, including Florida and much of the Gulf Coast. Propagate pitpit by cuttings and division. Harvest can begin five months from planting, and clumps will produce well for two to three years before needing division.

Note: Sugarcane is also a perennial edible crop, though not a vegetable by my definition. To enjoy fresh sugarcane, peel the outer sheath of the stalks (watch out for serious paper cuts!). Chew on a section of the pith, sucking out the sugary juice. Then spit out the fibrous pulp that remains.

Polygonaceae: The Smartweed Family

Rheum x cultorum • Rhubarb

Synonyms
- *Rheum rhabarbarum*

Aspects
- Clumping herb
- Edible leafstalks
- Edible flowerbuds
- Full sun
- Moist, well-drained soil

General Overview, History, and Ecology: Rhubarb is considered by many gardeners to be a fruit-like vegetable. Most people in the United States and Canada grow rhubarb as the sour component of sweet pies and sauces, adding lots of sugar or fruits like strawberries to offset its tartness. But rhubarb has a long history of being grown in the chilly regions of Asia as a vegetable, used in soups and stews. It is hard to imagine rhubarb served with lamb, but its red color and sorrel-like taste are very nice in stews. Rhubarb is currently undergoing a renaissance in restaurants as a gourmet vegetable.

The leafstalks (or petioles) are usually cooked. They can also be eaten raw in small amounts. The large flowerbuds can be eaten, and have the texture of cauliflower but a strong sour flavor. The flow-

erbuds, and indeed even the leafstalks to a lesser extent, should only be eaten in moderation.

It is well known that the leaves and roots of rhubarb are poisonous. They can cause nausea, dizziness, convulsions, and even death. Make sure to train any children who might be in your garden to avoid eating anything but the stalks of rhubarb. The stalks contain only the relatively harmless oxalic acid (see the article on page 120).

Crop Description: Rhubarb is a familiar garden vegetable with enormous leaves. It grows as a large clump perhaps 3–5 feet wide, with flower stalks 5–6 feet. Most have red leafstalks, but there are many varieties of rhubarb, including some with green stalks.

Climate: Rhubarb is a plant for cold and cool climates. It can be grown in the coldest places in Canada and Alaska, being hardy to Zone 1 (–50°F and colder). In the West rhubarb can be grown throughout the Pacific Northwest and in cooler areas of California that get some frost. In the Midwest and East it grows south through Zone 7, but the intense summer heat and humidity of the South is too much for it. In warm and tropical regions it can be grown as a cool-season annual. For example, in Florida rhubarb can be grown as a winter annual, planting seedlings (or presumably divisions) in August and harvesting from March to May.

Tolerances and Preferences: Rhubarb should be grown in full sun. It is a heavy feeder and should

Rhubarb is good for more than just pies—the stalks are great in stews and other dishes.

be planted in rich soil that is amended frequently with compost or well-rotted manure for best production.

Naturalization Status: Rhubarb has naturalized in much of the eastern and central United States and Canada.

Pest, Disease, and Weed Problems: Rhubarb has few pests or diseases to report, although it is susceptible to anthracnose.

Propagation and Planting: Propagation is usually by division of clumps. Rhubarb can also be grown from seed, but seedlings will have wide variation in flavor and leafstalk color. If you want to maintain your deep red stalks, use vegetative propagation. Plant rhubarb at least 3 feet apart.

Other Cultivation Information: Some sources recommend removing the flower stalks when they appear. This coincides nicely with harvesting the edible cauliflower-like buds.

Harvest and Storage: Rhubarb leafstalks can be cut or twisted off. Make sure not to accidentally get any of the poisonous rootstock at the base of any leafstalks, and remove any part of the leaf as well.

Uses: Rhubarb stalks can be cooked in the familiar sauces and pies, and can also be used as a tart, celery-like vegetable.

Related Species and Breeding Potential: Rhubarb is not in much need of breeding work, unless it would be to develop less poisonous varieties. There are many edible species in the genus *Rheum*. Turkey rhubarb (*R. palmatum*) is an enormous species, with leaves reaching 6 feet high and flower stalks to 10 feet. Its enormous leaves resemble maple leaves, and the leafstalks are said by some to be superior to ordinary rhubarb. Also worthy of mention is Himalayan rhubarb (*R. australe*), which apparently has apple-flavored leafstalks.

Rumex and *Oxyria* spp. • Sorrel

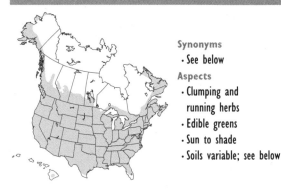

Synonyms
- See below

Aspects
- Clumping and running herbs
- Edible greens
- Sun to shade
- Soils variable; see below

General Overview, History, and Ecology: These closely related plants have long been popular perennial vegetables in Europe. Their leaves have a strong lemony tang and a delicate texture. Sorrels add a zesty flavor to salads, or can be cooked in many dishes, most famously in cream of sorrel soup. The leaves are edible nearly year-round in mild temperate climates, and here in my cold northern garden they are among the first greens available in spring and one of the last in fall. By continually cutting back the flowering stalks you can keep them producing tender greens long into the summer.

Sorrels are tough, reliable perennials that can become weedy in the garden. Some species have naturalized widely in the United States and Canada. I have seen a large clump of garden sorrel successfully holding its own against quack grass in a garden that had been abandoned for 10 years. Recently a nonflowering variety of garden sorrel named 'Profusion' has become available. The flavor of this variety stays excellent all season long, since it never bolts. It also will certainly never become weedy! My 'Profusion' plants have a delicious flavor and have grown very well, and have been a favorite stop for browsing and harvesting in my garden since I planted them this spring. An alternative technique to minimize weediness

The sorrel cultivar 'Profusion' never flowers and puts out fresh tangy leaves even under the snow.

would be to grow only male plants. Just grow out some plants from seed and rogue out all that produce female flowers and set seed. The males will not produce seed, although their flavor will still temporarily diminish when they flower.

Sorrels owe their sour flavor in part to oxalic acid (see page 120). They are also high in vitamin C.

Sorrel plants make good companions for other plants. Their roots dig deep in the soil and mine for calcium, phosphorus, and potassium. Over the years, as their leaves and roots decompose, they improve the soil around them, to the benefit of neighboring plants. Surely these low-maintenance, soil-building, delicious vegetables deserve a place in your garden.

O. digyna (Mountain Sorrel). This species is native to alpine and arctic areas around the Northern Hemisphere. It forms a medium-sized clump (1–2 feet) and has rounded leaves. The leaves are markedly larger in partial shade. They have a delicate flavor and texture. This species is probably hardy to Zone 1 or 2.

R. acetosa (Garden Sorrel, French Sorrel). This sorrel is the one most commonly cultivated in the United States and Canada. It has tall, lance-shaped leaves. The flower spikes grow up to 3 or 4 feet high. The nonflowering variety 'Profusion' belongs to this species. Just to make things confusing, not only this species but also *R. acetosella* and *R. scutatus* are all known as French sorrel.

R. acetosella (Sheep Sorrel, French Sorrel). This species is a very common weed in gardens, and

has naturalized extensively in disturbed areas, particularly areas with dry, acidic soils. To my taste buds, the flavor is as good as that of any of the cultivated species. The leaves are smaller and somewhat tedious to harvest. Sheep sorrel is low growing and spreads aggressively by runners to form large colonies, and also drops lots of seed. This is a case where having a male plant that cannot set seed would make a lot of difference in weediness within your garden. Such plants would make a useful edible groundcover—otherwise be very careful where you introduce this species.

R. scutatus (Silver Shield Sorrel, Buckler-Leaf Sorrel, French Sorrel). This species has replaced garden sorrel as the sorrel of choice in France, the world center of sorrel cuisine. The French feel that the flavor is superior, and I am inclined to agree, although my plants have not been as vigorous as garden sorrel (they seem to take a few years to get established, and don't abide competition). Their flavor and texture are definitely a bit more delicate, although the leaves are smaller than garden and mountain sorrel, making for more work in harvesting and washing. Silver shield sorrel has not yet caught on in the United States, but is a tasty addition to the garden.

Crop Description: Sorrels are perennial herbs. See the individual species descriptions for more details.

Tolerances and Preferences: Sorrels will grow in full sun to part shade, and prefer a somewhat acidic soil.

Climate: Sorrels grow in temperate and cold climates, and most are hardy in Zones 3–9.

Naturalization Status: Mountain sorrel is native to high altitudes in North America. Sheep sorrel is a pernicious weed and has naturalized aggressively. Garden sorrel has naturalized mildly. Silver shield sorrel has not naturalized.

Pest, Disease, and Weed Problems: Sorrels do not have too many pest or disease problems, although in wet weather they can have trouble with slugs. Leaf miners can be problematic. They can themselves become weeds in the garden.

Propagation and Planting: Sorrels grow readily from seed. They can propagate easily by division. Most species should be set 12–18 inches apart.

Other Cultivation Information: Plants should be divided every few years to rejuvenate them.

Harvest and Storage: Sorrel leaves do not store well, and should be used soon after harvest.

Uses: Sorrels are used in any way you would spinach, fresh or cooked, although the intensity of their flavor is a bit much if you make a salad just from them. Try mixing them with other greens to make a salad. They are also used in many soups, sauces, and other dishes. Sorrels cook down dramatically, so pick a lot if you are going to be cooking with them as a centerpiece of your meal.

Related Species and Breeding Potential: There are many edible species in the genus *Rumex*, including some that have been cultivated like patience dock (*R. patiencia*), monk's rhubarb (*R. alpinum*), and the attractive red-veined bloody dock (*R. sanguineus*). As far as breeding goes, however, the species profiled here are frankly already quite delicious and useful. Perhaps a running groundcover like sheep sorrel with much larger leaves could be developed.

Solanaceae: The Nightshade Family

Lycium barbarum and *L. chinense* • **Wolfberry**

Synonyms
- Matrimony vine
- Box thorn
- Goji berry

Aspects
- Suckering viney shrub
- Edible leaves and fruit
- Full sun to part shade
- Moist, well-drained soil

Wolfberry is a popluar leaf crop in China and among the few cold-hardy tree and shrub vegetables.

Wolfberry is a multipurpose perennial vegetable, featuring both edible leaves and fruit. The leaves are used in Chinese cooking, and are described as having a watercress-peppermint flavor. Sounds intriguing, but to me they taste more nutty, musky, and mildly mustard. I like them raw as well as cooked in soups. The fruit is very small and red, with a flavor incorporating cherry tomato and licorice, with just a hint of bitterness.

Wolfberry is one of the few hardy woody leaf crops, as well as being the only hardy perennial vegetable in this important garden family. It does have its drawbacks—it grows rampantly into a suckering viney shrub 6–12 feet tall and wide, with thorns on older growth. It has naturalized a bit in parts of the United States. A rhizome barrier might be a good idea to control the root suckers, while regular pruning or coppicing will keep the aboveground growth under control. Wolfberry also tip-layers, so don't let the branches contact the soil if you don't want it to spread. In fact, if you harvest leaves and shoots frequently enough that will keep it from taking over your garden.

The plant is easily grown from seed, cuttings, or division. My plants are quite susceptible to powdery mildew, so make sure to plant somewhere with good airflow. Apparently slugs can be a problem in areas where they are common. Wolfberry

> ### Stir-fried Greens
>
> This recipe works nicely with wolfberry leaves, but can be used for most greens profiled in this book.
>
> I clove garlic
> Peanut oil
> ¼ pound greens (about a double handful)
> Tamari
> Roasted sesame seeds
>
> Sauté garlic in peanut oil until golden, and then add chopped greens. Stir frequently, and splash with tamari once or twice. Garnish with roasted sesame seeds. Shredded ginger can also be used along with or instead of the garlic. Serves 4.

can be grown in sun to part shade, and is hardy from Zones 5 or 6 through 8. A number of named varieties are grown in China—such as 'Hemp Leaf' with large red fruit, and 'Yellow Acute Head' with very sweet yellow fruit (for detailed information and illustrations of cultivars see Hu's excellent *Food Plants of China*). These varieties should be imported for cultivation here. Perhaps someday wolfberry could be used in a wide cross to develop a hardy perennial tree tomato of some kind.

Physalis spp. • Ground Cherry and Goldenberry

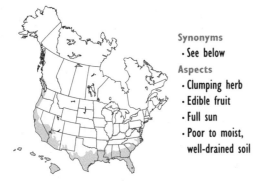

Synonyms
- See below

Aspects
- Clumping herb
- Edible fruit
- Full sun
- Poor to moist, well-drained soil

General Overview, History, and Ecology: Around the world there are many edible species in the genus *Physalis*, including the zesty tomatillo (*P. ixocarpa*). Here we will consider two very similar species, the tender perennial goldenberry (*P. peruviana*) and the self-seeding annual ground cherry (*P. pruinosa*). Both species are sprawling, woolly-leaved herbs somewhat resembling tomatoes or eggplants. The sweet yellow fruits are encased in a papery sheath like the related Chinese lantern (*P. alkekengei*). Fruits are usually ½–¾ inch, although some varieties of goldenberry are larger. The unique flavor of the fruits is sweet, slightly nutty, reminiscent of a tomato, and a bit musky. Ground cherries are delicious eaten fresh and are also excellent in sauces, especially when poured hot over ice cream. You can also peel back the paper husk and use it as a handle to dip the fruits in chocolate.

P. peruviana (Goldenberry, Cape Gooseberry, Ground Cherry, Poha). This perennial *Physalis* originates in the Andes. It is grown in gardens in mild climates around the world, and may soon become a major cultivated crop. Researcher David Klinac reports (as quoted in *Lost Crops of the Incas*), "If you're nice to it, you get a jungle. You get vast numbers of fruits per bush, but the effort of cutting your way in is enormous. It's best to be as hard on the plant as possible." For this reason plants are usually grown in poor soils, where they fruit quite well. Goldenberry will not set fruit well in intense heat and humidity, but requires warm nights. Plants are hardy through Zone 8, but need a long growing season to ripen fruit. If started indoors they can also be grown as annuals in colder climates, although some varieties have too short a season. Their climate limitations make them well suited for parts of California and upland Hawaii, but they are not well adapted to the rest of the United States or Canada. By cutting back plants after harvest, their productive life can be stretched out to about four years. Named cultivars include 'Giallo Grosso', 'Golden Nugget', and 'Goldenberry'. Some fruits of the cultivar 'Goldenberry' reach 2 inches across.

P. pruinosa (Strawberry Tomato, Husk Tomato, Ground Cherry). This annual species is a prolific self-seeder, making it functionally perennial in most gardens. Plants can also be started indoors to get a jump on the season. For gardeners unable to grow *P. peruviana*, this species is a good substitute. The flavor is excellent and there are

The delicious strawberry-tomoto-pineapple flavored fruits of golden berry. PHOTO BY BROCK DOLMAN.

several named cultivars available, including 'Aunt Molly's', 'Cossack Pineapple', and 'Goldie'. This species is also known as *P. pubescens*.

Crop Description: Both species are straggly, shrublike herbs with woolly leaves.

Climate: Goldenberry (*P. peruviana*) requires long seasons free of excessive heat or cold. It is best suited to southern and coastal California and upland Hawaii. It can be grown elsewhere to some degree, but often will not fruit well. It is hardy to Zone 8 as a perennial and can be grown as an annual in long-season areas. Strawberry tomato (*P. pruinosa*) can be grown in much of the United States and Canada. Some varieties fruit in as little as 60 days from seed. Starting plants indoors can give you an extra boost.

Tolerances and Preferences: Both species should be grown in full sun. Apparently they should get plenty of water when growing vegetatively and little water when fruiting. Goldenberry should be grown in poor soils for the most manageable fruit production.

Naturalization Status: Goldenberry has naturalized in California, Hawaii, and (surprisingly) Kentucky, New Jersey, and Massachusetts. Strawberry tomato is native to most of North America and has naturalized in Hawaii.

Pest, Disease, and Weed Problems: Both species are affected to some degree by the common pests and diseases of solanaceous crops (see the article on page 191).

Propagation and Planting: Both species are easy to grow from seed. Goldenberry is also grown from cuttings, although only about a third of cuttings take. Goldenberry can also be air-layered (see page 167). Cuttings and air layers fruit more quickly than seedlings. Space ground cherries at 3–4 feet.

Other Cultivation Information: Plants should be staked or grown in tomato cages for ease of harvest.

Harvest and Storage: Fruits fall off the plant when ripe. Their husk protects the fruits from getting dirty. Fruits can also be picked when the husks turn dry and papery. Spreading a cloth under plants and shaking is also effective. Fruits that are still slightly green can be ripened inside. Yields can be very high. Fruit stored in a cool, dry place will last for several weeks.

Uses: The fruits are delicious raw and can also be cooked to make sweet or savory sauces. They can be sun-dried like raisins. For a fruit, the protein and phosphorus contents are very high. Fruits are also high in vitamins A and C. *Note:* The leaves and unripe fruits are toxic.

Related Species and Breeding Potential: Breeding longer-lived and hardy ground cherries for home gardens would be interesting. There are several hardy perennial *Physalis* species with edible (though inferior) fruits. All have a running habit and form colonies. Especially interesting is the ornamental Chinese lantern (*P. alkekengi*). The Chinese lantern botanical variety 'Franchetti' has larger fruits and would be a good choice for crossing. (*Note:* The husks of Chinese lantern are poisonous.) The widespread native perennials *P. heterophylla* and *P. subglabrata* would be good hardy perennial parents as well. Heat- and drought-resistant plants could be bred from the southwestern native edible *P. crassifolia*. Ground cherries are apparently difficult to cross with the related tomatillos (*P. ixocarpa* and *P. philadelphica*).

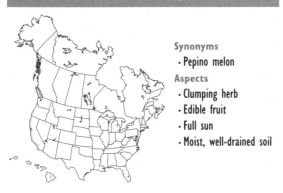

Solanum muricatum · Pepino Dulce

Synonyms
- Pepino melon

Aspects
- Clumping herb
- Edible fruit
- Full sun
- Moist, well-drained soil

General Overview, History, and Ecology: The pepino has been cultivated in the cool tropical and subtropical uplands of the Andes for at least 2,500 years. In the last decades pepino has become a minor cultivated crop in Chile, New Zealand, Australia, California, and Hawaii. Its prospects elsewhere are limited, as it has very particular climate requirements.

Pepino fruits are beautiful, tomato-sized and larger with a cream or yellow skin featuring attractive purple, gray, or green stripes. The flesh tastes very similar to cantaloupe and other melons. The fruits are mostly water, and have little nutritional value beyond vitamins A and C, but on a hot day they are very refreshing. Unripe fruits are also eaten, and are similar to cucumbers.

Pepino plants resemble tomatoes and are grown similarly, except that they will produce well for several years. There are a number of named varieties that are propagated by cuttings. These attractive plants are on their way to becoming a more common vegetable in those parts of the United States where they can be grown.

Crop Description: Pepinos are herbaceous perennials with a somewhat woody base. They resemble bushy potato plants.

Climate: Pepinos are from in the cool tropical uplands of the Andes. They need warm but not hot weather to set fruit, even at night. They are killed to the ground by temperatures below 28°F, though they will resprout if the roots are protected from freezing. A long, warm, frost-free season of five to eight months is required to set and mature fruit. Pepinos are well suited to much of Hawaii. They are successfully grown in central and Southern California, as well as coastal California in the Bay Area and farther north along the coast. Plants can also be grown in containers.

Tolerances and Preferences: Pepinos will grow in poor soil; in fact, too rich a soil will encourage vegetative growth instead of fruiting. They have a shallow root system and need frequent watering.

Naturalization Status: Pepino has not naturalized here.

Pest, Disease, and Weed Problems: Unfortunately pepinos are susceptible to many of the pests and diseases that other solanaceous crops are. Pests such as Colorado potato beetle, cutworm, and tomato hornworm can cause damage. Among the many potential disease problems are early and late blight, bacterial spot, and anthracnose. For more information, see the article on page 191.

Propagation and Planting: Propagate named varieties of pepino by cuttings. Cuttings should be 3–5 inches long, and root easily although some sources recommend using rooting hormone. Pepinos can also be easily grown from seed, although the seedlings will not be identical to the parent and may be of inferior quality. Space plants about 2 feet apart.

Other Cultivation Information: Plants are usually grown as annuals in climates outside of the tropics, but can be productive for several years. Like tomatoes, pepinos often need staking. Some growers trellis and prune their plants for maximum production. Pepinos do not require pollinators to set fruit, but growing more than one variety will increase yields.

Pepino is a melo-flavored perennial in the tomato family.

Harvest and Storage: Pepinos can be picked when fully mature for fresh eating. Pick them just before maturity for better storage. Almost-ripe fruits will store for three to four weeks in a refrigerator. Fruits are ripe when their skin turns yellow.

Uses: Unripe pepinos can be used like cucumbers. Ripe fruits taste extremely similar to cantaloupe, and are eaten the same way.

Related Species and Breeding Potential: Selecting for pepinos that are adapted to a wider range of climates, at least including hotter summers, should be a priority. Disease and pest resistance are also major issues. Crossing with tomatoes, eggplants, or other heat-loving relatives might develop heat-resistant pepino hybrids. Perhaps pepino could be crossed with the shrubby naranjilla (*S. quitoense*) to create a unique delicious new shrub fruit. It might also be crossed with tamarillo (*S. betaceum* or *Cyphomandra betacea*), a tomato-like tree fruit that is usually cooked rather than eaten raw. Like tomato and eggplant, pepino could be crossed with hardier relatives, but care should be taken as most of those have poisonous fruits. A longer-lived perennial might also be the goal of selection or crossing with long-lived perennial *Solanums* with edible fruits like naranjilla or the "bush tomatoes" of Australia (*S. centrale* and *S. chippendalei*).

Capsicum, Lycopersicon, and Solanum spp. • Peppers, Tomatoes, Eggplants & Potatoes

Aspects
- Clumping herbs or shrubs
- Edible fruits or tubers
- Full sun
- Moist, well-drained soil

Many of the common solanaceous crops grown in cold climates are actually short-lived perennials in the tropics. To my knowledge no breeding work has gone into developing productive, long-lived perennial varieties of these species.

The ají dulce, the long-lived national pepper of Puerto Rico.

This may be because of the susceptibility to diseases so common in this family, which would make perennials lose productivity early in their lives anyway. Nonetheless this sort of breeding work would be an interesting project. There are also many hardy perennials in this family that are closely related to these crops, although many of them are poisonous and thus poor breeding stock. Meanwhile, gardeners outside the tropics can continue to grow these crops as annuals.

***Capsicum* spp.** (Sweet Peppers). Ordinary sweet peppers sometimes persist for several years as perennials in the tropics. The only productive, reliably perennial bell pepper I am aware of is an Australian variety called 'Perennial Capsicum', which lives for three to four years. There are a number of longer-lived tropical perennial pepper species. The ají dulce (a variety of *C. chinense*) is the national pepper of Puerto Rico. Ají dulce is a long-lived perennial shrub, in the same species as the fiery habanero, with small sweet peppers with the rich aroma of their spicy cousins but only a mild warmth. There are also many perennial hot peppers, though to me these are culinary herbs rather than vegetables. They include tabasco peppers (*C. frutescens*) and wild hot peppers (*C. annum aviculare*), both hardy to about Zone 9, and the rocoto (*C. pubescens*), which lives for up to 10 years. The rocoto has large, fleshy hot fruits, and is the most cold-tolerant of cultivated peppers. It would be an excellent parent in a breeding program. Remember that sweet peppers are descended from fiery hot peppers themselves.

Lycopersicon spp. (Tomato). In the tropics tomatoes will sometimes persist as short-lived perennials. Many varieties, especially cherry tomatoes, self-sow prodigiously even in cold climates. The tiny wild cherry tomato *L. pimpinellifolium* is an excellent self-seeder. Tomatoes are sometimes classed in the genus *Solanum*, and are closely enough related that they can be grafted on potatoes (*S. tuberosum*). Perhaps tomatoes could be crossed with a hardy *Solanum* species. Unfortunately most hardy *Solanums* have poisonous fruits, so breeding work would have to be cautious. Tropical prospects are more promising. The naranjilla (*S. quitoense*) is a shrub cultivated for its delicious dessert-type fruits. Perhaps a woody form of tomato might be developed. Tomato could also potentially be crossed with pepino (*S. muricatum*) to create an interesting new short-lived perennial for warm climates. It is also possible that tomato could be crossed with the tamarillo or tree tomato (*S. betaceum* or *Cyphomandra betacea*) to develop a quite tomato-like tree fruit.

Solanum melongena & spp. (Eggplant). In the tropics eggplants are short-lived perennials, sometimes becoming woody shrubs. Like tomatoes, the potential for hardy perennial eggplants is handicapped by the lack of cold-loving edible relatives, which would make for a slower and more cautious breeding project. By crossing with the sweet naranjilla (*S. quitoense*) or savory tomato-like tamarillo (*S. betaceum* or *Cyphomandra betacea*), a tree eggplant could be developed.

S. tuberosum & spp. (Potato). Cultivated potatoes are a classic example of perennials grown as annuals. In warm enough climates potatoes left in the ground will resprout the following year. However, the many pest and disease problems facing potatoes mean that rotating potatoes through different parts of the garden is essential for good yields. Oikos Tree Crops offers a semi-wild potato variety that survives their Michigan winters and has overwintered in my Zone 6 garden. There are many hardy, marginally edible relatives, including the western natives *S. fendleri* and *S. jamesii*. Any potato to be grown in situ as a perennial would have to have excellent disease and insect resistance. A running, colony-forming habit, rather than a clumping one, would also be useful. There are a number of additional cultivated potato species in the Andes. Most have limiting day-length and climate requirements, but they may have valuable traits to offer to a perennial potato-breeding project.

Pests and Diseases of the Nightshade Family

Many pests and diseases specialize in this succulent family of crop plants. Here are a few of the worst, and some ideas you can use to protect your perennial nightshades from them. Rotation is effective with some diseases of this family, so make sure to plant your perennial Solanaceae in soils that have been free of members of this family (tomato, potato, eggplant, pepper) for at least three years. *Note:* Plants in this family are also susceptible to many other generalist pests and diseases; see page 50 for more information.

Colorado potato beetle is a devastating pest of the Nightshade family. The larvae and beetles skeletonize or completely devour leaves. Controls include the use of row covers in early season, lots of handpicking, rotenone, neem, and Bt sprays.

Early blight causes lesions, yellowing of foliage, leaf drop, and rotting fruit. It can be prevented by planting resistant varieties, purchasing disease-free seed and plants, and garden practices like good air circulation, drip irrigation to keep foliage dry, and crop rotation (which may be over a longer period with perennials). If early blight does show up on your perennial nightshades, remove and destroy the affected material, or use copper spray.

Late blight also causes lesions, along with white mold, and a slimy breakdown of plant parts. Good garden sanitation, like cleaning up and composting all nightshade residues in winter, can help to prevent it. Remove and destroy all plant parts with symptoms of late blight, or use copper spray.

Tobacco mosaic virus causes misshapen, mottled leaves, dying branches, and yellow, wrinkled fruits. It can be carried in cigarettes, so don't smoke near plants, and make sure all smokers wash their hands before handling plants or seeds. Infected plants should be pulled up and destroyed. Some reports indicate that spraying seedlings with skim milk is helpful.

Tomato hornworm is an enormous species of caterpillar, leaving large holes and dark barrel-shaped droppings on leaves. Hornworms can be controlled with Bt spray, soap spray with hot pepper, rotenone, and pyrethrins. See the picture on page 56 of a hornworm in my garden that has been parasitized by tiny wasps.

Tetragoniaceae: The New Zealand Spinach Family

Tetragonia tetragonioides • New Zealand Spinach

Synonyms
- *Tetragonia expansa*
- Warrigal greens

Aspects
- Mat-forming herb
- Edible greens
- Sun to part shade
- Dry to moist soil

New Zealand spinach is a wild edible of the beaches and plains of Australia, New Zealand, and many Pacific islands. It has been brought into cultivation in the last few hundred years, and has naturalized on many of the world's tropical and subtropical beaches. New Zealand spinach (under the name *warrigal greens*) has recently become a popular mainstay of "bush tucker" native wild-food cuisine in Australia.

The leaves and the top 3–4 inches of the new shoots are eaten. Even if you are not going to eat it you should keep it picked every week to ensure production of fresh new growth. Small amounts can be eaten raw, but the leaves contain oxalates and saponins and should be cooked if eaten in quantity. To keep the brilliant green color, steam or boil leaves and shoots briefly, then immerse them in cold water to cool them. Strain them out and eat them. The flavor is somewhat similar to spinach, though a bit inferior to my taste.

New Zealand spinach will grow well in northern summers, but it cannot handle true tropical heat. Even in the Deep South of the United States it should be grown in partial shade to protect it. Many gardeners outside the tropics grow it as annual summer spinach. The leaves and shoots are fast growing, and the more you pick the faster they grow. Some individual plants are perennial, and some are annual. All will readily self-sow in the subtropics. Their low-growing,

dense mats make a good groundcover below other types of vegetation. Plants are drought-tolerant and love sandy soils, also tolerating salt. New Zealand spinach is evergreen in mild climates. It has managed to naturalize not only in Hawaii and coastal California (as might be expected) but also as an annual in Massachusetts, Wisconsin, and other cold locations.

New Zealand spinach grows in full sun, or partial shade in intensely hot areas. Few pests or diseases affect this rugged plant. New Zealand spinach is propagated by cuttings or grown from seed. For best germination, soak the seeds in water for 24 hours before planting. Germination is somewhat erratic.

New Zealand spinach is a truly low-maintenance crop. These plants have come back for years in my garden in an area saturated with road salt every winter.

Tiliaceae: The Linden Family

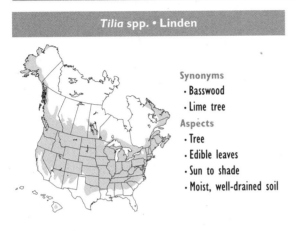

Tilia spp. • Linden

Synonyms
- Basswood
- Lime tree

Aspects
- Tree
- Edible leaves
- Sun to shade
- Moist, well-drained soil

Linden is one of the few hardy trees with edible leaves. In spring the tender young leaves have a mild flavor and tender, somewhat mucilaginous flavor. I was surprised by how much I liked them. Martin Crawford of the Agroforestry Research Trust recommends eating them in sandwiches like lettuce. Some botanists class the genus *Tilia* in the Mallow family with the similar edible cranberry hibiscuses. All *Tilia* species are edible, but the flavor varies. Apparently *T. cordata* is particularly good.

Lindens are very large trees, with most leaves out of reach. They do produce many sprouts at the base, easily accessible for harvest. Or, if you are serious about linden leaves and want to be able to harvest them all season long, you can use a technique called coppicing (see page 49). Cut the trees down to about 6 inches above the ground every two years or so. They will produce a great abundance of suckers, which will grow quickly and produce fresh leaves all season. Leaves will also be in easy reach for harvesting. Crawford is growing linden leaves in this fashion at his research farm in Devon, England, and they are among his favorite perennial vegetables.

Many species and hybrids of *Tilia* are available. Taste tests to determine the best species should be conducted by the curious. It is conceivable that trees with superior flavor exist, and could be crossed with one another to truly develop linden leaves as a new woody leaf crop for cold climates. There are species hardy from Zone 3 through Zone 8. Native species include *T. americana* and *T. heterophylla*.

Tropaeolaceae: The Nasturtium Family

Tropaeolum tuberosum • Mashua

Synonyms
- Añu
- Tuberous rooted nasturtium

Aspects
- Clumping herb
- Edible tubers
- Edible leaves and flowers
- Full sun
- Moist, well-drained soil

General Overview, History, and Ecology: This beautiful relative of nasturtium has been cultivated since ancient times in the cool tropical highlands of the Andes. It has a reputation for thriving on neglect, is virtually immune to pests and diseases, and can yield up to an astonishing 8 pounds of tubers per plant in a single growing season. Mashua has produced crops as far north as Vancouver on the West Coast.

While not as delicious as some of the other Andean root crops like yacon and oca, mashua roots are nutritious and productive. Tubers come in a variety of colors, ranging from white to yellow to beautiful bright red. The flesh is yellow. The tubers are usually cooked due to their strong peppery nasturtium-watercress taste when eaten raw. You may want to peel them before cooking. Mashua can be used as a generic root crop in many recipes, particularly in soups. They are most often boiled, after which most varieties have a mild or sweet flavor. Freezing them after cooking also makes them sweeter. These tubers are high in protein and vitamin C. *Note:* They can apparently cause goiter if consumed in very large quantities by people deficient in iodine, but this is very unlikely in the United States and Canada. The young leaves and flowers are also eaten, like the common annual nasturtium grown in gardens.

Mashua is a striking ornamental, with 5- to 10-foot vines bearing red and yellow nasturtium-like flowers. Technically it is hardy from USDA Zones 7 or 8 to 10, but mashua is a bit more picky then that. Its ideal climate is misty or cloudy, avoiding extremes of cold or heat, and rainy, with a long growing season. A particular challenge with mashua is that most varieties are day-length-sensitive and will not begin to form tubers until sunlight lasts about 12 hours. Since tubers can take six to eight months to mature after that point, that does not allow enough time for tubers to size up and produce a crop in cold climates.

Fortunately, a day-length-neutral variety (developed as an ornamental) is available, known as 'Ken Aslet'. This should enable mashua to be grown more widely—although its range is still limited because it cannot abide heat. 'Ken Aslet' should thrive in much of the Pacific Northwest, from northern California through Vancouver to the Alaska panhandle. On the other hand, if you live in an area with hot summers and mild winters, you could try it as a winter crop, planting tubers just after the heat of summer is over.

In these suboptimal climates tubers should be brought inside after harvest and stored like dahlia tubers until better weather returns. Mashua also makes a fine container plant, and has been suggested as a hanging edible ornamental.

Crop Description: Mashua resembles an aggressive perennial nasturtium, growing as a vine up to 10 feet high.

Climate: Mashua's foliage can withstand light frosts, and plants can handle temperatures in Zones 7 or 8. The issue is day length. Mashua should grow well in the Hawaiian uplands. Otherwise you will probably want to grow the day-length-neutral 'Ken Aslet' variety. It should be viable anywhere with a long, cool growing season.

Tolerances and Preferences: Within an acceptable climate, according to *Lost Crops of the Incas*, mashua is "almost unaffected by poor management." It can produce well in poor soils, tolerating pH from 5.3 to 7.5. It can grow in full sun or partial shade.

Naturalization Status: Mashua has not naturalized in the United States or Canada.

Pest, Disease, and Weed Problems: Mashua climbs over and smothers weeds, and has few pest problems. In fact, it contains insecticidal, nematocidal, and bactericidal compounds. Traditionally it is interplanted with other root crops like oca and potatoes to repel insects.

Propagation and Planting: Mashua is usually grown

Mashua is a productive, low maintenance root crop. PHOTO BY BROCK DOLMAN.

from tubers, although it can apparently be grown from seed as well. Plant mashua tubers 3–4 feet apart. As they begin to grow slowly (at least in Britain), you can grow a quick crop of lettuce or other annuals between mashua plants in spring.

Other Cultivation Information: Several times during the season, beginning when they are at least 6 inches high, plants should be "earthed up" with soil as they grow to provide room for more tubers. Plants are usually allowed to climb up stakes, trellises, or cornstalks, but can be allowed to sprawl on the ground.

Harvest and Storage: Apparently, like sunchokes it is difficult to find all the tubers, ensuring a perennial harvest in favorable climates. Otherwise harvest them all and select the best for replanting for the following season. The remainder of your tubers can be eaten or stored for later consumption. They will store for up to six months in a cool, dark, well-ventilated place.

Uses: Mashua roots are cooked like potatoes or other root crops. They have a peppery taste but can be sweetened up by freezing them after cooking and then reheating them. The leaves and flowers are eaten like ordinary annual nasturtiums, and have a strong watercress flavor.

Related Species and Breeding Potential: Perhaps mashua could be crossed with annual nasturtium (*Tropaeolum majus*) to develop a more heat-resistant, day-length-neutral root crop.

Urticaceae: The Nettle Family

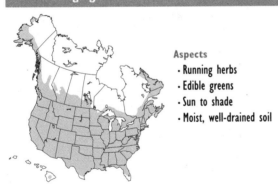

**Urtica dioica and Laportaea canadensis •
Stinging Nettle and Wood Nettle**

Aspects
- Running herbs
- Edible greens
- Sun to shade
- Moist, well-drained soil

General Overview, History, and Ecology: The first time I heard that nettles were edible I just couldn't believe it. Like many people, I had been stung many times by brushing past the plants, and I avoided them carefully. Now someone was proposing to actually pick the young nettles in spring and eat them? Ridiculous. However, always willing to try a new interesting food plant, I cautiously sampled a tiny piece of boiled nettle and found it delicious. Ten years later nettles are a spring tradition for me. I look forward to them as the very first green vegetable to come up in spring, often when there is still snow on the ground. I go out with gloves and scissors to harvest the green and purple shoots when they are only a few inches tall, and then for weeks afterward (they can be eaten until they start to flower).

Stinging nettles (*Urtica dioica*) and their native relative wood nettle (*Laportaea canadensis*) are both covered with stinging hairs that work like little syringes, injecting a painful mix of chemicals including formic acid, which is likewise present in the stings of ants and bees. Nettles need this defense because their leaves are so nutritious. Their roots draw up nutrients from the subsoil, enriching the plant itself and also its neighbors as its leaves decompose in winter. In fact, a recent study found that nettles increased the content of fragrant oils in herbs grown alongside them, perhaps due to the richer soil. Nettle leaves are rich in protein, vitamins A and C, iron, magnesium, calcium, potassium, and fiber. Still not convinced? Nettles have a rich, nutty spinach flavor, making them excellent alone or in many dishes, including my favorite, nettle quiche. Nettles have also been cultivated as fiber plants, and are used medicinally and in biodynamic compost preparations. Finally, nettle is a favorite

Once cooked, nettles make a tasty and delicious leaf crops. Harvest with gloves on!

Nettle Quiche

1 9-inch piecrust (use your own recipe or buy one)
1 cup grated cheddar cheese
4 eggs
1½ cups milk
3 cups spring nettle shoots
Salt and pepper to taste

Place a layer of cheese on the crust. Whisk eggs, and mix with milk. Boil nettles for 1 minute, then strain and chop. (Make sure to use gloves or caution with bare hands when handling uncooked nettles!) Add nettles to egg and milk mixture, and whisk in salt and pepper. Pour into piecrust. Bake at 375°F for 35–40 minutes or until golden brown. Serves 5.

habitat of many important beneficial insects, so it will help keep pests controlled in your garden!

Laportaea canadensis (Wood Nettle). Wood nettle is a more benign garden inhabitant than its more common cousin. This native woodland species grows in part to full shade, and has a less intense sting and arguably better flavor than its cousin. It spreads slowly to form a large colony over many years. I have seen large patches in old-growth forests.

Urtica dioica (Stinging Nettle). Stinging nettles are cultivated as a vegetable in Italy, and used as a wild edible throughout the cold and temperate regions of the world. The subspecies *U. d.* ssp. *gracilis* is native in much of North America, as are several other species. They spread by rhizomes to form a dense patch in sun or part shade, and spread by seed as well if you do not cut off the seed heads before they ripen.

Crop Description: Both species are perennial herbs that form colonies. Wood nettles grows 2–4 feet tall and stinging nettle 3–6 feet.

Climate: Nettle species can be grown in most of the United States and Canada, with the exception of the warmest parts of Florida. They are hardy through USDA Zone 3 or 4.

Tolerances and Preferences: Both species are hardy from the colder parts of Zone 9 to Zone 3. Both like rich soils. Stinging nettle prefers full sun to part shade, and wood nettle from part to full shade.

Naturalization Status: Wood nettle is native to eastern and central North America, and has not naturalized west of the Rockies. *Urtica dioica* ssp. *gracilis* is native to most of the United States and Canada, and there are several other native subspecies. The Eurasian *U. dioica* has naturalized extensively and is a weed of many farms and gardens.

Pest, Disease, and Weed Problems: There are very few pests or diseases to worry about. Stinging nettle itself is likely to become a weed in your garden, spreading both by rhizomes and by seed, and should be carefully managed.

Propagation and Planting: Stinging nettle is very easily grown from seed. It is also easy to divide plants and to dig up a clump from a colony. Apparently it can also be grown from cuttings, although I am not sure why anyone would go to the trouble. Wood nettle can also be grown from seed and divisions. Both species should be spaced 18–24 inches to fill in within a year or two.

Harvest and Storage: Although I know many people who harvest nettle leaves (from both species) without gloves, I have not mastered the art. Apparently if you hold the leaves tightly and go with the direction of the hairs, you don't get stung. Personally, I always use gloves and scissors and cut the leaves and young tops (the top 3 inches or so) into a bag to be carefully washed later.

Uses: Nettles just need to be cooked for a minute or two to destroy their stinging power. Accomplish this by boiling, steaming, or any kind of wet cooking (like baking in a casserole or quiche). Their flavor is strong and spinach-like, but they have more texture than spinach and do not reduce as much in size when cooked.

Related Species and Breeding Potential: Breeding for reduced stinging would be nice, although of course you then make the plants more vulnerable to pests. My neighbor Steve Breyer of Tripple Brook Farm propagates and sells a nettle clone that has fewer stinging hairs than usual. What would really be nice would be a sterile *Urtica* clone that would not spread by seed. Most plants have both male and female flowers on the same plant, while some have only female—perhaps some rare individuals produce or could be bred to produce only male flowers, thus preventing the formation of seed. Both *Laportaea* and *Urtica* nettles could presumably be bred for improved yield and flavor.

Part III

Resources

Perennial Vegetables for Each Climate Type

Here you will find lists of perennial vegetables for each of the climate types described on page 24. Some species are hardy throughout the entire area of the climate type. Others will grow only in the warmer (or sometimes colder) portions, or will only survive with protective mulch or in a microclimate. Species that can be grown as annuals (but not perennials) are also included for each climate type.

Please note that these ratings are somewhat speculative and should not be treated as though carved in stone by any means.

Extreme Cold: High Mountains and Frozen Northlands

This region covers most of inland Canada as well as the northern U.S. plains and the Rockies. It corresponds with USDA Zones 1–3, and Sunset Zones 1, 44, and 45. Note that heavy snow cover can provide excellent insulation in this zone, but the short season and lack of hot summers are serious limiting factors.

Perennial in all of the extreme cold zone:

Helianthus tuberosus, sunchoke
Hemerocallis spp., daylily
Matteuccia struthiopteris, ostrich fern
Nasturtium officinale, watercress
Oxyria digyna, mountain sorrel
Rheum x cultorum, rhubarb
Sagittaria latifolia, arrowhead

Perennial in warmer parts of the extreme cold zone, or perennial with protection:

Allium fistulosum, Welsh onion
Allium tricoccum, ramps
Allium tuberosum, garlic chives
Apios americana, groundnut
Aralia cordata, udo
Asparagus officinalis, asparagus
Bunias orientalis, Turkish rocket
Chenopodium bonus-henricus, good king Henry
Cicorium intybus, chicory
Crambe maritima, sea kale
Dioscorea japonica, jinenjo
Dioscorea opposita, Chinese yam
Laportaea canadensis, wood nettle
Levisticum officinale, lovage
Oenanthe javanica, water celery
Petasites japonicus, fuki
Phytolacca americana, pokeweed

Polygonatum biflorum var. *commutatum*, giant Solomon's seal
Rumex acetosa, French sorrel
Rumex acetosa, 'Profusion' sorrel
Rumex acetosella, sheep sorrel
Rumex scutatus, silver shield sorrel
Scorzonera hispanica, scorzonera
Sium sisarum, skirret
Stachys affinis, Chinese artichoke
Taraxacum officinale, dandelion
Tilia spp., linden (as a dieback perennial in colder areas)
Urtica dioica, nettles

Can be grown as annuals in the extreme cold zone:

Brassica oleracea acephala, 'Western Front' perennial kale
Diplotaxis spp., sylvetta arugula
Solanum tuberosum & spp., potato

Cold Temperate: East, Midwest, and Mountain West

This is a large and highly populated region covering much the eastern and central United States, as well as much of the warmer parts of Canada. This region corresponds with USDA Zones 4–7, and Sunset Zones 2–4, 6, 11, and 32–43.

Perennial in all of the cold temperate zone:

Allium fistulosum, Welsh onion
Allium tricoccum, ramps
Allium tuberosum, garlic chives
Apios americana, groundnut
Aralia cordata, udo
Asparagus officinalis, asparagus
Bunias orientalis, Turkish rocket
Camassia cusickii, Cusick's camass

Globe artichokes are truly a gourmet perennial vegetable.

Camassia leichtlinii, Leichtlin's camass
Camassia quamash, camass
Camassia scillioides, wild hyacinth
Chenopodium bonus-henricus, good king Henry
Cicorium intybus, chicory
Crambe maritima, sea kale
Dioscorea japonica, jinenjo
Dioscorea opposita, Chinese yam
Helianthus tuberosus, sunchoke
Hemerocallis spp., daylily
Laportaea canadensis, wood nettle
Levisticum officinale, lovage
Malva moschata, musk mallow
Matteuccia struthiopteris, ostrich fern
Nasturtium officinale, watercress
Oenanthe javanica, water celery
Oxyria digyna, mountain sorrel
Petasites japonicus, fuki
Phytolacca americana, pokeweed
Polygonatum biflorum var.
    commutatum, giant Solomon's seal
Rheum cultorum, rhubarb
Rumex acetosa, French sorrel
Rumex acetosa, 'Profusion' sorrel
Rumex acetosella, sheep sorrel
Rumex scutatus, silver shield sorrel
Sagittaria latifolia, arrowhead
Scorzonera hispanica, scorzonera
Sium sisarum, skirret
Stachys affinis, Chinese artichoke
Taraxacum officinale, dandelion
Tilia spp., linden
Urtica dioica, nettles

Perennial in warmer parts of the cold temperate zone, or perennial with protection:
Allium ampeloprasum, perennial sweet leek
Allium cepa aggregatum, potato onion
Allium cepa aggregatum, shallot
Allium cepa proliferum, walking onion
Arundinaria gigantea, canebrake bamboo
Asphodeline lutea, yellow asphodel
Atriplex halimus, saltbush (try as a dieback
    perennial)
Beta vulgaris maritima, sea beet
Brassica oleracea acephala, 'Tree Collards',
    'Walking Stick Kale'
Brassica oleracea acephala, tropical tree kale

Brassica oleracea acephala, 'Western Front'
    perennial kale
Brassica oleracea botrytis, perennial broccoli, including
    '9 Star'
Brassica oleracea ramosa, branching bush kale,
    including 'Dorbenton'
Brassica oleracea, wild cabbage
Canna edulis, achira
Colocasia esculenta, taro and 'Celery Stem' taro (with
    protection, in warmest parts, as a leaf crop only)
Cyperus esculentus var. *sativa*, chufa
Dioscorea bulbifera, air potato
Diplotaxis spp., sylvetta arugula (probably as
    dieback perennial in warmer areas)
Lycium spp., wolfberry
Nelumbo nucifera, water lotus (hardy as long as roots
    are below freeze line)
Toona sinensis, fragrant spring tree

These bamboos are fully hardy in the warmest areas of the cold temperate zone, may lose their leaves in the middle portions, and can be tried as dieback perennials in the coldest areas:
Phyllostachys spp., running bamboos
Sasa kurilensis, chishima-zasa bamboo
Semiarundinaria fastuosa, temple bamboo

Can be grown as annuals in the cold temperate zone:
Abelmoschus manihot, edible hibiscus
Alternanthera sissoo, sissoo spinach
Basella alba, Malabar spinach
Brassica oleracea alboglabra, gai lon
Capsicum annum, 'Perennial Capsicum' sweet pepper
Cnidoscolus chayamansa, 'Stingless' chaya
Coccinia grandis, 'Sterile' perennial cucumber
Colocasia esculenta, taro, cocoyam, eddo, dasheen (as
    a leaf crop only)
Cynara scolymus, 'Imperial Star' globe artichoke
Diplotaxis muralis & spp., sylvetta arugula
Eleocharis dulcis, water chestnut
Gynura crepioides, Okinawa spinach
Hibiscus acetosella, cranberry hibiscus
Ipomoea aquatica, water spinach
Ipomoea batatas, sweet potato
Lablab purpureus, hyacinth bean
Lycopersicon spp., tomato
Manihot esculenta, cassava (as a leaf crop only)
Momordica charantia, bitter melon

Moringa oleifera, moringa
Moringa stenopetala, moringa
Neptunia oleralea, water mimosa
Oxalis tuberosa, oca (with fall season extension)
Phaseolus coccineus, runner bean
Phaseolus lunatus, lima bean
Phaseolus polyanthus, cache bean
Physalis peruviana, goldenberry
Physalis pruinosa, ground cherry
Psophocarpus tetragonobolus, 'Day Length Neutral' winged bean
Sagittaria sinensis, Chinese arrowhead
Sauropus androgynous, katuk
Smallianthus sonchifolia, yacon (needs long season)
Solanum melongena & spp., eggplant
Solanum tuberosum & spp., potato
Tetragonia tetragonioides, New Zealand spinach
Xanthosoma brasiliense, belembe
Xanthosoma saggitifolium, tannier, yautia, malanga (as a leaf crop only)
Xanthosoma violaceum, violet-stem taro (as a leaf crop only)

Cool Maritime: The Pacific Northwest

From San Francisco north to Vancouver and the Alaska panhandle is a narrow, highly populated coastal region. This region corresponds with USDA Zones 8–9, and Sunset Zones 5 and 17.

Perennial in all of the cool maritime zone:

Allium ampeloprasum, perennial sweet leek
Allium cepa aggregatum, shallot
Allium cepa aggregatum, potato onion
Allium cepa proliferum, walking onion
Allium fistulosum, Welsh onion
Allium tricoccum, ramps
Allium tuberosum, garlic chives
Allium ursinum, ramson
Apios americana, groundnut
Aralia cordata, udo
Arundinaria gigantea, canebrake bamboo
Asparagus officinalis, asparagus
Asphodeline lutea, yellow asphodel
Atriplex halimus, saltbush
Beta vulgaris maritima, sea beet
Brassica oleracea, wild cabbage
Brassica oleracea acephala, 'Western Front' perennial kale

Brassica oleracea acephala, 'Tree Collard', 'Walking Stick Kale'
Brassica oleracea acephala, tropical tree kale
Brassica oleracea alboglabra, gai lon
Brassica oleracea botrytis, perennial broccoli, including '9 Star'
Brassica oleracea ramosa, branching bush kale, including 'Dorbenton'
Bunias orientalis, Turkish rocket
Camassia cusickii, Cusick's camass
Camassia leichtlinii, Leichtlin's camass
Camassia quamash, camass
Camassia scillioides, wild hyacinth
Canna edulis, achira
Chenopodium bonus-henricus, good king Henry
Cicorium intybus, hicory
Colocasia esculenta, 'Celery Stem' taro
Colocasia esculenta, taro, cocoyam, eddo, dasheen
Crambe maritima, sea kale
Cyperus esculentus var. *sativa*, chufa
Dioscorea bulbifera, air potato
Dioscorea japonica, jinenjo
Dioscorea opposita, Chinese yam
Diplotaxis spp., sylvetta arugula
Helianthus tuberosus, sunchoke
Hemerocallis spp., daylily
Laportaea canadensis, wood nettle
Levisticum officinale, lovage
Lycium spp., wolfberry
Malva moschata, musk mallow
Matteuccia struthiopteris, ostrich fern
Nasturtium officinale, watercress
Nelumbo nucifera, water lotus
Oenanthe javanica, water celery
Opuntia spp., spineless nopale cactus
Oxyria digyna, mountain sorrel
Petasites japonicus, fuki
Phyllostachys spp., running bamboos
Phytolacca americana, pokeweed
Polygonatum biflorum var. *commutatum*, giant Solomon's seal
Qiongzhuea tumidissinoda, running bamboo
Rheum x cultorum, rhubarb
Rumex acetosa, French sorrel
Rumex acetosa, 'Profusion' sorrel
Rumex acetosella, sheep sorrel
Rumex scutatus, silver shield sorrel
Sagittaria latifolia, arrowhead

Sagittaria graminea, Chinese arrowhead
Sasa kurilensis, chishima-zasa bamboo
Scorzonera hispanica, scorzonera
Semiarundinaria fastuosa, temple bamboo
Sium sisarum, skirret
Stachys affinis, Chinese artichoke
Taraxacum officinale, dandelion
Tilia spp., linden
Toona sinensis, fragrant spring tree
Tropaeolum tuberousum, 'Ken Aslet' mashua
Urtica dioica, nettles

Perennial in warmer parts of the cool maritime zone, or perennial with protection:

Bambusa spp., clumping bamboos
Cynara scolymus, globe artichoke
Moringa oleifera, moringa (dieback perennial)
Moringa stenopetala, moringa (dieback perennial)
Musa x paradisica, 'Rajapuri' banana
Oxalis tuberosa, oca
Phaseolus coccineus, runner bean
Phaseolus lunatus, lima bean
Physalis peruviana, goldenberry
Smallianthus sonchifolia, yacon
Solanum muricatum, pepino dulce

Can be grown as annuals in the cool maritime zone:

Abelmoschus manihot, edible hibiscus
Alternanthera sissoo, sissoo spinach
Basella alba, Malabar spinach
Capsicum annum, 'Perennial Capsicum' sweet pepper
Cnidoscolus chayamansa, 'Stingless' chaya
Coccinia grandis, 'Sterile' perennial cucumber
Cucurbita ficifolia, Malabar gourd
Eleocharis dulcis, water chestnut
Gynura crepioides, Okinawa spinach
Hibiscus acetosella, cranberry hibiscus
Ipomoea aquatica, water spinach
Ipomoea batatas, sweet potato
Lablab purpureus, hyacinth bean
Lycopersicon spp., tomato
Manihot esculenta, cassava (as leaf crop only)
Momordica charantia, bitter melon
Moringa oleifera, moringa
Moringa stenopetala, moringa
Neptunia oleracea, water mimosa
Oxalis tuberosa, oca
Phaseolus coccineus, runner bean

Phaseolus lunatus, Lima bean
Phaseolus polyanthus, cache bean
Physalis peruviana, goldenberry
Physalis pruinosa, ground cherry
Psophocarpus tetragonobolus, 'Day Length Neutral' winged bean
Sauropus androgynous, katuk
Smallianthus sonchifolia, yacon
Solanum melongena & spp., eggplant
Solanum muricatum, pepino dulce
Solanum tuberosum & spp., potato
Tetragonia tetragonioides, New Zealand spinach
Ullucus tuberosus, ulluco
Xanthosoma brasiliense, belembe
Xanthosoma saggitifolium, tannier, yautia, malanga
Xanthosoma violaceum, violet-stem taro

Hot and Humid: The Southeast

This warm band extends from eastern Texas through the coastal Carolinas. This region corresponds with USDA Zones 8–9 and Sunset Zones 26–28 and 31.

Perennial in all of the hot and humid zone:

Allium ampeloprasum, perennial sweet leek
Allium cepa aggregatum, shallot
Allium cepa aggregatum, potato onion
Allium cepa proliferum, walking onion
Allium fistulosum, Welsh onion
Allium tuberosum, garlic chives
Apios americana, groundnut
Aralia cordata, udo
Arundinaria gigantea, canebrake bamboo
Asparagus officinalis, asparagus
Asphodeline lutea, yellow asphodel
Atriplex halimus, saltbush
Bambusa spp., clumping bamboos
Brassica oleracea acephala, tropical tree kale
Bunias orientalis, Turkish rocket
Camassia scillioides, wild hyacinth
Canna edulis, achira
Cnidoscolus spp., bull nettles
Colocasia esculenta, 'Celery Stem' taro
Colocasia esculenta, taro, cocoyam, eddo, dasheen
Cynara cardunculus, cardoon
Cynara scolymus, 'Purple Sicilian' globe artichoke
Cyperus esculentus var. *sativa*, chufa
Dioscorea bulbifera, air potato
Dioscorea japonica, jinenjo

Dioscorea opposita, Chinese yam
Diplotaxis spp., sylvetta arugula
Helianthus tuberosus, sunchoke
Hemerocallis spp., daylily
Lycium spp., wolfberry
Malva moschata, musk mallow
Nasturtium officinale, watercress
Nelumbo nucifera, water lotus
Oenanthe javanica, water celery
Opuntia spp., spineless nopale cactus
Petasites japonicus, fuki
Phyllostachys spp., running bamboos
Phytolacca americana, pokeweed
Polygonatum biflorum var. *commutatum*, giant
   Solomon's seal
Qiongzhuea tumidissinoda, running bamboo
Rumex acetosa, French sorrel
Rumex acetosa, 'Profusion' sorrel
Rumex acetosella, sheep sorrel
Rumex scutatus, silver shield sorrel
Sagittaria latifolia, arrowhead
Sagittaria graminea, Chinese arrowhead
Sasa kurilensis, chishima-zasa bamboo
Scorzonera hispanica, scorzonera
Semiarundinaria fastuosa, temple bamboo
Stachys affinis, Chinese artichoke
Taraxacum officinale, dandelion
Tilia spp., linden
Toona sinensis, fragrant spring tree

Perennial in colder parts of the hot and humid zone:
Allium tricoccum, ramps
Chenopodium bonus-henricus, good king Henry
Cicorium intybus, chicory
Crambe maritima, sea kale
Laportaea canadensis, wood nettle
Levisticum officinale, lovage
Matteuccia struthiopteris, ostrich fern
Urtica dioica, nettles

Perennial in warmer parts of the hot and humid zone, or perennial with protection. Most of these species can also be grown as annuals in the colder parts of this zone.
Abelmoschus manihot, edible hibiscus (as dieback
   perennial)
Alternanthera sissoo, sissoo spinach
Arracacia xanthorhiza, arracacha
Basella alba, Malabar spinach

Brassica oleracea, wild cabbage
Brassica oleracea acephala, 'Western Front' perennial kale
Brassica oleracea acephala, 'Tree Collards', 'Walking
   Stick Kale'
Brassica oleracea alboglabra, gai lon
Brassica oleracea botrytis, perennial broccoli, including
   '9 Star'
Brassica oleracea ramosa, branching bush kale,
   including 'Dorbenton'
Capsicum annum, 'Perennial Capsicum' sweet pepper
Carica papaya, papaya
Coccinia grandis, 'Sterile' perennial cucumber
   (probably as dieback perennial in colder parts)
Cnidoscolus chayamansa, chaya (as dieback perennial)
Cucurbita ficifolia, Malabar gourd
Dendrocalamus spp., clumping bamboos (probably
   as dieback perennial even in warmest parts)
Dioscorea alata, white yam
Dioscorea esculenta, Asiatic lesser yam
Dioscorea trifida, cush cush yam
Eleocharis dulcis, water chestnut
Gigantochloa spp., clumping bamboos (probably as
   dieback perennial in bad winters)
Gynura crepioides, Okinawa spinach
Hibiscus acetosella, cranberry hibiscus
Ipomoea aquatica, water spinach
Ipomoea batatas, sweet potato
Lablab purpureus, hyacinth bean
Momordica charantia, bitter gourd
Manihot esculenta, cassava
Moringa spp., moringa (as dieback perennial)
Musa x paradisica, 'Rajapuri' banana (warmest parts,
   with long-season protection)
Nastus elatus, clumping bamboo
Oxalis tuberosa, oca
Phaseolus coccineus, runner bean
Phaseolus lunatus, lima bean
Phaseolus polyanthus, cache bean
Physalis pruinosa, ground cherry
Psophocarpus tetragonobolus, 'Day Length Neutral'
   winged bean
Psophocarpus tetragonobolus, winged bean
Saccharum edule, pitpit
Sauropus androgynous, katuk (as dieback perennial)
Sechium edule, chayote
Smallianthus sonchifolia, yacon
Solanum tuberosum & spp., potato
Tetragonia tetragonioides, New Zealand spinach

Trichostigma octandrum, basket vine (as dieback
perennial)
Xanthosoma brasiliense, belembe
Xanthosoma saggitifolium, tannier, yautia, malanga
(roots need long season)
Xanthosoma violaceum, violet-stem taro (roots need
long season)

Can be grown as annuals in the hot and humid zone:
Lycopersicon spp., tomato
Neptunia oleracea, water mimosa
Physalis peruviana, goldenberry
Rheum cultorum, rhubarb (cool season)
Solanum melongena & spp., eggplant
Tropaeolum tuberousum, 'Ken Aslet' mashua (as winter
annual?)

Arid and Hot: The Southwest

This region covers the low and mid-elevation deserts
and hot, dry lands of Texas, New Mexico, Arizona,
and southwestern California. This region corresponds with USDA Zones 8–10 and Sunset Zones
10, 12, 13, 29, and 30.

This region can grow all the species listed for the
hot and humid zone if sufficient irrigation is provided. In addition, the following species are drought-
tolerant.

Perennial in all of the arid and hot zone without substantial irrigation:
Atriplex halimus, saltbush
Cnidoscolus spp., bull nettles
Opuntia spp., spineless nopale cactus

Perennial without irrigation in warmer parts of the arid and hot zone, or perennial with protection. Most of these species can also be grown as annuals in the colder parts of this zone.
Cnidoscolus chayamansa, 'Stingless' chaya (as dieback
perennial)
Lablab purpureus, hyacinth bean
Manihot esculenta, cassava
Moringa oleifera, moringa (as dieback perennial)
Moringa stenopetala, moringa (as dieback perennial)
Phaseolus lunatus, lima bean
Tetragonia tetragonioides, New Zealand spinach

Mediterranean and Mild Subtropical: Southern and Coastal California

Southern and central California has a mild climate
well suited to perennial vegetables. This region corresponds with USDA Zones 8–10 and Sunset Zones
7–9, 14–16, and 18–25.

Perennial in all of the Mediterranean and mild subtropical zone:
Allium ampeloprasum, perennial sweet leek
Allium cepa aggregatum, shallot
Allium cepa aggregatum, potato onion
Allium cepa proliferum, walking onion
Allium fistulosum, Welsh onion
Allium tuberosum, garlic chives
Arundinaria gigantea, canebrake bamboo
Asparagus officinalis, asparagus
Asphodeline lutea, yellow asphodel
Atriplex halimus, saltbush
Bambusa spp., clumping bamboos
Beta vulgaris maritima, sea beet
Brassica oleracea, wild cabbage
Brassica oleracea acephala, 'Tree Collards', 'Walking
Stick Kale'
Brassica oleracea acephala, tropical tree kale
Brassica oleracea acephala, 'Western Front' perennial
kale
Brassica oleracea alboglabra, gai lon
Brassica oleracea botrytis, perennial broccoli, including
'9 Star'
Brassica oleracea ramosa, branching bush kale,
including 'Dorbenton'
Bunias orientalis, Turkish rocket
Canna edulis, achira
Chenopodium bonus-henricus, good king Henry
Cicorium intybus, chicory
Cnidoscolus spp., bull nettles
Colocasia esculenta, 'Celery Stem' taro
Colocasia esculenta, taro, cocoyam, eddo, dasheen
Crambe maritima, sea kale
Cucurbita ficifolia, Malabar gourd
Cynara scolymus, globe artichoke
Cyperus esculentus var. *sativa*, chufa
Dioscorea bulbifera, air potato
Diplotaxis spp., sylvetta arugula
Helianthus tuberosus, sunchoke
Hemerocallis spp., daylily

Lycium spp., wolfberry
Malva moschata, musk mallow
Nasturtium officinale, watercress
Nelumbo nucifera, water lotus
Oenanthe javanica, water celery
Opuntia spp., spineless nopale cactus
Phyllostachys spp., running bamboos
Physalis peruviana, goldenberry
Phytolacca americana, pokeweed
Polygonatum biflorum var. *commutatum*, giant
  Solomon's seal
Qiongzhuea tumidissinoda, running bamboo
Rumex acetosa, French sorrel
Rumex acetosa, 'Profusion' sorrel
Rumex acetosella, sheep sorrel
Rumex scutatus, silver shield sorrel
Sagittaria latifolia, arrowhead
Sagittaria graminea, Chinese arrowhead
Sasa kurilensis, chishima-zasa bamboo
Scorzonera hispanica, scorzonera
Semiarundinaria fastuosa, temple bamboo
Stachys affinis, Chinese artichoke
Taraxacum officinale, dandelion
Toona sinensis, fragrant spring tree
Urtica dioica, nettles

Perennial in some of the Mediterranean and mild subtropical zone or with protection:

Abelmoschus manihot, edible hibiscus (as dieback
  perennial)
Allium ursinum, ramson
Alternanthera sissoo, sissoo spinach
Apios americana, groundnut
Aralia cordata, udo
Arracacia xanthorhiza, arracacha
Basella alba, Malabar spinach (as dieback perennial)
Capsicum annum, 'Perennial Capsicum' sweet pepper
Carica pentaphylla, babaco papaya
Cnidoscolus chayamansa, 'Stingless' chaya (as dieback
  perennial)
Coccinia grandis, 'Sterile' perennial cucumber (as
  dieback perennial)
Dioscorea alata, white yam
Dioscorea esculenta, Asiatic lesser yam
Dioscorea trifida, cush cush yam
Eleocharis dulcis, water chestnut
Gigantochloa spp., clumping bamboos

Gynura crepioides, Okinawa spinach
Hibiscus acetosella, cranberry hibiscus (as dieback
  perennial)
Ipomoea aquatica, water spinach
Ipomoea batatas, sweet potato
Lablab purpureus, hyacinth bean
Laportaea canadensis, wood nettle
Levisticum officinale, lovage
Momordica charantia, bitter melon
Moringa oleifera, moringa (as dieback perennial)
Moringa stenopetala, moringa (as dieback perennial)
Musa x *paradisica*, 'Rajapuri' banana
Musa x *paradisica*, plantain, banana (only in warmest
  areas)
Nastus elatus, clumping bamboo
Oxalis tuberosa, oca
Phaseolus coccineus, runner bean
Phaseolus lunatus, lima bean
Phaseolus polyanthus, cache bean
Psophocarpus tetragonoblus, 'Day Length Neutral'
  winged bean
Rheum x *cultorum*, rhubarb
Saccharum edule, pitpit
Sauropus androgynous, katuk (as dieback perennial)
Sechium edule, chayote
Sium sisarum, skirret
Smallianthus sonchifolia, yacon
Solanum melongena & spp., eggplant
Solanum muricatum, pepino dulce
Solanum tuberosum & spp., potato
Tetragonia tetragonioides, New Zealand spinach
Trichostigma octandrum, basket vine (as dieback
  perennial)
Tropaeolum tuberousum, 'Ken Aslet' mashua
Ullucus tuberosus, ulluco
Xanthosoma brasiliense, belembe
Xanthosoma saggitifolium, tannier, yautia, malanga
Xanthosoma violaceum, violet-stem taro

Can be grown as annuals in the Mediterranean and mild subtropical zone:

Carica papaya, papaya (in warmest areas)
Lycopersicon spp., tomato
Manihot esculenta, cassava
Neptunia oleracea, water mimosa
Physalis pruinosa, ground cherry

Tropical Lowlands: Hawaii and South Florida

Lowland Hawaii and South Florida are proper tropical climates, completely free of frost all year. This region corresponds with USDA Zones 10–12 and Sunset Zone 25.

Note: There are many more fine perennial vegetables for the tropical lowlands, which unfortunately were excluded from this book due to its North American focus. See Recommended Reading for ideas.

Perennial in all of the tropical lowlands:

Abelmoschus manihot, edible hibiscus
Allium cepa aggregatum, shallot
Allium tuberosum, garlic chives
Alternanthera sissoo, sissoo spinach
Artocarpus altilis, breadfruit
Bambusa spp., clumping bamboos
Basella alba, Malabar spinach
Brassica oleracea acephala, tropical tree kale
Brassica oleracea alboglabra, gai lon
Canna edulis, achira
Capsicum annum, 'Perennial Capsicum' sweet pepper
Carica papaya, papaya
Cnidoscolus chayamansa, 'Stingless' chaya
Cnidoscolus spp., bull nettles
Coccinia grandis, 'Sterile' perennial cucumber
Colocasia esculenta, 'Celery Stem' taro
Colocasia esculenta, taro, cocoyam, eddo, dasheen
Cyperus esculentus var. *sativa*, chufa
Dendrocalamus spp., clumping bamboos
Dioscorea alata, white yam
Dioscorea bulbifera, air potato
Dioscorea esculenta, Asiatic lesser yam
Dioscorea trifida, cush cush yam
Eleocharis dulcis, water chestnut
Gigantochloa spp., clumping bamboos
Gynura crepioides, Okinawa spinach
Hibiscus acetosella, cranberry hibiscus
Ipomoea aquatica, water spinach
Ipomoea batatas, sweet potato
Lablab purpureus, hyacinth bean
Lycopersicon spp., tomato
Manihot esculenta, cassava
Momordica charantia, bitter melon
Moringa oleifera, moringa
Moringa stenopetala, moringa
Musa x *paradisica*, 'Rajapuri' banana
Musa x *paradisica*, plantain, banana
Nasturtium officinale, watercress
Nastus elatus, clumping bamboo
Nelumbo nucifera, water lotus
Neptunia oleracea, water mimosa
Opuntia spp., spineless nopale cactus
Phaseolus coccineus, runner bean
Phaseolus lunatus, lima bean
Phaseolus polyanthus, cache bean
Phyllostachys spp., running bamboos
Phytolacca americana, pokeweed
Psophocarpus tetragonobolus, 'Day Length Neutral' winged bean
Psophocarpus tetragonobolus, winged bean
Saccharum edule, pitpit
Sagittaria graminea, Chinese arrowhead
Sauropus androgynous, katuk
Sechium edule, chayote
Smallianthus sonchifolia, yacon
Solanum melongena & spp., eggplant
Toona sinensis, fragrant spring tree
Trichostigma octandrum, basket vine
Xanthosoma brasiliense, belembe
Xanthosoma saggitifolium, tannier, yautia, malanga
Xanthosoma violaceum, violet-stem taro

Perennial in cooler parts of the tropical lowlands:

Asparagus officinalis, asparagus
Oenanthe javanica, water celery
Tetragonia tetragonioides, New Zealand spinach

Can be grown as cool-season annuals in the tropical lowlands:

Allium fistulosum, Welsh onion
Helianthus tuberosa, sunchoke
Oenanthe javanica, water celery
Rheum x *cultorum*, rhubarb

The Hawaiian Upland Tropics

Within the United States and Canada, this region occurs only in Hawaii over 6,600 feet, although worldwide it is an important climate type. Please note that I have little experience in this area and cannot say with certainty just how high in the upland tropics these crops will grow. No doubt some of the other perennial vegetables profiled in this book will also succeed in the upland tropics.

Perennial in the upland tropics zone:

Allium ampeloprasum, perennial sweet leek

Allium cepa aggregatum, shallot

Allium fistulosum, Welsh onion

Allium tuberosum, garlic chives

Arracacia xanthorhiza, arracacha

Asparagus officinalis, asparagus

Basella alba, Malabar spinach

Beta vulgaris maritima, sea beet

Brassica oleracea acephala, tropical tree kale

Brassica oleracea alboglabra, gai lon

Canna edulis, achira

Carica pentaphylla, babaco papaya

Cicorium intybus, chicory (some cultivars)

Colocasia esculenta, taro (roots slow to develop)

Cucurbita ficifolia, Malabar gourd

Cyperus esculentus var. sativa, chufa

Dioscorea alata, white yam

Dioscorea bulbifera, air potato

Erythrina edulis, basul

Ipomoea batatas, sweet potato

Nasturtium officinale, watercress

Oenanthe javanica, water celery

Oxalis tuberosa, oca

Petasites japonicus, fuki

Phaseolus coccineus, runner bean

Phaseolus lunatus, lima bean

Phyllostachys spp., running bamboos

Physalis peruviana, goldenberry

Phytolacca americana, pokeweed

Psophocarpus tetragonobolus, winged bean

Rheum x cultorum, rhubarb

Rumex acetosa, French sorrel

Rumex acetosa, 'Profusion' sorrel

Rumex acetosella, sheep sorrel

Rumex scutatus, silver shield sorrel

Saccharum edule, pitpit

Scorzonera hispanica, scorzonera

Smallianthus sonchifolia, yacon

Solanum muricatum, pepino dulce

Solanum tuberosum & spp., potato

Stachys affinis, Chinese artichoke

Taraxacum officinale, dandelion

Tropaeolum tuberousum, 'Ken Aslet' mashua

Tropaeolum tuberousum, mashua

Ullucus tuberosus, ulluco

Can be grown as an annual in the upland tropics zone:

Physalis pruinosa, ground cherry

Recommended Readings

Note: The bibliography features complete information on all of the books listed here.

Useful Plants

African Indigenous Vegetables: An Overview of the Cultivated Species. Schippers, R. R.
   A very interesting and useful guide including many perennial species (such as lablab beans, air potatoes, and cranberry hibiscus), as well as some unique and fascinating perennial veggies that unfortunately did not make the cut for this book focused on North America, such as coleus potatoes and oyster nuts.

Bamboo World: The Growing and Use of Clumping Bamboos. Victor Cusack.
   A very thorough guide to production and use of tropical and subtropical clumping and moso bamboos.

Conserving and Increasing the Use of Neglected and Underutilized Crops series. International Plant Genetic Resources Institute.
   Very detailed and informative, including publications on aibika (edible hibiscus), chayote, breadfruit, mashua, and "Andean tubers" (incuding arracacha and yacon), this series is available online from the International Plant Genetic Resources Institute at www.biodiversityinternational.org. These are listed in the bibliography by author: Grau (mashua), Hermann (arracacha and yacon), Preston (edible hibiscus), Ragone (breadfruit), and Saade (chayote).

Food Plants of the World. Ben-Erik Van Wyk.
   Great descriptions of over 300 cultivated plants from around the world, with beautiful photos.

Fruits of Warm Climates. Julia Morton.
   This book is a compendium of tropical and subtropical fruits, with tons of useful information on papaya, banana, goldenberry, pepino, and more.

Global Gardening: Increasing the Diversity of Plants in Your Own Garden While Feeding a Hungry World. Hank Bruce and Tomi Jill Folk
   A fantastic guide, mostly to tropical perennials, available from www.echonet.org.

Gourmet Gardening: 48 Special Vegetables You Can Grow for Deliciously Distinctive Meals. Anne Halpin.
   A review of rare and underutilized vegetable crops for U.S. and Canadian gardeners.

Growing Unusual Vegetables: Weird and Wonderful Vegetables and How to Grow Them. Simon Hickmott.
   A wealth of practical information for the British (cool maritime) climate from the former owner of the late lamented Future Foods nursery.

Hardy Bamboos for Shoots & Poles: Thirty Varieties of Bamboo for Farms in USDA Zones 7, 8, 9. Daphne Lewis.
   A guide to production of hardy edible bamboos.

How to Make a Forest Garden. Patrick Whitefield.
   In addition to being a great guide to forest gardening, this book has excellent write-ups on temperate perennial vegetables based on the author's own experience.

Lost Crops of the Incas: Little-Known Plants of the Andes with Promise for Worldwide Cultivation. National Research Council.
   A classic featuring many perennials for temperate to tropical climates. Viewable online at www.nap.edu/books /030904264X/html.

Watercress is a popular crop throughout the world.

Neglected Crops: 1492 from a Different Perspective. J. E. Hernández Bermejo and J. León.
 Focuses on New World crops; nice section on New World beans, including perennial beans.

Oriental Vegetables: The Complete Guide for the Gardening Cook. Joy Larcom.
 Features many perennials, including aquatics.

Plants for a Future: Edible & Useful Plants for a Healthier World. Ken Fern.
 An excellent guide for temperate climate perennials. Also check out the fantastic PFAF online database at www.pfaf.org.

PROSEA: Plant Resources of Southeast Asia.
 Incredible multivolume set on crops of Southeast Asia. Volumes on vegetables (no. 8) and starch plants (no. 9) are fantastic resources.

PROTA: Plant Resources of Tropical Africa.
 Similar to PROSEA but focused on Africa. Some volumes are incomplete, but there is an incredible vegetable database online at www.prota.org.

Specialty and Minor Crops Handbook.
 Coverage of a wide range of herbs and vegetables for U.S. market gardeners.

The Tropical Perennial Vegetable series. Jay Ram.
 Very informative and practical series, covering 'Celery Stem' taro, chaya, chayote, moringa, Okinawa spinach, sissoo spinach, sweetleaf bush (katuk), and tropical tree kale.

The Vegetable Garden. M. M. Vilmorin-Andrieux.
 Written in the 1880s, this guide to vegetable crops includes many rare perennials and much lost information (six pages on sea kale production, for example).

Vegetables from Amaranth to Zucchini: The Essential Reference. Elizabeth Schneider.
 Cookbook featuring recipes for a great many perennial vegetables.

Permaculture and Edible Landscaping

The Complete Book of Edible Landscaping: Home Landscaping with Food-Bearing Plants and Resource-Saving Techniques. Rosalind Creasy.
 Nice overview of design and implementation of edible landscapes, with coverage of useful species, including some perennial vegetables.

Designing and Maintaining Your Edible Landscape Naturally. Robert Kourik.
 Hard-core manual for edible and ecological landscape design.

Edible Forest Gardens Vols. I and II. Dave Jacke with Eric Toensmeier.
 Food production modeled on the ecology of the eastern forest. Very detailed design process for developing permaculture and edible landscape systems, and coverage of a great many major and minor hardy perennial vegetables.

Food Not Lawns: How to Turn Your Yard into a Garden and Your Neighborhood into a Community. Heather Flores.
 Guerrilla gardening, seed saving, biodiverse gardening, and much more from another socially engaged plant geek.

Gaia's Garden: A Guide to Home-Scale Permaculture. Toby Hemenway.
 The first permaculture guide for North America.

Introduction to Permaculture. Bill Mollison and Reny Mia Slay.
 Excellent overview to an essential practice for the 21st century.

Permaculture: A Practical Guide for a Sustainable Future. Bill Mollison.
 Comprehensive guide to permaculture design, including perennial polycultures of useful plants.

Permaculture: Principles and Pathways Beyond Sustainability. David Holmgren.
 The co-originator of permaculture's 12 principles of design: practical, insightful, based in decades of experience.

History, Ecology, Native and Nonnative Species

The Eternal Frontier: An Ecological History of North America and Its Peoples. Tim Flannery.
   History of the last 65 million years of North America. Sets a proper context for the invasive species debate.

Guns, Germs and Steel: The Fates of Human Societies. Jared Diamond.
   A remarkable book, including a fascinating history of the origins of agriculture and crop domestication in different regions.

Invasion Biology: Critique of a Pseudoscience. David Theodoropoulos.
   A fascinating, controversial take on the nonnative species issue. Read it with an open mind.

Out of Eden: An Odyssey of Ecological Invasion. Alan Burdick.
   Eloquent and nuanced take on the invasive species issue.

Stalking the Wild Amaranth: Gardening in the Age of Extinction. Janet Marinelli.
   A thought-provoking examination of conservation gardening and nonnative species.

Weeds or Wild Nature? David Holmgren.
   The forthcoming book from co-originator of permaculture, on "ecosynthesis" of native and nonnative species.
   A short article by the same title is available on his Web site at www.holmgren.com.au.

Garden Climates and Microclimates

Canadian Climate Map
http://sis.agr.gc.ca/cansis/nsdb/climate/hardiness/intro.html
   Much more sophisticated than USDA maps, and similar to the Sunset Garden maps profiled below.
   A valuable resource for Canadian gardeners.

Growing Food in the Southwest Mountains: A Permaculture Approach to Home gardening Above 6,500 feet in Arizona, New Mexico, Southern Colorado and Southern Utah. Lisa Rayner.
   This guide should be required reading for gardeners in its region. Includes recommendations of a number of perennial vegetable species adapted to this unique climate.

Hot Plants for Cool Climates: Gardening with Tropical Plants in Temperate Zones. Susan Roth and Dennis Schrader.
   Guide to growing tropical and "tropicalesque" plants in northern gardens. Not focused on perennials or food crops, but contains highly relevant information for those wishing to grow tropical perennial crops in the North, and profiles of some perennial vegetables like taro.

Palms Won't Grow Here and Other Myths: Warm-Climate Plants for Cooler Areas. David Francko.
   Great ideas for growing a wider range of tropical and "tropicalesque" plants in the North—highly relevant and very practical.

Sunset Garden Books
   This series features detailed climate maps and gardening recommendations by region. The maps far surpass USDA Hardiness Zone maps, and incorporate heat, seasonal rainfall, length of growing season, and other factors, in addition to winter minimum temperatures. The series includes Sunset National Garden Book, Southern Living Garden Book, Sunset Western Garden Book, Sunset Northeastern Garden Book, *and* Sunset Midwest Top 10 Garden Guide. *I recommend picking up the national guide or the appropriate regional edition for your area.*

The Weather-Resilient Garden: A Defensive Approach to Planning & Landscaping. Charles Smith.
   Great ideas for garden design and microclimate utilization to protect plants from heat, cold, rain, fire, and more.

General Gardening Techniques

See also the Sunset Garden Books listed above, as well as many of the other books profiled here.

Amaranth to Zai Holes: Ideas for Growing Food Under Difficult Conditions. Laura Meitzner and others.
   Collection of articles from the ECHO newsletter, covering a wide range of low-tech sustainable practices. Focuses on warm climates, but full of many great ideas for any garden.

Drip Irrigation for Every Landscape and All Climates: Helping Your Garden Flourish, While Conserving Water! Robert Kourik.
  Guide to a water-saving, disease-preventing irrigation technique ideal for perennial vegetables.

How to Grow More Vegetables: And Fruits, Nuts, Berries, Grains, and Other Crops than You Ever Thought Possible on Less Land than You Can Imagine. John Jeavons.
  The guide to bio-intensive gardening that produces very high yields through (labor-intensive!) double-digging and other practices. Double-digging is a great way to prepare soil for long-lived perennial vegetables.

Lasagna Gardening: A New Layering System for Bountiful Gardens: No Digging, No Tilling, No Weeding, No Kidding! Patricia Lanza.
  Outlines the steps to crating a sheet mulch garden—a technique to turn lawns or parking lots into instant gardens.

Planting Green Roofs and Living Walls. Nigel Dunnett and Nöel Kingsbury.
  A remarkable book covering techniques for gardening on the surfaces of buildings. The section on working with vines is highly applicable for use with perennial vegetable vine crops.

Start with the Soil: The Organic Gardener's Guide to Improving Soil for Higher Yields, More Beautiful Flowers, and a Healthy, Easy-Care Garden. Grace Gershuny.
  An excellent guide to building and caring for organic soil.

The Xeriscape Handbook: A How-To Guide to Natural, Resource-Wise Gardening. Gayle Weinstein.
  The bible of water-saving garden practices for dry (and not-so-dry) climates.

Water Gardening

Also check out sections on water gardening in *Oriental Vegetables: A Guide for the Gardening Cook* and *Plants for a Future* under Useful Plants, on page 211.

Grow Your Own Chinese Vegetables. Geri Harrington.
  Features a chapter on edible water gardens.

Low-Maintenance Water Gardens. Helen Nash with Steve Stroupe.
  Guide to designing, installing, and maintaining water gardens.

Plants for Water Gardens: The Complete Guide to Aquatic Plants. Helen Nash.
  Good introduction to water gardening and the range of plants, including some that happen to be perennial vegetables.

Pests and Diseases

American Horticultural Society Pests and Diseases: The Complete Guide to Preventing, Identifying, and Treating Plant Problems. Pippa Greenwood and Andrew Halstead.
  Handbook for handling pests and diseases in the garden.

Garden Insects of North America: The Ultimate Guide to Backyard Bugs. Whitney Cranshaw.
  Phenomenal guide to identification and ecology of beneficial and pest insects in the garden.

The Gardener's A–Z Guide to Growing Organic Food. Tanya Denckla.
  Encyclopedia of crops, pests, and diseases, with organic prevention and control methods.

Rodale's Illustrated Encyclopedia of Perennials. Ellen Phillips and C. Colston Burrell.
  Includes a nice section on identifying and managing pests and diseases of perennials.

Propagation

American Horticultural Society Plant Propagation: The Fully Illustrated Plant-by-Plant Manual of Practical Techniques.
Alan Toogood.
  Handbook of plant propagation.

Breed Your Own Vegetable Varieties: The Gardener's and Farmer's Guide to Plant Breeding and Seed Saving. Carol Deppe.
  Excellent guide to backyard breeding. Deppe is a big fan of perennial vegetables and talks about them a good bit. Many perennial crops are in great need of breeding work, and backyard amateurs are the ones to do it.

Native Trees, Shrubs, and Vines and *The New England Wild Flower Society Guide to Growing and Propagating Wildflowers of the United States and Canada.* William Cullina.
  In addition to excellent coverage of native plant species, these guides have splendid information on propagation (cuttings, division, cold stratification, etc.) from a true expert.

Seed to Seed: Seed Saving Techniques for the Vegetable Gardener. Suzanne Ashworth.
  The bible of seed saving, including information on a good number of perennial crops.

Helpful Organizations and Web Sites

Action Group on Erosion, Technology, and Concentration
431 Gilmour St., 2nd Floor
Ottawa, ON K2P 0R
Canada
(613) 241-2267
www.etcgroup.org
  Nongovernmental organization working to fight consolidation in the seed industry, loss of diversity, and genetic engineering.

Agroforestry Research Trust
46 Hunters Moon
Dartington, Totnes
Devon, TQ9 6JT
England
+44 (0) 1803 840776
www.agroforestry.co.uk
  Permaculture and forest garden research and demonstration site. Producers of many great publications and promoters of useful perennials.

American Bamboo Society
750 Krumkill Rd.
Albany, NY 12203-5976
www.americanbamboo.org
  Association of bamboo enthusiasts.

American Community Garden Association
c/o Franklin Park Conservatory
1777 East Broad St.
Columbus, OH 43203
(877) ASK-ACGA
www.communitygarden.org
  Great resource for community gardeners; also can advise on lead testing issues for urban and suburban gardeners.

California Rare Fruit Growers Council
c/o The Fullerton Arboretum—CSUF
P.O. Box 6850
Fullerton, CA 92834-6850
www.crfg.org
  Fruit enthusiasts, experts on growing tropical plants in California, and their Web publications and conferences can plug you in to growing methods for subtropicals like pepino, papaya, and banana in California.

The Cucurbit Network
www.cucurbit.org
  Cucurbit enthusiasts share information and resources. Great information and photos on rare cucurbits, including perennial crop types.

Doubleday Research Center
Heritage Seed Library
c/o Garden Organic
Ryton Organic Gardens
Coventry
Warwickshire CV8 3LG
England
www.gardenorganic.uk.org
   *British organic gardening society, including a rare seed
   library for members only.*

Edible Forest Gardeners' Network
www.edibleforestgardens.com
   *Online networking and resources for anyone experimenting
   with edible forest gardens and perennial polycultures. Space to
   report on experiences with perennial vegetables.*

Edible Plant Project
www.edibleplantproject.com
   *Volunteer effort to propagate and promote useful plants for north
   Florida region, including many tree vegetables.*

Educational Concerns for Hunger Organization
www.echonet.org
   *Christian organization dedicated to sending free seeds of useful
   plants to tropical development projects. ECHO's farm site in
   Fort Myers, Florida, is one of the world's best places to see edible
   landscaping, including perennial vegetables in action.*

Food Not Lawns
www.foodnotlawns.com
   *Workshops, seeds, and information for Oregon Cascades area
   and beyond.*

International Plant Genetic Resources Institute
www.ipgri.cgiar.org
   *An international organization focused on preservation of crop
   diversity, including a special focus on "neglected and underutilized" crops. Excellent publications on their Web site.*

La'Akea Gardens
P.O. Box 1071
Pahoa, HI 96778
(808) 443-4076
www.permaculture-hawaii.com
   Permaculture demonstration and education center.

North American Native Plant Society
P.O. Box 84, Station D
Etobicoke, ON M9A 4X1
Canada
(416) 631-4438
www.nanps.org
   *Resources for native plant enthusiasts in the United States and
   Canada.*

Occidental Arts and Ecology Center
15290 Coleman Valley Rd.
Occidental, CA 95465
(707) 874-1557
www.oaec.org
   Workshops and demonstration center with fantastic gardens.

Pacific Northwest Palm and Exotic Plant Society
10310 Hollybank Dr.
Richmond, BC V7E 4S5
Canada
(604) 271-9524
www.hardypalm.com
   *Network of gardeners pushing the limits of hardiness in
   northwestern North America.*

The Permaculture Activist
www.permacultureactivist.net
   *Quarterly North American permaculture magazine listing
   courses, workshops, and events.*

Permaculture Magazine
www.permaculture.co.uk
   *Quarterly European permaculture magazine listing courses,
   workshops, and events.*

Plants for a Future
www.pfaf.org
   *Remarkable online database of more than 7,000 useful plants,
   including many perennial vegetables. PFAF operates several
   demonstration sites in southern Britain with great useful plant
   collections.*

PROSEA: Plant Resources of Southeast Asia
www.prosea.org
   *Web site and publication profiling hundreds of useful plants
   grown in Southeast Asia.*

PROTA: Plant Resources of Tropical Africa
www.prota.org
   *Similar to PROSEA, but focused on sub-Saharan Africa; great
   online vegetable database.*

Seeds of Diversity Canada
P.O. Box 36, Station Q
Toronto, ON M4T 2L7
Canada
(866) 509-SEED
www.seeds.ca
   Canadian seed-saving program and seed exchange.

Seed Savers Exchange
3094 North Winn Rd.
Decorah, IA 52101
(563) 382-5990
www.seedsavers.org
   International seed-saving and exchange network.

Southeastern Palm and Exotic Plant Society
www.sepalms.org
   Network of gardeners pushing the limits of hardiness in the southeastern United States.

USDA Plants Database
http://plants.usda.gov
   Database featuring native and naturalized plants of the United States with distribution maps by county.

Sources of Plants and Seeds

Perennial vegetables can be hard to find. The nurseries and seed companies that stock them are usually small and run by highly dedicated enthusiasts. In some cases only one or two companies in North America offer the species you are looking for. Be prepared for some quirky or technical catalogs—but ones that are chock-full of fascinating plants.

Someday perennial vegetables may be available through mainstream companies. While this will help many more people grow them, please don't forget the pioneering companies and organizations that first made these crops available to you.

During the course of writing this book two of the finest perennial vegetable nurseries—Oregon Exotics and Future Foods—went out of business. This should be a lesson to us all not to hold back on ordering something rare, because it may be very difficult to find it again if a company goes under.

Several books and organizations can help you track down rare plants and seeds. Check out the following:

Andersen Horticultural Library Plant Information Online.
   An online subscription service helping you find sources for 88,000 species from over 700 sources. Online at http://plantinfo.umn.edu.

Cornucopia: A Sourcebook of Edible Plants. Steven Facciola.
   Listing of 3,000 species and thousands more varieties of edible plants, cross-linked to over 1,300 companies and institutions that offer them.

Garden Seed Inventory: An Inventory of Seed Catalogs Listing All Nonhybrid Vegetable Seeds Available in the United States and Canada.
   Listing of commercially available vegetable cultivars, compiled by Seed Savenuers Exchange. Sixth edition features 8,500 varieties and over 250 seed companies and nurseries.

The Seed Search. Karen Platt.
   Book and online resource with sources for over 43,000 species and varieties. Online at www.seedsearch.demon.co.uk/books.html.

North American Sources

AgroHaitai Ltd.
P.O. Box 78051
Hamilton, Ontario L9C 7N5
Canada
(519) 647-2280
www.agrohaitai.com
   Asian vegetables including fragrant spring tree, water spinach, and winged bean.

J. D. Andersen Nursery
2790 Marvinga Ln.
Fallbrook, CA 92028
(949) 361-3652
www.jdandersen.com
   Tremendous banana selection for California.

Baker Creek Heirloom Seeds
2278 Baker Creek Rd.
Mansfield, MO 65704
(417) 924-8917
www.rareseeds.com
 Many perennial vegetables including such rarities as
 'Day Length Neutral' winged beans, green hyacinth beans,
 and goldenberry.

Bamboo Garden Nursery
1507 Southeast Alder St.
Portland, OR 97214
(503) 647-2700
www.bamboogarden.com
 Hardy bamboos.

Bamboo Headquarters
(866) 293-2925
www.bambooheadquarters.com
 Excellent selection of bamboos for California.

The Banana Tree
715 Northampton St.
Easton, PA 18042
(610) 253-9589
www.banana-tree.com
 Specializing in unusual tropical plants including many banana
 varieties as well as air potato.

Edible Plant Project
www.edibleplantproject.com
 Volunteer-run nursery propagating useful perennials adapted to
 northern Florida. Sales through Gainesville farmers' market.

Educational Concerns for Hunger Organization (ECHO)
17391 Durrance Rd.
North Fort Myers, FL 33917
(239) 543-3246
www.echonet.org
 ECHO is one of the best sources for tropical perennial vegetables.
 Their seed company ships anywhere, but unfortunately to get
 plants from their nursery you need to go there in person. ECHO
 has a wider selection of rare useful plants that are shipped free to
 development projects in developing countries, but are not avail-
 able elsewhere due to limited seed availability.

Evergreen YH Enterprises
P.O. Box 17538
Anaheim, CA 92817
(714) 637-5769
www.evergreenseeds.com
 Asian vegetable seeds including many perennials.

Fedco Seeds
P.O. Box 520
Waterville, ME 04903
(207) 873-7333
www.fedcoseeds.com
 Sunchokes, shallots, good king Henry, and more.

Florida Bamboo Company
Gainesville, FL
(352) 665-2175
www.floridabamboo.com
 Clumping bamboos for tropical and subtropical Florida.
 Not mail order.

G&N Ramp Farm
Box 48
Richwood, WV 26261
(304) 846-4235
 Specializing in ramps; also offering several booklets on
 growing and cooking with ramps.

Heronswood Nursery
7530 Northeast 288th St.
Kingston, WA 98346
(360) 297-4172
www.heronswood.com
 Fascinating collection, including udo and fuki.

Horus Botanicals
HCR Route 82, Box 29
Salem, AR 72576
 Fascinating collection of useful plants, including
 many rare tropical vegetables.

J. L. Hudson
Star Route 2, Box 337
La Honda, CA 94020
www.jlhudsonseeds.net
 "Native plants from around the world," including chufa
 and others. Authors of Invasion Biology: Critique of a
 Pseudoscience.

Johnny's Selected Seeds
955 Benton Ave.
Winslow, ME 04901
(207) 861-3900
www.johnnyseeds.com
   Wide range of vegetables, including many perennials.

Karchesky Canna Collection
(724) 466-0979
www.karcheskycanna.com
   Offering achira (edible canna), which they call "anchiras."

Lilypons Water Gardens
6800 Lilypons Rd.
P.O. Box 10
Adamstown, MD 21710
(800) 999-5459
www.lilypons.com
   Aquatic vegetables like water celery and arrowhead.

Moore Water Gardens
P.O. Box 70
4683 Sunset Rd.
Port Stanley, ON N5L 1J4
Canada
(519) 782-4052
www.moorewatergardens.com
   Fine selection of edible aquatic plants.

Mountain Gardens
546 Shuford Creek Rd.
Burnesville, NC 28714
(828) 675-5664
www.mountaingardensherbs.com
   Large collection of useful plants.

Occidental Arts and Ecology Center
15290 Coleman Valley Rd.
Occidental, CA 95465
(707) 874-1557
www.oaec.org
   Many species adapted to California, including tree collards and Andean root crops. On-site sales only.

Peace Seeds
2385 Southeast Thompson St.
Corvallis, OR 97333
(541) 752-0421
   Numerous interesting plants, including achira.

Perennial Pleasures
P.O. Box 147
East Hardwick, VT 05836
(802) 472-5104
www.perennialpleasures.net
   Hardy perennials, including a superior skirret clone.

Peters Seed and Research
P.O. Box 1472
Myrtle Creek, OR 97457
(541) 874-2615
www.psrseed.com
   They breed their own unique varieties of perennial vegetables including perennial grains and brassicas.

Plant Delights Nursery
9241 Sauls Rd.
Raleigh, NC 27603
(919) 772-4794
www.plantdelights.com
   "Tropicalesque" hardy plants for colder climates.

Pond Plants and More
P.O. Box 155
Bentleyville, PA 15314
(724) 239-6673
www.pondsplantsandmore.com
   Aquatic vegetables including water mimosa and water chestnut.

Richters Herbs
P.O. Box 26
Goodwood, ON L0C 1A0
Canada
(905) 640-6677
www.richters.com
   Fantastic catalog offering many perennial vegetables.

Rivenrock Gardens
c/o John & Vickie Dicus
P.O. Box 196
Nipomo, CA 93444
www.rivenrock.com
   Specializing in spineless nopale cactus varieties.

Sand Hill Preservation Center
1878 230th St.
Calamus, IA 52729
(563) 246-2299
www.sandhillpreservation.com
   Many neat crops, including incredible diversity in sweet potato varieties.

Seeds of Diversity Canada
P.O. Box 36, Station Q
Toronto, ON M4T 2L7
Canada
(866) 509-SEED
www.seeds.ca
Sea kale, skirret, groundnut, and more.

Seed Savers Exchange
3094 North Winn Rd.
Decorah, IA 52101
(563) 382-5990
www.seedsavers.org
Grassroots network of seed savers sharing seeds and plants by mail. The "Miscellaneous" section of their annual yearbook includes many rare perennial vegetables. Joining SSE is highly recommended! SSE also has a much more limited commercial catalog of seed varieties for sale; don't confuse this with their full listing of thousands of varieties, which is only available to members. Listing an astounding 11,848 varieties in 2006.

Southern Exposure Seed Exchange
P.O. Box 460
Mineral, VA 23117
(540) 894-9480
www.southernexposure.com
Collection of varieties adapted to the hot, humid South, including multiplier onions.

Sow Organic Seed
P.O. Box 527
Williams, OR 97544
(888) 709-7333
www.organicseed.com
Andean tubers and more.

Taro and Ti
Lakeland, FL
(877) 889-5088
www.taroandti.com
Specializing in edible taro varieties including low-oxalate "luau leaf" types needing only minimal cooking.

Thomas Jefferson Center for Historic Plants
Monticello
P.O. Box 316
Charlottesville, VA 22902
(804) 977-9821
www.monticello.org/shop
Crops grown by Jefferson, including edible hibiscus and heirloom lima and scarlet runner varieties.

Tripple Brook Farm
37 Middle Rd.
Southampton, MA 01073
(413) 527-4626
www.tripplebrookfarm.com
Great selection of useful cold-hardy plants, many perennial vegetables.

Underwood Gardens
1414 Zimmerman Rd.
Woodstock, IL 60098
(815) 338-6279
www.underwoodgardens.com
Many interesting plants, including cranberry hibiscus.

USDA Germplasm Resources Information Network (GRIN)
www.ars-grin.gov
National collection of plant materials for hundreds of crops and thousands of wild crop relatives. Free seeds and plants available for research purposes (including backyard research). Includes rarities like saltbush and earthnut pea.

Van Bourgondien
P.O. Box 1000
Babylon, NY 11702
(800) 622-9997
www.dutchbulbs.com
Source for the day-length-neutral mashua cultivar 'Ken Aslet'.

Van Engelen Inc.
23 Tulip Dr.
P.O. Box 638
Bantam, CT 06750
(860) 567-8734
www.vanengelen.com
Bulk bulb purchases; excellent camass prices.

Hawaiian Sources
Agrinom LLC
Box 174, 31–469 Mamalahoa Hwy.
Hakalau, Hawaii 96710
(808) 963 6771
www.agrinom.com
Authors of the excellent Tropical Perennial Vegetable series (see the bibliography). On-site sales only.

Fukuda Seed Store, Inc.
1287 Kalani St.
Honolulu, HI 96817
(808) 841-6719
Sole legal source of water spinach seed in the United States.

Gaia Yoga Nursery
RR2 No. 3334
Pahoa, HI 96778
(808) 965-5664
www.gaiayoga.org/nursery
   Breadfruit, bamboos, perennial leaf crops, and more.

La'Akea Gardens
P.O. Box 1071
Pahoa, HI 96778
(808) 443-4076
www.permaculture-hawaii.com
   Permaculture nursery featuring many perennial vegetables.

Overseas Sources

Agroforestry Research Trust
46 Hunters Moon
Dartington, Totnes
Devon, TQ9 6JT
England
+44 (0) 1803 840776
www.agroforestry.co.uk
   Research center with nursery and seed company, featuring useful
   plants for cool temperate climates.

B&T World Seeds
Paguignan
34210 Aigues-Vives
France
00 33 (0) 4 68 91 29 63
www.b-and-t-world-seeds.com
   Unbelievable seed company offering 35,000 listings. If no one
   else has it, B&T usually does, though it may take them awhile to
   track it down.

Chiltern Seeds
Bortree Stile
Ulverston
Cumbria LA12 7PB
England
www.chilternseeds.co.uk
   Many species including good king Henry and sea kale.

Doubleday Research
Heritage Seed Library
c/o Garden Organic
Ryton Organic Gardens
Coventry
Warwickshire CV8 3LG
England
www.gardenorganic.uk.org
   Rare seeds available to members, including branching bush kales
   like 'Dorbenton'.

Earthcare Enterprises
P.O. Box 500
Maleny, Queensland 4552
Australia
07 5499 9599
www.earthcare.com.au
   Great bamboos, achira, taro, cassava, water chestnut, and more.

Herb Garden and Historical Plants Nursery
Pentre Berw, Gaerwen
Anglesey LL60 6LF
Wales
01248 422208
www.historicalplants.co.uk
   Many interesting plants, including saltbush and wild cabbage.

Poyntz field Herb Nursery
Black Isle
By Dingwall IV7 8LX
Ross & Cromarty
Scotland
+44 (0) 1381 610352
www.poyntzfieldherbs.co.uk
   Offerings include sea kale, oca, mashua.

Sources of Garden Supplies and Materials

While obtaining the seeds or plants of perennial vegetables requires perusing exotic catalogs, most of the tools and supplies you need are easy to get at your local hardware store, garden center, or farm supply store. Some items, like organic soil amendments and pest-control products, drip irrigation supplies, and water garden materials, are harder to track down. I have included a short list of mail-order suppliers that can fill in where your garden center leaves off.

Dripworks
190 Sanhedrin Circle
Willits, CA 95490
(800) 522-3747
www.dripworksusa.com
   Supplies for drip irrigation and other water-saving practices.

Fedco
P.O. Box 520
Waterville, ME 04903
(207) 873-7333
www.fedcoseeds.com
   Gardening supplies including organic pest controls, soil amendments, and drip irrigation.

The Green Spot
93 Priest Rd.
Nottingham, NH 03290
(603) 942-8925
www.greenmethods.com
   Organic pest control and live beneficial insects.

Harmony Farm Supply
3244 Highway 116 North
Sebastopol, CA 95472
(707) 823-9125
   Gardening supplies, including organic pest controls, soil amendments, and drip irrigation. Also soil and water testing, live beneficial insects.

Johnny's Selected Seeds
955 Benton Ave.
Winslow, ME 04901
(207) 861-3900
www.johnnyseeds.com
   Gardening supplies, including organic pest controls, soil amendments, and drip irrigation.

Lilypons Water Gardens
6800 Lily Pons Rd.
P.O. Box 10
Adamstown, MD 21710
(800) 999-5459
www.lilypons.com
   Water garden supplies.

Moore Water Gardens
P.O. Box 70
4683 Sunset Rd.
Port Stanley, ON N5L 1J4
Canada
(519) 782-4052
www.moorewatergardens.com
   Water garden supplies.

Peaceful Valley Farm Supply
P.O. Box 2209
Grass Valley, CA 95945
(530) 272-4769
www.groworganic.com
   Gardening supplies, including organic pest controls, soil amendments, and drip irrigation. Also live beneficial insects, and bird- and bat houses.

Planet Natural
1612 Gold Ave.
Bozeman, MT 59715
(800) 289-6656
www.planetnatural.com
   Gardening supplies, including organic pest controls, soil amendments, and drip irrigation. Also live beneficial insects.

Pond Plants and More
P.O. Box 155
Bentleyville, PA 15314
(724) 239-6673
www.pondsplantsandmore.com
   Water garden supplies.

Bibliography

Ashworth, Suzanne. *Seed to Seed: Seed Saving Techniques for the Vegetable Gardener.* Decorah, IA: Seed Savers Exchange, 1991.

Aung, Louis H., Amelia Ball, and Mosbah Kushad. 1990. "Developmental and Nutritional Aspects of Chayote," *Journal of Economic Botany* 44, no. 2 (1990): 157–64.

Bailey, Liberty Hyde. *Hortus Third: A Concise Dictionary of Plants Cultivated in the United States and Canada.* New York: Macmillan, 1976.

Bender, Steve. *The Southern Living Garden Book.* Birmingham, AL: Oxmoor House, 1998.

Bermejo, J. E. Hernández, and J. León, eds. *Neglected Crops: 1492 from a Different Perspective.* Rome: FAO, 1994.

Blackmon, W. J., and B. D. Reynolds. "The Crop Potential of *Apios americana*—Preliminary Evaluations." *HortScience* 21, no. 6 (1986): 1334–6.

Blogett, Bonnie. *Sunset Midwest Top 10 Garden Guide.* Menlo Park, CA: Sunset Garden Publishing, 2003.

Brenzel, Kathleen Norris. *Sunset Western Garden Book.* Menlo Park, CA: Sunset Garden Publishing, 2001.

Bruce, Hank, and Tomi Jill Folk. *Global Gardening: Increasing the Diversity of Plants in Your Own Garden While Feeding a Hungry World.* Fort Myers, FL: Winner Enterprises, 2001.

Brücher, Heinz. *Useful Plants of Neotropical Origin and Their Wild Relatives.* Berlin: Springer-Verlag, 1989.

Burdick, Alan. *Out of Eden: An Odyssey of Ecological Invasion.* New York: Farrar, Straus and Giroux, 2006.

Cebenko, Jill Jesiolowski, and Deborah Martin, eds. *Insect, Disease & Weed I.D. Guide: Find-It-Fast Organic Solutions for Your Garden.* Emmaus, PA: Rodale Press, 2001.

Cranshaw, Whitney. *Garden Insects of North America: The Ultimate Guide to Backyard Bugs.* Princeton, NJ: Princeton University Press, 2004.

Creasy, Rosalind. *The Complete Book of Edible Landscaping: Home-Landscaping with Food-Bearing Plants and Resource-Saving Techniques.* San Francisco: Sierra Club Books, 1982.

Cullina, William. *The New England Wild Flower Society Guide to Growing and Propagating Wildflowers of the United States and Canada.* Boston: Houghton Mifflin, 2000.

Cusack, Victor. *Bamboo World: The Growing and Use of Clumping Bamboos.* Sydney, Australia: Kangaroo Press, 1999.

Denckla, Tanya. *The Gardener's A–Z Guide to Growing Organic Food.* North Adams, MA: Storey Publishing, 2003.

Deppe, Carol. *Breed Your Own Vegetable Varieties: The Gardener's and Farmer's Guide to Plant Breeding and Seed Saving.* White River Junction, VT: Chelsea Green, 2000.

Diamond, Jared. *Guns, Germs and Steel: The Fates of Human Societies.* New York: W. W. Norton, 1997.

DiSabato-Aust, Tracy. *The Well-Tended Perennial Garden: Planting and Pruning Techniques.* Portland, OR: Timber Press, 1998.

Dunnet, Nigel, and Nöel Kingsbury. *Planting Green Roofs and Living Walls.* Portland, OR: Timber Press, 2004.

España, B. Pascual, et al. *El Cultivo de la Chufa (Cyperus esculentus L. var. sativus Boeck.): Estudios Realizados.* Ciutat de Ferrol: Generalitat Valenciana, 1997.

Eyre, Suzanne Normand. *Sunset National Gardening Book.* Menlo Park, CA: Sunset Garden Publishing, 1997.

Facciola, Stephen. *Cornucopia: A Source Book of Edible Plants.* Vista, CA: Kampong Publications, 1998.

Facemire, Glen. *Ramps: From the Seed to the Weed.* Self-published, 1997.

Fern, Ken. *Plants for a Future: Edible & Useful Plants for A Healthier World.* East Mean, Hampshire, England: Permanent Publications, 1997.

Flach, M., and F. Rumwas, eds. *PROSEA: Plant Resources of South-East Asia No. 9: Plants Yielding Non-Seed Carbohydrates.* Leiden, Netherlands: Backhuys Publishers, 1996.

Flannery, Tim. *The Eternal Frontier: An Ecological History of North America and Its Peoples.* Melbourne, Australia: Text Publishing, 2001.

Flores, Heather C. *Food Not Lawns: How to Turn Your Yard into a Garden and Your Neighborhood into a Community.* White River Junction, VT: Chelsea Green, 2006.

Foster, Steven. *Herbal Renaissance: Growing, Using & Understanding Herbs in the Modern World.* Salt Lake City: Gibbs Smith, 1993.

Francko, David. *Palms Won't Grow Here and Other Myths: Warm-Climate Plants for Cooler Areas.* Portland, OR: Timber Press, 1993.

Gershuny, Grace. *Start with the Soil: The Organic Gardener's Guide to Improving Soil for Higher Yields, More Beautiful Flowers, and a Healthy, Easy-Care Garden.* Emmaus, PA: Rodale Press, 1993.

Grau, Alfredo, et al. *Mashua (Tropaeolum tuberosum).* Rome: International Plant Genetic Resources Institute, 2003.

Greenwood, Pippa, and Andrew Halstead. *American Horticultural Society Pests and Diseases: The Complete Guide to Preventing, Identifying, and Treating Plant Problems.* New York: DK Publishing, 2000.

Griffiths, Mark. *Index of Garden Plants.* Portland, OR: Timber Press, 1994.

Halpin, Anne. *Gourmet Gardening: 48 Special Vegetables You Can Grow for Deliciously Distinctive Meals.* Emmaus, PA: Rodale Press, 1981.

Halpin, Anne. *Sunset Northeastern Garden Book.* Menlo Park, CA: Sunset Garden Publishing, 2001.

Harrington, Geri. *Grow Your Own Chinese Vegetables.* North Adams, MA: Garden Way Publishing, 1984.

Harrington, H. D. *Edible Native Plants of the Rocky Mountains.* Albuquerque: University of New Mexico Press, 1967.

Hemenway, Toby. *Gaia's Garden: A Guide to Home-Scale Permaculture.* White River Junction, VT: Chelsea Green, 2001.

Hendrick, U. P. *Sturtevant's Notes on Edible Plants.* Albany, NY: J. B. Lyon Company, 1919. Facsimile reprint published in 1972 by Dover Publications, New York.

Herklots, G. A. C. *Vegetables in Southeast Asia.* London: Allen and Unwin, Ltd., 1972.

Hermann, M., and J. Heller, eds. *Andean Roots and Tubers: Ahipa, Arracacha, Maca and Yacon.* Rome: International Plant Genetic Resources Institute, 1997.

Hickmott, Simon. *Growing Unusual Vegetables: Weird and Wonderful Vegetables and How to Grow Them.* Bristol, England: Eco-Logic Books, 2003.

Hodgson, Wendy. *Food Plants of the Sonoran Desert.* Tucson: University of Arizona Press, 2001.

Holmgren, David. *Permaculture: Principles and Pathways Beyond Sustainability.* Hepburn, Victoria, Australia: Holmgren Design Services, 2002.

Holmgren, David. "Weeds or Wild Nature." *Permaculture International Journal* 61 (1996): [PAGE NUMBERS?].

Hu, Shiu-ying. *Food Plants of China.* Hong Kong: Chinese University Press, 2005.

Jacke, Dave, and Eric Toensmeier. *Edible Forest Gardens.* 2 vols. White River Junction, VT: Chelsea Green, 2005.

Jeavons, John. *How to Grow More Vegetables: And Fruits, Nuts, Berries, Grains, and Other Crops than You Ever Thought Possible on Less Land than You Can Imagine.* Berkeley, CA: Ten Speed Press, 2002.

Jones, Samuel, and Leonard Foote. *Gardening with Native Wild Flowers.* Portland, OR: Timber Press, 1990.

Kallas, John. "Wapato, Indian Potato." *The Wild Food Adventurer* 1, no. 4 (1996): page 1.

Kallas, John. "Edible Blue Camas—Preparation Old and New." *The Wild Food Adventurer* 3, no. 2 (1998): page 1.

Kindscher, Kelly. *Edible Wild Plants of the Prairie: An Ethnobotanical Guide.* Lawrence: University Press of Kansas, 1987.

Kirk, Donald. *Wild Edible Plants of Western North America.* Happy Camp, CA: Naturegraph Publishers, 1975.

Kourik, Robert. *Designing and Maintaining Your Edible Landscape Naturally.* Santa Rosa, CA: Metamorphic Press, 1986.

Kourik, Robert. *Drip Irrigation for Every Landscape and All Climates: Helping Your Garden Flourish, While Conserving Water!* Santa Rosa, CA: Metamorphic Press, 1992.

Lanza, Patricia. *Lasagna Gardening: A New Layering System for Bountiful Gardens: No Digging, No Tilling, No Weeding, No Kidding!* Emmaus, PA: Rodale Press, 1998.

Larkcom, Joy. *Oriental Vegetables: The Complete Guide for the Gardening Cook.* New York, Kodansha: 1991.

Lewis, Daphne. *Hardy Bamboos for Shoots & Poles: Thirty Varieties of Bamboo for Farms in USDA Zones 7, 8, 9.* Seattle, WA: Daphne Works, 1998.

Low, Tim. *Wild Food Plants of Australia.* Pymble, Sydney, Australia: Angus and Robertson, 2000.

Mangan, Frank. *Worldcrops: World Crops for the Northeastern United States* (www.worldcrops.org). Amherst: University of Massachusetts, 2006.

Marinelli, Janet. *Stalking the Wild Amaranth: Gardening in the Age of Extinction.* New York: Henry Holt, 1998.

Martin, Franklin. *Selecting the Best Plants for the Tropical Subsistence Farm.* Fort Myers, FL: Educational Concerns for Hunger Organization, Inc., 1998.

Martin, Franklin. "Tropical Yams and Their Potential." *USDA Agricultural Handbook* no. 466, 1976.

Martin, Franklin, Ruth Ruberté, and Victor E. Doku. *ECHO's Inventory of Tropical Vegetables.* Fort Myers, FL: Educational Concerns for Hunger Organization, Inc., *year unknown.*

Martin, Franklin, Ruth Ruberté, and Laura Meitzner. *Edible Leaves of the Tropics.* Fort Myers, FL: Educational Concerns for Hunger Organization, Inc., 1998.

Meitzner, Laura, et al. *Amaranth to Zai Holes: Ideas for Growing Food Under Difficult Conditions.* Fort Myers, FL: Educational Concerns for Hunger Organization, 1996.

Merideth, Ted Jordan. *Bamboo for Gardens.* Portland, OR: Timber Press, 2001.

Mollison, Bill. *Permaculture: A Practical Guide for a Sustainable Future.* Washington DC: Island Press, 1990.

Mollison, Bill, and David Holmgren. *Permaculture One: A Perennial Agriculture for Human Settlements.* Winters, KY: International Tree Crops Institute, 1981.

Mollison, Bill, and Reny Mia Slay. *Introduction to Permaculture.* Sisters Creek, Tasmania, Australia: Tagari, 1997.

Morton, Julia. *Fruits of Warm Climates.* Miami, FL: Self-published, 1987.

Nash, Helen. *Low-Maintenance Water Gardens.* New York: Sterling, 1998.

Nash, Helen, with Steve Stroupe. *Plants for Water Gardens: The Complete Guide to Aquatic Plants.* New York: Sterling, 1999.

National Research Council. *Lost Crops of the Incas: Little-Known Plants of the Andes with Promise for Worldwide Cultivation.* Washington, DC: National Academy Press, 1989.

Nugent, Jeff. *Permaculture Plants: Agaves & Cacti.* Nannup, Western Australia: Sustainable Agriculture Research Institute, 1999.

Ochse, J. J. *Vegetables of the Dutch East Indies (Edible Tubers, Bulbs, Rhizomes and Spices Included): A Survey of the Indigenous and Foreign Plants Serving as Pot-Herbs and Side-Dishes.* Amsterdam: Asher & Co, 1980.

Peterson, Lee Allen. *A Field Guide to Edible Wild Plants of Eastern and Central North America.* Boston: Houghton Mifflin, 1997.

Phillips, Ellen, and C. Colston Burrell. *Rodale's Illustrated Encyclopedia of Perennials.* Emmaus, PA: Rodale Press, 2004.

Picq, Claudia. *Bananas/Les Bananas.* Paris: International Network for Improvement of Banana and Plantain, 1998.

PROTA: Plant Resources of Tropical Africa Database. www.prota.org (accessed December, 2006).

Plants for a Future Database. www.pfaf.org (accessed December, 2006).

Platt, Karen. *The Seed Search*, 3rd ed. Sheffield, England: Karen Platt, 1998.

Preston, Stephen. *Aibika/Bele (Abelmoschus manihot (l.) Medik)*. Rome: International Plant Genetic Resources Institute, 1998.

Ragone, Diane. *Breadfruit (Artocarpus altilis)*. Rome: International Plant Genetic Resources Institute, 1997.

Ram, Jay. *Celery Stem Taro: A Prolific and Easy to Grow Vegetable*. Tropical Perennial Vegetable Series. Hakalau, HI: Tropical Rural and Island/Atoll Development Experiment Station, 1994.

Ram, Jay. *Chaya: A Highly Productive Leafy-Green Vegetable*. Tropical Perennial Vegetable Series. Hakalau, HI: Tropical Rural and Island/Atoll Development Experiment Station, 1994.

Ram, Jay. *Chayote: Perennial Squash and Leafy-Greens for the Tropics*. Tropical Perennial Vegetable Series. Hakalau, HI: Tropical Rural and Island/Atoll Development Experiment Station, 1994.

Ram, Jay. *Moringa: A Highly Nutritious Vegetable Tree*. Tropical Perennial Vegetable Series. Hakalau, HI: Tropical Rural and Island/Atoll Development Experiment Station, 1994.

Ram, Jay. *Okinawan Spinach: A Reliable, Low-Input Tropical Vegetable*. Tropical Perennial Vegetable Series. Hakalau, HI: Tropical Rural and Island/Atoll Development Experiment Station, 1994.

Ram, Jay. *Sissoo Spinach: A Pleasant-Tasting Vegetable Groundcover*. Tropical Perennial Vegetable Series. Hakalau, HI: Tropical Rural and Island/Atoll Development Experiment Station, 1994.

Ram, Jay. *Sweetleaf Bush: A Popular and Productive Tropical Vegetable*. Tropical Perennial Vegetable Series. Hakalau, HI: Tropical Rural and Island/Atoll Development Experiment Station, 1994.

Ram, Jay. *Tree Kale: A Nutritious and Versatile Food Plant*. Tropical Perennial Vegetable Series. Hakalau, HI: Tropical Rural and Island/Atoll Development Experiment Station, 1994.

Rayner, Lisa. *Growing Food in the Southwest Mountains: A Permaculture Approach to Home Gardening Above 6,500 feet in Arizona, New Mexico, Southern Colorado and Southern Utah*. Flagstaff, AZ: Flagstaff Tea Party, 2002.

Reynolds, B. D., et al. "Domestication of *Apios Americana*." In *Advances in New Crops*. Portland, OR: Timber Press, 1989.

Roth, Susan, and Dennis Schrader. *Hot Plants for Cool Climates: Gardening with Tropical Plants in Temperate Zones*. Boston: Houghton Mifflin, 2000.

Rubatzky, Vincent, and Mas Yamaguchi. *World Vegetables: Principles, Production, and Nutritive Values*, 2nd ed. New York: Chapman and Hall, 1997.

Saade, Rafael Lira. *Chayote, Sechium edule*. Rome: International Plant Genetic Resources Institute, 1996.

Schippers, R. R. *African Indigenous Vegetables: An Overview of the Cultivated Species*. Chatham, England: Natural Resources Institute, 2000.

Schneider, Elizabeth. *Vegetables from Amaranth to Zucchini: The Essential Reference*. New York: HarperCollins, 2001.

Seed Savers Exchange. *Garden Seed Inventory: Inventory of Seed Catalogs Listing All Non-Hybrid Vegetable Seeds, Available in the United States and Canada*, 6th ed. Decorah, IA: Seed Savers Exchange, 2005.

Siemonsma, J. S., and Kasem Piluek, eds. *PROSEA: Plant Resources of South-East Asia No. 8: Vegetables*. Wageningen, Netherlands: Pudoc Scientific Publishers, 1993.

Smith, Charles. *The Weather-Resilient Garden: A Defensive Approach to Planning & Landscaping*. North Adams, MA: Storey Publishing, 2004.

Smith, Keith, and Irene Smith. *Grow Your Own Bushfoods*. Sydney, Australia: New Holland Publishers, 1999.

Smith, Miranda. *Complete Home Gardening: Cutting-Edge Techniques for Gardeners*. Upper Saddle River, NJ: Creative Homeowner, 2006.

Specialty and Minor Crops Handbook, 2nd ed. Davis, CA: University of California, 1998.

Sunset National Garden Book. Menlo Park, CA: Sunset Garden Publishing, 1997.

Swindells, Philip. *The Master Book of the Water Garden: The Ultimate Guide to Designing and Maintaining Water Gardens.* Boston: Bulfinch Press, 2002.

Theodoropoulos, David. *Invasion Biology: Critique of a Pseudoscience.* Blythe, CA: Avvar Books, 2003.

Tilford, Gregory. *Edible and Medicinal Plants of the West.* Missoula, MT: Mountain Press Publishing, 1997.

Toogood, Alan. *American Horticultural Society Plant Propagation: The Fully Illustrated Plant-by-Plant Manual of Practical Techniques.* New York: DK Publishing, 1999.

Tull, Delena. *Edible and Useful Plants of Texas and the Southwest.* Austin: University of Texas Press, 1987.

USDA, NRCS. *The PLANTS Database.* http://plants.usda.gov/ (accessed December, 2006).

Van Wyk, Ben-Erik. *Food Plants of the World: An Illustrated Guide.* Portland, OR: Timber Press, 2005.

Vilmorin-Andrieux. *The Vegetable Garden.* English Edition. London: Hazel, Watson, and Viney Ltd., 1905.

Weinstein, Gayle. *The Xeriscape Handbook: A How-To Guide to Natural, Resource-Wise Gardening.* Golden, CO: Fulcrum Publishing, 1999.

Whitefield, Patrick. *How to Make a Forest Garden.* East Meon, Hampshire, England: Permanent Publications, 1997.

Index